SECRETS OF AUTHORITY

SECRETS OF AUTHORITY

ANDREW MURRAY

WHITAKER
HOUSE

Editor's note: This book has been edited for the modern reader. Words, expressions, and sentence structure have been updated for clarity and readability.

All Scripture quotations are taken from the King James Version (KJV) of the Bible.

SECRETS OF AUTHORITY

Titles included in this anthology:

The Blood of the Cross	ISBN: 0-88368-103-X	© 1981 by Whitaker House
Receiving Power from God	ISBN: 0-88368-647-3	© 1984 by Whitaker House
Covenants and Blessings	ISBN: 0-88368-748-8	© 1984 by Whitaker House
Divine Healing	ISBN: 0-88368-642-2	© 1982 by Whitaker House
God's Plans for You	ISBN: 0-88368-512-4	© 1983 by Whitaker House
Reaching Your World for Christ	ISBN: 0-88368-500-0	© 1997 by Whitaker House

ISBN: 0-88368-853-0
Printed in the United States of America
© 2002 by Whitaker House

Whitaker House
30 Hunt Valley Circle
New Kensington, PA 15068
Visit our web site at: www.whitakerhouse.com

Library of Congress Cataloging-in-Publication Data

Murray, Andrew, 1828–1917.
 Secrets of authority / by Andrew Murray.
   p.   cm.
 ISBN 0-88368-853-0 (trade pbk. : alk. paper)
 1. Christian life. 2. Authority—Religious aspects—Christianity. I. Title: On
   the believer's authority. II. Title.
 BV4501.3 .M875 2002
 248.4—dc21

2002014039

1 2 3 4 5 6 7 8 9 10 11 12 13 / 09 08 07 06 05 04 03 02

Contents

Book One

——◆——

The Blood of the Cross

Contents

Preface

————◆◄——

I have published these messages because I am deeply convinced that we Christians can never know too much about
the truths the blood proclaims. There can be no freedom of
approach to God, nor fellowship with Him, apart from a truly
vital and powerful experience of the blood of Christ. Its power
is a hidden, divine, spiritual reality; therefore, it can be experienced only in a heart that is humbly and entirely submitted
to the Spirit of God. And in the same proportion that we have
an insight into the inner nature that inspired Christ to shed His
blood, we will understand what the power is that can produce
that same nature in us.

Reconciliation and deliverance from guilt will become our
blessed entrance into a life in which the blood—as it was translated into heaven and abides there—will be truly the power of a
divine life abiding in us.

It is not without some hesitancy that I publish these meditations. There is always the danger, when one attempts to explain
divine mysteries in human words, of leading souls away from
the one thing that can bring blessing to them: waiting on God
for His Spirit to reveal these truths. I have endeavored to remember that just as the blood is the deepest mystery of redemption,
so its power can be experienced only in a nature similar to the
nature of Christ who shed that blood.

I cherish the hope that, for those who read these pages with
a desire for that nature, these addresses may be a help and

blessing to them, and that the reader might give careful consideration to this truth that is truly the center of God's wondrous counsel of redemption.

It is my prayer that the Lord our God may lead all His people, including me, ever deeper into the blessed experience of a heart and walk in which the blood manifests its power, and into a communion with God in the liberty and intimacy that the blood can bring about. May He cause us to experience and manifest what it means to say that we have washed our garments and made them white in the blood of the Lamb (Rev. 7:14). So may it be.

—ANDREW MURRAY

Chapter 1

———◆———

The Spirit and the Blood

There are three that bear witness in earth, the Spirit, and the water, and the blood: and these agree in one.
—1 John 5:8

*B*efore considering the blood of Jesus Christ and the glorious results that it accomplishes in us, there is a difficulty that must be overcome. We do not always enjoy the blessings and power of Christ's blood because we do not clearly understand what those benefits are or how the blood accomplishes them. Or, even if we do understand in some measure, it is not possible for us always to experience the blood's power because we do not always actively cooperate with it. Such difficulties arise because we do not remember that God has provided that the blood, as a vital power, automatically and ceaselessly carries on its work within us. He has so inseparably bound together the Holy Spirit and the blood that we may rely on Him to make the power of the blood ceaselessly effective in us by the power of the Spirit.

This is the thought expressed in the above Scripture verse used for the text of this chapter. The apostle had in the previous verses (see 1 John 5:4–5) spoken about faith in Jesus, and then he directed attention to the testimony on which that faith rests. (See verses 8–11.) He mentioned three witnesses:

- The water: this refers to an outward and human act commanded by God to be observed by those who, turning from their sins, present themselves to Him in baptism.
- The blood: in this we see what God has done to bring about a real and living cleansing.
- The Spirit: it is by the Spirit that the witness of both the others is confirmed.

In this chapter we will confine our attention to the truth that the united witness of the Spirit and the blood is the foundation of our faith. Let us notice the unbroken union of these witnesses, first, in the work of redemption; second, in our personal experience.

The Union of the Spirit and the Blood in the Work of Redemption

What first demands our attention here is that it is through the Spirit alone that the blood has its power. We read in Hebrews 9:14, *"How much more shall the blood of Christ, who through the eternal Spirit offered himself without spot to God, purge your conscience from dead works to serve the living God?"* The blood possesses its power to cleanse and to make us fit to serve the living God by the eternal Spirit who was in our Lord when He shed His blood. This does not mean merely that the Holy Spirit was in the Lord Jesus and bestowed on His person and His blood a divine worth. It is much more than that: it indicates that the shedding of His blood was brought about by the eternal Spirit, and that the Spirit lived and worked in that blood. As a result, when the blood was shed, it could not decay as a dead thing; but, as a living reality, it could be taken up to heaven, to exercise its divine power from there.

It is expressly for this reason that the Spirit is here called *"the eternal Spirit." Eternal* is one of the words of Scripture that everyone thinks he understands, but there are few who realize what a deep and glorious meaning it has. It is supposed that eternal is something that always continues, something that has no end. This explanation is merely a negative one and tells us only what eternal is not; it teaches us nothing about its nature and being.

Everything that exists in time has a beginning and is subject to the law of increase and decrease, of becoming and decaying. What is eternal has no beginning and knows no change or weakening because it has in itself a life that is independent of time. In what is eternal, there is no past that has already disappeared and is lost, and there is no future not yet possessed. It is always a glorious and endless present.

Now, when Scripture speaks of eternal life, eternal redemption, eternal joy, it means much more than to say merely that they will have no end. By the word *eternal,* we are taught that he who has a share in eternal blessedness possesses something in which the power of an endless life is at work. It is something in which there can be no change, nor can it suffer any diminution; therefore, we may always enjoy it in the fullness of its life-bestowing blessings.

The objective of Scripture in using that word is to teach us that if our faith lays hold of what is eternal, it will manifest itself in us as a power superior to all the fluctuations of our minds or feelings, with a youth that never grows old, and with a freshness that does not for a moment wither.

From this Scripture we are taught something also about the blood of Jesus, *"who through the eternal Spirit offered himself without spot to God."* Not only had the act of shedding His blood an eternally availing worth, the blood itself has Spirit and life in it. The blood is made effective by the power of an eternal life. This is why the epistle to the Hebrews lays much emphasis on the work of Christ as being *"once for all"* (Heb. 10:10) and *"eternal"* (Heb. 9:12). Notice the expressions in Hebrews: Christ is *"a priest for ever after the order of Melchisedec"* (Heb. 7:17). He is a *"priest who is made...after the power of an endless life"* (v. 16). He has an *"unchangeable priesthood"* (v. 24). *"Wherefore he is able also to save them to the uttermost that come unto God by him, seeing he ever liveth to make intercession for them"* (v. 25). He is *"the Son, who is consecrated for evermore"* (v. 28). Further on we read, *"By his own blood he entered in once into the holy place, having obtained eternal redemption for us"* (Heb. 9:12), and, *"By one offering he hath perfected for ever them that are sanctified"* (Heb. 10:14). Hebrews 13:20 speaks of *"the blood of the everlasting covenant."* By the eternal Spirit, the blood has obtained an eternal, ever-availing, ever-fresh, independent, imperishable power of life.

But the correlative is also true. As the blood possesses its power through the Spirit, so the Spirit manifests His full power and works effectively among men only through the blood.

We know that the outpouring of the blood was followed by the outpouring of the Spirit. And we know the reason for this. By sin, a middle wall of partition separated God and man. The flesh was the veil that made true union impossible. As long as sin was not atoned for, God, by His Spirit, could not take up a settled abode in the heart of man. Until the power of the flesh was broken and subdued, the Spirit could not manifest His authority. For this reason, there is no mention in the days of the Old Testament of an outpouring of the Spirit of God except as a prediction of what would be in the last days. Also, though He greatly loved His disciples and longed to bless them, our Lord Jesus was not in a position to bestow upon them the Spirit with whom He had been baptized, even though He took them into the closest fellowship with Himself.

Our Lord had to die before He could baptize with the Holy Spirit. The blood is the life of man; the Spirit is the life of God. Man must sacrifice his sinful life, bear the penalty of his sin, and surrender himself entirely to God before God can dwell in him with His life. What man himself could not do, the Lord Jesus, the Son of Man, did for him. He shed His blood; He gave His life in entire surrender to the will of God as a satisfaction of the penalty of sin. When that was accomplished, it was possible for Him to receive the Spirit from the Father so that He might pour Him out. The outpouring of the blood rendered possible the outpouring of the Spirit.

This is declared in the Scriptures in such words as these: *"The Spirit...was not yet given; because...Jesus was not yet glorified"* (John 7:39), and, *"He showed me a pure river of water of life, clear as crystal, proceeding out of the throne of God and of the Lamb"* (Rev. 22:1). It was when the Lamb took possession of the throne with the Father that the Spirit could flow out as a river. In the preaching of John the Baptist these were, also, the two statements he made about Jesus: *"Behold the Lamb of God, which taketh away the sin of the world"* (John 1:29), and, *"The same is he which baptizeth with the Holy Ghost"* (v. 33).

It was necessary for our High Priest to enter into *"the Holiest"* (Heb. 9:3) with His blood and, having come out again, to appear before the throne with that blood. Only then could He bestow the Spirit from the throne as the seal that His work in the Holiest had brought about a perfect reconciliation. The blood and the Spirit are inseparable, for only through the blood can the Spirit dwell in man.

In the execution of the work of redemption, also, the activities of the blood and the Spirit are inseparably connected. This is why we find in Scripture that what in one place is ascribed to the Spirit is in another place ascribed to the blood, and the work of sanctification is ascribed to both the blood and the Spirit. Life also is ascribed to both. Our Lord said, *"Whoso eateth my flesh, and drinketh my blood, hath eternal life"* (John 6:54), adding afterward, *"It is the spirit that quickeneth; the flesh profiteth nothing"* (v. 63). We find similar expressions in the epistle to the Ephesians. After having said, *"Ye...are made nigh by the blood of Christ"* (Eph. 2:13), a little later Paul declared, *"We...have access by one Spirit unto the Father"* (v. 18). So also in the epistle to the Hebrews, the scorning of the blood and of the Spirit is treated as one act. We read of those who *"counted the blood of the covenant...an unholy thing, and hath done despite unto the Spirit of grace"* (Heb. 10:29).

We have noticed that *blood* is a word chosen by God as a concise way of expressing certain thoughts, powers, and characteristics that are, as it were, included in it. It is not always easy, either in preaching or in personal exercise of faith, to find a perfect expression of these thoughts, powers, and characteristics. But this is what the Holy Spirit undertakes as His work, especially where faith is exercised about the blood.

He will explain, and make living, the full and glorious meaning of the word. By enlightening our understanding, He will make clear to us the great thoughts of God that are contained in the words, *the blood.* Even before the understanding can lay hold of them, He will make their power active in the soul. And where a heart desiring salvation is humbly and reverently seeking for the blessings they bring, He will bestow them. He will not only send the power of the blood to the heart, but will so reveal it in the heart that the same inner nature that inspired Jesus in the shedding of His blood will be awakened in us, as it is written: *"They overcame him by the blood of the Lamb,...and they loved not their lives unto the death"* (Rev. 12:11).

It is the great work of the Holy Spirit to glorify Jesus, to make Him glorious in human hearts, by bestowing the blessed experience of His redemption. And because the blood is the central point of redemption, the Holy Spirit will make the blood appear especially glorious to us and will glorify it in us. We can form some idea of the blood that was shed on earth in connection with the sin offering, but we have little conception of the blood that in the Holiest on high speaks and works in the power of eternal life. The Holy Spirit, however, comes with His heavenly, life-giving power to enable us to take hold of that which is eternal and to make it a real, living, inward experience in us.

Faith in the atoning power of the blood and in the personality of the Holy Spirit are two truths that are both denied when the church turns aside to error, while both of them are held fast by the true church of God. Where the blood is honored, preached, and believed in as the power of full redemption, there the way is opened for the fullness of the Spirit's blessing. And in proportion as the Holy Spirit truly works in the hearts of men, He always leads them to glory in the blood of the Lamb. *"And I beheld, and, lo, in the midst of the throne...stood a Lamb as it had been slain, having...seven eyes, which are the seven Spirits of God"* (Rev. 5:6). The blood and the Spirit proceed together from the Lamb, and together they bear witness to Him alone.

The Union of the Spirit and the Blood in our Personal Experience

We lay emphasis on this to show what rich comfort and blessing this truth contains for us. We must once again notice the two sides of this truth: the blood exercises its full power through the Spirit, and the Spirit manifests His full power through the blood.

The blood exercises its full power through the Spirit. We have here a glorious answer to the questions that at once arise in the minds of seekers after salvation. I have no doubt that by what has been written on the power of the blood of Jesus—about the rich, full blessing that is found in that blood—questions have arisen, such as

- How is it that the blood does not produce more results in my life?
- How can I experience its full power?
- Is there any hope for a person as weak as I am, and one who understands so little, to expect that fullness of blessing?

Listen to the answer, all you who heartily and sincerely long for it. The Holy Spirit dwells within you, and it is His office to glorify the Lamb and the blood of the Lamb. The Spirit and the blood bear witness together. The mistake we make is in thinking of the blood as if it alone bare witness. We think of the shedding of the blood as an event that occurred two thousand years ago on which we are to look back and, by the exercise of faith, represent it as present and real. But since our faith is always weak, we feel that we cannot do this as it ought to be done. As a result of this mistaken idea, we have no powerful experience of what the blood can do.

This weakness of faith arises, in the case of honest hearts, from imperfect conceptions concerning the power of the blood. If I regard the blood, not as something that lies inactive and must be roused to activity by my faith, but as an almighty, eternal power that is always active, then my faith becomes, for the first time, a true faith. Then I will understand that my weakness cannot interfere with the power of the blood. I have simply to honor the blood by exalted ideas of its power to overcome every hindrance. The blood will manifest its power in me because the eternal Spirit of God always works with it and in it.

Was it not through the eternal Spirit that, when Jesus died, His blood had power to conquer sin and death, so that Jesus was *"brought again from the dead...through the blood of the everlasting covenant"* (Heb. 13:20)?

Was it not through the eternal Spirit that the blood penetrated the regions of holy light and life to heaven itself and bears there its special relationship to God the Father and to Jesus the Mediator?

Is it not through the eternal Spirit that the blood ever continues to manifest its power on the innumerable multitude that is being gathered together?

Is it not the eternal Spirit who dwells in me as a child of God, on whom I may rely to make the blood of Jesus glorious in me also? Thank God, it is so. I have no need to fear. In the childlike heart, conscious of its weakness and wholly surrendered to the Lamb of God in order to experience the power of His blood, the Holy Spirit will do His work. We may confidently rely on the Spirit to reveal in us the omnipotent effects of the blood.

But there is another difficulty. Even once we recognize that the blood is omnipotent in its effects, we often limit the continuance of its activities to the period of our own active cooperation with it. You imagine that, so long as you can think about it and your faith is actively engaged with it, the blood will manifest its power in you. But there is a very large part of your life during which you must be engaged with earthly business, and you do not believe that, during these hours, the blood can continue its active work quite undisturbed. And yet it is so. If you have the necessary faith, if you definitely commit yourself to the sanctifying power of the blood for those hours during which you cannot be thinking about it, then you can be sure that your soul may continue undisturbed under the blessed activities of the blood. That is the meaning, the comfort, of what we said about the word *eternal* and the eternal redemption that the blood has purchased.

Eternal is that in which the power of an imperishable life works ceaselessly every moment. Through the eternal Spirit, the precious blood possesses this ceaselessly effective power of eternal life. The soul may, with even greater confidence, entrust itself to Him for every hour of business engagements, even in the midst of the hustle and bustle of life, for the activity of the blood will continue without hindrance. Just as a fountain that is supplied by or from an abundant store of water streams out day and night with a cleansing and refreshing flow, so the blessed streams of this fountain of life will flow over and through the soul that dares to expect it from his Lord.

And just as the Holy Spirit is the life-power of these omnipotent and ever-flowing streams of the blessed power of the blood, so it is He also who prepares us and makes it possible for us to recognize and receive these streams by faith.

Spiritual things must be spiritually discerned. Our human thought cannot comprehend the mysteries of the Holiest in heaven. This is especially true concerning the unspeakable glory of the holy blood in heaven. Let us with deep reverence entrust ourselves to the teaching of the Spirit, waiting on Him in holy stillness and awe that He may witness with, and of, the blood.

As often as we longingly pray for the holy power of the blood, let us with great tenderness open our hearts to the influences of the Spirit; the Spirit and the blood always bear witness together. Through the eternal Spirit, the full power of the blood will be exercised in us.

There is another glorious side to this truth: the Spirit attains His full power in us through the blood. Just as the outpouring of the Spirit followed the outpouring of the blood and its translation into heaven, so it is also in the heart. In proportion as the blood obtains a place in the heart and is honored there, so the Spirit is free to carry on His work.

At Easter time we remember the Passion and resurrection of our Lord, and we look forward to Pentecost and the days of prayer during which we wait on the Lord that we may be filled by His Spirit. Each year we are thus reminded that it is the will of Him who baptizes with the Holy Spirit that His disciples should be filled with the Spirit. Being full of the Holy Spirit is not set forth in Scripture as the privilege of a particular time, or of a certain people, but is plainly represented as the privilege of every believer who surrenders himself to live wholly for, and in fellowship with, Jesus. Pentecost is not just a remembrance of something that happened once and then passed away, but it is the celebration of the opening of a fountain that ever flows. It is the promise of that which is always the right, and the characteristic of those who belong to the Lord. We ought to be, and we must be, filled with the Holy Spirit.

The lesson that the Word of God has taught us shows the preparation necessary for the baptism of the Spirit. For the first disciples, as well as for the Lord Jesus, the path to Pentecost ran by Golgotha. The outpouring of the Spirit is inseparably bound up with the previous outpouring of the blood. With us also it is a new and deeper experience of what the blood can accomplish that will lead us to the full blessing of Pentecost.

If you long for this blessing, consider, I beseech you, the immovable foundation on which it rests. Take such a word as that from John: *"The blood of Jesus Christ his Son cleanseth us from all sin"* (1 John 1:7). The cleansed vessel can be filled. Come with all the sins of which you are conscious and ask the Lamb to cleanse you in His blood. Receive that word with a perfect faith, with a faith that rejoices over all feeling and experience, and believe that it has taken place for you. Faith acts as possessing what it does not feel; it knows how, in the Spirit, to take possession of that which only later on will be realized in the soul and in the body.

Walking in the light, you have a right to say with perfect liberty, "The blood of Jesus Christ cleanses me from all sin." Rely on your great High Priest to manifest in your heart also, by His Spirit, the heavenly wonder-working power that His blood has exercised for cleansing in the Holiest. Rely on the blood of the Lamb that destroyed the authority and effect of sin before God, in heaven, to destroy it also in your heart. Let your song of joy, by faith, be *"unto him that loved us, and washed us from our sins in his own blood"* (Rev. 1:5), and count on receiving the fullness of the Spirit. It is by the Spirit that the blood was offered up. It is by the Spirit that the blood has had its power and is still producing results in your heart. It is by the Spirit that your heart, through the blood, has been made a temple of God. Know, with full assurance of faith, that a heart that is through Him "by blood made clean" is prepared, as a temple, to be filled with the glory of God. Count on the fullness of the Spirit as your portion.

Oh, the blessedness of a heart made clean by the blood of the Lamb and filled with the Spirit! Full of joy and full of love, full of faith and full of praise, full of zeal and full of power—for the work of the Lord. By the blood and the Spirit of the Lamb, that heart is a temple where God dwells on His throne of grace, where God Himself is the light, where God's will is the only law, where the glory of God is all in all. Oh, children of God, come and let the precious blood prepare you for being filled with His Spirit, so that the Lamb who was slain for you may have the reward of His labor—labor marked by blood. And He and you together may be satisfied in His love.

Chapter 2

---◆---

The Blood of the Cross

*The Father..., having made peace through the blood
of his [Son's] cross, by him to reconcile all things
unto himself; by him, I say, whether they be things
in earth, or things in heaven.*
—Colossians 1:19–20

*H*ere the apostle Paul used an expression of deep significance: *"the blood of his cross."* We know how greatly he valued the expression *"the cross of Christ"* (1 Cor. 1:17; Gal. 6:12; Phil. 3:18). It expressed, in a brief phrase, the entire power and blessing of the death of our Lord for our redemption. It was the subject of Paul's preaching and the hope and glory of his life. By the expression used here, Paul showed how, on the one side, the blood possesses its value from the cross on which it was shed, and, on the other side, that it is through the blood that the cross reveals its effect and power. Thus, the cross and the blood reflect light on one another. In our inquiry concerning the power of the blood, we will find it of great importance to consider what this expression has to teach us, what is meant by the blood as *"the blood of his cross."* It will enable us to view from a new standpoint the truths that we have already discovered in that phrase *"the blood."*

Let us fix our attention on the following points: first, the nature of the cross; second, the power of the cross; third, the love of the cross.

The Nature of the Cross

In speaking about the cross of Christ, we are so accustomed to think only of the work that was done there for us that we take too little notice of the Source from which that work derives its value—the inner nature of our Lord, of which the cross was only the outward expression. Scripture does not place in the foreground, as most important, the weighty and bitter sufferings of the Lord that are often emphasized for the purpose of awakening religious feelings. But Scripture does emphasize the inner nature of the Lord, which led Him to the cross and inspired Him while on it. Neither does Scripture direct attention only to the work that the Lord accomplished for us on the cross. It directs special attention to the work that the cross accomplished in Him, and the work that through Him must yet be accomplished in us also.

This appears not only from our Lord's words that He spoke from the cross, but also from what He said when on three different occasions He told His disciples that they must take up their cross and follow Him. More than once He spoke in this way when foretelling His own crucifixion. The thought He wished especially to impress upon them in connection with the cross was that of conformity to Him. That this did not consist in merely outward sufferings and persecutions, but in an inward quality of character, appears from what He often added: "Deny yourselves and take up the cross." This is what He desires His disciples to do. Our Lord further teaches us that neither for Him nor for His disciples does the bearing of the cross begin when a material cross is laid upon the shoulders. No! He carried the cross all through His life. What became visible on Golgotha was a manifestation of the character that inspired His whole life.

What then did the bearing of the cross mean for the Lord Jesus? And what end could it serve for Him? We know that the evil of sin appears in the change it brought about both in the relationship of man with God, as well as in that of God with man. With man it resulted in his fall from God, or enmity against God; with God it resulted in His turning away from man, or His wrath. In the first we see the terribleness of its tyranny over man; in the second, the terribleness of the guilt of sin, demanding the judgment of God on man.

The Lord Jesus, who came to deliver man from sin as a whole, had to deal with the power of sin as well as with its guilt; first the one, and then the other. For although we separate these two things for the sake of making truth clear, sin is ever a unity. Therefore, we need to understand not only that our Lord by His atonement on the cross removed the guilt of sin, but that this was made possible by the victory He had first won over the power of sin. It is the glory of the cross that it was the divine means by which both these objectives were accomplished.

The Lord Jesus had to bring the power of sin to nothing. He could do this only in His own person. Therefore, He came in the closest possible likeness of sinful flesh, in the weakness of flesh, with the fullest capacity to be tempted as we are. From His baptism with the Holy Spirit and the temptation of Satan that followed, up to the fearful soul agony in Gethsemane and the offering of Himself on the cross, His life was a ceaseless striving against self-will and self-honor, against the temptation of trying to reach His goal—the setting up of His kingdom—by fleshly or worldly means. Every day He had to take up and carry His cross. That is, to lose His own life and will by going out of Himself and doing and speaking nothing except what He had seen or heard from the Father.

That which took place in the temptation in the wilderness and in the agony of Gethsemane—at the beginning and end of His public ministry—is only a clear manifestation of the inner nature that characterized His whole life. He was tempted to the sin of self-assertion, but He overcame the temptation to satisfy lawful desires—from the first temptation, to obtain bread to satisfy His hunger, until the last, that He might not have to drink the bitter cup of death—so that He might be subject to the will of the Father.

Thus He offered up Himself and His life; He denied Himself and took up His cross; He learned obedience and became perfect. In His own person He gained a complete victory over the power of sin, until He was able to testify that the evil one, *"the prince of this world cometh, and hath nothing in me"* (John 14:30).

His death on the cross was the last and most glorious achievement in His personal victory over the power of sin; from this the atoning death of the cross derived its value. A reconciliation was necessary if guilt was to be removed. No one can contend with sin without at the same time coming into conflict with the wrath of God. These two cannot be separated from one another. The Lord Jesus desired to deliver man from his sin. He could not do this except by suffering death as the Mediator, and in that death suffering the curse of God's wrath against sin and bearing it away. But His supreme power to remove guilt and the curse did not lie merely in the fact that He endured so much pain and suffering of death, but that He endured it all in willing obedience to the Father for the maintenance and glorification of His righteousness. It was this inner nature of self-sacrifice, the bearing of the cross willingly, that bestowed on the cross its power.

So the Scripture says, *"He became obedient unto death, even the death of the cross. Wherefore God also hath highly exalted him, and given him a name above every name"* (Phil. 2:8–9). It also says, *"Yet learned he obedience by the things which he suffered; and being made perfect, he became the author of eternal salvation unto all them that obey him"* (Heb. 5:8–9). It is because Jesus broke down and conquered the power of sin first in His personal life that He can remove from us the guilt of sin, and thus deliver us from both its power and guilt. The cross is the divine sign proclaiming to us that the way, the only way, to the life of God is through the yielding up in sacrifice of the self-life.

Now, this spirit of obedience, this sacrifice of self, which bestowed on the cross its infinite value, bestowed that value also on the blood of the cross. Here again, God reveals to us the secret of the power of that blood. That blood is the proof of obedience unto death by the Beloved Son—proof of the inner nature that chose to offer the blood, to shed it, to lose His own life rather than commit the sin of pleasing Himself. It is the sacrifice of everything, even life itself, to glorify the Father. The life that dwelt in that blood, the heart from which it flowed, glowing with love and devotion to God and His will, was one of entire obedience and consecration to Him.

And now, what do you think? If that blood, living and powerful through the Holy Spirit, comes into contact with our hearts, and if we rightly understand what the blood of the cross means, is it possible that that blood should not impart its holy nature to us? But as the blood could not have been shed apart from the sacrifice of self on the cross, so it cannot be received or enjoyed apart from a similar sacrifice of self. That blood will bring to us a self-sacrificing nature. And in our work there will be a conformity to, and an imitation of, the Crucified One, making self-sacrifice the highest and most blessed law of our lives. The blood is a living, spiritual, heavenly power. It will cause the soul that is entirely surrendered to it to see and know by experience that there is no entrance into the full life of God, except by the self-sacrifice of the cross.

The Power of the Cross

As we pay attention to this, we will have a deeper insight into the meaning of the cross and the blood of the cross. The apostle Paul spoke of the *"preaching of the cross"* as *"the power of God"* (1 Cor. 1:18).

We need to know what the cross as the power of God can accomplish. We have seen the twofold relationship our Lord has toward sin. First, He must in Himself, as man, subdue its power; then He can destroy its effects before God as guilt. The one was a process carried on through His whole life; the other took place in the hour of His passion. Now that He has completed His work, we may receive both blessings at the same time. Sin is a unity, and so is redemption. We receive in an equal share both deliverance from the power of sin and acquittal from its guilt at the same time. As far as consciousness is concerned, however, acquittal from guilt comes earlier than a clear sense of the forgiveness of sins. It cannot be otherwise. Our Lord first had to obtain the blotting out of guilt through His victory over sin, and then He entered heaven. The blessing comes to us in the reverse order. Redemption descends upon us as a gift from above, and therefore restoration of a right relationship to God comes first, and we receive deliverance from guilt. Along with that, and flowing from it, comes deliverance from the power of sin.

This twofold deliverance we owe to the power of the cross. Paul spoke of the first, deliverance from guilt, in the words of our text. He said that God has become reconciled, *"having made peace by the blood of the cross,"* with a view to reconciling all things to Himself.

Sin had brought about a change in God, not in His nature, but in His relationship toward us. He had to turn away from us in wrath. Peace has been made through the cross of Christ. By reconciliation for sin, God has reconciled us with and united us to Himself.

The power of the cross in heaven has been manifested in the entire removal of everything that could bring about a separation from God or awaken His wrath. Now, in Christ we are granted the utmost freedom of entrance to and the most intimate relationship with God. Peace has been made and proclaimed; peace reigns in heaven. We are perfectly reconciled to God and have been received again into His friendship.

All this is through the power of the cross. Oh, that we had eyes to see how completely the veil has been torn in two! How free and unhindered is our access to God! How freely His blessing may flow toward us! There is now nothing, absolutely nothing, to hinder the fullness of the love and power of God from coming to us and working in us, except our unbelief, our slowness of heart.

Let us meditate upon the power that the blood has exercised in heaven until our unbelief itself is conquered, and our right to these heavenly powers by faith fills our lives with joy.

But the powerful effect of the cross in the blotting out of guilt and our renewed union with God is, as we have seen, inseparable from that other effect—the breaking down of the authority of sin over man by the sacrifice of self. Therefore, Scripture teaches us that the cross not only works out a desire to make such a sacrifice, but it also bestows the power to do so and completes the work. This appears with wonderful clearness in the epistle to the Galatians. In one place the cross is spoken of as the reconciliation for guilt: *"Christ hath redeemed us from the curse of the law, being made a curse for us: for it is written, Cursed is every one that hangeth on a tree"* (Gal. 3:13). But there are three other places where the cross is even more plainly spoken of as the victory over the power of sin; as the power to put to death the "I" of the self-life, of the flesh, and of the world. *"I am crucified with Christ: nevertheless I live; yet not I, but Christ liveth in me"* (Gal. 2:20). *"And they that are Christ's have crucified the flesh with the affections and lusts"* (Gal. 5:24). *"But God forbid that I should glory, save in the cross of our Lord Jesus Christ, by whom the world is crucified unto me, and I unto the world"* (Gal. 6:14). In these passages, our union with Christ, the Crucified One, and the conformity to Him resulting from that union are represented as the result of the power exercised on us by the cross.

To understand this we must remember that when Jesus chose the cross, took it up and carried it, and finally died on it, He did this as the Second Adam, as the Head and Surety of His people. What He did had and retains power for them and exercises that power in those who understand and believe this. The life that He bestows on them is a life in which the cross is the most outstanding characteristic. Our Lord carried His cross all through His entire life as Mediator. By dying on that cross as Mediator, He obtained the life of glory. As the believer is united to Him and receives His life, he receives a life that, through the cross, has overthrown the power of sin; henceforth, he can say, *"'I am crucified with Christ.'* I know that my old man is crucified with Christ. I am dead to sin. I have crucified the flesh. I am crucified to the world." (See Galatians 2:20; Romans 6:6, 11.)

All these expressions from God's Word refer to something that occurred in a time now past. The Spirit and life of Jesus bestow on believers their share in the victory over sin that was achieved on the cross. And now, in the power of this participation and fellowship, they live as Jesus lived. They live always as those crucified to themselves, as those who know that their "old man" and "flesh" are crucified so as to be put to death. In the power of this fellowship, they live as Jesus lived. They have the power in all things and all times to choose the cross in spite of the "old man" and the world, to choose the cross and to let it do its work.

The law of life for Jesus was the surrender of His own will to that of the Father by giving up that life to death. Therefore, He entered upon the heavenly life of redemption through the cross to the throne. So, as surely as there is a kingdom of sin, under the authority of which we were brought by our connection with the first Adam, so surely has there been set up a new kingdom of grace, in Christ Jesus, under the powerful influence of which we are brought by faith. The marvelous power by which Jesus subdued sin on the cross lives and works in us, and not only calls us to life as He lived, but also enables us to do so, to adopt the cross as the motto and law of our lives.

Believer, the blood with which you have been sprinkled, under which you live daily, is the blood of the cross. It obtains its power from the fact that it was the complete sacrifice of a life to God. The blood and the cross are inseparably united. The blood comes from the cross; it bears witness to the cross; it leads to the cross. The power of the cross is in that blood. Every touch of the blood should inspire you with a fresh ability to take the cross as the law of your life. *"Not my will, but thine, be done"* (Luke 22:42) may now, in that power, become a song of daily consecration. What the cross teaches you, it bestows on you; what it imposes upon you, it makes possible for you. Let the everlasting sprinkling of the blood of the cross be your choice. Then, through that blood, the nature as well as the power of the cross will be seen in you.

The Love of the Cross

We must now fix our attention on the love of the cross if we are to learn the full glory of the blood of the cross. We have spoken of the inner nature of which the cross is the expression and of the powerful influence that inner nature exercises in and through us if we allow the blood of the cross to have its full power over us. The fear, however, often arises in the mind of the Christian that it is too much of a burden always to preserve and manifest that inner quality. And even the assurance that the cross is *"the power of God"* (1 Cor. 1:18) that produces that quality does not entirely remove the fear. This is because the exercise of that power depends to some extent on our surrender and faith, and these are far from being what they ought to be. Can we find in the cross a deliverance from this infirmity, the healing of this disease? Cannot the blood of the cross make us partakers always, without ceasing, not only of the blotting out of guilt, but also of victory over the power of sin?

It can. Draw near to hear once more what the cross proclaims to you. It is only when we understand aright and receive into our hearts the love of which the cross speaks that we can experience its full power and blessing. Paul indeed bore witness to this when he said,

> *I am crucified with Christ: nevertheless I live; yet not I, but Christ liveth in me: and the life which I now live in the flesh I live by the faith of the Son of God, who loved me, and gave himself for me.* (Gal. 2:20)

Faith in the love of Him *"who gave himself for me"* on the cross enables me to live as one who has been crucified with Him. The cross is the revelation of love. He saw that there was no other way by which His love could redeem those whom He so loved, except by shedding His blood for them on the cross. It is because of this that He would not allow Himself to be turned aside by the terror of the cross, not even when it caused His soul to tremble and shudder.

The cross tells us that He loved us so truly that His love surmounted every difficulty—the curse of sin and the hostility of man—that His love has conquered and has won us for Himself. The cross is the triumphant symbol of eternal love. Because of the cross, love is seated on the throne, so that from the place of omnipotence it can now do for the beloved ones all that they desire.

What a new and glorious light is thus shed on the demand the cross makes on me, on what it offers to do for me, on the meaning and glory and life of the cross to which I have been called by the Word! I, whose flesh is so disposed to go astray that even the promise of the Spirit and the power of heaven seem insufficient to bestow on me the courage I need. But here is something that is better still than the promise of power. The cross points out to me the living Jesus in His eternal, all-conquering love. Out of love for us, He gave Himself up to the cross, to redeem a people for Himself. In this love, He accepts everyone who comes to Him in the fellowship of His cross, to bestow on them all the blessings that He had obtained on that cross. And now He receives us in the power of His eternal love, which does not cease for one moment to work out in us what He obtained for us on the cross.

I see it! What we need is a proper view of Jesus Himself, and of His all-conquering, eternal love. The blood is the earthly token of the heavenly glory of that love; the blood points to that love. What we need is to behold Jesus Himself in the light of the cross. All the love manifested by the cross is the measure of the love He bears to us today. The love that was not terrified by any power or opposition of sin will now conquer everything in us that would be a hindrance. The love that triumphed on the accursed tree is strong enough to obtain and maintain a complete victory over us. The love manifested by *"a Lamb as it had been slain"* (Rev. 5:6) in the midst of the throne, bearing always the marks of the cross, lives solely to bestow on us the inner nature, power, and the blessing of that cross.

To know Jesus in His love, to live in that love, and to have a heart filled with that love is the greatest blessing that the cross can bring to us. It is the way to the enjoyment of all the blessings of the cross. Glorious cross! Glorious cross that brings to us and makes known to us the eternal love! The blood is the fruit and power of the cross; the blood is the gift and bestowal of that love. In what a full enjoyment of love those may now live who have been brought into such wonderful contact with the blood, who live every moment under its cleansing. How wondrously that blood unites us to Jesus and His love!

He is the High Priest, out of whose heart that blood unites us to Him and His love. He is the High Priest, out of whose heart that blood streamed, to whose heart that blood returns, who is Himself the end of the sprinkling of the blood. He Himself perfects the sprinkling of the blood in order that by it He may take possession of the hearts that He on the cross had won. He is the High Priest who in the tenderness of love now lives to perfect everything in us, so that the nature that the cross has established as the law of our lives, and the victory that the cross offers us as the power of our lives, may be realized by us.

Beloved Christian, whose hope is in the blood of the cross, give yourself up to experience its full blessing. Each drop of that blood points to the surrender and death of self-will, of the "I" life, as the way to God and life in Him. Each drop of that blood assures you of the power obtained by Jesus on the cross to maintain that inner nature, that crucified life, in you. Each drop of that blood brings Jesus and His eternal love to you, to work out all the blessing of the cross in you, and to keep you in that love.

May each thought of the cross and the blood bring you nearer to your Savior and into a deeper union with Him to whom they point you.

Chapter 3

---◆---

The Altar Sanctified by the Blood

Seven days thou shalt make an atonement for the altar,
and sanctify it; and it shall be an altar most holy:
whatsoever toucheth the altar shall be holy.
—Exodus 29:37

*O*f all the articles in the furnishing of the tabernacle, the altar was in many respects the most important. The golden mercy seat on which God manifested His visible glory in the Most Holy Place within the veil was more glorious. It was, however, hidden from the eyes of Israel, being the representation of the hidden presence of God in heaven. Only once each year was Israel's active faith intentionally fixed on it. But at the altar, on the other hand, God's priests were continually engaged every day. The altar might be likened to a door of entrance to all the service of God in the Holy Place.

Before there was either a temple or tabernacle, an altar served as a place for the worship of God, as in the case of Noah and the patriarchs. Man may worship God without a temple, if he has an altar. But he may not worship God without an altar—even if he has a temple. Before God spoke to Moses at Sinai about a tabernacle where He might dwell among the people, He had already spoken to him about sacrificial worship. The service of the altar was the beginning, the center, indeed the heart of the service of the tabernacle and temple.

Why was that? What was the altar? And why did it occupy such an important position? The Hebrew word for *altar* gives the answer. It means, specifically, the place of putting to death, of killing. Even the place of incense—where there was no slain victim—bore the name of altar because gifts offered in sacrifice to God were laid on it. The chief thought is this: man's service for God consists in the sacrifice and consecration of himself and all he has to God. To this end there had to be a separated place, ordered and sanctified by God Himself.

Because the altar was ordered and sanctified by Him, it sanctifies and makes the gift that is laid on it acceptable. The one who gives the offerings brings to it not only the sacrifice that is to atone for his sins, but also the thank offering that follows reconciliation. This is the expression of his love and thankfulness, of his desire for closer fellowship with God and for the full enjoyment of His favor. The altar is the place of sacrifice, of consecration, and also of fellowship with God.

The altar of the Old Testament must have an antitype in the New Testament, something that in spiritual worship is the perfect reality of which the Old Testament altar was only the shadow. *"We have an altar,"* we read in Hebrews 13:10. In the eternal activities of heaven, there is also an altar. *"And another angel came and stood at the altar, having a golden censer;... and the angel took the censer, and filled it with fire of the altar"* (Rev. 8:3, 5). That altar in the New Testament, no less than those of the Old Testament, was a place for putting to death, a place of sacrifice. It is not difficult to tell where that place is that is spoken of in the New Testament. It is the altar where, *"once for all"* (Heb. 10:10), the Lamb of God was sacrificed as the great sin offering, where also each believer must present himself with all that he has as a thank offering to God. That altar is the cross.

In our text we learn that the altar itself had to be sanctified by blood if it was to possess the power of sanctifying whatever touched it. Our text tells us of two things: first, the altar sanctified by blood, and second, the offering sanctified by the altar.

May the Spirit of God open our eyes to see the full power of the blood of the cross. May we see the sanctification of the cross as the place of our death, and the place where we also may be consecrated to God.

The Altar Sanctified by Blood

It is in the midst of the instructions concerning the consecration of Aaron as high priest (his sons being consecrated with him as priests) that the words of the text appear. A priest must have an altar. But just as the priest himself had to be sanctified by blood, so was it also with the altar. God commanded that a sin offering should be prepared to cleanse the altar and to make atonement for it.

For seven days Moses had to carry on this work of making atonement for the altar. We read:

> *And Moses took the blood* [of the sin offering], *and put it upon the horns of the altar round about with his finger, and purified the altar, and poured the blood at the bottom of the altar, and sanctified it, to make reconciliation upon it.* (Lev. 8:15)

By this *"reconciliation,"* not only was the altar sanctified and made holy, but it was also made most holy—a Holy of Holies. This expression is the same as that used to describe the inner shrine of the tabernacle where God dwelt. It is used here of the altar, which had a similar, special measure of holiness. The one was the hidden, the other the approachable holy of holies. Then we read: *"Whatsoever toucheth the altar shall be holy"* (Exod. 29:37). By the sevenfold atoning with blood, the altar had obtained such a holiness that it had the power of sanctifying everything that was laid on it. The Israelite had no need to fear that his offering might be too small or too unworthy; the altar sanctified the gift that was laid on it. Our Lord referred to this as a well-known fact when He asked, *"Whether is greater, the gift, or the altar that sanctifieth the gift?"* (Matt. 23:19). The altar, by the sevenfold sprinkling of the blood, sanctified every offering that was laid on it.

What a glorious, fresh light this word sheds on the power of the blood of Jesus and on His cross that is sanctified by it. As blood—proof of the surrender of the life of Christ in obedience unto death—it has power to make reconciliation and to obtain victory over sin. But notice that here a fresh glory of the blood is revealed to us. The cross on which it was shed is not only the altar on which Jesus was sacrificed, but it has been consecrated by that blood as an altar on which we also may be sacrificed and made acceptable to God. It is the cross alone, as sanctified by blood (yes, sanctified to be a holy of holies, which sanctifies everything that touches it), that has this power.

In heathen worship, people are often taught a doctrine about a cross, that by self-imposed suffering and self-sacrifice they may become pleasing to God. But they seek a value in the sufferings themselves, as a putting to death of the flesh. They do not understand that everything that man does, whether it be suffering or sacrifice, is stained by sin and is thus incapable of really conquering sin or pleasing God. They do not understand that even the cross itself, as the means of self-sacrifice, must first be sanctified. Before the sufferings of a cross can sanctify us, it must itself first be sanctified.

For this purpose God made a most glorious provision. He caused an altar to be erected for which a sevenfold, and thus a perfect, reconciliation had been made, so that whatever touched that altar was holy. By the blood of the Son of God, the cross has become most holy—a holy of holies—with power to sanctify us.

We know how this has been accomplished. We cannot speak or think about it too often, nor believe it or be thankful enough for it. By shedding His precious, divine blood as a sacrifice for our sin, by surrendering Himself in perfect obedience to the will of the Father, by a personal victory over sin, by bearing our punishment and curse, Jesus has conquered sin and rendered it powerless for us, also.

What Jesus did and suffered on the cross, He did and suffered as the Second Adam, as our Surety, our Head. At the cross, He showed us that the only way to be freed from the flesh—in the likeness and weakness of which He came—so as to enter into the life of God and of the Spirit was by surrendering the flesh to the righteous judgment of God. The only way into the life of God was through the death of the flesh.

He did not merely show us that this was the only way, but by His death He also obtained the right and power to enable us to walk in that very way. Our natural life is so entirely under the authority of sin that we cannot be delivered from it by any sufferings or sacrifices or endeavors of our own. But the life and sufferings of Jesus have such a divine power that by them the authority of sin has been entirely destroyed. Now everyone who seeks the way to God and to the life of God, through sacrifice and death in fellowship with Him, will find that way and be enabled to walk in it.

Through the blood of Jesus, through the perfect reconciliation and the power of an eternal life that His blood has revealed, the cross of Jesus has been sanctified forever as an altar on which alone everything that is presented to God must be offered.

The cross is an altar. We have seen that the altar is the place for slaying, the place of sacrifice. The place where the incense was offered was also called an altar. On both the altar of sacrifice and the altar of incense a fire burned. What is presented to God must first pass through death and then be consumed by fire. In its natural condition it is unclean. By death, judgment upon sin must be executed; it must be consumed by fire and in a new spiritual form be borne heavenward.

What the cross, the altar of sacrifice, proclaims about Christ is the law in the temple of a Holy God; there is no way to God except through death, through the sacrifice of life. There is no way to God or to heaven for us except by the cross.

And the cross is not merely that cross on which we are to believe that Jesus died for our sins. No, it is the cross on which we must die. The Lord Jesus early and repeatedly warned His disciples that He must be crucified, and that they must bear their cross after Him. Each must be prepared to be crucified even as He was. He did not mean by that merely outward suffering or death. No, He spoke of the inner self-denial, of the hating and losing the self-life as the fellowship of His cross. This was before His crucifixion.

The Holy Spirit teaches us by the apostle Paul how we are to speak about the cross after Jesus had been put to death on it: *"I am crucified with Christ"* (Gal. 2:20); *"They that are Christ's have crucified the flesh with the affections and lusts"* (Gal. 5:24); *"God forbid that I should glory, save in the cross of our Lord Jesus Christ, by whom the world is crucified unto me, and I unto the world"* (Gal. 6:14). These three passages in the epistle to the Galatians teach us that we are not to regard the sufferings on the cross as being only the atonement of our guilt, but also the characteristic and the power of our lives.

In the cross, the life of Jesus on earth attained its purpose, its climax, its perfection. Apart from the cross He could not have been the Christ. The life of Christ from heaven bears the same characteristic in us; it is the life of the Crucified One. The phrase *"I am crucified with Christ"* (Gal. 2:20) is inseparable from and coupled with the other that follows: *"Christ liveth in me"* (v. 20). Each day and hour we must abide in the place of crucifixion. Each moment the power of the cross of Christ must work in us. We must be made *"conformable unto his death"* (Phil. 3:10). Then the power of God will be manifested in us; the weakness and death of the cross is ever coupled with the life and power of God. Paul said, *"For though he* [Christ] *was crucified through weakness, yet he liveth by the power of God. For we also are weak in him, but we shall live with him by the power of God toward you"* (2 Cor. 13:4).

Many Christians do not understand this. The cross in which they glory differs from that in which Paul gloried. He gloried in a cross on which not only Christ was crucified, but on which he himself was also crucified. They glory in a cross on which Christ died, but they are not willing to die on it themselves. Yet this is what God designs. The very blood that atoned for us on the cross has sanctified the cross so that we might find the way of life.

Notice how clearly this distinction and this connection between the blood of atonement and the sacrifice of the flesh is taught us in this well-known passage:

> *Having therefore, brethren, boldness to enter into the holiest by the blood of Jesus, by a new and living way, which he hath consecrated for us, through the veil, that is to say, his flesh;...let us draw near.* (Heb. 10:19–20, 22)

The *"new and living way"* is a different thing from *"boldness"* through the blood. It is the way in which Jesus Himself walked, tearing the veil of His flesh when He shed His blood. This way always passes through the torn veil of the flesh. The crucifixion and sacrifice of the flesh was the way in which the blood was shed. Everyone who obtains a share in that blood is, by that blood, brought into this way. It is the way of the cross.

Nothing less than the entire sacrifice of one's self-life is the way to the life of God. The cross with its entire renunciation of self is the only altar on which we can consecrate ourselves to God. The cross has been sanctified by the blood of Jesus as the altar on which we may become a sacrifice, holy and acceptable to God.

And now we see the meaning of the phrase that is connected with the altar and also with the cross, *"Whatsoever toucheth the altar shall be holy."* The smallness or unworthiness of the offering of him who brought it did not render it unacceptable to God. The altar, sanctified by blood, had the power to make it holy. And thus, when I fear that my self-sacrifice is not perfect, or that in my dying to self I may not be entirely honest and true, my thoughts must be turned away from myself and fixed on the wonderful power that the blood of Jesus has bestowed on His cross, to sanctify all that touches it. The cross—the crucified Jesus—is the power of God. When I, by increasing insight into what the cross means, really choose it and hold it fast, then there proceeds from the cross a power of life to take me up and hold me fast so that I may live as one who has been crucified.

I can walk in the consciousness of my crucifixion each moment. There is a renunciation of self because the Spirit of the Crucified One makes His cross the death of the self-life and the power of the new life of God. From the cross, as a sanctified altar, a sanctifying power is exercised over me. From the moment that I trustfully surrender myself to the cross, I become a sanctified person—one of God's saints. And to the degree that I believe in the sanctifying power of the cross and seek to live in fellowship with it, I become partaker of a progressive and increasing holiness. The cross on which I have been crucified with Jesus becomes daily the altar that sanctifies everything that touches it and sanctifies me, too, with a divine sanctification. The altar sanctified by blood sanctifies the gift laid on it.

The Offering Sanctified by the Altar

Now let us closely consider that the altar is sanctified by blood, so that in time it may sanctify the gift that is laid on it. What is the gift that we have to lay on the altar? We find the answer in a word of Paul written to the Romans: *"I beseech you therefore, brethren, by the mercies of God, that ye present your bodies a living sacrifice, holy, acceptable unto God"* (Rom. 12:1). The body of the victim was laid on the altar. Christ bore our sins in His body on the tree (1 Pet. 2:24). Our bodies are the sacrifices that we have to present to God on the altar. The body has many members and is a wonderful union of several powers. Each of these separately, and all together, must be laid on the altar.

The body has a head; we speak of the head with the brains as the seat of understanding. The head with all its thoughts must be laid on the altar. I must consecrate my understanding entirely to the service of God, placing it entirely under His control and direction to be used by Him: I must bring *"into captivity every thought to the obedience of Christ"* (2 Cor. 10:5).

The head has its members also, the eyes and mouth and ears. Through the eyes, I come into contact with the visible world and its desires. The eyes must be turned away from vanity and be wholly His, to see, or not to see, according to His will. Through the ears, I enter into fellowship with my fellowmen. The ears must be consecrated to the Lord and are not to listen to language or conversation that pleases my flesh, but they are to be attentive to the voices that the Lord sends to me. By my mouth, I reveal what is in me, what I think and seek and will. By it I exercise an influence over others. My mouth, tongue, and lips must be consecrated so that I will not speak anything except what is in accordance with God's will and to His glory. The eyes, ears, mouth, and the head—and all belonging to it—must be laid on the altar to be purified and sanctified by the cross.

I must renounce every right to manage them. I must acknowledge my utter sinfulness and lack of strength to control or sanctify them. I must believe that He who purchased them will accept them and guard them in the fellowship of His cross and of His entire surrender of Himself. In that faith, I must offer them to God upon the altar. The blood has sanctified the altar and made it the holy of holies: all that touches the altar becomes holy. The act of touching is a living, spiritual, real, and, for faith, an ever-enduring thing. The reconciliation of the cross has opened the way for the fellowship of the cross. The blood has sanctified the cross as my altar.

The body also has hands and feet. The hands represent power to work. My handiwork, my business, my service, my possessions must all be placed upon the altar to be sanctified, cleansed from sin, and consecrated to God. My feet represent my ways and my walk, the paths I choose, the companionship I cultivate, and the places I visit. The feet, sanctified by the altar, cannot go their own way any longer. They have been presented to God to be in all things under His leading and at His service.

And they must be *"beautiful"* (Isa. 52:7) to carry the good news and to bring help to the sorrowful and the lost. With hands and feet bound, the body must be laid on the altar, not having the least freedom to stir, until He enables the soul to cry out, *"I am thy servant...: thou hast loosed my bonds"* (Ps. 116:16).

Our Savior hung on the cross, nailed to it by hands and feet. In wonderful spiritual union with Him, our hands and feet are crucified with Him. The natural, sinful use of them is condemned and abides daily under that sentence. In the sanctifying power of the cross of the living Christ, they are free, holy, and fit to work for God.

The body has a heart, the center of life, where the blood, in which the soul dwells, flows in and out. In the heart is the meeting place of all the desires and endeavors of men, of all they will or choose, of love and hatred. The heart of Jesus was pierced on the cross. Everything that flows in or out of our hearts must be laid on the altar. I must renounce the right to seek or will anything after my own wishes, to love or hate after my own desires. In the case of Jesus the cross meant, "My will is of no account: the will of God is everything. The will of God, cost what it may, must be done, even if it costs My life." In the smallest as well as in the greatest things, God's will must be done. In nothing must my will be done—in everything, God's will.

That is the purpose behind the cross that Jesus sanctified as an altar for us. The will is the kingly power of the heart. It is governed by our love or hatred, and by it, in turn, the whole man is governed. When the will is on the altar, that is, on the cross, the fellowship of the cross will soon extend its power over the whole man. My will, sinful and blind; my will, condemned and freely surrendered to death; my will, put to death on the cross; my will in fellowship with Jesus living again, raised to life again, and made free; my will now entirely submitted to His leading and authority. This is the way in which the believing heart comes to understand what it means to be on the cross as on an altar. And the believer experiences that the two seemingly opposed conditions are united in a glorious union: his will bound to the cross and yet free; his will dead on the cross and yet alive. And so the truth now becomes glorious even for him: *"I am crucified with Christ:...Christ liveth in me:...I live by... faith"* (Gal. 2:20).

Heart and head, hands and feet—together they form one body. They are united in that wonderful structure of flesh in which the soul has its lodging. It was created at first to be the servant of the soul, to be kept in subjection to the guidance of the spirit; sin subverted this order. The sensual body became the seducer or tempter of the soul and has dragged the spirit down into servitude. The only way for the restoration of the order that God ordained is for the body to be placed upon the altar, the body by the Holy Spirit to be nailed to the cross. The body with its eating and drinking, with its sleeping and working, with its wonderful system of nerves by which the soul comes into contact with the world—the body must go to the altar. The power of the cross of Christ that, by the Holy Spirit, becomes at once and continuously active must have authority over the entire body. The body, with the soul and spirit dwelling in it, must become a living sacrifice to God. Thus that word of deep significance obtains its fulfillment: *"The body...for the Lord; and the Lord for the body"* (1 Cor. 6:13).

Beloved Christian, when we gather at the Lord's Table—to meet with Him, to receive Him who was sacrificed on the cross for us—what our Lord asks us to do is to offer ourselves to Him and for Him. What will He do for us? He will receive us into the fellowship of His cross as the most glorious thing He possesses, by which He entered into the glory of the Father. In the statement concerning the altar that is sanctified by the blood so that it may in turn sanctify the gift, He points out the way and the place where we may find Him.

Are you willing to ascend the altar, the place of death? Are you willing to make the cross your abode, the place where you will pass every hour of your life in fellowship with the crucified Jesus? Or does it seem to you to be too hard to surrender your self, your will, your life so utterly up to death, so as to bear about daily the dying of the Lord Jesus? I pray you, do not think this is too hard for you. It is the only way to close fellowship with the blessed Jesus and through Him a free entrance to the eternal Father and His love.

It does not need to be too difficult for you! In fellowship with Jesus, it will become joy and salvation. I pray you, become willing; let us ascend to the altar to die, so that we may live. Or is it your fear that you are not fit to complete such a sacrifice? Listen then to the glorious comfort that the Word of God gives you today: the altar sanctifies the gift. By the sevenfold reconciliation, even the Old Testament altar had power to sanctify every gift that was laid on it. *"How much more shall the blood of Christ, who through the eternal Spirit offered himself without spot to God"* (Heb. 9:14) sanctify the cross as an altar on which the sacrifice of your body may be sanctified? You have learned about the wonderful power of the precious blood, how it has conquered sin and has opened the way into the Holiest. As the blood has been sprinkled before God in that Most Holy Place, it has made His throne a throne of grace.

The very same word is used concerning both that inner Most Holy Place and the altar. Both are called the Holy of Holies. What the blood has accomplished by its wonderful power in the unseen Holy of Holies in destroying the authority of sin in God's sight is also accomplished in the Holy of Holies on which you are to be offered up. In the Holy of Holies where God dwells, the blood, by its wonderful power, has perfected everything. In your Holy of Holies where you must dwell, the blood works with no less power.

Lay yourself down on that altar. Trust the sanctifying power of the blood communicated to the altar. Believe that the blood and the cross are inseparable from the living Jesus, as High Priest, and from His Spirit, as fire. You will receive the assurance that the sanctifying of the gift by the altar is so divine and powerful that you will count on a victory over all your uncleanness and weakness. Lay yourself down upon the altar as the altar of consecration and approval. The altar is the place of the blessed presence of God. Dying with Christ leads to a life with Him in the love of the Father.

It has sometimes been said that as Jesus is Priest and Offering, He must also be the altar. There is a truth in this representation. The cross does not exist apart from the crucified Christ. At the cross the living Christ is found. If this representation helps your faith, take the crucified Christ as your altar and lay down your body with all that it contains, with all the life that dwells in it, on Him, before the Father. Then you are a living, holy sacrifice, acceptable to God. Then you will reach the full fellowship of which the Lord's Supper is the type.

The bread that we break, is it not the fellowship of the body of Christ? The cup that we drink, is it not the fellowship of the blood of Christ? Full fellowship with the crucified flesh and the shed blood is what He desires to give us. This fellowship is found when we give ourselves over entirely to die as He died so that we may live with Him, the Crucified One. We lay ourselves on the altar, giving up ourselves to the cross, to become one by faith with the crucified Jesus.

Friends, we have an altar; the altar sanctifies the gift. Everything that touches the altar is sanctified. I beseech you by the mercies of God to *"present your bodies a living sacrifice, holy, acceptable unto God"* (Rom. 12:1).

Chapter 4

———◆———

Faith in the Blood

*Whom God hath set forth to be a propitiation
through faith in his blood.*
—Romans 3:25

*F*aith in the blood of Christ is the one thing that makes the
doctrines of the holiness and grace of God, of the divine and
human nature of Christ, of our deliverance from sin and union
with God intelligible. In the history of the kingdom of God, as
well as in the experience of each believer, it becomes clear that
we have in the blood of Christ the supreme revelation of the
wisdom, the power, and the love of God.

Let us gather up what we have already learned and
endeavor to set forth briefly and clearly its practical importance, taking by way of introduction the words of our text:
"through faith in his blood." The apostle used these words
with special reference to one particular effect of the blood—
reconciliation—which, as we have seen, underlies all its other
effects. And so these words may be confidently applied to
everything that Scripture elsewhere teaches concerning the
blood. If we obtain a better understanding and make a fuller
inward appropriation of these words, our labor will not be in

vain. May the Lord our God grant us the teaching of His Holy Spirit while we consider, first, faith to partake in the blessings of the blood, and, second, faith in the all-encompassing power of the blood.

Faith to Partake in the Blessings of the Blood

"According to your faith be it unto you" (Matt. 9:29). We know that this foundation law of the kingdom of grace is applicable to every circumstance of the spiritual life. Faith is the inner nature of the heart without which God's most glorious blessing is offered to us in vain, but by which all the fullness of God's grace can be most certainly received and enjoyed. It is, therefore, of great importance for us to remind ourselves of those things that are necessary for a right exercise of that faith in the precious blood. It is by faith alone that we can press through to the enjoyment of all that the blood has obtained for us. But before considering these things, it must be noted that faith is born from a sense of need.

The great event that moved heaven, earth, and hell, for which the world had to be prepared and for which it had to wait for four thousand years, the results of which will endure forever—the shedding of the blood of the Son of God on the cross—had an unspeakably great purpose: it was to bring about the destruction of sin itself and of its consequences.

Only he who is in agreement with this purpose, and who seeks to attain it, is capable of entering into the full fellowship of faith in the blessing of that blood. He who desires to be delivered only from the punishment of sin, or from sin as far as it makes him unfit for heaven, is certainly not in a condition to take hold by a strong faith what the Word promises through the blood. But when the soul truly seeks, above everything else, to be cleansed from sin itself and to live in abiding fellowship with a holy God, it possesses the first requisites of a true faith in that blood.

The deeper the dissatisfaction with what is wrong and deficient in our spiritual lives, the stronger the longing to be really delivered from sin. The more lively the desire to have unbroken communion with God in the Holiest, so much the more is such a soul prepared to receive by faith what God promises and will bestow. Oh, if our eyes were only opened to see what God is willing to become to us; if wandering and alienation from God became entirely unbearable; if the whole soul thirsted and cried out for the living God and His love; then salvation *"through faith in his blood"* would acquire a new meaning, and a new desire for it would be awakened.

Where the sense of need exists, the first requirement for a full faith in the blood is a spiritual knowledge of the Word of God. As surely as mere knowledge of the Word by itself profits but little, so surely faith cannot grow and become strong apart from the Word applied by the Holy Spirit. Many think that, as they have always hoped in the blood as the grounds of their salvation, there could not be much more for them still to learn about it. They are convinced that they are well acquainted with and hold fast the teachings of the church. They do not expect the Word to unlock anything new for them about the blood. They think so because they have so little understanding of what it means to place themselves under the guidance of the Holy Spirit, so that He, by His heavenly teaching, might inspire the well-known words or truths of Scripture with a new meaning. They forget that it is only *"the anointing"* that teaches *"of all things"* (1 John 2:27), and that *"we have received...the spirit which is of God; that we might know the things that are freely given to us of God"* (1 Cor. 2:12).

The believer who desires to understand completely the blessed power of the blood must submit entirely to the teaching of the Word through the Holy Spirit in private. He must understand that the words of God have a much wider meaning than man himself can attach to them and that the matters on which God speaks have a reality and power and glory of which he himself can form no conception. But the Holy Spirit will teach him to understand these things—not at once, but as he devotes time and takes trouble to learn.

Believing in the rich, spiritual, living content of each Word of God, the learner must understand that the blood of the Son of God is a subject the glory of which God alone knows, and He alone can reveal. He must believe it is possible for each facet that is ascribed to the blood to be brought about by a manifestation of divine power that is beyond our conception. In this attitude of mind, he should meditate on what one portion of Scripture says about the blood, and then what another portion says, so that the Holy Spirit may apply to his soul something of its life-giving power. It is only by such a use of the Word, in dependence upon the teaching of the Holy Spirit, that faith can be strengthened so as to recognize and receive what the blood has to bestow.

By this means we realize how necessary it is to devote time to these things. Time must be found for meditation on the Word in private, so that it may sink into the heart. To read a portion, to get hold of a fresh thought, and then to go away in the hope that a blessing will follow is of little use. The soul must give the Word time, in silence before God, to get it fixed in the heart. Otherwise it will be driven away again by the rush of the world. The thought may remain, but there will be no power. Time must be given, not merely occasionally, but regularly and persistently. Day after day, perhaps week after week, I must place myself under and give myself up to the Word that I desire to appropriate. It can become in reality the possession of my soul only by obtaining a lodging place in, and by becoming part of, my spiritual being. It is in this way that *"faith cometh...by the word of God"* (Rom. 10:17).

Faith is the ear that hears and receives the Word of God. It listens attentively to understand what God says. Faith is the eye that seeks to place before itself, as an object of vital importance, what would otherwise remain only a thought. Faith thus sees the invisible. It observes the things that are not seen. It is the sure evidence of these things (Heb. 11:1). Faith is accustomed to surround itself with, and to dwell in the midst of, those things that the Word leads the understanding to regard as heavenly realities. So it seeks to behold, in the Spirit, the blood being brought into heaven and sprinkled upon the throne and, by the Spirit, sprinkled upon the soul, with powerful results.

But faith is not only an ear and eye to ascertain; it is also a hand and mouth to receive. What it hears from the Word, what it in the Spirit beholds, it appropriates to itself. Faith surrenders itself to the impression produced by what is heard, places itself under the influence of invisible objects, until they have secured for themselves a lodging in the heart, in their heavenly, life-giving power. Faith accepts it as a certainty that what the Word of God says, the power of God is prepared to make objectively real.

Faith knows that when it accepts the Word, but has not yet had the longed-for experience, it is only because it is not yet strong enough to become inwardly a partaker of what it has appropriated. It does not permit this in any way to dishearten it, but only devotes itself the more to persevere, until the undivided soul opens itself to receive the blessing. It knows that trust must always be coupled with surrender, and if there is postponement, it is only until the surrender is complete. Then faith will surely be crowned.

It is not difficult for us to obtain the appropriation of all the blessings of full salvation *"through faith in his blood."* Of each different word that is used in Scripture concerning the blood— *"redeemed," "cleansed," "sanctified," "purchased," "made nigh by the blood"*—faith says, "These words contain a heavenly, divine meaning, richer and deeper than I am able to grasp, but the blessing in their heavenly power is mine. God Himself will, by His divine power, make this matter real to me. I dare confidently to believe that this blessing, in a sense that surpasses all human understanding, is mine. I must simply await God's time. I have only to live after the Spirit, and be led by Him, surrendering myself wholly, so that God may take possession of me. He Himself will bring this blessing to me in its full power."

It is in fellowship with the Lord Jesus Himself that faith can be exercised and strengthened. It is a matter too little understood that God bestows salvation upon us in no other way than in—not just *through,* but *in*—the Savior. The living Jesus is salvation. He who gave and now imparts His blood, it is in Him that we must daily find our life and our salvation. Further, it is only in living in direct fellowship with Him that our faith can increase and triumph. Many Christians take great pains in endeavoring to reach a life of full faith by earnest association with the Word, or by straining all their powers to believe, yet they see but little fruit as the result of their efforts. The reason often is that, in studying the Word, and in trying to believe, they have not first of all found rest themselves in the love of the Savior.

Faith in God is an act of the spiritual life. It is Christ who is our life and who imparts faith to us. He does this, however, not as an act or gift separate from Himself. It is in fellowship with Him that faith is active. He is *"the author and finisher of our faith"* (Heb. 12:2). Those who walk with Him learn from Him to exercise faith. In the face of Jesus, the light that leads to the *"full assurance of faith"* (Heb. 10:22) is always found. To gaze upon His face, to sit still at His feet so that the light of His love may shine upon the soul, is a sure way of obtaining a strong faith. He who longs for such a faith in order to come to the knowledge of the full power of the blood needs only to practice this fellowship.

The shedding of His blood was the proof of His unspeakable love toward us. Jesus *"gave himself for us, that he might redeem us from all iniquity, and purify unto himself a peculiar people"* (Titus 2:14). His blood is the power by which He takes possession of us for Himself, to sanctify us. All that is necessary for the more powerful operation of the blood in us is that faith in it should become wider, brighter, and stronger. He who longs for such a full faith will find it only, but find it certainly, in fellowship with Jesus. It is His work to impart the blood; it is His work also to increase faith. Let there be an undivided surrender to the Lord Jesus, the sacrifice of the self-life, in order to walk with Him; in that walk unbelief will wither.

This undivided surrender, however, is indispensable. True faith always includes entire surrender. To believe with the whole heart means to surrender with the whole heart to Jesus, in whom life and salvation are found. The will and the law of the Lord Jesus are inseparable from His person and from His love. We can neither know nor receive Him without knowing and receiving His will: obedience is the one sure characteristic of the surrender of faith. Faith that is not coupled with obedience is an imagination or pretense; there is not a true surrender to Christ. But the faith in which this true surrender is found presses ever on to a deeper insight into what the blood means and to the experience of what it can do.

Faith in the All-encompassing Power of the Blood

I will not repeat what has already been said about the different effects of the blood, but I will point out some special characteristics of the way in which the blood accomplishes its work. Faith, however, must first be roused to recognize and appropriate the fact that the blessed effects of the blood make all things possible and are ever-enduring and all-inclusive. All things are possible: the blood has a divine power to produce results in us today.

Several times I have spoken of the wonderful power that the blood of Jesus manifested immediately after He had shed it. It was by that blood that Jesus, in His holy, triumphal march, broke open the doors of death and Hades and carried its prisoners out with Him, that, as Conqueror, He might see the doors of heaven thrown open for "the blood," and that He might take possession of the Holy of Holies of God on our behalf. The blood works today with a similar wonderful power to that which the blood manifested then in making reconciliation for sin, in removing its curse, in opening the Holiest, in restoring fellowship with God. With the very same power that was manifested then in those supreme things—concerning sin and its authority, concerning God and His law, concerning hell and heaven—with the very same power, the divine blood works now when sprinkled on a single soul.

We must confess that its divine power in our individual hearts is too little experienced. But this is because of our unbelief. If it were not for this unbelief, the mere thought of being ransomed and cleansed by the blood of God's own Son would cause our souls to leap for joy and to overflow with love. Would not every exercise of faith in the blood cause the sense of the favor and nearness of God and the glory of deliverance from the curse and dominion of sin to flow through the soul?

Alas, we may hear and think and sing about the blood, while it exercises almost no influence over us! Even the very thought that the blood always manifests such wonderful divine power seems strange and unreal to many, and so no wonderful work is done in us because of unbelief.

Our faith must be quickened to expect the all-conquering power of the blood. Even if a change in our feelings does not come at once, nor any sensation of new blessing, let us commence in perfect quietness to fix our hearts on these truths of God. When the blood becomes effective through the Spirit, it operates with the divine power either for reconciliation or union with God or sanctification. Let us believe and still believe and ever keep on believing in the infinite power of the blood. Such faith will not be in vain. Although it may not be in the way or at the time we expected, we will be brought into a new and deeper experience of salvation *"through faith in his blood."* Let us seek with our whole hearts to hold fast this truth: what the blood does, it does with a divine power.

Next to its power to make all things possible, our faith must be assured that the power of the blood endures forever. We have already seen on what foundation faith is grounded. By the eternal Spirit, the blood was offered *"once for all"* (Heb. 10:10). By the eternal High Priest, it is administered in *"the power of an endless life"* (Heb. 7:16). The power of the blood is eternally active. There is no single moment in which the blood is not exerting its full power. In the heavenly Holy of Holies where the blood is before the throne, everything exists in the power of eternity, without cessation or diminution. All activities in the heavenly temple are on our behalf, and the effects are conveyed to us by the Holy Spirit. He is Himself the eternal Spirit and has been bestowed on us to make us partakers of all that has been or will be done for us by our Lord Jesus. He is able to make us partakers, in a very powerful and blessed way, of the continuous activities of the blood, which never for one moment cease.

We long to abide always in the full enjoyment of close fellowship with God, whom we serve as priests. We desire to experience the constant cleansing of our souls from the stains of sin by the blood. We wish to know the peace and joy and power of the cross of Jesus in the fellowship of His blood. All these things are possible because the eternal, never-ceasing activities that the blood exercises in heaven may be exercised also in our hearts here on earth.

The blessedness of a clear insight into these truths is very great. The general complaint made by believers about their spiritual lives is that they are conscious of their instability. They have a strong desire that the glorious experiences of special hours should be the continuous state of their mind, and it is God's will that it should be so. If you who desire this will only set your hearts on something surpassing all that you have hitherto experienced and if you will fix your attention on the Holy of Holies now opened, with its heavenly life and eternal redemption, and on the unchangeable priesthood of your Lord Jesus, then you will see that the divine provision for your unbroken enjoyment of His fellowship is perfect.

In the morning before you go out to work and to meet the distractions of the day, commit yourself to Him who ever remains the same, that He may reveal in you the ever-living activity of His blood, and He will do it.

During the hours of business, when you can think of nothing else, the blessed results of the sprinkling of the blood and the nearness of God, of cleansing, of victory over sin, will be made yours. Our activity of faith must be an abiding thing, but not in the sense that we must anxiously take care to think about it every moment. Instead, from the depths of our souls, we cherish a quiet and steadfast confidence that eternal redemption has taken possession of us and holds us fast by its heavenly activity if only we are trustful. Thank God, we do not need to fear. Each moment, without ceasing, we may live here below in the enjoyment of the blessing that the blood has procured for us because the effects of the blood are ever-enduring.

Not less are we to believe in the all-embracing, all-penetrating power of the blood. When the priests were separated to their ministry, the blood was placed upon the tip of the ear, on the thumb of the hand, and on the toe of the foot. Possession was taken of the entire man for God. All his powers were sanctified: his ears to listen to and for God; his hands to work by and for God; his feet to walk with God and to go out in His service. In the case of the believer, the precious blood of Christ will exercise a similar authority over every power, to sanctify it for the service of the Lord.

Christians have often had to complain about a divided life: there are certain portions of life or of work that are a hindrance in a walk with God. The only way to obtain deliverance from this is to see that the blood covers everything. *"Almost all things are by the law purged with blood"* (Heb. 9:22). The entire person of the believer, with all his circumstances and affairs, must be brought into the Holy of Holies.

For one to enjoy such an experience, it is evident that a most complete surrender to the Lord is necessary. The priest who was marked by blood on the ear, hand, and foot, so that all the activities of these members might be sanctified, had to recognize that he had been separated to the service of God. The believer must give himself up no less wholly to be and live only for Jesus.

In each relationship of a Christian's life—his home, his business, commercial or political affairs—he must give himself up to be led by the Holy Spirit, to live according to the law of God and for His glory. Then, the blood in its reconciling, cleansing, and sanctifying power will embrace everything. The peace of God, and the consciousness of His nearness will reveal itself in all things, by the power of the heavenly life. He will experience the completeness of his deliverance from the authority of sin, of his liberty to enter upon a walk in the light and love of a Holy God. But always on this one condition: everything must be brought into the Holy of Holies and set right there. The whole life must be spent there, for that is where the blood is and where it exercises its power. This again, is by faith—faith that is absorbed in what the blood has accomplished in the Holy of Holies, and what power it now exercises there. And that faith maintains, on the authority of the Word, that all this power can be brought into uninterrupted contact with the personal life.

And then, to the degree that the believer learns in his own experience how far-reaching the effects of the all-including blood are, his heart will be opened to long for a widespread experience of the power of the blood in the world around him.

It pleased the Father that in him should all fulness dwell; and, having made peace through the blood of his cross, by him to reconcile all things unto himself; by him, I say, whether they be things in earth, or things in heaven.
(Col. 1:19–20)

The power of the blood avails for every creature, for those also who have *"counted the blood of the covenant, wherewith he was sanctified, an unholy thing"* (Heb. 10:29), and for those who are *"denying the Lord that bought them"* (2 Pet. 2:1). The experience of what the blood can accomplish for those who believe will teach them to regard their fellowmen as living under the tender mercy of God, under redemption, and under the call to salvation through the precious blood. It will fill them with an irresistible impulse to devote their lives, which have been bought by the blood, to be fellow workers with God. They have been consecrated to bear witness to the blood by word and by prayer, so that the blood may have the honor that belongs to it. That they *"were not redeemed with corruptible things, as silver and gold,...but with the precious blood of Christ"* (1 Pet. 1:18–19) will become for them the all-inclusive thing to which they devote their lives.

A Christian writer has testified that the insight into what the blood can do in its ever-cleansing power was the beginning of a new experience in her spiritual life. Sometime later she wrote, "I see more and more clearly that it is only by the abiding indwelling of the Holy Spirit that this hidden power of the blood can be revealed and experienced." May our lives also be under the teaching of the Holy Spirit, so that He may constantly keep us also in the heavenly blessedness and joy that the blood has procured for us.

Chapter 5

——————————◆——————————

The Blood of the Lamb

These are they which came out of great tribulation,
and have washed their robes, and made them white
in the blood of the Lamb.
—Revelation 7:14

*I*n our meditations on the precious blood of Christ, we have already considered the question of what it really is that bestows such value on the blood. Scripture has given us an answer from more than one viewpoint. It is because of His eternal Godhead, His true manhood, His infinite love, and His perfect obedience. In all these we find a reason why His blood exercises such an immeasurable power with God and men.

The Scripture quoted above calls us to the consideration of this subject from still another side. The new name given to the blood here is *"the blood of the Lamb."* We need to learn what the peculiar characteristics and results of the blood are that can be revealed only by the expression, *"the blood of the Lamb."*

When our Lord Jesus is called the Lamb of God, two leading thoughts are bound up with that name. One is that He is the Lamb of God because He was slain as a sacrifice for sin. The second is that He was lamblike, gentle, and patient. The first emphasizes the work that He as a Lamb had to accomplish; the second emphasizes the gentleness that characterized Him as Lamb. The first of these views is the more general one. We have often had the opportunity of speaking about the value of the blood from that point of view, as for instance in the chapter, "The Altar Sanctified by the Blood." The second has too often been lost sight of. Let us on this occasion fix our attention specifically on it, in order that we may obtain our share of the rich blessing that is contained in it. Taking as our point of view the inner nature that inspired our Lord as the Lamb of God, we will see that it is just this that makes the blood so precious—it is the blood of the gentle Lamb of God.

We will consider what it means that in heaven they praise the blood as the blood of the Lamb. First, it bestows on the blood its value. Second, it reveals the true nature of redemption. Finally, it assures us of a perfect salvation.

The Value of the Blood

When Jesus was on earth He said, *"Come unto me....Learn of me; for I am meek and lowly in heart: and ye shall find rest unto your souls"* (Matt. 11:28–29). He did not mention meekness as one of several other virtues that were to be learned from Him, but as the one that was His chief characteristic, the one that they must learn if they were to find rest for their souls. He who takes the trouble to understand this correctly will have a vision of the true inwardness of the work by which our redemption has been obtained.

The Lord came to deliver us from sin. In what does sin really consist? In self-exaltation, or pride. This was the sin of the angels who fell. They were created to find their life in God alone. With pride, they began to view themselves and the wonderful gifts that God had bestowed upon them. They began to consider that their dependence on God and subjection to Him were a humiliation, a curtailment of their liberty and enjoyment. They exalted themselves against God, seeking their own glory instead of God's. At that moment, they fell into the abyss of destruction.

Pride and self-seeking changed them from angels into demons, cast them from heaven to hell, and turned the light and the blessedness of heaven into the darkness and flames of hell.

When God created a new world to repair the destruction brought about by the fall of the angels, with man created for it, Satan came to lead man into the same opposition to God. The temptation that the serpent presented to the woman was intended to draw man away from subjection to God. Along with the words that Satan whispered in Eve's ear, he breathed into her soul the deadly poison of pride. And since man listened to him, self-exaltation became in his case, also, the root of all sin and sorrow. Consequently, his life is made up of self-love, self-will, and self-pleasing. Self—I—is the idol he serves. Self is a thousand-headed monster that, in the forms of self-seeking, self-pleasing, and prideful self-confidence and self-esteem, is the fruitful mother of all the sin and misery that are to be found in the world. The authority of Satan is exercised over and the fire of hell burns in all that belongs to self, I, and pride; the soul becomes consumed with a thirst that can never be quenched.

If the Lord Jesus is to become our true Savior, one thing is most necessary—He must deliver us from ourselves. He must bring about a death to self, to the self-life, and lead us again to live for God, so that we may live no more to ourselves. *"For none of us liveth to himself"* (Rom. 14:7). This is the only way by which man can become truly blessed. And there is, further, no other means by which this way can be prepared for us, except by the Lord Jesus opening the path for us, obtaining a new life for us, and imparting it to us. Of that life, denial of self and self-humili-ation should be the chief characteristics and the inner blessed-ness. In this way God might again take up His rightful place and become our All in all in that new life.

This is the reason why the Lord Jesus had to come into the world as the Lamb of God. He had to bring back again to earth the meekness and lowliness of heart in which true submission to God is manifested. It was no longer to be found on earth. He brought it from heaven. In heaven He humbled Himself as

Son before the Father, so that He might be sent as a servant into the world. He humbled Himself to become man. As man He *"humbled himself...unto...the death of the cross"* (Phil. 2:8). As the Lamb of God, He denied Himself with a heavenly meekness that surpasses all our thoughts to become a servant of God and man, so that He might please God and man. This was the inner quality that inspired Him and constituted the true nature of His sufferings, which made Him a complete victor over sin. It was as the Lamb of God that He took away the sin of the world (John 1:29).

This is what bestows such virtue upon His blood. He inflicted a deadly wound on sin, gaining the victory in His own person. He subjected Himself to the will of God. And through His whole life, under the severest temptations, He sacrificed Himself for the glory of God with a lowliness, patience, and meekness that were the delight of the Father and of all the holy angels. He did all this as *"the Lamb of God."* He crowned all this when He shed His blood as the Lamb of God for the reconciliation of sin and for the cleansing of our souls. This is why praise is offered in heaven for His blood, as the blood of *"the Lamb of God."* This is why the Father has placed Him *"in the midst of the throne"* (Rev. 5:6) as the *"Lamb* [that]...*had been slain"* (v. 6). This is why believers, in tender astonishment and love, glorying in the blood of the Lamb, praise His meekness and lowliness as their greatest joy and their one desire. The blood of the Lamb possesses virtue and power for complete redemption.

The True Nature of Redemption

The Lord Jesus came to do in His own person what we could not do. He also came to make us, who did not possess it, partakers of the treasure that He had procured. His lowliness is the gift that He brought from heaven. His lowliness is what He wishes to bestow upon us. And as the blood was the manifestation and the result of the divine meekness in Him, so it is also in us the manifestation and result of our contact with the blood.

Our fellowship in His blood—what is it but fellowship in His death? And His death was the culmination of His humiliation and sacrifice. It was a proof that there was no other way by which to attain to the fullness of the life of God—resurrection life—except through death. And so the blood—as a fellowship in His death, as a participation of the inner power of His death—calls us to give ourselves over to death, through His humiliation and self-sacrifice, as the only way to the life of God. A Christian who thinks that he is trusting in the blood often gives way to pride, self-will, and self-exaltation. But if he really knew that the blood of the Lamb is at work in him every moment, in living power, then he would recognize in this fact a decided call, coupled with a supply of power to enable him to manifest his faith in that blood with the meekness of Christ.

This is a subject upon which the attention of Christians must be much more fixed than is generally the case. We must learn that there is no way to heaven except by lowliness, by entirely dying to our pride, and by living entirely in the lowliness of Jesus.

Pride is from hell: it is the poison of Satan in our blood. Pride must die or nothing of heaven can live in us. Under the banner of this truth, we must surrender ourselves to the Spirit of the meek and lowly Lamb, to the Lamb of God, the Victor over all pride.

Each exercise of faith in the Lamb of God, each act of thanksgiving for the love and the blessedness brought to us by it, ought to powerfully encourage us to desire supremely to know and to manifest the humility of the Lamb of God. All our worship of God from hearts cleansed and saturated by the blood ought to strengthen us in the blessed certainty that where the blood of the Lamb is, there He is Himself in His meekness, to sanctify our hearts as temples of God.

We must not only recognize that this meek spirit, which in God's sight is of great value, must be the object of our desire and effort, but we must also believe that it is really possible for us to obtain a share in it. Jesus Christ is the Second Adam, who restores what the First Adam lost. Our pride and self-seeking, everything that self does or produces, and all the sorrow that arises from our self-will and self-love are only a continuation of that first turning away from God, when Adam fell under the authority of Satan.

There can be no thought of any redemption or approach to God without an entire turning back to a life of decided dependence, humility, and submission to God. The only way for redemption from the condition of pride is by death; dying to the life of self, the surrender of the self-life to death, to make room for the new life. And there is nothing in the entire universe that can make that death possible for us, and work out a new life in us, except such a heavenly lowliness as the Lamb of God brought from heaven, and which He made transferable to us by His death. What He was when He died, such He was when He arose from the dead. As the Lamb of God, He is the Second Adam, our Head, and He lives to bestow His Spirit upon us.

Yes, by His Spirit the Lamb of God will certainly bestow this meekness and will work it out in the heart of everyone who surrenders his life entirely to the power of the blood. We have already seen that the shedding of the blood was followed by the shedding forth of the Spirit, and that the Spirit and the blood bear witness together. Where the blood reaches there also is the Spirit. John saw the Lamb in the midst of the throne standing as if slain, *"having...seven eyes, which are the seven Spirits of God sent forth into all the earth"* (Rev. 5:6). The Spirit works as the Spirit of the Lamb. He works with a hidden but divine power, breathing into the heart of His own people that which is the divine glory of the Lamb—His meekness.

Do you desire to understand how these effects of the blood and the Spirit may be experienced? Do you complain that you know but little about them? Do you fear that in you perhaps it may never be possible? You may learn how it is possible, if you are a believer, that the Spirit is in you as a seed of God. That seed appears small and dead; its life-power is hidden and not yet active. Begin to esteem that seed of the divine nature. Keep calm, so that you may quietly believe that the Spirit is in you. Believe that the gentleness of the Lamb is also in you as a seed, a hidden power of the Spirit. Begin in that faith to pray to God to strengthen you by His Spirit in the inner man. Take any hour of the day—say nine o'clock—when you will (even if it is but for one moment) send up a prayer for the bestowal upon you of your inheritance, the meekness and gentleness of the Lamb. Cultivate the virtue of welcoming everything that calls for or helps you to humility. You may rely upon it that the hitherto hidden seed, the Spirit of Jesus, will open out and spring up on you. And it will become your experience that the blood of the Lamb has brought you into contact with a lowliness that is powerful and blessed beyond all thought.

Assurance of a Perfect Salvation

We would have thought that, in calling our Lord the Lamb, this name would have been used only in respect to His humiliation in His earthly life. Yet in Scripture it is used most often in reference to His glory in heaven. John saw Him stand in the midst of the throne as a Lamb that had been slain. The four living creatures, the twenty-four elders, and the hosts of heaven praise Him as the Lamb who purchased us unto God by His blood. *"Salvation to our God...and unto the Lamb"* (Rev. 7:10). It is the Lamb who executes judgment, who conquered Satan and all his power. The Lamb is the Temple and the Lamp of the New Jerusalem. It is from beneath the throne of God and of the Lamb that the river of the water of life flows. In heaven, through eternity, the Lamb is All in all. He is the glory and joy of heaven. Eternity will echo the song of His praise: *"Worthy is the Lamb that was slain to receive power, and riches, and wisdom, and strength, and honour, and glory, and blessing"* (Rev. 5:12).

And why is all this? *"Thou art worthy...for thou wast slain, and hast redeemed us to God by thy blood"* (v. 9). It is the blood of the Lamb that bestows this glory upon Him. By His own blood He has entered into the Holy of Holies and is seated at the right hand of the Majesty in heaven. His blood has accomplished this. Because He humbled Himself to death, God has so highly exalted Him (Phil. 2:8–9). As the Lamb of God, meek and lowly of heart, He glorified God even to the pouring out of His life. Therefore, He is esteemed to be worthy of being praised forever by the song of the universe. *"Salvation to our God which sitteth upon the throne, and unto the Lamb"* (Rev. 7:10). The blood has brought this about.

The blood will be effective for us, also. All on whom the precious blood has been sprinkled must come to that place where the Lamb is and where the blood is, where all those who have been bought and cleansed by the blood will honor and praise the Lamb forever. All on whom the precious blood has been sprinkled will come to the place where the Lamb will lead them to the fountains of living water and will perfect the salvation that He began in them, as they obtain a share in the Marriage Supper of the Lamb and forever worship God where the Lamb is the Temple and the Light. Yes, certainly the blood of the Lamb is the only, but the certain, pledge of a perfect salvation. And that not only in eternity, but here on earth in this life. The more we meditate on the glory of eternity and contemplate the unspeakable blessedness that He bestows, the more settled our faith will become that the blood that accomplishes such incomprehensible things there is able to effect here also a heavenly and thought-surpassing power in us.

Yes, the blood of the Lamb that was powerful enough to destroy sin, to open heaven for sinners, and to bring their salvation to such perfection, that blood surely has power to cleanse our hearts, to saturate and fill them, with all the power and joy that the Lamb on the throne will, even here, pour out upon us.

That blood is powerful to cleanse us from pride and to sanctify us with the holiness of the Lamb, His heavenly gentleness and humility. In Him we see humility crowned by God and all-conquering gentleness exalted to the throne. He is able to reveal this in our hearts.

The blood of the Lamb is the pledge of a perfect salvation! Oh, that we in deep astonishment and worship might let our hearts be filled with this truth! Our faith must take time to nourish itself by the reality of what is revealed to us, the reality of what takes place in heaven today and will continue forever, the reality of the powerful activities that stream forth from the blood here on earth every moment. In that faith, we must present ourselves before Him, who Himself has cleansed us by His blood and made us *"kings and priests"* (Rev. 5:10). He Himself will keep alive in us an effective application of the blood. Just as a garment that is to be dyed must be plunged in the liquid that contains the color and become saturated by it, so the soul that constantly bathes and cleanses itself in the blood of the Lamb becomes entirely saturated with those characteristics that the blood carries. The gentleness and the humility of the Lamb will become the adornment of that soul. He Himself will cause us to experience through the blood, as priests, a living entrance to God, an ever-abiding communion with God. He Himself will bestow on us, as kings, sovereignty and victory through the blood of the Lamb.

Yes, He Himself will make His blood the pledge of a perfect salvation. Oh, that we might give glory to the blood of the Lamb! Oh, that each day our hearts might sing, "In Jesus' blood is power!" Oh, that each day our confidence might be this: "The blood that is powerful in heaven is powerful in my heart. The blood that works wonders in heaven works wonders also in my heart. The blood of the Lamb is my life, my song, my joy, my power, my perfect salvation!" For that blood has come forth from His heavenly gentleness and humility, that blood bestows on me also the heavenly gentleness and humility through which I enter heaven. We have learned that it is because it is the blood of the Lamb that it has such a divine worth and power. It is the Lamb in His gentleness and humility who has redeemed us. It is gentleness and humility that constitute the power and the inner nature of redemption. It is in the way of gentleness and humility that He sacrificed His own will and life and died, and so has received a new life from God.

Learn, I pray you, that here is your way to eternal blessedness. Let each contact with the blood be contact with the Lamb, more particularly with His gentleness and meekness. Let your faith touch just the hem of His garment, and power will go out from Him. Self is our one sin and sorrow; wholly and always denial of self is our only redemption. Fellowship with the death of the Lamb of God is our only entrance into the life that He bestows. If only we knew what a sweet, heavenly, heart-changing power there is in a humility like that of the Lamb of God, which moved Him to give His blood. How this would drive the poison of Satan and pride out of our fallen nature; how this would bestow on us the Water of Life, to extinguish the fire of our self-seeking! Would we not rather sacrifice everything than fail to possess it in full measure? How we should praise the blood of the Lamb as the revelation, the impartation, and the eternal glory of humility!

Chapter 6

---◆---

The Blood-bought Multitude

*And they sung a new song, saying, Thou art worthy to take the
book, and to open the seals thereof: for thou wast slain, and
hast redeemed us to God by thy blood out of every kindred, and
tongue, and people, and nation.*
—Revelation 5:9

When we lay our gifts for the work of the Lord upon His altar,
it should not be done from mere custom or without serious thought. Every penny that comes into His treasury has a
value corresponding to the intention with which it is offered to
Him. Only true love to Him and His work transforms our gifts
into spiritual offerings. It would be well for us to learn what God
thinks and says about missionary work if we are to think and act
according to His will.

The work of the missionary is always a work of faith—faith
that is sure evidence of things man cannot see. It is guided
in everything by what is seen or heard in the unseen world.
The outstanding value of missionary work lies in the fact that
it is a work of faith. It has always been something beyond
mere human comprehension, for mere human wisdom cannot
understand it, and the natural man has no love for it. He cannot

imagine how it is possible for a heathen to be tamed and renewed by nothing save the message of the love of God in Christ.

The men who in all ages have stood at the head of the great missionary undertakings have received from heaven, by the Word and Spirit of God, the light and power needed for their work. It was the eye of faith fixed on Jesus as King that opened their hearts to receive His command and His promise, in which they found both the impulse and the courage for their work.

Our text tells us of a vision of things in the heavenlies that sheds the light of eternity upon the work of missions. We hear the song of the redeemed who praise the Lamb that He had redeemed them to God by His blood. And in their song, what is mentioned as of prime importance after the praise of the Lamb—or rather that is one part of that praise—is the fact that they were gathered together out of *"every kindred, and tongue, and people, and nation."* This is mentioned in praise of the power that the blood had exercised. There was no kindred or nation that did not have its representatives among those redeemed by the blood of the Lamb. There was no division of language or nationality of which the breach had not been healed. All were united in one spirit of love, and in one body, before the throne.

What else is that vision except a heavenly revelation of the high calling and glorious result of mission work? Without mission work that vision could not have become fact, nor could that song have been sung. In that song is set forth the divine right of missionary work and the heavenly supply that empowers it. Every time a friend of missions, or the people of God, hear the notes of that song, they receive a loud call to fresh courage and renewed consecration and to fresh joy in the glorious work of gathering together the *"great multitude, which no man* [can] *number"* (Rev. 7:9).

In these chapters on the power of the blood, we have fixed our attention chiefly on its effects in the individual soul. It is right that we should now inquire into the far-reaching extent and wonderfully powerful effects of His blood in the world.

Missionary work will appear in a new light to us when we see in what relationship it stands to the blood that is so precious to us, and we will be strengthened to serve the missionary cause if we understand that the power behind it is nothing less than the power of the blood of Jesus. We will learn that in order to carry on that work, we must ever regard it as a work of faith—a work that receives its recommendation, not from what is seen on earth, but from what is heard from heaven.

In order to understand this better, let us consider mission work in light of the blood that bestows its power. It is in this that faith finds its power. In the song of the great multitude gathered as a result of missionary activity, we hear that it is the blood of the Lamb by which they were redeemed, to which they owe their participation in salvation. Let us consider how that blood is, in truth, the power of the missionary movement. It is that blood alone that bestows the courage, awakens the love, and provides the weapons to which missions owe their victory.

The blood bestows courage. How else could weak men and women have dared to attempt to attack the power of Satan in heathendom and rob him of his prey? If the thought had come from great statesmen, from warriors who had conquered the peoples of the heathen world and intended in this matter also to conquer them, or from men of learning who believe in the power of knowledge and civilization, then we might perhaps have understood it. But no, these men were generally the fiercest opponents of the work. The thought was conceived and cherished in the quietness of hidden circles, of those who were of no consideration or influence in the world.

What was it, then, that gave them the needed courage? It was nothing else than the blood of Christ and faith in the power of that blood. They saw in the Word of God that God had *"set forth* [Christ] *to be a propitiation through faith in his blood"* (Rom. 3:25)—a propitiation *"for the sins of the whole world"* (1 John 2:2). They saw that that blood availed for every kindred and tongue and nation. It was granted to them to perceive that the blood had been carried into heaven and is now set down before the throne as the ransom for the deliverance of souls for whom it had been lawfully paid. They heard the voice of the Father to the Son, *"Ask of me, and I shall give thee the heathen for thine inheritance"* (Ps. 2:8). They knew that no power of hell could prevent the Lord Jesus from reaching all those for whom His blood was shed. Satan was conquered by that blood and was cast out of heaven; that blood had power to conquer him on earth also and to deliver his prisoners out of his hand. By the sprinkling of that blood in heaven, the power of sin was forever broken. And all that could hinder the outflowing of the love or blessing of God toward the most unworthy was removed, and the way opened for His people, through faith and prayer, to obtain heavenly power, so that in their weakness they might perform wondrous things. They knew with certainty that the blood of Jesus Christ, God's Son, was the pledge that men from every people and tongue should bow before Jesus.

The blood that bestowed courage to believe this also awakened love to act on that belief. We, here on earth, speak of blood relationships as being the strongest that exist. The blood of Jesus awakens the sentiment of a heavenly blood relationship, not only among those who are already cleansed, but also for those for whom that blood was shed. The blood of Christ expresses the surrender of love, even to death. It is, therefore, the death of selfishness, and it opens the fountain of an eternal love in the heart.

The more deeply the believer lives in the power of the blood of Christ, the more clearly he views mankind, even the heathen, in the light of redemption. That the blood has been shed for the most degraded bestows a value on every person and forms the band of a love that embraces all.

The confidence of faith—that the blood will obtain its recompense out of every tongue and nation—should be followed by a purpose of love. I, who myself owe everything to that blood, must bear witness to it and make it known to those who have not yet heard of it.

The blood that is for all is also for me. By faith in that word the soul obtains a share in its blessing. The blood that is for me is also for all. By faith in that word, love for my fellowman burns and sacrifices self to reveal the power of the blood to others. Yes, that blood is the power of mission work, for it is those who live in the full fellowship of that blood who are driven by the love of Christ to carry the tidings to others of that glorious portion that belongs to them.

The friends of missions need nothing less than love with its super-earthly power. It is this love alone, brought down to earth, that is able to embrace the wretched ones and to persevere when all hope seems lost. There are mission fields where God's servants have labored for twenty or thirty years without seeing any fruit for their labor, and supporters of societies in Europe have asked if it did not appear to be God's will not to open a door there. But love of souls enabled them to persevere, and later on a rich and blessed harvest has been reaped.

In spite of all the difficulties among us by which mission work seems at times to be surrounded, the heart that burns with love for Christ refuses to relinquish it. The laborer may be imperfect, and the work evidently gives but a small return at home, and abroad it may appear to the eye of flesh that loss, rather than gain, is the result; but love is not frightened. Souls who have been redeemed by the blood of Christ are too dear; love will wrestle on through all difficulties to save those of one blood in the Second Adam. It is the blood, the blood that speaks of the love of the Lamb, that is the power of missionary endeavor.

The blood is at the same time the weapon used by missionaries engaged in the battle. It is not enough that the believer has courage and love for the work, and power to begin it and persevere with it. Where can he obtain power to really touch the darkened heart so as to incline and to move it to forsake the gods of its forefathers, to receive the teaching of the cross along with the sacrifice of everything that the natural man desires, and listen to the call to a heavenly and spiritual life? That power the missionary movement finds in the blood of the cross.

That blood is the proof of a love that surpasses all understanding. That blood is the pledge of a reconciliation and pardon that the wakened soul needs. That blood brings a peace and a cleansing that break the power of sin and banish it. The Holy Spirit bears witness along with that blood, as He opens the heart for this love and this redemption. Just as the veil was once torn by that blood, so also now the thick veil on the most sinful heart is destroyed by that blood. It is by the preaching of the grace of God toward the ungodly that their hearts have been broken and renewed and have become the temple of God.

The history of missions supplies the most touching proofs of this. Thus, we learn that in the beginning of mission work in certain countries, the missionaries thought that they must first teach the people about God and His law, about sin and righteousness. They did that for more than twenty years without awakening them out of their deadly carelessness. On a certain evening, a brother read a portion of the New Testament that he had translated to a single heathen who had visited him. It was the story of the agony in Gethsemane. "Read that again," said the man. When he had reread it, he asked the missionary what it meant. When the missionary began to explain the sufferings and death of God's Son, the heathen's heart was broken. He was immediately enabled to believe, and then followed a glorious work. The blood of the cross had won the victory.

It is more than one hundred years since that occurred. But every mission field supplies proof that what the wisdom of this world cannot do has been done through simple men and women, by their message about the blood of the Lamb. And it is because there are thousands of God's children who heartily believe this that they will not allow themselves, by any means, to be turned away from their love for the glorious, precious work of missions. It is by this work that the *"multitude, which no man [can] number"* (Rev. 7:9) is gathered together to sing the new song in praise of the Lamb that redeemed them to God by His blood. Beloved Christians, there is one question that presses itself upon all of us who profess to be redeemed by the blood of Jesus. The question is, "What is the value of that blood to us?"

Is it of sufficient value to lead us to offer ourselves as a sacrifice to the love that caused it to be shed, and to bear witness to it? Is it indeed to us the most glorious thing in heaven or on earth, so that we have surrendered everything for it, so that the precious blood may have its full authority over the whole earth? Is it worth so much to us that we long that every creature on earth should know about it and obtain a share in it? Is it worth so much to us, this mission work by which alone the unnumbered multitude redeemed by that blood can be gathered together to sing the praises of the Lamb and to satisfy His love? Is the blood worth this to us, that in us the missionary movement has true, warm, praying, helpful friends?

Oh, that it may be so! In spite of all its deficiencies, mission work is God's work. Already God has done great things through it. Throughout the world there are those redeemed out of heathenism who have lived to truly honor our Lord and whose testimonies have borne out that they pleased God. Do not, I pray you, allow yourselves to be led astray by the talk of those who judge only by the eye of the flesh or in the light and interest of time.

He who does not love Jesus cannot understand mission work, for he knows nothing about the secret blessing of missions and the redemption of souls. Mission work is the work of eternity; therefore, it is a work of faith. Just as the Lord Jesus Himself was despised when He was on earth and not esteemed, yet the glory of God was in Him, so also is it with mission work. God is with it; He is in it. Do not allow yourselves to be misled by its outward weakness and deficiencies to misunderstand it. Live for it; give to it; work for it; speak for it; pray for it. If you are a Christian, also be a friend of missions. He who knows the power of the blood in his own heart cannot be anything else than a friend of missions.

The Blood of the Cross

I pray you, by the blood of the Lamb, by your hope of one day joining in the song of the Lamb, by your hope of being welcomed by the unnumbered multitude as a companion in redemption, live as one of the witnesses of the blood of Jesus. As you live only *by* the blood, live also only *for* the blood, and give yourself no rest until all His purchased ones know of His glory.

Chapter 7

———◆———

"When I See the Blood"

The blood shall be to you for a token upon the houses
where ye are: and when I see the blood, I will pass over
you, and the plague shall not be upon you to destroy you,
when I smite the land of Egypt.
—Exodus 12:13

*T*he story of the Passover is well-known to us all. The Lord was about to lead His people out of Egypt and, in the night of their departure, to inflict judgment upon Egypt. The Lord considered Israel as His firstborn son among the nations. Egypt had transgressed against Him by ill treatment of this firstborn son, and so punishment must fall on "the firstborn" of Egypt. In every house the firstborn would be smitten by the destroying angel, who, at midnight, would pass through the land of Egypt.

The Egyptians and the Israelites in many cases dwelt near one another, and so a sign must be set on the door of every Israelite house, so that the destroying angel might not enter there to slay. That sign was to be the blood of a lamb, slain by the father of the family, according to the commandment given by God. *"The blood shall be to you for a token"*—so God had said. It was to be a sign, an assurance by which the Israelite might have entire confidence concerning the safety of his family. It would be a sign also before God of the spiritual condition of the father of the house regarding his obedience of faith through which God would spare his house: *"When I see the blood, I will pass over you."*

We know why it is that the blood, and nothing else, was established by God as a sign. Although Israel was God's people, they were also, alas, a sinful people. As far as sin was concerned, if it was to be treated as it deserved, then the destroying angel must exercise judgment on Israel, also. But the blood was to be a token of redemption. The death of the lamb that was slain was considered as taking the place of the death that man had earned by his sin. The redemption of Israel, however, was not to take place simply by the exercise of power, but according to law and righteousness. Therefore, the punishment of the sin of each Israelite home had to be warded off by the blood of the paschal lamb. (The paschal lamb is the lamb slaughtered on the eve of Passover. It is a foreshadowing of the Paschal Lamb that is Jesus Christ.) Each father of a household, by the sprinkling of blood on the door of his house, had to give proof of his recognition of his sinfulness and need of deliverance. He showed his confidence in God's promise of redemption by his willing obedience to God's command. All this was in a remarkable way represented by the blood of the paschal lamb.

In the New Testament we read: *"Christ our passover is sacrificed for us"* (1 Cor. 5:7). The outstanding name that He bears in heaven, the Lamb of God, refers chiefly to what He, as our Paschal Lamb, has done for our redemption. And if we wish to declare in the most simple manner how His blood obtains our salvation, then we cannot teach it in a better way than by the type of the Passover in Egypt. Up until now, in explaining the power of Jesus' blood in these chapters, we have dealt chiefly with believers. We now address ourselves to the simplest and most unlearned in spiritual things, to those who, as yet, understand nothing about this blood. May God grant to them a knowledge of the preciousness of the blood of Christ by the glorious type supplied by the Passover!

Our attention will be drawn, first, to the danger to be averted by the blood; second, the deliverance brought by the blood; and, third, the blessings we may obtain by the blood.

The Danger to be Averted by the Blood

- The danger was awful. The eternal God was about to send the destroying angel with his sword through the land.
- It was general: no house was to be spared. Each family was to be robbed of its crown: the firstborn must die.
- It was certain: no power of man could procure redemption.
- It was unexpected: it portrayed a terrible picture of the danger that threatens us and from which there is no deliverance except by the blood of the Lamb.

That danger is awful. A hiding place, a means of redemption, has no value if danger is not realized. The blood of Jesus, however precious it is in the eyes of God and of the redeemed, has no value for him who has not realized his danger. The world is under the wrath of God. However happily life is spent, however we boast about our present civilization and prosperity and progress, there hangs over this world a heavy, dark cloud, more terrible than that which hung over Egypt. There is a Day of Judgment approaching, when anger and wrath, tribulation and anguish will be recompensed to all disobedience and sin. Christ will appear in flaming fire, taking vengeance on those who *"know not God, and that obey not the gospel"* (2 Thess. 1:8). He will pronounce that terrible sentence upon all who do not belong to Him: *"Depart from me, ye cursed, into everlasting fire, prepared for the devil and his angels"* (Matt. 25:41). *"Behold, the day cometh, that shall burn as an oven"* (Mal. 4:1), and who shall stand when He appears?

It is general. No house in Egypt was to be passed by. From the palace of the king to the hut of the beggar, the firstborn had to die. There was no distinction: rich and poor, godless and fashionable, friends and enemies of Israel, innocent children, those who were kind, as well as the cruelest oppressors of the people—that night there was no difference among them. The nation had sinned; the judgment must come upon all, without exception.

It will be just the same with the judgment that is coming upon the world. We all have sinned; we all are under a curse and wrath. No one—unless God Himself in a miraculous manner redeemed him—will escape a judgment that he cannot endure. No reader of these words, whoever he is, can escape standing before God's throne, to be cast into the outer darkness on account of his sins, if God's mercy has not worked out for him a miracle of grace.

This judgment is certain. We are living in the days of which Scripture has spoken, when scoffers, walking after their own lusts, say, *"Where is the promise of his coming? for...all things continue as they were from the beginning of the creation"* (2 Pet. 3:4). God is longsuffering and extends the days of grace, but the Day of Judgment will surely come. No power or force, no wisdom or cunning, no riches or honor can enable man to escape it. It comes certainly. As surely as there is a God in heaven who is a righteous Judge, as surely as there is sin on earth opposed to God's holy law, as surely as there is in every child of man consciousness that sin must be punished by a judge, with the same certainty, that Day will come. Although the thought of the millions who then will be lost, and of the terribleness of the breaking loose of the pent-up fire of God's wrath, and of the misery of an eternal destruction from God's presence is too terrible to rightly apprehend or bear—it is true and certain. There hangs over the whole world, and over every soul, a dark cloud of the wrath of God that will speedily break loose and burn with a fire that through eternity will not be extinguished.

The danger is unexpected. In Egypt they were busy buying and selling, building and trading, living luxuriously and boasting about their power and wisdom, when in one night the whole land was plunged into the deepest sorrow. *"And Pharaoh rose up in the night, he, and all his servants, and all the Egyptians;*

and there was a great cry in Egypt" (Exod. 12:30). It was in Egypt, as in the days of the flood, and of Sodom and Gomorrah; in an hour when they thought not, the angel of destruction came.

It will ever be so. The devil lulls men to sleep by the business and enjoyments of this world: Death comes unexpected. Judgment comes unexpected. While one still puts off to a more convenient season, while another comforts himself with the assurance that he will yet sometime be delivered, while still others do not trouble themselves at all about these things— judgment ever draws nearer. It has happened more than once that a man has fallen asleep on the railway line; everything around him seemed restful and still; suddenly the express train came rushing on and crushed him to death.

God's judgment draws near with incomprehensible rapidity and power. Because everything around you is quiet and safe and appears joyous, I beseech you, do not deceive yourselves: judgment comes unexpectedly, and then—then it is forever too late. Believe this, I pray you, the danger is greater and nearer than you imagine; make haste to be delivered.

The Deliverance Brought by the Blood

Deliverance is planned by God Himself. Let this be a settled conviction with you, that no human wisdom is of any avail here. It is from God's judgment, which is so terrible, that we must flee. It is God alone who can point out the way of escape. Deliverance by the blood of the Lamb was the outcome of divine wisdom. If a sinner desires to be delivered, then he must learn in this matter to be entirely submissive to God and entirely dependent on Him. He must see that he has to deal with what is really a divine purpose, and that, as sure and powerful as the destruction is, just as sure and powerful is the deliverance that has been prepared for him.

Deliverance is through substitution. That was the meaning of the blood of the slaughtered paschal lamb. The Israelite was just as sinful as the Egyptian. If the destroying angel came, he would have the right—yes (if we must go by right) it would be his duty to enter each house of Israel. But if on the door of the Israelite he found the blood—what does that mean?

When the Israelite took the lamb and raised the knife to slay that innocent creature for the sake of its blood, which he needed for his deliverance, he had only one thought in his mind: "I am sinful; my house is sinful. The angel of God's wrath is coming tonight. If he acts according to what I deserve, then death would enter my house; but I offer this lamb to die for me and my house." That phrase "for me," "in my place," was the one thought in his heart.

This lamb was typical: *"God will provide himself a lamb"* (Gen. 22:8). He has done this. He has—oh, wonder of wonders!—given His own Son to die in our place. The death that Jesus died was my death. He bore my sins. Now, I do not need to die. The deliverance that God has prepared is through substitution. Jesus, my Substitute, has paid all—all my indebtedness to God's law—and has done everything for me. He has entirely broken the power of sin and death, and I can now, at once, be entirely acquitted and be freed from all my sins. Deliverance is through substitution.

Deliverance is by means of the sprinkling of blood. The blood of the lamb had to be sprinkled on the doorposts. It was not enough that the lamb should be slain and its blood shed; the blood must be personally applied. The father of the family had to take the blood and sprinkle it on the door of his house. And so the Scripture says that our consciences must be cleansed and our hearts must be sprinkled. *"Let us draw near...having our hearts sprinkled from an evil conscience"* (Heb. 10:22).

In this deliverance, God and man meet one another; each has his share in the work. God provided the Lamb—His own Son. God, through the eternal Spirit, prepared Him to be a sacrifice. God promised to accept the blood. God bestows on us, by the blood, justification, cleansing, and sanctification. All this is the work of God. Our work is to believe in that blood and, in faith, to submit ourselves to the sprinkling of it. The result is real and eternal.

Deliverance is through the obedience of faith. For the Israelite it was a new and hitherto unheard-of thing, that the destroying angel was to come, and that the blood on the door would deliver him. But he believed God's Word, and in that belief he did what he had been commanded. This is just what you who are longing for deliverance from eternal death have to do. Exercise faith in the blood. Be assured that if God tells you the blood of His Son cleanses you from all sin, it is the truth. The blood has a supernatural, heavenly, divine power to cover and blot out sin before God immediately and forever. Accept this as God's truth and rest upon it. Then be obedient and appropriate the blood that accomplishes such wonders. Be assured that it was shed for you. Humble yourself before God, so that the Holy Spirit may apply it to you and cleanse your heart by it. Simply believe in that blood as shed for you. The almighty God is faithful and will accept you for the sake of the blood. Jesus will cleanse you by His blood and will work out in you the cleansing and impart to you the joy and the power that the blood alone can bestow.

The blood brings about an immediate deliverance from the judgment of God. The blood delivered the Israelites immediately and entirely from the threatened danger of that night.

From the moment that you are sprinkled by that blood, you are justified from your sins, and the judgment of God is averted from you. This blessing is so great, so divine, that it appears to man too great to be true. We desire to see in ourselves some token of improvement, to feel something as a proof that God has received us. It seems incredible that God could thus justify the unrighteous immediately, and yet it is so. This is the divine glory of redemption through the blood of the Lamb. That blood has such a divine and life-giving power that the moment a person believes in it, he is cleansed from all his sins. You who desire to be saved from sin and judgment may rely on this. The blood brings about an immediate redemption. The blood is so unspeakably precious to God, as the proof of the obedience of

His Son, that He, for Jesus' sake and because of His pleasure in Him, immediately forgives and receives you, if only you trust in that blood.

The blood is the beginning of a new life. You know that the Feast of Unleavened Bread was closely connected with the Feast of the Passover. If leaven was used, it came from a portion of the old lump of dough of a previous baking. Leavening is a process of corruption. Israel had to use unleavened bread during the Passover Feast and the seven following days as a proof that they would no longer have anything to do with the old leaven of Egypt; everything must become entirely new. The sprinkling with the blood of Christ is the commencement of an entirely new life. The blood and the Spirit of Christ are inseparable. When the sinner is brought near to God by the blood, he is renewed and sanctified by the Spirit. The blood is the beginning and pledge of a life in the service of God.

The blood gave assurance of the love and guidance of God. Israel was delivered by the sprinkling of the blood from the power of the destroying angel and also from the power of Pharaoh. The Red Sea, the pursuit by Pharaoh, and the desert, were still to come, but the blood was the pledge that God would be responsible for everything.

The blood of Christ gives you a share in the love, the guidance, and the protection of God. Oh, if you only understood this—the God who has provided the blood of His Son, who has received you because of that blood—He has become your God! He who has given His Son for you, how will He not with Him also freely give you all things (Rom. 8:32)? This is the blessing and power of the blood—it brings you into an eternal covenant with God; He becomes your leader and your portion.

The blood is the pledge of a perfect redemption. The God who delivered Israel from Egypt by the blood was not satisfied until He had brought Israel into Canaan. God bestows on you not only the blood of Christ, but also the living Christ Himself. Because He ever lives, He can save to the uttermost (Heb. 7:25). Each moment of your life, He will care for you. He undertakes to provide for your every weakness and need. He will, here in this life, lead you into the full blessedness of God's love. He becomes surety for your arrival in eternal glory. His blood is the eternal and undeniable proof that all God the Father and Christ see needful, they will do, and that they will not forsake you until they have accomplished their work in you from beginning to end. All the blessedness and all the glory of redemption are securely founded on the precious blood. Oh, you who up until now have had no part in that blood, let me persuade you to seek for salvation in the blood of the Lamb of God. Do not rest until you have the assurance, the perfect certainty, of your redemption.

The Blessings We May Obtain by the Blood

When the Israelite had sprinkled the blood on the top and sides of the doorframe of his house, he knew that he was safe. God had given him a promise of protection, and he was able trustfully to await the terrible visit of the destroying angel. He could listen peacefully to the great cry in the streets around him. His safety lay in God, who had said, *"When I see the blood, I will pass over you."*

How much more may we, who now do not have the blood of an earthly lamb but that of the Lamb of God from heaven— how much more may we be assured of our redemption? You who read this, give, I pray you, an answer to the question I now ask: do you have this assurance? Are you truly sheltered from the day of wrath, under the protection of the blood? Do you have the assurance that you also have been redeemed by that blood? If not, hasten, without delay, to receive this blessing. The danger is so terrible. The redemption is so glorious. The conditions are so full of grace. Let nothing keep you back from obtaining a share in it. You must be sure about it, or you will have no rest for your soul.

It is recorded that on the Passover night, there was an old gray-haired man who lived in the house of his firstborn son, and he himself was the firstborn son of his father. His son also had a firstborn son. Thus, there were three firstborn sons in the house who all must die if the destroying angel entered the house. The old man was lying on his bed sick, but he heard with interest everything his son told him about God's command to Moses. Toward evening he was often restless as he thought of their danger, and he said, "My son, are you sure that you have done everything that has been prescribed?" His answer was, "Yes, father, everything."

For a moment he was satisfied. Then he asked again, "Are you sure? Has the blood been sprinkled on the door?" Again the answer was, "Yes, father. Everything has been done according to the command." The nearer it came to midnight, the more restless he became. Finally, he cried out, "My son, carry me out if you please, that I may see it myself, and then I can rest." The son took his father up and carried him to where he could see the blood on the side posts and the lintel. "Now I am satisfied," he cried. "Thank God! Now I know that I am safe!"

My reader, can you say that—"Thank God, now I know that I am safe. I know that the blood was shed for me and has been sprinkled on me"? If not, I beseech you, by the terror and certainty of the judgment of God, make haste this day to heed God's Word. Turn away from your sin and place your trust in the blood. Oh, I pray you, do not add to all your other sins that of despising, rejecting, or treading upon the blood of the Son of God. I beseech you by the mercy of God and the wondrous love of the Son of God, flee from the wrath to come and seek shelter under the blood that alone can redeem. Believe, I beseech you, that no prayer, no worship, no works, no endeavor will avail you anything. But God has said, *"When I see the blood, I will pass over you."* Let that be your confidence. If He does see the blood on you, He will spare you. Come now, today, to this dear Savior, who lives to cleanse you with His blood, and who never once has rejected anyone who came to Him.

Chapter 8

———◆———

Purchased by the Blood

Thou art worthy...for thou wast slain,
and hast redeemed us to God by thy blood.
—Revelation 5:9

B ought: that word is understood by everybody. Buying and selling occupy a great place in our lives. We are all so constantly engaged in the process that the ideas attached to it are understood by everyone. The right that the buyer obtains over that which previously had not been his; the value that he attaches to it after its price has been paid; the certainty that what he has bought will be given to him; and the use that he will make of his purchase—all these things are obvious. Daily, in a thousand ways, they take place within the life of the community.

The words of our text, taken from a heavenly hymn of praise, *"Thou...hast redeemed us to God by thy blood,"* invite us to see in the mirror of earthly trade what the blood of the Lamb has done for us and what a clear knowledge of this fact entails. The right to us that our Lord Jesus, the Lamb of God, has obtained, and the claim that we now have in regard to Him, what we may expect from Him, what He expects from us—all these things will become plain to us. If the Holy Spirit teaches us to regard the blood in the light of these points, our hearts surely will take up the song of heaven with new joy: *"Thou art worthy...for thou wast slain, and hast redeemed us to God by thy blood."*

Let us notice some additional thoughts: first, the right to us that Christ has obtained; second, the claim He makes on us; third, the joy with which He will receive us; and, finally, the certainty that He will protect and care for us.

The Right to Us That Christ Has Obtained

"Thou...hast redeemed us to God by thy blood." This Scripture indicates the right to us that Christ has obtained. As Creator, the Lord Jesus has a right to every soul of man. Through Him God has bestowed life upon men, so that they might be His possession and inheritance. Never on earth has any maker had such a right over his own work as Jesus has over us; we belong to Him.

Someone has said, "It has often happened among men that one has had to buy back what really belonged to him but had been taken from him by a hostile power. Many times people have had to buy back their land and freedom by their blood. After that, land and liberty become of increased value."

Thus, the Son of God has ransomed us from the power of Satan. God, at Creation, had placed man under the government of His Son. By yielding to the temptations of Satan, man fell from God and became entirely subject to the authority of the tempter; he became his slave. It was the law of God that prohibited sin and threatened punishment. When man sinned, it was this law that bestowed upon Satan his authority. God has said, *"In the day that thou eatest"* (Gen. 2:17), you will fall into the power of death. God Himself gave man up to be a slave in the prison of Satan. For man there was no possibility of redemption except by ransom—by the payment of the price that the law must righteously demand as ransom for the redemption of prisoners.

You know that word *redemption*. In old times when it was the custom that prisoners of war were made slaves, sometimes a very high price was paid by the friends or rulers of the prisoners as ransom for their deliverance from slavery. Jesus Christ has purchased, with His own blood, our freedom from the prison and slavery of Satan. It is that prison in which he, as our enemy, had lodged us and to which the law of God had condemned us.

To purchase, to ransom, always means that one valuable thing is given for another. Our souls needed redemption: the law demanded the payment of a ransom. We were under its power and condemnation. We were held as prisoners until what we owed was paid, a recompense for the wrongs we had done—a perfect righteousness. Jesus came and gave Himself in our place: His soul for our souls. He bore our punishment of death, our curse of death. He shed His blood as reconciliation for our sin. That blood was the ransom price by which we are redeemed. He gave His life for our lives. His blood gave Him an eternal right to us. And now the message comes to us as from heaven—Jesus has bought us by His blood. He and none else has a right to us. Not Satan, not the world, not ourselves, have any right to us. The Son of God has bought us with His blood. He alone has a right to us; we belong to Him.

Oh, friend, be still and listen, and recognize that right. Perhaps you have never known this or have never meditated on it. An eternal price has been paid for you. A price has been paid for you of more value than the whole world—the blood of God's Son. You have been redeemed from the power of Satan. God proclaims you to be now the possession of His Son. And the Son comes today to take possession of what belongs to Him. He asks you, "Do you know that you belong to Me? Will you recognize My right?" His blood, His love, God as Judge, the Law as creditor, Satan as executioner—all agree. The Lord who has redeemed you by His blood has a right to you. Oh, let your heart respond: "Yes, Lord, I acknowledge that You, and You alone, have a right to me."

The Claim Christ Makes on Us

"Thou...hast redeemed us to God by thy blood." These words remind us of the claim that He makes on us. A person may have a right to something without exercising that right; he lays no claim to it. But it is not so with Jesus Christ. He comes to us with the urgent request that we should surrender ourselves to Him. You know how, in every ordinary purchase, the buyer has the right to ask that what he has purchased will be given to him. It is carefully stated when and where the delivery will take place. Jesus Christ sends His servants with the request that without delay—that at the hour and in the place where the message is delivered—there the persons, as His purchased possession, should hand themselves over and become subject to Him. That message comes to you again today. He entreats you to say farewell to all foreign authority that has ruled over you and to become His sole possession.

Chief among those foreign powers is sin. By our descent from fallen Adam, sin has a terrible authority over us. It has soaked to the deepest roots of our nature. It is thoroughly at home in us; it has become our nature. However strongly we may be inclined to forsake sin, whether by the voice of God, our own conscience, or some desire to do good, sin refuses to release us. As slaves of sin, we have no power to break the bonds that bind us. But Jesus, who has bought us by His blood, now calls on us to give ourselves to Him. However deeply we experience that we have been sold under sin and that the law of sin always holds us prisoners, He promises to deliver us from its tyranny. He promises that He will Himself bestow on us the power to serve and follow Him as Lord. He asks only for the choice of our hearts, the honest declaration of our wills, that we recognize His right and yield ourselves to Him. He will see to it that the authority of sin will be destroyed.

Another of the foreign powers that has exercised authority over us is the world. The needs and business of the world are so manifold and so urgent, they lay claim to our lives and all our powers. The promises, the enjoyments, and the temptations that the world presents to us are so flattering, and exercise such an unconscious influence upon us, that it is impossible for us to offer resistance to them in our own strength. The favor and assistance of the people we associate with, their displeasure and contempt if we separate ourselves from them to live only for God, work out in many an enslavement to the world. It rules over them and demands their obedience. Satan is the ruler of this world and through it exercises his power over them. Jesus Christ comes as Conqueror of Satan and the world and asks us to choose whom we wish to serve—Him, or this enemy of His. He asks this of us, as those who belong to Him. He points us to His blood, to the right to us that He has obtained, and asks that we should recognize this right and surrender ourselves as His possession.

There is another power, a still stronger one, foreign and hostile to Christ. It is the power of self. It is here that sin has worked its most terrible ruin. The doing of our own wills, seeking our own pleasure and our own honor, are so deeply rooted in us that, apart from an entire revolution, it can never be otherwise. Body and soul, understanding and imagination, inclination and love—all are subject to the terrible power of self-pleasing, to the tyranny of self. Jesus Christ asks that self should be pulled down from the throne and condemned to death. He asks that in all things His will and not ours should be supreme. He beseeches us to make an end of slavery to other lords and to give ourselves up to Him as His purchased possessions.

Each of us must deal with this claim, this request of the Lamb of God. How you deal with it will decide what your life will be in time and in eternity. A voice comes to us from heaven, saying, "He is worthy; He has been slain. He has purchased us to God by His blood." Oh, that our hearts might no longer hesitate, but by faith in that divine blood respond to His call and reply, "You are worthy, O Lord! Here I am. Take what You have purchased. I yield myself to You as Your possession."

The Joy with Which He Will Receive Us

"Thou...hast redeemed us to God by thy blood" gives us the pledge of the joy with which He will receive us. When a sinner has been urged to give himself to the Lord, and he declares his willingness to do so, he is, alas, often hindered by the fear that he is unworthy to be received. He feels himself so sinful, so dead. He feels he is so greatly lacking in humility and real earnestness, and in that heartfelt love that befits one who desires to give himself to such a Lord, that he cannot believe the Lord will receive him so instantly, so fully, and so eternally. He cannot understand it; still less does he feel in his heart that it is true.

What a glorious answer to all these questionings is in this word, *"Thou...hast redeemed us to God by thy blood."* Do you not know that if a person buys anything he will surely take possession of it if it is brought to him? You have, I suppose, at some time bought something. As you have paid your money for it and it was given or brought to you, were you not willing to receive it and take possession of it? The higher the price you paid for it, the less was there any doubt that you would take possession of what you had paid for.

"But"—you will perhaps answer—"if I buy something, I know what it is, and that it is worth the price I paid. But I, with my sinful heart, with everything so dead and miserable—there is reason for me to fear that He who purchased me will not receive me. I am not what I ought to be. When I buy an article and another of less worth is sent to me, I refuse to receive it. I send it back with the message: 'This is not what I bought and for which I have paid.'"

You are right, but consider what the difference is between Him who has bought us by His blood and human purchasers. He bought what He knew was bad, because it was bad, and which He will accept as bad, so that His love may have the joy and glory of making it good. How wonderful this is! It is nevertheless true; the worse you are, and the deeper you have sunk in the helplessness of your sin, the more fit you are for Him. Scripture says, *"Christ died for the ungodly....While we were yet sinners, Christ died for us"* (Rom. 5:6, 8). It says, further, that the price of Christ's blood was paid for those who denied the Lord, for those who sold Him, even for His rejecters. Understand, I pray you, that Jesus has paid an eternal price for you, as one who is an enemy, as one who is a lawful slave of Satan, as one entirely dead in sin. He comes to you who are in this condition with the request that you will surrender yourself to Him, and with a promise that He will receive you just as you are.

I pray you, do not allow yourself to be kept by Satan from your Lord and Savior any longer. It is Satan who whispers to you that you are too unworthy, that mercy is not for you because you are so sinful. It is a lie—a lie born in hell. You are utterly unworthy, but not too unworthy, for mercy is only for unworthy persons. If you have no desire to serve this Lord, if His love and His blood have no value in your eyes, say so openly and refuse to give yourself to Him as His purchased property. But if your heart acknowledges that you by right belong to Him—oh, come, I pray you, and believe that He will receive you instantly. And let every doubt depart under the power of that one word: "You have purchased me with Your blood."

It is impossible for the Lord Jesus to refuse to receive you. Between Him and the Father there is an eternal covenant concerning you. The Father has given Him right and authority over you. He has paid your ransom at the great price that has freed you from the tyranny of Satan. He has been constantly calling you to come to Him. He now entreats you again to give yourself up to Him. How can you be so foolish as to think that He will not receive you? Then doubt no longer. Although you are devoid of feeling, and everything appears cold and dead, come and cast yourself down before Him. Declare to Him that since He has bought you, you rely upon Him to receive you. He will certainly do so.

The Certainty That He Will Protect and Care for Us

"Thou...hast redeemed us to God by thy blood." This assures us that He will preserve us and care for us. The man who has purchased something of value, for instance, a good horse, not only receives it when it is brought to him, but he appreciates it, he takes care of it, and he provides for it. He exercises it and uses it. He does all this so that he may have the utmost service and pleasure out of it. When Jesus Christ receives us—however glorious that is—it is only the beginning. We can rely on Him who bought us by His blood to complete His work in us (Phil. 1:6).

It is just the lack of insight into this truth that holds many troubled persons back from surrender and causes many of weak faith to live always in trouble and worry. They do not apply to spiritual things what they understand so well in earthly affairs. When a man has paid a high price for something, even if only a horse or a sheep, he takes it for granted that he must care for it so that he may have pleasure and service from it. And the Lord Jesus—how is it that you do not understand it?— takes it upon Himself to care for you, and so to order things that He may attain His purpose in you. You cannot guard yourself against temptation or going astray. You cannot manage yourself or make yourself fit for His service. You cannot direct yourself so that you may know how to act in everything according to His will and that of the Father. You cannot do it. But He can; He will, as the One who has bought you with His blood.

My fellow believer, the right that the Lord Jesus has obtained to you is so infinitely high, so broad, so unlimited, that if you will only think about it, you will respond to it. Just as I desire that every member of my body—the eye, the ear, the hand, the foot—should always be at my service, so the Lord desires that you, as a member of His body, along with every power and faculty, should always without a moment's break serve Him. You are so far from being able to do this that you do not even comprehend it. Cease trying to do it, and begin each day by committing yourself to the almighty preservation and control of your

Lord. Just as a horse or a sheep with each new day must be cared for afresh by its owner, even more so must you, as the property of the Son of God, be cared for by Him. Christ is not an owner who is outside you, or who is only in heaven above; He is your Head. And just as the First Adam lives within you with his sinful nature, so Christ, as the Second Adam, lives in you with His holy nature and by His Holy Spirit. And the one thing to which He calls you is to trust Him, to wait on Him, to rely confidently upon Him to finish in the outward things of our lives His hidden and unnoticed work of protection and perfection. I pray that each one of us might know what is implied by our being accepted as the blood-bought possession of Jesus.

It implies that He has set a very high value on us, and so He will not allow any evil to befall us. He will manifest His love to us. He has need of us for His work and glory, and it is His desire and joy to adorn us with His salvation and to fill us with His unspeakable joy. Meditate on this until it becomes fixed firmly in your mind.

It implies that our great need is to recognize ourselves as His possession and, by a reverent confession of this, to have our hearts filled by the consciousness of it. Just as a faithful dog often shows so great an attachment to his owner that he will not cease following him, let the wonderful ownership of Jesus, His blood-bought right, so possess you that it will every moment be the keynote of your life and the power of an enduring attachment to Him.

Also, it implies that we should cultivate trust in Him, and let it completely control our whole souls and every thought as to how we are to spend our lives and do our work. A possession is preserved and cared for by the owner. Jesus is my heavenly and almighty Owner, who has bought me for Himself by His blood and prizes me as the dear purchase of that blood. He will surely protect me; He will surely make me fit for all things in which He intends to make use of me.

"Thou...hast redeemed us to God by thy blood." Oh, my readers, listen, I pray you, to the song of heaven, and let it begin

to sound in your heart. Let it be the heart confession of your relationship to the slain Lamb. Remember that the blood is the power that binds us to Jesus in bonds that cannot be loosened.

Let him who has not yet acknowledged the claim of Christ do so today, and let him now say, "You are worthy; for the sake of Your blood You shall have me."

Let him who has already acknowledged the Lord's claim abandon himself to the heavenly influences of the Holy Spirit for the destruction of all doubt and slowness of heart and for the enduement of power to live wholly for the Lamb of God.

Meditate on and adore God for this divine wonder, that you have been bought by the blood of the Son of God. Let your life become a testimony of the song: *"Thou art worthy...for thou wast slain, and hast redeemed us to God by thy blood."*

Chapter 9

─────◆◆◆◆─────

The Blood and the Trinity

*To the...elect according to the foreknowledge of God the
Father, through sanctification of the Spirit, unto obedience and
sprinkling of the blood of Jesus Christ: Grace unto you, and
peace, be multiplied.*
—1 Peter 1:1–2

*T*he Tri-unity of the Godhead is often considered as merely a
matter of doctrine and having no close relationship to the
Christian life. This is not the view of the New Testament when it
describes the work of redemption or the idea of the life of God.
In the Epistles the three Persons are constantly named together,
so that in each activity of grace all three together have a share in
it. God is triune; but in everything that He does, and at all times,
the Three are One.

This is in entire agreement with what we see in nature. A
trinity is found in everything. There is the hidden, inner nature,
the outward form, and the effect. It is not otherwise in the
Godhead. The Father is the eternal being—I AM—the hidden
foundation of all things and fountain of all life. The Son is the
outward form, the express image, the revelation of God. The
Spirit is the executive power of the Godhead. The nature of the

hidden unity is revealed and made known in the Son, and it is imparted to us and is experienced by us through the agency of the Spirit. In all their activities the Three are inseparably One.

Everything is of the Father, everything is in the Son, and everything is through the Spirit.

In the words of our text that Peter wrote to believers to whom also he sent his greetings, we find the relationship in which each redeemed one stands to the three Persons of the Godhead is clearly set forth.

They are *"elect according to the foreknowledge of God."* The source of our redemption is in the counsel of God.

They are chosen *"through sanctification of the Spirit"*: the entire carrying out of the counsel of God is through the Holy Spirit and the sanctification and the impartation of divine holiness that He works.

They are elect *"unto obedience and sprinkling of the blood of Jesus Christ."* The final purpose of God is the restoration of man to a state where the will of God will be done on earth as it is done in heaven. Then everything will reflect the glory of the free grace that has been revealed so gloriously in the death and blood of the Son of God.

The place that the *"sprinkling of the blood"* takes is most remarkable. It is mentioned last, as the great final end in which, according to the foreknowledge of the Father, the sanctification of the Spirit, and the submission to the obedience of Christ, it finds completion.

In order that we may understand its place and worth in redemption, let us consider it in the light of three things: first, the glorious purpose of the triune God; second, the mighty power by which that purpose was attained; and, third, the counsel in which everything originated.

The Glorious Purpose of the Triune God

Christians are described as *"elect...unto obedience and sprinkling of the blood of Jesus Christ."* In the Holy Trinity the place occupied by the Lord Jesus is characterized by the name that He bore as *"the only begotten Son of God"* (John 3:18). He is literally and really the only One with whom God the Father can or will have anything to do. As the Son, He is the Mediator through whom God worked in creation, and by whom the creature can draw near to God. God dwells in the hidden and unapproachable light of a consuming fire: Christ is the Light of Lights, the Light in which we can view and enjoy the Deity. And the eternal election of God can have no higher purpose than to give us a share in Christ and, through Him, approach to the Father Himself.

Because of sin there was no possibility for man to be brought near to God again, except through reconciliation by means of the sprinkling of the blood of Christ. Scripture speaks of Him as the *"Lamb slain from the foundation of the world"* (Rev. 13:8). It is stated that we are *"elect...unto...sprinkling of the blood of Jesus Christ."* This means that God ever and always saw that the only way by which salvation could be made possible for us, the only needful thing by which the door of heaven could be opened for us, and the right procured for us to obtain a share in all the blessings of His love, was by the sprinkling of the blood. Scripture tells us further that when the blood occupies the place in our eyes and hearts that it occupies in the eyes and heart of God, then we will certainly enter into the full enjoyment of what He has acquired for us by it.

What these blessings are is clearly revealed to us in the Word of God. *"Ye who sometimes were far off are made nigh by the blood of Christ"* (Eph. 2:13). We have liberty *"to enter into the holiest by the blood of Jesus"* (Heb. 10:19). He has *"washed us from our sins in his own blood"* (Rev. 1:5). *"How much more shall the blood of Christ...purge your conscience...to serve the living God?"* (Heb. 9:14). *"The blood of Jesus Christ...cleanseth us from all sin"* (1 John 1:7). Many such statements show us that the cleansing and fitness to draw near to God, that the true and living entrance into fellowship with Him, is the blessed effect of the *"sprinkling of the blood"* on our hearts and consciences. In the depths of eternity, that blood of sprinkling was the object of the unspeakable good pleasure of the Father as the means of redemption of His elect. It is obvious that when that blood becomes the good pleasure and joy of a sinner, and he seeks life and salvation in that blood, then the heart of God and the heart of the sinner meet one another. It is there that an inner agreement and fellowship, which nothing can break, is found in the blood. The Father has elected us to the sprinkling of the blood, so that we may heartily accept it and find our entire salvation in it.

There is still another word to consider: *"Elect...unto obedience and sprinkling of the blood of Jesus Christ."* Here the two sides of the life of grace are placed together for us in a most striking way. In the *"sprinkling of the blood,"* we learn what Christ has done for and to us. In *"obedience,"* we have what is expected from us. The creature can have no other blessedness than that found in the will of God, and in doing it as it is done in heaven. The Fall was simply the turning away of man from God's will to do his own will. Jesus came to alter this and to bring us again into obedience. And God lets us know that He, in His eternal choice, had these two things in view: *"obedience"* and the *"sprinkling of the blood."*

The placing together of these two thoughts teaches us the very important lesson that obedience and the sprinkling of the blood are inseparably united. It was so with the Lord Jesus. Apart from His obedience, the shedding of His blood would have been of no value. The blood is the life. That life consists of inner nature and will. The power of Jesus' blood lies wholly in this, that He *"offered himself without spot to God"* (Heb. 9:14), to do His will, subjecting His own will utterly to the will of God. *"He...became obedient unto death....Wherefore God also hath highly exalted him"* (Phil. 2:8–9). He who receives the blood of Jesus receives with it, as his life, His inner nature of utter obedience to God. Obedience and sprinkling of the blood are inseparably bound together. The inner nature manifested by Christ in the shedding of His blood must become the nature of those on whom it has been sprinkled.

He who desires to have the benefit of the blood must first submit himself to an obedience of faith that must characterize his whole life. He must understand that the blood is constantly crying, "God's will must be done, even to death." He who truly experiences the power of the blood of Jesus will manifest it by a life of obedience. In the heart of God, in the life and death of Christ, in the heart and life of the true Christian, these two things will always go together.

If any Christian asks why he enjoys so little of the peace and cleansing of the blood, he may be almost certain that the reason is that he has not fully surrendered himself to be obedient. If anyone asks how he may obtain the full enjoyment of the power of the blood, the reply may be, "Set yourself resolutely to obey God. Let your motto be, 'My will in nothing; God's will in everything'; that is what the blood of your Redeemer teaches you." Do not separate what God from the beginning has joined together—obedience and the sprinkling of the blood—and you will thus be led into the fullness of blessing. From eternity God has elected you to both obedience and the sprinkling of the blood.

It may be that you shrink from this demand. Such obedience seems to you to be out of your reach, and as you hear about the power and blessedness obtainable by the sprinkling of the blood, even that seems to you to be out of reach. Do not be discouraged, but attend to what has yet to be said.

The Power by Which That Purpose Was Attained

The Spirit is the great power of God. In the Holy Trinity He proceeds from the Father and the Son. He, by His omnipotent but hidden activity, executes the divine purpose. He reveals and makes known the Father and the Son. In the New Testament the word *holy* is applied to Him more often than to the Father or the Son. He is almost always called the Holy Spirit because it is He who from the inward being of God transfers holiness to the redeemed. The life of God is where His holiness dwells. Where the Holy Spirit imparts the life of God, there He imparts and maintains the holiness of God, and thus is called the Spirit of sanctification. So the text says that we are *"elect...through sanctification of the Spirit, unto obedience and sprinkling of the blood of Jesus Christ."* It is committed to the Holy Spirit by His holy power to watch over us and to fulfill God's purpose in us. We are elect in sanctification of the Spirit unto obedience.

The Spirit of sanctification and obedience: these two go together in the purpose of God. Here we have also a solution to the difficulty already mentioned, that it is not possible for us to render the obedience that God demands. Because God knew this much better than we do, He has made provision for it. He bestows on us the Spirit of sanctification, who so renews our hearts and our inward nature and fills us with His holy and heavenly power that it becomes really possible for us to be obedient. The one necessary thing is that we should recognize and trust in the indwelling of the Holy Spirit and follow His leading.

His inward activity is so gentle and hidden, He unites Himself so entirely with us and our endeavors, that we still imagine that it is our own thinking or willing, where He has already been the hidden Worker. Through this disregard of Him, we cannot believe that when we have a conviction of sin, or a willingness to obey (both the result of His inward activity), that He also has the power to perfect that work in us. Let him, therefore, who really desires to be obedient, be careful persistently and quietly to maintain this attitude of trustful confidence: "The Spirit of God is in me." Let him bow reverently before God with the prayer that He would strengthen him *"with might by his Spirit in the inner man"* (Eph. 3:16).

The sanctification of the Spirit supplies the power that enables us to be obedient, and through which also we experience what the sprinkling of the blood means and imparts.

This is the reason why so many of God's people have to complain that after all they have learned and heard and thought and believed about the blood, they experience so little of its power. This is not to be wondered at, for that learning, hearing, thinking, and believing is in a great part only a work of the understanding. And even when prayer is made for the Holy Spirit, it is all in expectation that He will give us clearer ideas of the truth. No, this is not the way. The Spirit dwells in the heart: it is there He desires to do His first and greatest work. The heart must first be made right, and then the understanding will lay hold of the truth, not merely as a mental idea, but as an inner strength for the Christian life. We are chosen in sanctification of the Spirit—not in the activities of the understanding—to the sprinkling of the blood.

Everyone who desires to know the power of the blood of Jesus must remember that the Spirit and the blood bear witness together (1 John 5:8). It was by the shedding of the blood, and by the sprinkling of that blood before God in heaven, that the Spirit was free to come and dwell among us and in us. It was to assure the hearts of the disciples concerning the glorious result of the blood in heaven, in opening a free and bold entrance to God, and to make them partakers of the blessedness and power of the heavenly life that was now their portion, that the Holy Spirit was sent into their hearts.

The first Pentecost, in all its power and blessing, is our portion, also our inheritance. Would that we might cease to seek in our own strength the salvation and blessings purchased for us by the blood. If only we began to live as those who have been led in sanctification of the Spirit to the full experience of what the blood can do, we would have, as never before, a real entrance into an eternal abiding place near God and fellowship with Him. We would know what it is to have a conscience cleansed by the blood, to have the heart entirely cleansed from an evil conscience, and so have liberty for an abiding communion with God. The Holy Spirit, as we commit ourselves to His leading, is able, in a moment, to bring us into that relationship to Him in which we will expect everything from Him.

We have seen what is the work of the Son and of the Spirit; let us now ascend to see the place that the Father occupies.

The Counsel in Which Everything Originated

Peter wrote to the *"elect according to the foreknowledge of God the Father, through sanctification of the Spirit, unto obedience and sprinkling of the blood of Jesus Christ."* The counsel of the Father is the origin of everything, and that is in the Godhead as well as in the work of redemption. In the Godhead, the Son proceeds from the Father, and the Spirit proceeds from the Father and the Son. The whole counsel of redemption is also solely *"according to the purpose of him who worketh all things after the counsel of his own will"* (Eph. 1:11). From the greatest—the ordering of the work of the Son and of the Holy Spirit—to the least—the day-to-day occurrences in His kingdom—all this is the work of the Father. Sanctification of the Spirit, obedience, and the sprinkling of the blood are the portion of the elect, according to the foreknowledge of the Father.

You may, with the most entire confidence, reckon that He who has thought out this wonderful counsel so far, and gloriously carried it out in the sprinkling of the blood and the sending of the Spirit, will just as surely and gloriously carry it out in your soul. This is the right use of the doctrine of predestination—leading you to cast yourself down before God and to acknowledge that from Him, and through Him, and to Him are all things, and to expect everything from Him alone. Take your place before God, my fellow believer, in deep reverence and complete dependence. Do not imagine that now that God has revealed Himself in Christ and by the Spirit, that you, by making use of what you have learned from this revelation, can work out your own salvation. Let it not be thought of! God must work in you to will and to do before you can work it out. (See Philippians 2:12–13.) God must work in you by the Spirit, and by Him must reveal Christ in you. Give God the glory, and let the fullest dependence upon Him be the keynote of your life of faith. If God does not do everything in you, all is in vain. If you expect anything from yourself, you will receive nothing; if you expect all from God, God will do everything in you. Let your expectation be from God alone.

Apply this to all on which we have been meditating concerning obedience. *"Elect...unto obedience"*; how certain it is that obedience is indispensable, that it is possible, that in it lies salvation. The Son was obedient unto death. But this was because He had said, *"The Son can do nothing of himself"* (John 5:19). He submitted Himself to the Father in order that the Father might do everything in Him. Let every desire to do the will of God, every fear of your own weakness, drive you to Him who has elected you to obedience. Predestined to obedience: that gives assurance that you can be obedient. God Himself will accomplish His purpose in you. Become nothing before Him; He will become all.

Apply it especially to the blessed *"sprinkling of the blood of Jesus Christ."* It was this that led me to the choice of this text. Your heart is longing with great desire—is it not?—to live every day under the clear consciousness: "I have been sprinkled with the eternal, precious, divine blood of the Lamb." Your heart longs after all the blessed effects of that blood—redemption, pardon, peace, cleansing, sanctification, drawing near to God, joy, victory—all of which come through the blood. Your heart longs to experience constantly these blessings in full measure. Cast fear aside—you have been elected by God to the sprinkling of the blood of Christ Jesus. You must steadfastly rely on the fact that God, as God, will bestow it on you. Wait continually upon Him in patience of soul, and confidently expect it. He *"worketh all things after the counsel of his own will"* (Eph. 1:11); He Himself will surely work it out in you.

Apply this also to the sanctification of the Spirit. He is the link that binds together the middle and the end. His is the power that brings together the eternal purpose of God and a life of obedience and the sprinkling of the blood. Do you feel that this is the one thing that you desire and for which you must wait so that you may inherit the full blessing? Understand that it is God Himself who bestows the Spirit, who works through the Spirit, who will fill you by the Spirit. How can God who elected you *"through sanctification of the Spirit"* allow you to lack that without which His purpose cannot be carried out? Be confident about this; ask and expect it with utter boldness. It is possible to live in the sanctification of the Spirit because it has been designed for you from eternity.

The sprinkling of the blood is the light or revelation of the Trinity—how wonderful and glorious it is! The Father designed the sprinkling of the blood and elected us to it. The Son shed His blood and bestows it on the obedient from heaven. The Spirit of sanctification makes it our own, with abiding power, and imparts to us all the blessings that He has obtained for us. Blessed sprinkling of the blood! Revelation of the triune God! May this be our joy and our life each day.

Chapter 10

———◆———

Washed in His Blood

*Unto him that loved us, and washed us from our sins
in his own blood, and hath made us kings and priests
unto God and his Father; to him be glory and dominion
for ever and ever. Amen.*
—Revelation 1:5–6

*T*he apostle John dwelt in spirit before the doors of an open heaven when he was in Patmos. Time after time he saw in divine visions the glory of God and of the Lamb and of the redeemed. Of all the things that he saw, the most wonderful was that which caused the four living creatures, the four and twenty elders, the angels, the redeemed, and the whole creation to fall down repeatedly in ecstasy and adoration—the vision of the Lamb standing as it had been slain, in the midst of the throne. And of everything that he heard, what most deeply impressed him was the frequent mention made in heaven of the blood of the Lamb. In the hymn of praise of the redeemed, he had heard the words, *"Thou art worthy..., for thou wast slain, and hast redeemed us to God by thy blood"* (Rev. 5:9). And in the reply of the elder to the question to which John could give no answer, he offered this explanation: *"These are they which...*

have washed their robes, and made them white in the blood of the Lamb" (Rev. 7:14).

John had been commanded to describe what he had seen and heard. He began his book with a greeting similar to those we find in the Epistles: *"Grace be unto you, and peace, from him which is, and which was, and which is to come"* (Rev. 1:4)—the eternal God. Then he mentioned the Spirit: *"and from the seven Spirits which are before the throne"* (v. 4); and then follow these words: *"and from Jesus Christ* [as he had seen Him]...*the first begotten of the dead, and the prince of the kings of the earth"* (v. 5).

The mention of the name of the Lord filled John's heart with joy and praise. Impressed by what he had heard in heaven, he cried out, *"Unto him that loved us, and washed us from our sins in his own blood, and hath made us kings and priests unto God and his Father, to him be glory and dominion for ever and ever. Amen."*

It is the blood, and being washed in that blood, that is the central point in his praise. The blessing seemed truly glorious and heavenly to John. He saw that blood linked with the love and salvation Christ has given us. And his heart, set on fire with a heavenly zeal, cried out, *"To him be glory and dominion for ever."*

We have for some time been meditating upon the blood of Jesus. If there is one thing that befits us, which would be a proof that we have recognized something of the glory and power of that blood, it would be that we also, as we think of it, cry out, *"To him be glory and dominion for ever and ever."*

In this chapter we will consider John's song of praise. May it be granted to us to see something of what he saw, to feel something of what he felt, to receive something of the fire that inspired him, and to bring something of the offering of praise that he brought. Let us to that end fix our attention on the place that the blood occupies in this thanksgiving and inquire into the meaning of the following: first, He has washed us in His blood; second, He has made us kings and priests; third, He loved us; and, finally, to Him be the glory and dominion forever and ever.

He Has Washed Us in His Blood

We know what the word *washing* means. We wash our bodies to cleanse them from the least defilement that adheres to us. Our clothes are washed to remove every stain or spot. Now, sin is not merely a transgression of the law of God that is reckoned to us as guilt from which we must obtain acquittal or pardon. Sin has an effect on our souls. It is a pollution that cleaves to us. The blood of Jesus procures for us more than the pardon for our guilt. When this has been powerfully brought to our hearts by the Holy Spirit, then at the same time the blood manifests the full deliverance of its cleansing power so that our souls know that they have been washed whiter than snow.

John spoke of this twofold work of grace in his first epistle. He wrote, *"If we confess our sins, he is faithful and just to forgive us our sins, and to cleanse us from all unrighteousness"* (1 John 1:9). To the same effect he had previously said, *"If we walk in the light, as he is in the light"*—that is in the pardoning and sanctifying love of God—*"we have fellowship one with another, and the blood of Jesus Christ his Son cleanseth us from all sin"* (v. 7). This refers to the abiding and uninterrupted cleansing of sin in the case of him who walks in the light, in fellowship with God.

Where does this washing take place, and what is it really that is washed? It is the heart. It is in the deep, hidden, inner life of man that this effect of the blood is experienced. Jesus said, *"The kingdom of God is within you"* (Luke 17:21). Sin has penetrated into the heart, and the whole nature has become saturated with it. The blood too must penetrate the heart; as deeply as the power of sin has gone, so deeply must the inner being be cleansed by the blood. We know that when some article of clothing is washed, the water with its cleansing power must soak in as deeply as the stain, if it is to be removed. Even so must the blood of Jesus penetrate to the deepest roots of our beings. Our hearts, our entire personalities, must be reached by the cleansing power of the blood. *"The blood...cleanseth us from all sin"* (1 John 1:7). Where sin has reached, there, too, must the blood follow; where sin ruled, there the blood must rule. The entire heart must be cleansed by the blood. However great may be the depth of the heart, however manifold and lively its activities may be, the blood is just as wonderful and penetrating in its effects. It is in our hearts that the cleansing by the blood of Jesus must take place. We are told, *"They...have washed their robes, and made them white in the blood of the Lamb"* (Rev. 7:14).

A person's position or character can often be told by his clothing. Royal robes are a sign of royal estate. Filthy or torn garments are a sign of poverty or carelessness. White robes indicate a holy character. Thus we read of the Lamb's bride, *"To her was granted that she should be arrayed in fine linen, clean and white: for the fine linen is the righteousness of saints"* (Rev. 19:8). (*"Righteousness"* here is the translation of a word that means "the righteous acts.")

The message of the Lord Jesus to the church at Sardis was, *"Thou hast a few names even in Sardis which have not defiled their garments; and they shall walk with me in white: for they are worthy"* (Rev. 3:4).

Out of the heart *"are the issues of life"* (Prov. 4:23); to the degree that the heart is cleansed, so the entire life is cleansed. The whole man inwardly and outwardly is cleansed by the power of the blood.

How is this washing brought about? It is done by our Lord Jesus Himself who *"washed us from our sins in his own blood."* The washing began in an act personally accomplished in us by our Lord. He alone can perfect the work that He carries on in us by the Holy Spirit. Sin invaded our lives. Our powers of thought, will, and feeling were all brought under its authority. This was not an authority exercised from without, or occasionally, but one that was so united with these powers of ours that they themselves became altogether sinful. But now the Holy Spirit takes possession of the place in which sin had become entrenched. *"The Spirit is life"* (Rom. 8:10), and He becomes the life of our lives. Through Him the Lord Jesus carries on His work in us. Through Him also the blood is constantly applied in its cleansing power.

Our Lord is a High Priest in *"the power of an endless life"* (Heb. 7:16), and thus the cleansing power of the blood of the Son of God is unceasingly conveyed to us. As we wash and cleanse ourselves daily, and thus are refreshed and invigorated, so the Lord bestows on the soul that trusts in Him the enjoyment of a constant sense of cleansing by the blood. It is He Himself who cleanses us from sin, while we on our part receive the cleansing by faith, by that faith through which at first we receive the pardon of sin. But faith's capacity is now enlarged by obtaining a spiritual view of the divine power and continuous activity of the blood. By this insight, faith obtains a spiritual understanding and becomes able to comprehend the fact that just as the blood has had an infinite effect in the Holiest in heaven, so sin has been completely and finally atoned for before God. Faith beholds the Lord Jesus, the great High Priest, living in the heart. He cleanses it in the blood that ever retains its power. Faith has learned that full salvation consists in one thing—Jesus Himself, who has cleansed us by His blood, is our life.

He Has Made Us Kings and Priests

This is the position for which we are prepared and to which we are exalted by the cleansing of the blood. In this the power of the blood is manifested. If we wish to fully comprehend the spiritual connection between these two positions that are ours through the blood, we must learn it from the experience of the Lord Jesus Himself.

It was only after He had shed His blood that He was able to enter the Holiest as Priest and to ascend the throne as King. It was His blood that conquered sin, and by it He was consecrated to enter into the Holiest, into God's presence as Priest.

The blood bestowed on Him the right, as Victor, to rule as King in the glory of God. Such is the heavenly and divine power that the blood possesses.

Now, when the blood comes into contact with us, and we by faith recognize its full power, it produces in us also the nature and fitness to become priests and kings. As long as we think that forgiveness of sins is all that is to be obtained by the blood, we will neither understand what the kingly priesthood means, nor will we have any desire for it. But when the Holy Spirit teaches and enables us to believe that the blood can accomplish in us also what it accomplished in the Lord Jesus personally, then the heart is opened to receive this glorious truth. The blood opens the way into a kingly priesthood. It was so to the Lord Jesus; it may be so with us, also.

Let us no longer be content with standing still at the beginning of things, but let us press on to perfection. Let us press on to the knowledge of the perfection prepared for us in the Lord Jesus—entrance by His power into the life in the Holiest, into a fellowship in the life of Jesus, our Priestly King.

What now does it mean that He, when He has cleansed us by His blood, also makes us priests and kings to God and His Father? The principal idea attached to the title "king" is that of authority and rule; to the title "priest," that of purity and nearness to God. The blood of Jesus makes us priests and gives us admission into the presence, the love, and the fellowship of God. We are so cleansed by the blood as to be prepared for this. Jesus so fills us with His Spirit, with Himself, that we in Him may truly draw near to God as priests.

The blood of Jesus carries in it so much of His victory over sin and death that it inspires us with the consciousness of His victorious power and bestows on us victory over sin and every enemy. He makes us kings. Jesus, the living, Priestly King on the throne, cannot manifest in us His full power by exercising it from above, or from the outside, but only by indwelling. When He, the Priestly King, takes up His abode within us, He makes us kings and priests.

Do we wish to know the purpose of this? The answer is not far to seek. Why is Jesus seated as Priest on the throne of the heavens? It is so that man may be blessed, and that God may be glorified in man. As Priest, He lives only for others, to bring them near to God. He lives as King only that He might reveal the kingdom of God in us and through us. He makes us priests so that we might serve the living God, that we might bring others near to Him, that we might be filled with his Spirit so as to be a blessing to others.

As priests through the blood of Christ we live for others, to pray for them, to work among them, to teach them, and to bring them to God. To be a priest is no idle self-seeking blessedness. It is a compelling power to enter into God's presence on behalf of others, the power to pray for blessings and to receive and carry and distribute them. He makes us kings to complete and perfect the priesthood. Because of this, the idea of authority stands out so prominently. Jesus fills us with a kingly nature; He enables us to rule over sin, over the world, over men. In the midst of all circumstances and difficulties, of all opposition or cruelty, the Christian who yields himself to be made king by Christ lives in the joyous certainty that he is one with Him who has won the victory, and that in Him he is more than a conqueror (Rom. 8:37).

He Loved Us

We have spoken of the blood in which Jesus has cleansed us and of the glory to which He has exalted us. Let us now ascend to the fountainhead from which all this flows out to us—it is that He loved us. If we desire really to understand the salvation that God bestows on us—to understand it so that it will tune our voices to sing like that of John, *"To him be glory"*—we must first of all understand that its origin and power are in the love of Jesus. Love is the greatest glory of salvation. As it springs from love as its source, it must lead us to that love as its object and nature. Love always suggests a personal, mutual attachment. This is the most wonderful thing in salvation, and it is almost impossible to fully comprehend—that the Lord Jesus desires to honor us with His love and His friendship. He wishes to have fellowship with us as His loved ones and to fill and satisfy our hearts with His divine love.

It is John especially who taught us what this love is. In his Gospel he told us the Lord Jesus Christ said that as the Father loved Him, so He also loved us (John 15:9). Our Lord was one with the Father in nature and life. It is difficult for us to form any idea of what that unity is. But love, as the revelation of this unity, helps us in some small measure to understand it.

In love the Father goes out of Himself and communicates Himself to the Son, in whom is His delight and life. He imparts to the Son all that He has and holds communion with Him in a life of giving and receiving. The Father has no life or delight or pleasure apart from the Son. That is the love with which Jesus loves His own. (See John 17:26.) He gave Himself for them, imparts Himself to them, lives in them. He wishes to have no life apart from them. From the beginning of His love, in pitying them and sympathizing with them, He passed on to the love of good pleasure and fellowship, with a view to a unity in which they would dwell in Him and He in them. His desire and rest was in them, and they learned *"to comprehend with all saints* [some idea of the]*...love of Christ, which passeth knowledge"* (Eph. 3:18–19). Only the Holy Spirit can lead the soul personally into that love. *"The love of God is shed abroad in our hearts by the Holy Ghost which is given unto us"* (Rom. 5:5).

The love of God is such a supernatural, heavenly power that we might be tempted to make it merely a matter of thought, and by that means create some impression of it in our hearts. But a real participation in that love from heaven is such a divine matter that only those who have with great tenderness and wholeheartedness yielded themselves to be led and taught by the Holy Spirit can come to the knowledge of it. The love of God is plainly declared in Scripture to be the result of Christ dwelling in the heart. Only where the inner communion with the Lord has become in a measure the joy and experience of every day can we know what the Lord meant when He said, *"Continue ye in my love"* (John 15:9). *"Unto him that loved us, and washed us from our sins in his own blood, and hath made us kings and priests unto God and his Father."*

Let us consider Jesus as He was when as man He suffered and died for us, to give His blood for us. Let us allow Him to reveal in us the meaning and heavenly power of that blood. He will teach us that the most glorious fact in all His work is that it is the gift and bearer of His eternal, unceasing love toward us. Let us think of where He is carrying us—it is to a full partnership in His kingly priesthood and glory. He allows us to enjoy a foretaste of the love that make us entirely one with Him and that will live forever in our hearts. Then our first and last thought about Jesus will be: Him who loved us.

To Him Be the Glory and Dominion Forever and Ever

The words of this song of praise are generally applied to God, but our Lord Jesus Christ is God, and they belong to Him also. He is worshipped here as our Redeemer. Now at the end of our series of meditations on His blood, and what He has obtained for us by that blood, these words of praise are a suitable expression for the feelings that ought to be ours—*"to him be glory and dominion for ever and ever."* These words came from a heart full of the joy of a personal experience of redemption. John wrote as one who was living in the full enjoyment of the love of his Lord, who knew and felt in his heart that he was cleansed in the blood, and who experienced that Jesus had made him a king and a priest. His thanksgiving is that of one who rejoices with *"joy unspeakable and full of glory"* (1 Pet. 1:8)—a joy kindled by the song of heaven to which he had been listening. Let us put this to our hearts. Nothing will equip us for taking a real share in this thanksgiving that was offered involuntarily from the depth of a joyful heart except a living experience of the love of Jesus, of the power of His blood to cleanse us, and of the kingly priesthood in which He enables us to live. If I would truly attribute glory and power to Jesus, my heart must be inwardly filled with that glory and power. *"Out of the abundance of the heart the mouth speaketh"* (Matt. 12:34). Think of how true this was on the Day of Pentecost. What was it that moved a band of one hundred and twenty to praise and glorify the Lord? The Holy Spirit, who is the glory and power of the Lord Jesus, had descended upon them. And because they were filled with that glory and power, their hearts could ascend in praise to Him, and from them streamed out blessings for others.

It is the glory and power of Jesus to bestow His love on a soul and to bring about its cleansing in His own blood and to appoint such a one to His kingly priesthood. Then the heart overflows spontaneously—*"to him be glory and dominion for ever and ever."*

You who have accompanied me through God's Word to discover what the glory and power of the blood of Jesus is—ought not your lives and walk every day be full of the notes of praise and worship—*"to him be glory and dominion"*?

This is possible. Jesus Himself is the center of this threefold blessing—the love, the blood, and the kingly priesthood. Jesus Himself will so reveal them to us by His Spirit that we will ceaselessly experience all these blessings.

Let us, as far as our knowledge goes, at every remembrance of His love, cry out, *"To him be the glory."* At times we are convicted that the praise we offer is too weak and too seldom heard, or that it has too little of the joy-note of heaven in it. But each conviction is a help to us if it drives us to seek after a fullness of Christ's presence within us that causes our hearts to overflow.

Yes, it is possible. Jesus lives, and Jesus has loved us and has Himself cleansed us in His blood. He bestows on us the disposition of kingship and priesthood by His indwelling.

It is possible. He can fill our lives with the experience that finds expression in the thanksgiving: "To Him be the glory and power."

My friends, we hope to meet one day amid that multitude who have washed their robes in the blood of the Lamb and who never weary in singing, *"Thou art worthy..., for thou...hast redeemed us to God by thy blood"* (Rev. 5:9). Let our exercises of preparation for that glory consist in the singing of that song: *"Unto him that loved us, and washed us from our sins in his own blood, and hath made us kings and priests unto God and his Father; to him be glory and dominion for ever and ever. Amen."*

Book Two

———◆◆———

Receiving Power
from God

Contents

Preface

A number of years ago I was asked to write a series of articles encouraging Christians to live a life of earnest devotion to God. At that time I was deeply involved in a study of the epistle to the Ephesians. I thought I could connect the teaching of the epistle with my thoughts on spiritual living to give some help for the believer's quiet time with the Lord.

I am deeply conscious of my imperfections in expressing what I have seen of the treasures God has stored in this epistle for His church. Nevertheless, I have compiled my thoughts in this book in the hope that God may use them to help some of His children realize the standard of the true Christian life. God is able and willing to make all the spiritual blessings and power that Paul's letter contains come true in our experience.

I send this book out with the prayer of Paul in his epistle, *"That the God of our Lord Jesus Christ, the Father of glory, may give unto you the spirit of wisdom and revelation in the knowledge of him"* (Eph. 1:17). Unless that Spirit is sought, received, and yielded to, the truths of the epistle will remain a mystery. With the Spirit's teaching, we will *"be filled with the knowledge of his will in all wisdom and spiritual understanding"* (Col. 1:9). We will discover that His power is actually able to do in us far above what we can ask or think.

—ANDREW MURRAY

Chapter 1

————◆◆————

The Spirit of Devotion

Pray to thy Father which is in secret; and thy
Father...shall reward thee openly.
—Matthew 6:6

We use the word *devotion* in two ways—with regard to prayer in our private devotions and with regard to that spirit of devotion, or devotedness to God, that is to mark our daily lives. If we meet our Father in the inner chamber, He will give us the open reward of grace to live our lives to His glory and devote our whole being to His will. The *act of devotion* secures the power for that *spirit of devotion* that is to fill our daily lives to His glory.

The classic passage on the law of devotion is Leviticus 27:28: *"No devoted thing, that a man shall devote unto the LORD..., shall be sold or redeemed: every devoted thing is most holy unto the LORD."* Devotion is the wholehearted and irrevocable giving up to God of something that may never be taken back again. The person or thing becomes *"most holy unto the LORD."*

Aids to devotion may be given in more than one way. The simplest would be to suggest helpful ways to prepare us for worshipping God in truth. We could discuss some of the chief hindrances to effective prayer and Bible study or some of the reasons that these hindrances have such power over us. We may read a series of Scripture meditations to strengthen faith. The Word will become a joy to us and give us the humble trust that our devotions are pleasing to God.

Another way is more difficult, but it has some advantages. It does not deal directly with the act of devotion, but with that spirit that is to rule us all day and fill every action with true devotion to God. The goal is to encourage the personal involvement of the worshipper, stirring him to inquire as to what is the true meaning of a life wholly given up to God, His will, and His glory. He may think of his successes or failures in the past and their causes. He can then determine the measure of effort and self-denial necessary to succeed in the pursuit of true devotion.

Learning to Think

The goal of a good teacher is to stimulate the mind of the pupil to action. When a pupil is awakened to realize his powers and led to taste the joy of victory over apparently insurmountable difficulties, he has been given the key to discover truths for himself. No one can do us a greater favor than stimulating our desire to seek with our whole hearts a spirit of life and devotion that is most pleasing to God.

Socrates has been called the greatest teacher (after Christ) that the world has ever seen. He communicated no knowledge directly. He simply asked questions and helped his scholars to see their own ignorance and then to know their powers of thought and reason. Finally, he led them to understand that the real value of knowledge lay in its moral power, as the truth was received in the heart and life.

Today, men claim to have little time for personal meditation on divine truth. Perhaps we need a Socrates to awaken us by his questions to find out whether we really understand the words we use and honestly believe the truths we profess. The unbelieving Socrates could teach many Christians the meaning of true religion and help us in our devotion.

Our lives must be as holy as our prayers. Our prayers prove their reality by the fruit they bear in the holiness of our lives. True devotion in prayer will assuredly be rewarded with the power to live a life of true devotion to Jesus and His service.

Let Jesus Christ Himself, our blessed Teacher, guide us to find out whether our devotion is what He desires from us: a full surrender to God and a full devotion to His glory every day.

Chapter 2

---◆---

The New Testament Standard

*Howbeit for this cause I obtained mercy, that in me
first Jesus Christ might show forth all longsuffering,
for a pattern to them which should hereafter believe
on him to life everlasting.*
—1 Timothy 1:16

*I*n any judgment we make, everything depends on our standard of measure. Many believers become content with the levels of ordinary Christianity. Although they may acknowledge that their own devotion is defective, there will be no deep conviction of sin or of the need and the possibility of any higher attainment.

But when we begin to see the standard of the New Testament and its universal obligation, we realize how far we have come short of it. We become convicted of the great sin of unbelief in the power of Jesus to keep us from sin and to enable us to walk pleasing to God. However impossible the standard is with men, it is not impossible with God because He works in us by the power of His Holy Spirit.

To discover the New Testament standard of devotion is not an easy matter. Our preconceived opinions blind us, and our environment exercises a powerfully deluding influence. Unless there is a sincere desire to know the whole will of God along with a prayerful dependence on the Holy Spirit's teaching, we may search in vain. But everyone who is truly willing to live entirely for God and desires in everything to please Him should be of good courage. God wants us to know His will and has promised by the Spirit to reveal it to us.

Paul—Our Example

Paul said that Christ made him a pattern for all believers, and he frequently admonished the churches to follow his example. In studying true New Testament devotion, Paul makes an excellent pattern. But why should we imitate Paul when God gave His Son as our perfect pattern? Many look upon Christ in His sinless perfection as utterly beyond what they can attain. Thus, His example loses much of its impact.

But Paul, the chief of sinners, was a man like us. Christ proved what He could do for a sinner in saving Paul and keeping him from sin. What Christ did for Paul, He can and will do for us, too. If we as Christians make a careful study of the life of devotion Christ enabled Paul to live, we will be one step nearer to the absolute devotion to God set before us in Scripture. We will know the true devotion that is essential to a Christian life.

Is there really a great difference between the standard of devotion in our churches and that of the New Testament? Our creeds honor God's Word, and we acknowledge Scripture as our only guide. A little reflection will suggest the answer.

Not long after the first generations of Christians had passed away, terrible corruption entered the church. In course of time, the church sank into the darkness of the Middle Ages. With the Reformation and the preaching of the doctrine of justification by faith, there was a great revival of Christian truth. But it lacked the corresponding revival of Christian life and practice. While we bless God for the Reformation, we must remember that *it was not Pentecost*. The spirit and power of Pentecost was infinitely greater.

Church history tells us that it sometimes took half a century and more before some of the great doctrines of our faith were fully understood and formulated. It was not given to one generation to develop more than one truth at a time. All the strength of the Reformers was required to free the great doctrine of justification by faith from the errors under which it had been buried. The full exposition of the doctrine of sanctification, of the power and work of the Holy Spirit, of the calling of the church to preach the Gospel to the heathen—these truths were left to later ages.

Even now in studying the true standard of spiritual devotion to God, we must beware of looking to the Reformation or to later ages for our answer. Our only safety is in careful study guided by the Holy Spirit and the teaching of Scripture. God gave Paul as an example and a pledge of what He could do for us. Therefore, we may be sure that his example of devotion, self-sacrifice, joy, and victory will help us find the path in which we can live pleasing to God.

Stepping into Spiritual Life

Private devotions give us a clearer insight into what God is absolutely willing to do for us. A life prepared for us by God Himself is waiting to be revealed in us by the Holy Spirit. We must only be ready to know and confess how much is lacking in our spiritual life.

The church today is characterized by the feeble workings of the Holy Spirit. The Bible promises us the mighty working of God's Spirit in the hearts of His children. Therefore, we should make a penitent confession of how little we have honored the Holy Spirit and lived up to what He is willing to work in us. Then our hearts will be drawn out to a new and stronger faith in the mighty workings of the Spirit that God has promised. Each day our devotions lead us out of the human standard we have been content with and into a life in the Spirit that God has provided and will certainly make real to us.

As we pursue our study, let us fix our attention on three simple questions:

1. Does Scripture really lay down a standard for those who wholly yield themselves to the Spirit and trust God's almighty power to work in them?
2. Is it true that the church as a whole does not live up to the standard that God has placed within our reach?
3. Are we ready to yield ourselves with our whole hearts to accept what God has prepared?

Chapter 3

---◆---

Finished and Unfinished Work

*Because ye are sons, God hath sent forth the Spirit of his Son
into your hearts, crying, Abba, Father.*
—Galatians 4:6

When God revealed His love for us in the gift of His Son, His great work was completed. When Christ was raised from the dead and seated on the throne of God, His work was also completed. The dispensation of the Spirit had begun.

The Spirit's job is to reveal all that the work of God and Christ had prepared. The work of the Holy Spirit has not yet been fully accomplished. For this reason, Christ sits upon the throne, waiting for all His enemies to be made His footstool (Ps. 110:1). The work of the Father and the Son was finished when salvation was prepared for man's acceptance. The office of the Holy Spirit is to impart the grace that enables men to live out what the Father and the Son have provided.

In this dispensation, the Spirit's work and man's work are linked together. The Spirit does His work through man, and whatever is to be done in the kingdom of God is done by man. The Holy Spirit can manifest Himself in no other way than in the spirit of man. In this dispensation we are to fulfill man's part in carrying out God's plan.

God's Glorious Plan

When Paul spoke of God in Christ reconciling the world to Himself, he immediately added, *"And hath committed unto us the word of reconciliation"* (2 Cor. 5:19). The responsibility of making the reconciliation known was entrusted to the church. The power that reconciliation works in the world depends on the faithfulness or failure of God's people. These thoughts suggest the glory of the ministry of the Spirit, the terrible failure on the part of the church, and the great need of restoration.

God's reason for sending the Spirit of Christ to take possession of the hearts of men was to restore their fellowship with Himself. All the work of God and Christ in redemption culminated in this one thing—the Holy Spirit was to communicate the salvation that had been provided and maintain unbroken fellowship in the hearts of God's children. He was to be the Spirit of life, leading them in the path of holiness and perfect conformity to Jesus Christ. He was to be the Spirit of power, preparing them for service as Christ's witnesses to the ends of the earth. The Holy Spirit was to be the perfect bond of union between the Father in heaven and the children on earth and between Christ and the perishing world.

In the power of the Spirit, every believer would be able to give his testimony of the love that had come to him. God's great purpose was that man should be saved by the witness of the men in whom He lived. The gift of the Spirit made this possible for everyone who yielded himself to God.

The church has failed in its high calling. How few there have been who, with Paul, have proved that absolute dependence on the Spirit secures the continual presence and working of God in a Christian's life. Long prayers are offered for the power of the Holy Spirit, but few are ready to yield to His control. They do not know the secret of coming under His full power—the faith that dies to self and counts on God to do His perfect work. When the church and the believer begin to understand what this submission to the Holy Spirit means, there will be hope for the true revival of the Spirit in divine power.

Temples of the Spirit

The Spirit has been poured out. He is yearning over us, and He is ready and able to take possession of His church. Let us be ready to confess honestly the current state of the church and the share we have in it. Let all who believe in the love and almighty power of God proclaim that God is longing to fill His redeemed people with the power of the Spirit. God will manifest Himself to all who are longing to be temples of the Holy Spirit, filled with His power, and ready for the service of the living God.

What is the connection between the indwelling Spirit and the devotion of daily life? Our aim in our secret devotions must be to cast aside the ordinary standard of religion and make God's standard our unceasing desire. The Spirit has been given to us to reveal Christ and His life in us. No true progress can be made until we choose to live in unceasing dependence on the power of the Spirit in every area of our lives.

We must avoid the great hindrances along the way. We need to realize God's right to have absolute control of our lives. Our faith in His gracious and tender love will accomplish His work of power in our hearts. Ignorance of the power of the world as the great enemy of the blessed Spirit is dangerous. Unwillingness to take up the cross of Christ and follow Him can be overcome only by the Spirit. We must maintain that deep conviction of what a holy and almighty work it is for the Holy Spirit to take possession of our lives and carry out His one desire: to make Christ live within us.

This great work is accomplished in our daily devotions. With God's help, we will grow strong in faith, giving glory to God, trusting in Him to carry out His work in us. The goal of God in the gift of the Holy Spirit was to enable His people to become what they could never become in the Old Testament.

God does not expect us to strengthen and maintain our own spiritual life. That is the work of His Holy Spirit. Only the soul who lives in entire surrender to and dependence on the blessed Spirit can effectively carry on God's mighty work and accomplish all His blessed purposes.

Chapter 4

Experiencing Life in Him

*Blessed be the God and Father of our Lord Jesus
Christ, who hath blessed us with all spiritual blessings
in heavenly places in Christ.*
—Ephesians 1:3

A study of the letter to the Ephesians will help us discover the New Testament standard of devotion. The opening words of the epistle not only give us a blessed summary of the truth of the Gospel, but also reveal, out of the depths of Paul's experience, what the true Christian life is.

First let us consider the grace of our Lord Jesus Christ. The God and Father of our Lord Jesus Christ has blessed us with all spiritual blessings "in Him." The expression "in Him" is the keynote of the epistle, occurring numerous times.

The words of our text are the beginning of a sentence that continues through verse 14. We find we are *"chosen...in him"* (Eph. 1:4), foreordained through Him (v. 5), accepted in Him (v. 6), and redeemed in Him (v. 7). The purpose of God is in Him (v. 9), all things are summed up *"in Christ"* (v. 10), and in Him *"we have obtained an inheritance"* (v. 11). In Him we believed, and in Him we were sealed with the Holy Spirit (v. 13). All our blessings are treasured up in Christ (v. 14), and we are in Him, too. As truly as the blessings are in Christ, so truly are our lives in Him—the two are inseparably intertwined. Abiding in Christ means abiding in the heavenly places and in all the spiritual blessings God has given to us in Him.

Faith in Christ is meant to be nothing less than unceasing dependence upon Him and fellowship with Him. From Him we receive every grace the soul can possibly need. Your soul may be kept in blessed fellowship with Jesus as constantly as you live and breathe. This is what Scripture means by the words, *"Christ, who is our life"* (Col. 3:4), *"Christ liveth in me"* (Gal. 2:20), and *"To me to live is Christ"* (Phil. 1:21). What riches of grace these are!

God's Gift of Love

Christ was the Father's gift to us, and all blessings are given by Him. God's purpose was to bring us back to Himself as our Creator. Our happiness can be found in His fellowship and glory alone. God satisfied the love of His own heart by bringing us into complete union with Christ, so that in Him we can be as near to God as Christ is. Oh, the mystery of the love of God!

Our text says, *"God...hath blessed us with all spiritual blessings."* More than one believer has found in these words the key that unlocks the treasury of blessing. As the light of the Spirit shines on these words, they come alive with new meaning. In Christ, God has blessed me with all spiritual blessings. Faith and wholehearted surrender are free to claim in Him, and the heart finds itself in the very center of blessing.

The revelation of the blessings and the faith that claims them lead to the adoring benediction, *"Blessed be the God and Father of our Lord Jesus Christ"*! It is the fountain from which the stream of blessings flows through the epistle. In our lives, too, may it be an unceasing song of praise, *"I will bless the LORD at all times: his praise shall continually be in my mouth"* (Ps. 34:1).

Spiritual blessings are simply the blessings of the Holy Spirit. He has the divine office of imparting to us all the fullness of blessing and blessedness in the divine life. He reveals them to us. He enables us to see, delight in, and accept them. He communicates them to our hearts, and we become spiritual people, clothed with the power of the Spirit.

Where the heart is fully yielded to Him, the Spirit does more than influence our thoughts and actions. He dwells within us in divine reality and power, making our hearts the temple of Christ. He imparts every grace and virtue that is in Christ to us. The seed sown in the earth needs the warmth of the sun and the rain from heaven to make it grow. Even so, as we believe that the seeds of grace and virtue are within us, we look up to Christ in whom we find our life. In the sunshine of His love, the spiritual blessings grow into our very being.

Throughout this letter to the Ephesians, the Holy Spirit is mentioned twelve times in different aspects of the work He does in the believer. As we study these, we will find a wonderful revelation of what God meant the life of His children to be. If we desire to discover the New Testament standard of true spirituality and devotion in our lives, we must have the courage to set aside every human standard and make God's purpose our only aim.

Begin with Praise

Let us begin by reading the benediction of the letter. It reveals the true life of spiritual blessing, and we can try to make it our own. Let us, in quiet meditation, wait on the Holy Spirit to work faith in our innermost consciousness. As one whom the Father has blessed in Christ with every spiritual blessing, humbly take your place before Him and say, "Blessed be God! Blessed be God!"

People may complain about the lack of spiritual life and pray for its deepening. Yet much ignorance remains concerning what is really needed to bring a Christian into a strong and joyous life in Christ Jesus. Let us learn the lesson from our text that nothing less than the adoring worship of the blessed Trinity can meet our need. Our expectation is to rest upon God, who has blessed us in Christ Jesus. God and His blessings are found in Christ if we continue in close and unceasing fellowship with Him.

Through the Spirit, the presence of the Father and the Son in divine power can be known. The Holy Spirit has been given to make Christ real to us and to make every spiritual blessing ours. A life entirely given up to the Holy Spirit and a heart full of faith and confidence that God will do His wondrous work within us will see miracles. A body yielded to God as a holy, living sacrifice on the altar for His service will surely be accepted. God will teach us to sing the song of praise, *"Blessed be the God and Father of our Lord Jesus Christ, who hath blessed us with all spiritual blessings in heavenly places in Christ."*

Chapter 5

◀◆▶

The Seal of the Spirit

In whom also after that ye believed, ye were sealed
with that holy Spirit of promise.
—Ephesians 1:13

The wonderful sentence that began in verse 3 listing the spiritual blessings we have in Christ closes with the blessed *sealing of the Holy Spirit.* When a king appoints an ambassador, his commission is sealed with the king's seal. The Holy Spirit Himself, by His life in us, is the seal of our sonship. His work is to reveal and glorify Christ in us, the image of the Father. By fixing our hearts and our faith on Him, He transforms us into His likeness.

What a wonderful thought! The Spirit of the Father and the Son, the bond of union between them, comes to us as the bond of our union with them. He gives us the witness of the divine life within us and enables us to experience that life here on earth. In the Christian life, everything depends on knowing the Holy Spirit and His blessed work.

Lord of All

First of all, we need to know that He comes to take the mastery of our whole being—spirit, soul, and body. Through it all, He reveals the life and the power of God as it works in our renewed nature. Christ could not be glorified and receive the Spirit from the Father for us until He died upon the cross and parted with the sin and weakness of our nature. Likewise, the coming of the Holy Spirit into our hearts in power implies that we must yield ourselves to the fellowship of the cross and consent to die to self and sin. Thus, through the Spirit, the new and heavenly life may take complete possession of us.

This entire mastery demands complete surrender and obedience on our part. Peter spoke of *"the Holy Ghost, whom God hath given to them that obey him"* (Acts 5:32). Christ humbled Himself to the perfect obedience of the cross that He might receive the Spirit from the Father for us. In the same way, our full experience of the Spirit's power rests entirely on our readiness to deny self and yield ourselves to His teaching and leading.

The reason that believers are feeble and ignorant of the blessings of the Spirit is that they never made a decision to yield themselves to the control of the Spirit at every moment. Pray that God's children might accept God's terms: complete mastery of the Spirit and the unhesitating surrender of the whole being to His control.

We especially need to understand that the degree in which the working of the Spirit is experienced may vary greatly. A believer may rejoice in one of the gifts of the Spirit, such as peace or boldness, and still be extremely deficient in other areas. Our attitude toward the Spirit must be that of perfect teachableness, waiting to be led by Him into the will of God. We must realize how much there still is within the heart that needs to be renewed and sanctified if He is to have the place and honor that belong to Him.

The Spirit's Transforming Power

Two great enemies obtained dominion over man when Adam sinned: the world and self. Of the world Christ said, *"The Spirit of truth; whom the world cannot receive, because it seeth him not, neither knoweth him"* (John 14:17). Worldliness is the great hindrance that keeps believers from living a spiritual life. Of self Christ said, *"Let him deny himself"* (Mark 8:34). Self, in all its forms—self-will, self-pleasing, self-confidence—renders life in the power of the Spirit impossible.

Nothing can deliver us from these two great enemies except the cross of Christ. Paul boasted in the cross by which he had been crucified to the world. He told us, *"They that are Christ's have crucified the flesh"* (Gal. 5:24). To live the spiritual life, we must completely give up the old life to make room for the blessed Spirit. He will then be free to renew and transform our whole being into the will of God.

Without the Spirit, we can do nothing acceptable to God. *"No man can say that Jesus is the Lord, but by the Holy Ghost"* (1 Cor. 12:3). No man can truly say, "Abba, Father" except by the Spirit of God's Son sent into our hearts. In our fellowship with God and with men, in our religious worship and our daily vocations, in the highest pursuit that life can offer, and in the daily care of our bodies—everything must bear the seal of the Holy Spirit.

Of the Son we read, *"Him hath God the Father sealed,"* (John 6:27). We are sealed *in Christ.* After the Spirit descended upon Jesus at His baptism, He was led by the Spirit into the wilderness, and He was led through His whole life to the cross. *"Through the eternal Spirit offered himself without spot to God"* (Heb. 9:14). We, too, are to live daily as those who are sealed by the Spirit.

These words are true of every believer: *"Him hath God the Father sealed."* The Son and every son has been sealed by the Father. The New Testament standard of the Christian life and its devotion is that everything we do bears the stamp of the Holy Spirit.

The Holy Spirit cannot inspire our devotion unless He inspires our daily lives. The Spirit of Christ must rule the whole person if He is to perform His blessed work in us. The indwelling of the Holy Spirit means that nothing is to be thought of, trusted, or sought after except continual dependence on His blessed work.

The way we live our daily lives will be the test of the sincerity of our hearts' devotion. As we mature spiritually, our confidence in God who works in us through His blessed Spirit will grow. Every thought of faith in the power of the Spirit must find its expression in prayer to God. He will surely give us His Spirit when we ask Him to work in us what we need.

A seal attached to a document gives validity to every word it contains. Even so, the Holy Spirit of promise who sealed us also ratifies every promise that is in Christ. This is one of the great differences between the Bible and the human standard of the Christian life. In the Bible, the seal of the Spirit is accepted in His control of every movement and every moment of our lives. Sadly, by human standards, we are content with partial surrender to His guidance.

Chapter 6

---◆---

The Spirit of Wisdom

*Making mention of you in my prayers; that the God
of our Lord Jesus Christ, the Father of glory,
may give unto you the spirit of wisdom and revelation
in the knowledge of him: the eyes of your understanding
being enlightened; that ye may know what is the hope
of his calling, and what the riches of the glory
of his inheritance in the saints.*
—Ephesians 1:16–18

*I*mmediately after Paul mentioned the Holy Spirit as God's
seal on believers, he spoke of his unceasing prayer that God
would give them the spirit of wisdom. It is not enough that the
believer has the Holy Spirit. The Spirit can do His work only in
answer to prayer.

Paul prayed unceasingly and taught us to pray unceasingly,
too, for the wisdom of the Spirit to enlighten the eyes of our
hearts. Just as a child needs education, the believer who has the
Spirit within him needs divine illumination daily to know God
and the spiritual life He bestows. Without spiritual wisdom and
understanding, we can never comprehend it.

Knowing Hope, Riches, and Power

In Ephesians 1:18–19, Paul listed three things that we need to know:

1. *"The hope of his calling"*—the holy calling in which we are to walk.

2. *"The riches of the glory of his inheritance in the saints"*—the unsearchable riches of the heavenly treasure that God has in His saints.

3. *"The exceeding greatness of his power to us-ward who believe, according to the working of his mighty power"*—the power by which we can fulfill our calling and possess our heritage.

This passage teaches many valuable lessons for those who are in the ministry. It points to the three great spiritual blessings that include all a Christian needs to know of what God has prepared for him. They remind us that to preach these truths to believers is not sufficient because human wisdom cannot grasp them.

If the knowledge is to come alive and be effective, it needs a special illumination of the Holy Spirit. Only the spiritual person can discover spiritual things. God Himself, the Father of glory, will give the Spirit of wisdom in answer to definite and persevering prayer. Such teaching and praying will lead believers to the full life that the letter to the Ephesians sets before them.

The life of the Christian is truly the life of God in the soul. Nothing that we do can maintain that life or renew it. The great need of the believer is to wait upon God for the Holy Spirit to show *"the exceeding greatness of his power to us-ward who believe."* No human mind can grasp it. The Holy Spirit living in the heart reveals it and teaches us to believe this truth. As Christians we are to depend on God every day to work in us according to the greatness of His strength in us who believe. When we accept the Holy Spirit's teaching in answer to prayer, He will keep us conscious of this mighty power working in us.

Obtaining the Power

The Holy Spirit shows us the work and nature of the mighty power dwelling within us. It is the power of God, *"according to the working of his mighty power, which he wrought in Christ, when he raised him from the dead, and set him at his own right hand"* (Eph. 1:19–20). This power works in us who believe and raises us from the power of death to a life in the glory of heaven. By the greatness of this power, our daily lives may be lived in fellowship with the Son of God.

God raised Christ from the dead because His death on the cross exhibited deep humility and perfect obedience. Because Jesus yielded Himself unreservedly to the power of God, He was raised from the dead and given glory. When we give ourselves over to die with Christ to sin and the world in humility and obedience, God will make us partakers of the resurrection power and of the Spirit of glory.

The life of the believer as an exhibition of the greatness of God's power is a theme that runs through all the writings of Paul. In his prayer for the Colossians, he asked that they may

> *walk worthy of the Lord unto all pleasing, being fruitful in every good work, and increasing in the knowledge of God; strengthened with all might, according to his glorious power, unto all patience and longsuffering with joyfulness.* (Col. 1:10–11)

As one thinks of the life of devotion that Paul described— always worthy of God and pleasing to Him—one feels that the standard is impossible. But then the thought comes in, *"Strengthened with all might, according to his glorious power"* (Col. 1:11), and we say, "No, if this is true, if God works this, the life is possible."

These same thoughts occur in Ephesians 3:20–21, *"Now unto him that is able to do exceeding abundantly above all that we ask or think, according to the power that worketh in us, unto him be glory."* These words lift our hearts to believe and expect something far beyond what we ask or think. The lives we are to live are to be supernatural ones—the resurrection life. We experience the heavenly life of Christ in glory maintained in us by the same working of the strength of His might that raised Christ from the cross to the throne.

The same almighty power that raised Christ from the dead as the Conqueror of sin and death is the power that works in our hearts to give us victory over every sin. To believe this with our whole hearts will immediately bring a sense of our own weakness, but we will also know with divine certainty that God will fulfill His purpose in us.

Reigning in Him

If the believer trusts the greatness of God's power and yields himself in entire subjection to let that power rule in his heart; if he will be content to trust the strength that is made perfect in weakness and count all things loss for the sake of this blessed prize; then God's Word is pledged that the power that raised Christ will work in him day by day until he knows what it means to live and reign with Christ in glory.

We are trying to grasp the New Testament standard of a life of true devotion and whether the accepted standard of our modern Christianity is in harmony with it. Try to realize the full meaning of Paul's prayer. Think of his private pleading for the Ephesians. Think of the standard of his own life as he spoke of God working in him. Think of what he wished his readers to take as their aim and expectation. Paul's heart was set upon two goals for every believer: to live every day under the teaching of the Holy Spirit and under the mighty power of God working in him.

Have your secret devotion, your confident faith, and your hope in daily life accepted and rejoiced in the life that is held out to you? Are you daily living out the greatness of God's power working in you as you yield yourself to the Holy Spirit and keep depending on His power?

May God help us to return again to this passage until it becomes to us the light of God shining in our hearts and the power of God working in our lives!

Chapter 7

---◆---

Drawing Near to God

*Through him we both have access by one Spirit
unto the Father.*
—Ephesians 2:18

C hrist and the Holy Spirit are united in a great work to make
the permanent and unceasing presence of God become a
blessed reality. Our text not only speaks of a right of access,
but of its actual experience and enjoyment as provided for us
through Christ and His Spirit.

Think of what Scripture teaches us. In the tabernacle, God
dwelt in the Holy of Holies, separated by a thick veil from the
priests who came daily to serve. Even the high priest could enter
that holy place only once every year. Access through the veil
was forbidden on pain of death.

When Christ died, this veil was torn in two. Christ Jesus
not only entered into God's presence with His blood, but also
opened a new and living way through the torn veil of His
flesh for us to enter. When Jesus entered heaven, the way was
opened for every believer to enter into God's holy presence and
dwell there every day. Jesus sent us the Holy Spirit to bring us

into that holy presence and enable us to live there. The unbroken enjoyment of God's presence is available to every believer who is willing to forsake all to possess it.

Unified by the Son and Spirit

Having access to God through Christ means more than Jesus being our Advocate who secures our acquittal and acceptance. Our High Priest lives and acts in the power of an endless, incorruptible life. He works in us through the power of His resurrection life and His entrance into glory. To have access to God through Christ means that we have been made alive with Christ and made to sit with Him in the heavenly places. (See Ephesians 2:5–6.) We live in Him, and we are one with Him. He keeps us in fellowship with God. The access through Christ brings us as near to God as Christ is, in intimate and divine fellowship.

The Spirit has been given to us that we may have the power to cry out to the Father, even as Christ did. The Spirit dwells in us to reveal Christ. Without Him, *"no man can say that Jesus is the Lord"* (1 Cor. 12:3). The Spirit takes possession of our whole lives and being. When He is yielded to and trusted, He maintains our fellowship with the Father through the Son.

The New Testament standard of Christian living consists of access to God's holy presence and love through the living union with Christ in the power of the Holy Spirit. The one thing needed to make it ours is the practice of the presence of God. When we give up our own lives, Christ's life may be carried out in us. Access through Christ in the Spirit will restore to us what Adam lost by sin.

A walk in the light of God can be as clear and natural as the enjoyment of feeling the warmth of the sun on our bodies. No thinking, feeling, or working can enable us to dispense with the daily privilege of access into the Holiest of all and of dwelling there.

Making an Impact on Your World

Most of us have heard the expression, "Take time to be holy." A missionary in China for more than twenty years often said to young missionaries,

> Preach the Gospel, and take time to be as holy as the preparation. The missionary must above everything else be a holy man. Unbelievers expect it of him. He must be more than a good person, and more than someone who takes time to master the language and the literature of the people. He must be holy.
>
> This is what we need if this world is to be moved by us. The throne of grace must be our refuge with the shadow of the Almighty as our dwelling place every hour. We must take time to be filled with His power. We must take time to be holy.

The person who takes time to fellowship with God will become holy, too. His private place of prayer is the school of true devotion.

Take time to be alone with the holy God. Take time with the Father, of whom it is said, *"The very God of peace sanctify you wholly....Faithful is he that calleth you, who also will do it"* (1 Thess. 5:23–24).

Take time with Christ, the holy One of God, who said, *"For their sakes I sanctify myself, that they also might be sanctified through the truth"* (John 17:19).

Take time with the Holy Spirit who makes you His holy temple. Give time to this holy fellowship, and God Himself will sanctify you entirely. Live in unbroken fellowship because through Christ we have our access in one Spirit to the Father.

Chapter 8

Spiritual Building Blocks

*Jesus Christ himself being the chief corner stone; in whom all
the building fitly framed together groweth unto an holy temple
in the Lord: in whom ye also are builded together for an
habitation of God through the Spirit.*
—Ephesians 2:20–22

The blessed Trinity is mentioned here again: the Father, for whom the habitation is built; Jesus Christ, the Chief Cornerstone; and the Spirit, the Builder through whom all the living stones are united with each other in perfect fellowship with God.

The main point of our text is *fellowship*—the fellowship of the Spirit. That fellowship is spoken of first as the fellowship of believers who are built up into one holy temple. Paul spoke of the Gentiles as strangers from the covenant of the promise who are now accepted by the blood of Christ. The enmity between Jews and Gentiles was nailed to the cross that we *both* might have access in one Spirit to the Father.

In verse 19 Paul said, *"Ye are no more strangers and foreigners, but fellowcitizens with the saints, and of the household of God."* Jew and Gentile have access by one Spirit to the Father, and by the same Spirit, they are built up into one temple.

The cross has ended all separation among Jews and Gentiles, Greek and barbarian, the wise and the foolish: all are one in Christ Jesus. National and social distinctions cannot stand against the unity of the Spirit. The cement that holds the living stones together, the bond that makes all members of one household and one body, is the Spirit and the life and the love of God Himself.

Our Bond of Love

Our fellowship with Christ, the Cornerstone, is also the work of the Holy Spirit. In Him, the believer on earth and the Father in heaven find their bond of union. Men think of pardon, peace, obedience, and holiness as an end in themselves. But they are only means to the great end of bringing God and man into perfect union. We prize the Atonement through the blood of Christ while we forget there is something higher: the presence and fellowship of God Himself.

God dwelt in the sanctuary in the midst of His people so that He could be their God. They enjoyed His guidance, His blessing, His mighty deliverance in their time of need, and His abiding presence. Fellowship with the Father and the Son, that intimate, holy, and unceasing communion, is the reason for man's creation. That fellowship has been restored to us in Christ Jesus.

As believers realize their dependence on Christ and their inseparable union with Him, they will trust the Spirit to maintain within them the faith of His presence. Then they will know that the presence and the power of God is the highest of all the blessings in Christ Jesus. Through the Spirit alone we can have access in Christ to the Father. He reveals Christ to us and the reality of our union with Him. We can experience the nearness to God He gives.

He not only builds the temple, but He reveals the indwelling God. He makes each heart a temple and reveals God's willingness to be and to do in our hearts what He is and does in heaven above. It seems impossible to many Christians that the presence of God can be with them and keep them. But it is indeed possible if we know and believe in the Holy Spirit as the power of God that works in us.

Loving the Brethren

The fellowship with God, with Christ, and with other believers constitutes the blessedness of being built as a habitation of God in the Spirit. The cross of Christ destroyed all selfishness. The love that seeks no life but giving itself for others has been made available to us.

Close fellowship with each other is as sacred and vital as our fellowship with God. Our spiritual life depends on it, and the only way of showing people our love for God and the reality of God's love for us is through our love for one another. Our Lord Jesus prayed, *"That they all may be one;...that the world may believe that thou...hast loved them, as thou hast loved me."* (John 17:21, 23). Jesus taught us that a divided church is powerless before the enemy. Only love for the brethren that is like God's and Christ's will give us the victory. The world will be compelled to acknowledge that Christ's love is present and working in us.

When the New Testament standard of spiritual life is lifted up and our love of the brethren proves the reality of our love for God, our lives will conform to the image of Jesus. Our prayers will be delivered from the selfishness that often hinders them. Our hearts will feel a new confidence that God will hear our prayers for the growth of a holy temple in the Lord. God's presence with us and our devotion to Him can be the mark of our daily lives.

Chapter 9

Proclaiming the Way of Life

By revelation he made known unto me [Paul] *the
mystery...of Christ...as it is now revealed unto his holy
apostles and prophets by the Spirit; that the Gentiles
should be fellowheirs, and of the same body,
and partakers of his promise in Christ by the gospel.*
—Ephesians 3:3–6

The more one studies Paul's letter to the Ephesians, the
deeper the impression becomes that the true standard of
New Testament faith is faintly realized in the church today. The
tone of the letter is intensely supernatural. Only a life identified
with the life of Christ and under the guidance of the Holy Spirit
can grasp its full meaning.

In the first chapter of Ephesians, Paul set before us the
source of the divine life. His unceasing prayer was that supernatural life would be revealed by the Holy Spirit in the hearts of
believers. In chapter two, we had the *communication* of that life.
God made us alive in Christ, and *"we are his workmanship, created in Christ Jesus unto good works"* (Eph. 2:10).

Now, we are taught that the *proclamation* of that divine life
is also the work of God and His Spirit. As definitely as the origin

and communication of His life is supernatural, so the provision for its being made known in the world is entirely supernatural, too. God's grace is set before us in a new light.

In chapter one, we had *"his grace, wherein he hath made us accepted in the beloved....In whom we have...the forgiveness of sins, according to the riches of his grace"* (vv. 6–7). In chapter two, we had *"the exceeding riches of his grace"* (v. 7). Now in chapter three, we have *"the dispensation of the grace of God which is given...unto his holy apostles and prophets by the Spirit"* (vv. 2, 5). Paul was made a minister of this grace, *"according to the gift of the grace of God given unto me by the effectual working of his power"* (v. 7).

In the ministry of the Gospel, the riches of God's grace are greatly magnified. Paul spoke of the mystery of Christ and said that it has now been revealed by the Holy Spirit. The Gentiles are *"fellowheirs, and of the same body, and partakers of his promise in Christ"* (Eph. 3:6). Through the Spirit, the revelation of what had been hidden in God through the ages was revealed.

Led by the Spirit

Throughout the book of Acts, we read of the Spirit guiding the steps of Philip, Peter, Barnabas, and Paul. They spoke under the power and anointing of the Spirit, and many received the word with joy. The Holy Spirit was entrusted with the whole work of revealing and carrying out through the ages to come the riches of the glory of this mystery among the Gentiles: *"Christ in you, the hope of glory"* (Col. 1:27).

All mission work has been placed under the direction of the Holy Spirit. In every area of that work, His guidance is to be sought and can be counted on. Missions are indeed the work of the Holy Spirit.

Why is so little use made of the language of Scripture in our evangelism today? The Holy Spirit will reveal the great mystery of God in the heart, awaken its affections and its purpose, and empower it with all that is needed to carry out God's blessed will. It is not enough that the Spirit reveals this hidden mystery of God to preachers, so that through them the church may become acquainted with His plans. Each believer needs to receive the teaching of the Spirit personally if the blessed secret is to master him.

Answering Our Call

We consider it to be a great step forward when a congregation yields itself to the call to take part in the work of evangelizing the world. Yet this may come about from nothing more than a sense of duty and readiness to take part in all the activities of the church. Believers must realize that missions are the chief aim of the church, the one purpose for which every congregation and every believer exists. In preaching and in writing, in prayer and in Christian fellowship, all work within the church should train its members for its great calling: work on the mission field to win the unbelievers for Christ.

Dependence on the Holy Spirit is the first and essential element of success. By the Spirit, the church will be able to carry out the Lord's commands. When the Holy Spirit takes the place that was given to Him in the early church, we may expect His power to be manifested as it was in those days: *"Ye shall receive power, after that the Holy Ghost is come upon you: and ye shall be witnesses unto me...unto the uttermost part of the earth"* (Acts 1:8).

These were the last words of our Lord on the earth. The fullness of the Spirit will be given only in connection with the extension of the kingdom. The power for carrying the Gospel to those near or far depends on the measure of the Spirit's presence. Every prayer for the power of the Spirit to be revealed should have as its aim the power to testify for Jesus. As the number of believers increases who pray for the Spirit, the church will become strong for preaching the Gospel to every creature.

The School of Prayer

A close connection exists between these thoughts and our lives of secret devotion. Paul spoke to believers of the conflict he had in unceasing prayer for the churches who were struggling among the world of unbelievers. He asked them to strive with him in prayer for his work of preaching to the Gentiles. Prayer was to be not only for the supply of the needs of the spiritual life, but also a training school for the exercise of the highest power available to us in God's service.

Prayer brings us into conflict with the powers of darkness and into fellowship with the cross. It stirs our strength to take hold of God and prevail with Him for His blessing on men around us. Prayer causes believers to realize, amid their deep sense of unworthiness and helplessness, "I have power with God. He will listen to me. He will cause our mission work to triumph through the power of the cross on the battlefield in the world."

Let us test the effectiveness of our prayers by the influence they exercise on the fulfillment of the mystery of Christ in the world. Work can be done in the prayer closet that will count for eternity. There, the power can be received that will make itself felt wherever God sends us to establish His kingdom on earth. Let us not be afraid to say what Paul said of himself, *"Unto me, who am less than the least of all saints, is this grace given, that I should preach among the Gentiles the unsearchable riches of Christ"* (Eph. 3:8).

We may count on God to lead us into the riches of the glory of this mystery among the Gentiles. Our prayer will be for the power of the Holy Spirit to permeate all that is being done for mission work in the church and throughout the world.

Chapter 10

Opening the Door to Power

*I bow my knees unto the Father...that he would grant you,
according to the riches of his glory, to be strengthened with
might by his Spirit in the inner man; that Christ may dwell in
your hearts by faith.*
—Ephesians 3:14, 16–17

We see in this wonderful prayer the harmonious work of the blessed Trinity. The Father grants the Spirit of power. The Spirit reveals Christ in the heart. Through Christ and the Spirit, we are filled with all the fullness of God! As God dwells in heaven as the Three in One, even so He lives in our hearts.

Paul's prayer at the close of chapter one of Ephesians was that God would give us the Spirit of wisdom so that we might know Him in the greatness of His power to us who believe. Here we have the prayer for the Spirit of power to strengthen us with His might. The greatness of God's power is to be a permanent experience in our inner lives. Let us bow with deep reverence as we gaze upon this mystery of love.

Notice first the expression, *"That he would grant you, according to the riches of his glory."* Paul wanted us to take time and think of God's glory and inconceivable riches. Then, in faith, we can expect that God will do nothing less to us than according to the riches of that glory. Our inner man can experience the glory of God shining in our hearts and manifesting His power in what He does within us. Our faith cannot expect the fulfillment of the prayer until it enters into and claims that God will work in us according to the riches of His glory. Let us take time and see that nothing less than this is the measure of our faith.

"That he would grant you...to be strengthened with might by his Spirit in the inner man." The Spirit is indeed the mighty power of God. As the Spirit of wisdom, He reveals the greatness of God's power in us who believe—the power that lifted Christ from the cross to the throne. He teaches us to believe in the greatness of God's power in us. As the Spirit of power, He works in us, strengthening us in the inner man.

In His Word, God continually calls on His servants to be strong and courageous. God chooses the weak things of this world, but He wants them to be strong in faith and strong *"in the power of his might"* (Eph. 6:10). With strength of will, they can be ready to do all God says; and with strength of character, they will be bold for any sacrifice.

In a healthy body, strength is not something separated from the whole, but it fills the entire being and permeates every fiber. Likewise, *"to be strengthened with might by his Spirit in the inner man"* simply means that our whole being is under the sway of His mighty power.

Abiding in Christ

The purpose of this strengthening with might is that *"Christ may dwell in your hearts by faith."* The divine power enables and emboldens our faith to claim this precious privilege. The Spirit reveals Christ dwelling within us and gives the consciousness of His unceasing and omnipotent presence.

Just as God maintains the life of the body by supporting the heart in its action, the Holy Spirit, by His almighty power, strengthens our inner man daily to enable us to live the true spiritual life. Christ's dwelling in the heart is meant to be our portion. In speaking of his conversion, Paul wrote, *"It pleased God...to reveal his Son in me, that I might preach him among the heathen"* (Gal. 1:15–16). When he preached the unsearchable riches of Christ, he preached Him as dwelling in the heart. He would have none of his readers to be without it. He continually pleaded with God to strengthen them with might in their inner lives, so that nothing might keep them from this wonderful blessing.

It seems as if the church has lost the understanding of the reality of Christ's indwelling. Yet Paul's teaching is in harmony with that of our blessed Lord. When Jesus spoke of the gift of the Holy Spirit, He said, *"At that day ye shall know that I am in my Father, and ye in me, and I in you"* (John 14:20). He went on to add, *"If a man love me, he will keep my words: and my Father will love him, and we will come unto him, and make our abode with him"* (v. 23).

Our Lord speaks here of something far beyond the initial grace of pardon and regeneration. He speaks of what would be given to those who love Him and keep His commandments—of a special gift of the Holy Spirit dwelling and working in them. The blessing offered to us completes the spiritual life with the highest exhibition of what the mighty power of God can work in us.

Christ wants to dwell in the heart. Let us begin with urgent prayer for ourselves and for God's children around us. God will work according to the riches of His glory to lift us out of our feebleness and bring us into a new life that will be lived to His praise and glory.

When Jesus Christ is within us, we are *"rooted and grounded in love"* (Eph. 3:17). We can begin to comprehend the reality and the joy of the love of Christ that passes knowledge. This leads to being filled with the fullness of God. The Spirit of power fills the inner man, the presence of Christ fills the heart, and the fullness of God fills all.

No wonder Paul said, *"Now unto him that is able to do exceeding abundantly above all that we ask or think, according to the power that worketh in us, unto him be glory"* (Eph. 3:20–21). Faith in the promise of what the Father of glory will do, according to the riches of His glory, will teach us to worship, saying, "Glory! Glory to Him forever and ever."

Assured of God's Almighty Power

This doxology gives a revelation of what lies at the root of Paul's standard of prayer and expectation. He was confident that his prayer that believers *"be strengthened with might...in the inner man,"* according to the riches of God's glory, would be granted. Many say this was meant to be an ideal to stir our desires, but that its actual fulfillment in life in this world is beyond our reach. This thought cuts away the root of the faith in the supernatural power of God in our lives. Since it is absolutely secured in the promise, it is therefore possible in experience.

Paul dared any reader to say that what he asked for out of the riches of God's glory was too high and beyond what we dare think or ask. He knew what the greatness of God's power had done in his own life. He knew God was ready to do a miracle in anyone who would give himself up with his whole heart and life to trust God. He answered every doubt and encouraged every sincere soul who is willing to trust God for the fulfillment of the prayer to say with him, *"Now unto him that is able to do exceeding abundantly above all that we ask or think, according to the power that worketh in us, unto him be glory in the church by Christ Jesus throughout all ages, world without end. Amen."* (Eph. 3:20–21).

Here was Paul's standard of the New Testament life. Is it ours? Do I believe it with my whole heart and soul? Does it inspire my private devotion in the prayer closet? Does it make me realize that my life's devotion is the best and the happiest thing there is in the world?

Who will yield himself, like Paul, to be an intercessor? Who will plead not only with but also for the believers around him, that they may learn to expect the almighty power of God to work in them? What has previously appeared beyond their reach may become the object of their longing desire and their confident assurance: a life of faith in which Christ reigns in their hearts.

Chapter 11

————◆————

One in the Spirit

*I...beseech you that ye walk worthy of the vocation
wherewith ye are called, with all lowliness and meekness,
with longsuffering, forbearing one another in love;
endeavouring to keep the unity of the Spirit
in the bond of peace.*
—Ephesians 4:1–3

*T*he letter to the Ephesians is divided into two equal parts. In chapters one through three, we have the divine life in its heavenly origin as revealed in the heart of man by the Holy Spirit. In chapters four through six, we see the Christian life in the ordinary conduct of our daily walk. The two halves correspond to what we said of devotion as an act and as a habit.

The first three chapters begin with adoration: *"Blessed be the God...who hath blessed us"* (Eph. 1:3). They tell us what all those blessings are and end by glorifying Him who *"is able to do exceeding abundantly above all that we ask or think"* (Eph. 3:20). In every act of prayer and praise, the soul takes its place in the midst of all those riches and seeks to enter more fully into their possession.

The last three chapters begin with an admonition to walk worthy of our high calling. We are taught how to show our devotion as a habit in the common activities of daily life. Devotion lifts us up into the heavenlies to return to this earth charged with blessings. In all that we do or say, we will prove that our whole lives are devoted to God alone.

The Evidence of Our Calling

The opening words of the second half of the letter bring us down to the roots of the Christian life. The great mark of our high calling is a Christlike humility. The unity of the Spirit is to be maintained in our relationships with our fellow believers. Amid all diversity of character and all the temptations arising from the imperfections of those around us, the first mark of a life wholly devoted to God is this: *"Walk...with all lowliness and meekness."*

To realize the full impact of this command, first look at it in its connection with the first three chapters. Think of the heavenly blessings God has given us (Eph. 1:3). Think of the *"greatness of his power"* (v. 19) to us who believe and of the Holy Spirit who reveals that power in us. Through Him we have access to God in Christ (Eph. 2:18) and are built up as a *"habitation of God"* (v. 22). We are mightily strengthened by Him according to the riches of God's glory so that Christ can dwell in our hearts (Eph. 3:16–17).

Take time to form a true conception of the wonderful standard of spiritual life indicated in these words. The one fruit of this astonishing revelation of the grace of God and the one mark that you are truly a partaker of it will be a deep and never-ceasing humility. Your humility proves that God has revealed Himself to you and brought self and pride down into the dust.

Lowliness and meekness should characterize your attitude toward man as well as toward God. You can have no surer proof that God's spiritual blessings in Christ Jesus have reached and mastered a man than his lowliness and meekness in his relationships with his fellowmen. The greatness of God's power raised us out of the death with Christ Jesus to the throne. This same power makes us, like Christ, willing to wear the servant's robe and do the servant's work. What is impossible with men is possible with God.

Following Jesus' Example

We see the true Christlike disposition in Paul's words to the Philippians: *"Let nothing be done through strife or vainglory; but in lowliness of mind let each esteem other better than themselves"* (Phil. 2:3). The Master Himself, the meek and lowly Lamb of God, commanded us, *"Learn of me; for I am meek and lowly in heart"* (Matt. 11:29).

Paul emphasized what he had written by adding, *"Let this mind be in you, which was also in Christ Jesus: who...took upon him the form of a servant...and became obedient unto death, even the death of the cross"* (Phil. 2:5–8). The self-emptying in the heavenly glory, the form of a servant during His earthly life, and then the humbling death of the cross—this was the mind of Christ. Our salvation is rooted in the spirit and practice of a life like this. Through our lowliness and meekness, as we bear with one another in love, Christ will be magnified and our hearts sanctified. It will become obvious to all that we have been with Jesus.

The heart of a servant diligently works to keep the unity of the Spirit in the bond of peace. It is not what we know or say about the beauty of love, the unity of the body of Christ, and the power of the Holy Spirit that proves the true Christian life. Only through our meekness and lowliness in our daily dealings with our fellow Christians, even when they tempt and try us, do we show that we will sacrifice anything to maintain the unity of the Spirit. Jesus gives the name of *chief* to the servant of all. (See Matthew 20:27.) It may not be easy, but Christ came from heaven to bring humility back to this earth and to work it out in our hearts.

Is the church teaching the lowliness and meekness of Christ and giving it the place it holds in the will and Word of God? Do we make an effort to maintain this standard of Christian living and keep the unity of the Spirit from being disturbed by pride? In our own search after a deeper spiritual life, is this meekness and lowliness our hearts' desire and confident hope?

Let this be the first thing we ask of God: a heart humbled by His infinite love and yielded to His Holy Spirit to work out in us, and in His body around us, the blessed likeness of Jesus our Lord. By the Spirit's grace, humility can become the habit of a life devoted to God.

Let us not forget to link the thought of a Christlike lowliness with the Holy Spirit and His power. In the power of the Spirit, Christ humbled Himself on the cross as a sacrifice to God. As we fully yield ourselves to the life of the Spirit, the meekness and lowliness of our Lord can be found in us. Let us believe that He can and will work it in us.

Chapter 12

———————◆———————

Working Together in Christ

There is one body, and one Spirit.
—Ephesians 4:4

*I*n the last chapter, our subject was maintaining the *unity of the Spirit* in our relationships with fellow Christians. Here our subject is the *Spirit of unity.* The Holy Spirit is the source and the power in which believers, as members of one body in Christ Jesus, are to minister to each other to build up the body of Christ.

The knowledge of what the body of Christ means, the insight into its glory and its purpose, and the fulfilling of the place and ministry to which God has called us in the body have a deep connection with spiritual life. To receive the Spirit and the love of Christ means death to every vestige of selfishness. We must surrender our lives and love entirely to Christ and His body. The welfare of every member becomes the supreme object of our desire. Let us try to realize what this body is in which the blessed Spirit of God seeks to manifest Himself.

Masterpiece under Construction

We know what a masterpiece of divine workmanship a human body is. Made of dust, it is the instrument through which spiritual life can unfold and express itself. Our human bodies are a parable of the body of believers with Christ as the Head. God *"gave him* [Christ] *to be the head over all things to the church, which is his body, the fulness of him that filleth all in all"* (Eph. 1:22–23). The body is to contain and exhibit the divine fullness as it dwells in Christ. *"All the building fitly framed together groweth unto an holy temple in the Lord: in whom ye also are builded together for an habitation of God through the Spirit"* (Eph. 2:21–22).

We are reminded that *"Christ also loved the church, and gave himself for it...that he might present it to himself a glorious church, not having spot, or wrinkle, or any such thing"* (Eph. 5:25, 27).

An intimate union exists between our body and its head. The power of the head to move and use every member and the readiness of every member to yield itself to assist its fellow members is only a shadow of that mysterious power that links every believer to Christ. This power places the believer at the disposal of his fellow believers.

The body of Christ is the highest revelation of the glory of God. He manifested His power to make a creature of the dust, who had fallen under the power of sin and Satan, become the partaker of the holiness of the blessed Son. The Holy Spirit presides over this work today as He encourages each believer to carry out the eternal purpose: that they all should be one, even as the Father is one with the Son. (See John 17:21.) When the church yields itself to His divine working, the power of the Holy Spirit can be expected to work unhindered in the church and in its individual members.

United in Ministry

When He ascended on high, Christ gave His church the gifts of apostles, prophets, evangelists, pastors, and teachers (Eph.

4:8, 11), *"for the perfecting of the saints, for the work of the ministry, for the edifying of the body of Christ* (v. 12). The apostles and prophets and pastors are not called to build up the body of Christ. Their work is the *"perfecting of the saints...for the ministry"* of building up. Every saint is to be trained to take part in building up the body of Christ. Just as every member of your body helps to build the whole, every believer should know his place and work in the body of Christ in caring for every other member.

Each one of us needs the other. Each one is to feel linked to the whole body in the love of the Spirit. A Christian not only should avoid doing anything that is selfish or unloving, but also should actively yield himself to the Spirit to be the instructor and the comforter of all who are weak.

Then it follows—*"Till we all come in the unity of the faith...unto a perfect man, unto the measure of the stature of the fulness of Christ"* (v. 3). Nothing less than maturity is to be the aim of each believer, not only for himself, but for all around him. Then the body may experience the fullness of Him who fills all in all. We can

> *grow up into him in all things, which is the head, even Christ: from whom the whole body fitly joined together..., according to the effectual working in the measure of every part, maketh increase of the body unto the edifying of itself in love.* (vv. 15–16)

The significance of all this in our spiritual life is clear. As long as our prayers aim only at our own perfection and happiness, they defeat themselves. Selfishness prevents the answer. Only in the union with the whole body will each member be healthy and strong. Building up the body of Christ in love is vital to our spiritual health.

Let intercession, *"with all prayer and supplication in the Spirit...for all saints"* (Eph. 6:18), be the proof that the Spirit of unity dwells and prays in us. Let us love the brethren fervently with a pure heart. In our home life, in prayer meetings, and in all our fellowship with God's children, let our love watch over and encourage them. Always remember that we and they are indispensable to each other. Let the Spirit of unity inspire our secret devotions. Grace will be given to live in unceasing devotion to Christ to build up His glorious body in love.

Chapter 13

———— ►◆◄ ————

Enjoying God's Presence

Grieve not the holy Spirit of God.
—Ephesians 4:30

The words of Isaiah sadly sum up the history of Israel and the whole Old Testament covenant: *"They rebelled, and vexed his holy Spirit"* (Isa. 63:10). Stephen's scathing rebuke threw the high priests into a rage: *"Ye do always resist the Holy Ghost: as your fathers did, so do ye"* (Acts 7:51). In the New Testament, provision was made that this should no longer be the case. God promised His people a new heart and a new spirit. He wrote His law in their hearts and gave them His Spirit, so that they would keep His judgments and do them. (See Hebrews 10:16.)

The Spirit of God's Son is given to live in us and have mastery over us. Grieving Him should no longer be a matter of course. The warning, *"Grieve not the holy Spirit,"* is a promise because what grace commands, it enables us to perform. The believer who seeks to live as one who has been sealed with the Holy Spirit will find that his faith in the power and presence of the Spirit within makes it possible to live without grieving Him.

Perfect Harmony with God

The danger of grieving the Spirit is great unless we live entirely under His power. We need to heed the warning and make a study of all that can possibly hinder His blessed work in us.

The context of the words *"grieve not the holy Spirit of God"* speaks of falsehood, anger, stealing, corrupt speech, and transgressions of the law of love. (See Ephesians 4:25–29.) These things were to be put far away. Everything that is against God's law grieves His Holy Spirit.

The commands of the Lord Jesus include the Beatitudes pronounced on the poor in spirit, the meek, the merciful, and the pure in heart. (See Matthew 5:3–12.) He taught us to bear the cross, deny self, forsake the world, and follow Him. (See Matthew 16:24–26.) He instructed His disciples to love one another as He had loved them and to serve one another. (See John 13:34–35; Luke 22:25–27.) These are the marks of the heavenly life Christ came to bring. Everything that is not in harmony with these teachings grieves the Spirit and prevents the enjoyment of His presence.

Paul told us, *"Whatsoever is not of faith is sin"* (Rom. 14:23). While God's Word announces the major principles of our action, the Holy Spirit teaches the individual believer to apply those principles in daily life. In little things, in doubtful things, in things where opinions differ among Christians, the believer grieves the Spirit when he does not wait for His guidance and acts contrary to His mind. The whole life of the believer is to be under the Spirit's control with the heart watchful and ready to obey in everything. What is not of faith must be yielded to God at once, or it may become a cloud that darkens the light of the Spirit in His divine tenderness.

Scripture speaks of the struggle between the flesh and the Spirit. It tells us that the only way a believer can live the life in the Spirit is in the power of the truth. *"They that are Christ's have crucified the flesh"* (Gal. 5:24). Even as Christ yielded His life and His flesh to the death of the cross, so the believer accepts God's judgment on his whole sinful nature as embodied in the flesh. His own will, strength, and even his goodness have been given up to the power of the cross. He says by faith, *"I am crucified with Christ: nevertheless I live; yet not I, but Christ liveth in me"* (Gal. 2:20). Anything that yields to the flesh hinders and grieves the blessed Spirit. A tender, humble, watchful dependence on the blessed Spirit and His leading is necessary if we are to maintain His fellowship undisturbed.

The Revelation of Jesus

The great work of the Holy Spirit is to reveal Christ to the believer in the glory of His heavenly life and in His power at work in our hearts. As a preparation for this, His first work is to convict us of the sin of unbelief. The salvation God has prepared for us is complete in Jesus Christ. His life of humility and obedience has been prepared for us and can be received and lived through simple faith alone.

The great secret of the true Christian lies in the daily, unceasing faith in what Jesus will work in us each moment of our lives. When this faith is not exercised and sought after, the Christian life becomes feeble. Nothing grieves the Holy Spirit as much as the unbelief that prevents Jesus from showing His power to deliver people from the power of sin and the world.

We need to see the simplicity and the glory of the Gospel we profess. In Jesus Christ all that His life, death, and resurrection accomplished is stored up for us. The fullness of life that is in Jesus is reproduced in us, enabling us to grow into the likeness of His humility, love, and obedience.

This is not accomplished by any power in ourselves. The Holy Spirit is given and lives in us to communicate and maintain the life of Christ in the soul. Feel the urgency of the command: *"Grieve not the holy Spirit of God."* What an unspeakable blessing will come if we yield to Him!

We are in search of the New Testament standard of a life of devotion. Suppose we could ask Paul about his personal experience. He would answer, "I am sure that the child of God who is living fully in the power of the Holy Spirit can please God. There is no reason to grieve the Spirit every day."

The different standard of our modern Christianity is simply the result of ignorance and unbelief in the supernatural working of the Spirit in the heart. Paul lived his life of devotion in the fullness and the joy of the Holy Spirit. Is our standard limited because such an experience is seldom taught and lived? Is the reason for this that our knowledge is too intellectual and that the Holy Spirit is not honored as the only Teacher of spiritual truth? We need to return to the prayer in Ephesians 1:17–23. Let it teach us to receive the Spirit of wisdom as the only Teacher who can enable us to experience the heavenly life God has prepared for us.

Chapter 14

———————◆———————

Unlocking Your Spiritual Treasure

Be not drunk with wine,...but be filled with the Spirit;
speaking to yourselves in psalms and hymns
and spiritual songs.
—Ephesians 5:18–19

"*Grieve not the holy Spirit of God*" (Eph. 4:30)! *"Be filled with the Spirit"*! All our duty to the Spirit is included in these two commands. The one is negative, forbidding everything of the flesh or self that would lead to unbelief or disobedience of Christ Jesus. The other is positive, calling us to yield our whole being in surrender to Him who reveals and maintains the life of Christ within us.

To understand the command, *"Be filled with the Spirit,"* we need to turn to the Day of Pentecost. The disciples were all filled with the Holy Spirit, and we know the dynamic change He worked in their lives. For three years they had lived day and night in close fellowship with their Lord. His presence meant everything to them. When He spoke of His departure, their hearts were sad. He promised that the Spirit would come, not to take Jesus' place, but to reveal Christ as their Lord. Christ would be present with them as much as when He was on earth, only far more intimately and gloriously. He would now live and work in them, even as the Father lived and worked in Him on the earth.

To be filled with the Spirit meant that Christ on the throne would be an ever-present, living reality, filling their hearts and lives with all His heavenly love and joy. Their fellowship with Him on earth proved to be merely the shadow of that intense and unceasing union with Him that the Spirit revealed in power.

Our Part in Pentecost

The command, *"Be filled with the Spirit,"* that the disciples received and enjoyed at Pentecost is for us, too. The church has sunk down from the level of Pentecost to a life in which the spirit of the world and of human wisdom is far too prevalent. Few believe in the possibility of the constant presence of Christ dwelling in the heart and conquering sin. We despair of a life of devotion and perfect self-sacrifice by the fire of His love, guiding us into all His will and work by the leading of His blessed Spirit. The heavenly vision of Christ at the right hand of God, ministering salvation to the penitent and spiritual fulfillment to all He has sanctified, is scarcely known. As the result of this, few witness the greatness of His power toward us who believe.

The condition required for this blessing to be received can be studied in the disciples. They turned their backs on the world and gave up everything to follow Christ. They had learned to know and love Him and do His will. As our Savior said, *"If ye love me, keep my commandments. And I will pray the Father, and he shall give you another Comforter"* (John 14:15–16).

Jesus' disciples had remained with Him in His temptations. He carried them with Him through death and the grave. The joy and the power of the resurrection life filled their hearts with confidence and hope. Their whole being was yielded up and united with the ascended Lord on the throne. They were fully prepared to receive the wondrous gift that was to come upon them.

The church of our day is sadly lacking in that separation from the world. The intense attachment and obedience to Christ, the fellowship with His suffering and conformity to His death, and the devotion to Christ on the throne seem almost to be forgotten. Where is our confident expectation of the never-ceasing flow of living water from the throne of grace, which gives the assurance that the fullness of the Spirit will not be withheld? No wonder the mighty power of God is seldom known and felt in our churches!

Aglow with the Spirit

Let us turn once again to Pentecost and think of the great gift that was bestowed. The Spirit made the disciples see that He who had come to dwell in them was indeed the true God. Rivers of life flowed from Him, through them, and out to the world. Coming fresh from the throne of our Lord in heaven, He rested on them as the Spirit of glory and of God. He filled their hearts with the love and power of Christ in glory. As the mighty power of God dwelling in them, He convinced the world by their boldness and love that God was in their midst.

Most Christians' understanding of the Spirit is far different from the experience of the presence and power of Christ that God desires for us. The thought of the Spirit to them is little more than a mental conception or a passing emotion with a slight sense of power or happiness. Where is the consciousness that fills the soul with deep reverence, quiet rest, heavenly joy, and strength as the natural and permanent possession of the believer?

"Be filled with the Spirit." Before any filling can take place, two things are needed. First, the vessel must be clean, empty, and ready to receive the water that is waiting for it. Then the water must be near and ready to give itself in full measure to the waiting vessel. In the great transaction between God and man for the filling of the Spirit, man needs first of all to know how to surrender completely. The death to self and the world

and yielding up the whole being is essential. God is ready and able to take possession of our being and fill us with Himself.

Our Lord Jesus said, *"He that believeth on me...out of his belly shall flow rivers of living water"* (John 7:38). He named one condition of being filled with the Spirit to overflowing: simple faith in Himself. Faith is not an imagination or an argument or an intellectual conviction. It claims the whole heart and yields up the whole being. It trusts unreservedly in the power that seeks to take possession of it. The blessing is found in the life of faith and cultivated in secret fellowship and wholehearted surrender.

Let us pray that our blessed Lord will deliver us from all that could keep us back from a life of full faith and close fellowship with Him. Answer the call to worship and wait until the Spirit dwells within us, revealing the Father and the Son. He will work in our hearts even what is done in heaven above.

Chapter 15

————————◆————————

Prepared for Spiritual Warfare

Take...the sword of the Spirit, which is the word of God.
—Ephesians 6:17

*P*aul began the last section of his letter to the Ephesians
with the words, *"Finally, my brethren, be strong in the Lord,
and in the power of his might"* (Eph. 6:10). In chapter one, he
wrote of the *"exceeding greatness of his power to us-ward who
believe"* (v. 19)—the resurrection power that lifted Christ to the
throne. Again in chapter three, he spoke of being *"strengthened
with might by his Spirit in the inner man"* (v. 16). Believers are
to prove in their lives that all that has been said and written of
God's power manifesting itself in His church is a divine reality.
The Spirit is the mighty power of God, and the Spirit-filled Christian should be strong for God's service and the wars of His kingdom.

Paul told us, *"We wrestle not against flesh and blood, but
against principalities, against powers, against the rulers of the
darkness of this world, against spiritual wickedness in high
places"* (v. 12). To live victoriously, we must wear the whole
armor of God every day and stand strong in Christ and in the
strength of His might.

The believer not only has to face various temptations but also must take his place as one whom Christ leads in warfare against the kingdom of darkness. In the work of the church, the victory of the cross over the power of Satan is to be carried out in the same power through which Christ triumphed over the grave.

Defense and Offense

When Paul said, *"Take unto you the whole armour of God,"* (Eph. 6:13), he began by speaking of the various parts of defensive armor. The Christian first needs to see that he is perfectly safe in the protection of his Lord. Only then is he fit for acting on the offensive. Paul mentioned only one weapon of attack: the sword. That sword is the sword of the Spirit, the Word of God.

To know its power and how to use it effectively, we can look to our Leader, the Captain of the Lord's host. When Jesus Christ met Satan in the wilderness, He conquered him by the Word of God alone. As a man, He had studied the Word. He loved it, He obeyed it, and He lived in it. The Holy Spirit brought to His mind the familiar words He needed to meet and conquer every satanic suggestion.

To use the sword of the Spirit in the hour of battle means that I have lived in that Word and that it abides in me. I have given it the mastery of my whole being. The Spirit of Christ within me enables me by faith to cast out Satan by the Word.

The man who yields his whole being to the Word, who lives by every word that comes from the mouth of God, will be a good soldier of Jesus Christ. In the struggle with doubt and worldliness; with open or secret iniquity; with feeble, hopeless Christians; with dark superstition, nominal Christianity, or a backsliding church—the Word of God will always be the weapon of victory to those who know how to use it properly.

We learn to use our sword from the vision of John in Patmos. He saw One like the Son of Man, and *"out of his mouth went a sharp twoedged sword"* (Rev. 1:16). John heard

Him say, *"These things saith he which hath the sharp sword with two edges;....Repent; or else I will come unto thee quickly, and will fight against them with the sword of my mouth"* (Rev. 2:12, 16).

Christ has been revealed to us, calling us to repent of sin, especially the sin of our unbelief. He has fought against the evil in us with the sword of His mouth, so that the power of the Word will be revealed in us. Now we can be strong to wield the sword of the Spirit.

> *For the word of God is quick, and powerful, and sharper than any twoedged sword, piercing even to the dividing asunder of soul and spirit, and of the joints and marrow, and is a discerner of the thoughts and intents of the heart.*
> (Heb. 4:12)

The Word shows us the difference between the soulish and spiritual realms. It discovers our most secret intentions and inclinations in the light of God and His holiness. The branch that has been cleansed by the Word will bear much fruit. The soul that has fully yielded itself to the sword of His mouth will have faith and strength to wield it against every enemy.

Mobilized for Battle

Every believer is called to be a soldier in Christ's army. The spiritual powers of darkness are to be met and overcome by all who have learned that they are not to live for themselves, but wholly for Him who redeemed them. Jesus leads them as His conquering forces to rout the spiritual hosts of wickedness in heavenly places. Many Christians have never understood their calling and have never given their lives unreservedly for the one object of securing the triumph of our Redeemer in the world.

Listen to the summons that calls us to the war. Let us confess and repent that we seldom stand in the strength of the Lord *"and in the power of his might"* (Eph. 6:10), with our armor on day and night. Let our ears be opened to the call that comes from every church for men and women who will yield themselves to Christ for His service, whether in the home or on the mission field.

We are to prove first in our own life that God's Word has power with Him in prayer and intercession, and with us in surrender and cleansing. There we learn to use it. Our love for our Lord and for souls will rouse us to the war. The Word of God will become the sword of the Spirit that we carry to meet the enemy and to deliver his captives.

How helpless is the church of our day with its thousands of missionaries to meet the needs of millions of unbelievers. How strong it might be if every believer were trained to yield to the two-edged sword proceeding out of the mouth of the Son of Man. After it has done its work in his own heart, he could grasp it and use it to bring deliverance to those who are dying in bondage to sin.

Our private devotions have often been the vain attempt to find nourishment or joy in the Word of God. We failed because our first thought was the selfish one of seeking comfort or holiness for ourselves. Let us repent and learn that a Christian is saved so that Christ may use him for the welfare of the whole body and of those who have not yet been gathered into it.

May our devotions bear these two simple marks: the entire surrender to the Word of God as the two-edged sword and the surrender to wield that two-edged sword in the power of the Holy Spirit against every enemy of Christ and His kingdom.

Chapter 16

---◆---

Victory through Intercession

*Praying always with all prayer and supplication
in the Spirit, and watching thereunto with all
perseverance and supplication for all saints.*
—Ephesians 6:18

*T*he Christian's wrestling is against the spiritual hosts of wickedness in the heavenly places. He must put on his armor and wield the sword of the Spirit in complete dependence on God and with confidence in His all-sufficient grace. A life of constant prayer is the secret of a life of victory. Praying in the Spirit is the mark of the normal spiritual life.

Our lungs are kept breathing by the divine power that upholds our physical life. Likewise, the Holy Spirit will certainly breathe in us prayers that maintain the power of the divine life and the heavenly world. Salvation is not accomplished by works or struggling. We are God's *"workmanship, created in Christ Jesus unto good works, which God hath before ordained that we should walk in them"* (Eph. 2:10). The Bible tells us that we are a divine creation, not finished and left to ourselves, but with every moment of our lives upheld by the Word of His power. Unceasing prayer is possible and is commanded because the eternal Spirit causes it to become the heavenward breathing of the soul.

For What Should We Pray?

Praying at all times is by no means to be selfish, referring only to our own needs. *"Watching thereunto with all perseverance and supplication for all the saints."* Paul taught us the importance of unity in the body of Christ in love. In contrast to the wrestling of believers with the powers of darkness, he spoke of the unity of the saints as they form one great army of the Lord. This army has been made alive by one Spirit and is striving together to establish His kingdom in the world. Continual earnest prayer for all believers is our duty, but it is also vital for the welfare and the victory of the whole body.

We can learn the subject of our prayers from Paul's own petitions. In chapter one, he prayed for those who had already been sealed with the Spirit. He asked that God would give them the Spirit of wisdom and divine illumination that they might know the greatness of His power in all who believe.

Believers need to allow this great truth to take hold of their hearts and thoroughly possess them. Those who have sought this for themselves need to be reminded of their calling to make this request for others. The health of the church as a whole and the spiritual strength of individual believers or churches depends on our perseverance in prayer for all the saints.

True believers need the prayers of other believers. The prayer is to be specific, pleading for the Spirit of divine power to fill their inner man, that Christ may dwell in their hearts and that they may be rooted in love. All believers are to unite in pleading for all the saints.

The Secret of Revival

Prayer is to be marked by perseverance. Praying always in the Spirit for all saints is the secret of true revival in God's children. The minister who is pleading as an intercessor for his congregation also needs their prayers in return. As blood is purified by the fresh air we breathe, even so the Spirit of prayer breathes in the air of heaven and breathes up to heaven the unceasing supplication of love. This is essential to the health of the body of Christ, and the work of the ministry depends on it.

The minister should teach believers that intercession is one of their highest privileges. The work of the missionary who, like Paul, carries the Gospel to the ungodly depends on it. New power would fill our mission work if believers answered the call to pray at all times in the Spirit. Grace would be given to Christian workers as they boldly proclaim the mystery of the Gospel. Preaching the Word to the wise or to the ignorant, to the Greek or the Jew, reveals Christ—the power of God and the wisdom of God.

Paul gave us a great vision of the work to be done in our daily hour of devotion. We see the hosts of spiritual wickedness in heavenly places and Jesus Christ ruling over all and carrying out the triumph of the cross. Victory is won as the members of Christ labor together and wrestle in preaching and in prayer for the conquest of the world. Our devotions take on a new meaning and glory as we grow strong in the Lord and in the power of His might. We will no longer live for ourselves and our religious hopes and efforts but live in love, even as Christ loved us. Each believer can learn to give himself as an offering to God for the building up of the body of Christ.

May God help us to catch the fire of inspiration that Paul's letter to the Ephesians holds out to us. We can know the rewards of praying always in the Spirit for all the saints, and above all, for the ministers of the Gospel.

Chapter 17

———◆———

Fulfilled in God's Plan

*God...hath blessed us with all spiritual blessings
in heavenly places in Christ.*
—Ephesians 1:3

*I*n Paul's letter to the Ephesians, the expression *"heavenly places"* is used five times. In the heavenly places, God blessed us with every spiritual blessing in Christ. He set Christ at His right hand and made us sit with Christ. The wisdom of God is to be made known through the church to principalities and powers. We are ready to wrestle against the spiritual hosts of wickedness. No man or woman can live a Christian life except in the power of the heavenly world.

In his excellent letter, Paul revealed the mystery of God's will and His purpose in Christ. He helps us understand our resurrection and ascension with Christ, our new creation, and our glory as a part of the body of Christ. As the light of the Holy Spirit shines on one truth after another, we learn how truly divine and heavenly our lives on earth can be.

Knowing Our Heavenly Calling

We have studied the twelve passages in which the Holy Spirit is mentioned. Let us gather all their teaching into one and see if we can sketch a portrait of the man called to live by this heavenly standard.

The believer has been sealed in Christ by the Holy Spirit of promise. The Spirit is the down payment of his inheritance, the pledge of what he is and can become in Christ, and the divine assurance that every promise can be fulfilled. He has the seal of God on his forehead, and his whole being bears the stamp of the Holy Spirit.

The first blessing of the Spirit is that He enlightens our eyes to know our calling and the greatness of God's power to fulfill His plan in us. The Holy Spirit reveals God's power in raising Christ from the dead to the throne of glory as the pledge of what God will work in us each day.

The sealed one has been brought near to God by the blood of His Son and lives in the Holy Place. Through the Spirit he has a life of perfect fellowship with God in Christ Jesus.

The sealed one no longer lives for himself but as a member of the great spiritual temple built for God through the Spirit. The Spirit links the believer to the Chief Cornerstone and to all his fellow saints. He also knows the mystery of Christ among the Gentiles and counts them as fellow heirs to all the unsearchable riches of Christ. He lives for the kingdom and the conversion of the unbelievers as Christ's inheritance.

The sealed one has learned that only by God's almighty power can he live in the heavenly places. He continually prays that the power of the Spirit may strengthen him mightily. He wants Christ to dwell in his heart by faith and to be filled with love and with all the fullness of God. He asks for himself and for others that God may reveal His Son in them.

The sealed one bears the image of Jesus. He walks worthy of his heavenly calling, humbly maintaining the unity of the Spirit. He knows he can do this because God strengthens him with might in the inner man. His calling is to minister to the saints and build up the body of Christ in love.

Above everything else, he seeks never to grieve the Holy Spirit of God. In this way, he can partake of all the blessings in the heavenly places in Christ. He cultivates a tender spirit.

Walking in the Spirit

The more the believer knows about the scaling of the Spirit and the work that He does, the greater is his desire to yield himself completely to the Spirit's control. At the same time, he feels the need of a deeper vision of the riches of grace dispensed by the blessed Spirit. He sees that to be filled with the Spirit means peace, joy, health, and strength.

The seal of the Spirit includes the call to be a soldier and to be strong in the Lord and the power of His might. The believer understands that divine power is promised him so that he may wrestle against the powers of evil with the sword of the Spirit and rescue men for Christ and His service. He obeys the call to a life of continual prayer with perseverance for all saints and for all ministers of the Word. The Spirit makes it possible for him to be a true soldier and prayer warrior.

"Blessed be the God and Father of our Lord Jesus Christ, who hath blessed us with all spiritual blessings in heavenly places in Christ" (Eph. 1:3). Let us meditate on the blessings until we realize what a glorious salvation God has prepared for us. A believer who is sealed by the Spirit is taught to know the divine power working in him. He enjoys perfect fellowship with the Father, united with all his fellow saints as the temple of God.

Strengthened with might by the Spirit, Christ dwells in his heart, and he is filled with all the fullness of God. He walks in all meekness and lowliness in his daily life, keeping the unity of the Spirit. In the power of the Spirit, he works to build up the body in love. He hungers to be filled with the Spirit and never grieves Him. He fulfills the law of love in his daily life and is strong in the Lord and in the power of His might to wrestle with the powers of darkness, using the Word and praying for all saints.

It takes time, thought, prayer, and quiet waiting on the Spirit of God for anyone to keep the vision of the Spirit-sealed, Spirit-taught, Spirit-strengthened, and Spirit-filled believer. We must turn from self and the world to allow God to work in us according to the counsel of His own will.

Let us not forget our purpose in studying Paul's letter to the Ephesians. Let us believe in the divine standard of the Christian life that it sets before us. By the almighty power of God alone, it can become ours. If we are serious about seeking deliverance from worldly standards, we can count on the infinite mercy of God to work in us what otherwise appears to be utterly hopeless: a life filled with the Spirit.

Chapter 18

Because of Unbelief

*Why could not we cast him out? And Jesus said unto them,
Because of your unbelief.*
—Matthew 17:19–20

*D*o you think it is possible to carry out the Ephesians standard of spirituality in your own daily life? Some people would say that they do not see how it can be possible because of the sin in every believer that makes daily confession absolutely necessary. Others might answer that, although such a standard is possible for Paul and other spiritual men, it is not within the reach of all. Such a life is not for everyone. A large majority content themselves with the thought of an attractive yet unattainable ideal that exercises its elevating influence on those who remain far below it.

Surely Paul meant in all sincerity to testify of what God not only had shown him by revelation, but also had actually accomplished within him. He spoke in chapter one of the revelation of the Spirit to make us know the greatness of God's power through our faith in Christ raised from dead and seated on the throne. In chapter three he told of our being strengthened by the Spirit in the inner man, so that the great miracle of grace is perfected in us. Christ dwells in our hearts, filling us with all the fullness of God. He finally added the ascription of praise, *"Now unto him that is able to do exceeding abundantly above all that we ask or think, according to the power that worketh in us, unto him be glory"* (Eph. 3:20–21). Paul undoubtedly meant that this was his own experience, and he confidently urged his readers to believe that it can be theirs.

An Ideal or an Experience?

The greatness of God's power working in the heart from moment to moment, day by day, is the ground on which the standard of devotion rests. Paul held this standard out to us. Unceasing prayer is required to know this power, to believe it, and to receive it. Without prayer, we will regard the standard as an impractical one and continue in ignorance of what is offered for our acceptance.

Why is this mighty power of God working in us seldom taught and rarely experienced? Is the whole church in error in resting content with a far lower standard than what Paul's letter holds out to us? The answer to these questions will lead us to the root of the evil from which the church is suffering.

We all know that God gave Abraham to Israel as the great example of faith in Him. Abraham believed that God was able to raise the dead, both in his own case and in the sacrifice of Isaac. Yet we know how Israel, from the beginning of God's dealings in Egypt, continually grieved Him by unbelief. Their unbelief condemned them to forty years of wandering in the wilderness. Psalm 78 tells us their story and shows how they continually limited God by unbelief.

We know, too, how our Lord Jesus continually sought to cultivate faith in His disciples as the one condition for their seeing the power and the glory of God. He set Paul forth as a witness to the power of faith, not only in justification, but also in the whole of our spiritual life and service.

Yet just as Israel, despite the example of Abraham, utterly failed in trusting God, so in the church it became plain how little man knows to receive his salvation based on trust in God alone. We know how terribly the Galatians failed. The letter to the Hebrews warns above everything against unbelief. The church of the second century was brought into bondage under the law. The human heart naturally turns from grace and faith to the law and works.

In the lives of the church fathers, we find, with all their earnestness, how little they understood faith in the power of God as the one secret of a life pleasing to Him. They developed a religion in which the grace of God was connected with the confession of endless sins. The voice of Paul and his faith in God's mighty keeping and saving power was seldom heard. The generations that heard the Gospel of justification by faith hardly understood that sanctification is also by faith. The power of a holy life for victory over the world and the flesh can be found only in an unceasing exercise of faith in the greatness of God's power in us. We should not be surprised that one of the great causes of feebleness in the church today is the unbelief in the mighty power of Jesus.

Reasons for Power Failure

We often hear complaints of the lack of power in the church. It seems unprepared to guide its members to true devotion to Christ and to influence the unsaved multitude around us. The chief cause of all is often overlooked: a church that does not experience the power of Christ dwelling in the hearts of His people to overcome the power of sin cannot expect that mighty power in its conflict with Satan and his hosts.

The first great work of the Holy Spirit is to convict people of their unbelief. Where that work has not been fully done, nothing will happen until the church confesses that all its weakness is due to this one thing: not giving Christ His place of honor. Jesus said, *"All power is given unto me in heaven and in earth"* (Matt. 28:18). As the church believes and experiences this truth, it will learn to expect Him to do His mighty works.

Receiving Power from God

Ask yourself the question: do I believe in the power of God in Christ by His Spirit to work in me the life depicted in this epistle? Instead of mourning over the sins we cannot master—the pride, self-will, lack of love, or disobedience—let us come to the root of the matter and confess our terrible sin of unbelief. Let our faith grow in the greatness of God's power revealed in Christ. We will be strengthened by the Spirit with might and led on to the fullness of God. As we humble ourselves before God in the confession of our unbelief, He will reveal Christ in us. Our lives can indeed become the response to the divine call: *"Be strong in the Lord, and in the power of his might"* (Eph. 6:10).

Chapter 19

Harmony between God and Man

*Who then can be saved? And he said, The things which are
impossible with men are possible with God.*
—Luke 18:26–27

The great hindrance to the power of God's Word in the truth
we have found in Ephesians is this thought: God's standard
is an impossible one. Our only response to this doubt must be
to listen again to the voice of Christ as He tells us that what is
impossible with man is possible with God. God can do for us
what appears to be beyond His reach and ours. God can work
in us what He worked in Paul.

What is implied in the great gift of the Holy Spirit? No word
is used in such a variety of ways as the word *spirit*. It can mean
anything in which the mind of man exerts and proves its power,
or it can mean the highest revelation of God's holiness and love.
The same word is used, increasing the danger that each person
will understand it only according to his own point of view. We
often suffer from our defective view of what is really meant by
the Spirit of God and of Christ.

God sent His Son into the world as a man so that He would
work out in His life a holy nature. This nature could then be

imparted to believers in Christ as a thing already prepared and brought into existence for us. Just as the grain of wheat dies and reappears in the full ear of corn with its hundredfold reproduction of the seed, Christ died that He may live again in our lives here on earth.

When Jesus ascended to the throne, the Father gave Him the Spirit to pour down His life in the hearts of His people. The Spirit communicates the holy nature of Christ with a divine power to all who believe. They live by the Spirit and are led by the Spirit. The Spirit is their life.

Working with God

In the wonderful union of the divine and the human life in the believer, everything depends on the true relationship being maintained between God and man. God works all in all, and man receives all from God to work it out in trust and obedience. Where this relationship is not properly understood, man will use his own efforts to take the place that God wants to fill. He thinks that if he can secure God's help in his efforts, he has found the path to holiness and growth. He does not understand that the Spirit must have absolute control, and he must exercise direct and unceasing dependence on Him.

Two men may be praying that God would give them the Spirit of wisdom. The one may be thinking only of the ordinary measures of help he has connected with the thought of the Spirit. But the other is expecting that God will do more than he can ask or think.

The great secret of the Christian life is found in dying to self and being brought to nothing by the cross of Christ. Before our Lord Jesus could receive the new life from the Father and impart the gift of the Holy Spirit to His people, He had to give up the life He lived on earth. He had to take His place among the dead in weakness and helplessness before He could live again by the power of God. His death on the cross was indispensable to the life of the Spirit.

As it was with Christ, so it must be with us. As we yield ourselves to be united with Him in the likeness of His death, we can
share with Him in the glory and power of the life of the Spirit. To
know what the Holy Spirit means implies knowing what death
means. The cross and the Spirit are inseparable. The soul that
understands that death to self is the gate to true life is ready to
learn what and who the Holy Spirit is.

Why is our understanding of what the Holy Spirit can and
will do for us so limited? The great mark of the New Testament
church was the presence of the Holy Spirit in power. Today we
see only a feeble representation of the Spirit's work. Our conversions, preaching, fellowship, life, aggressive work for God and
His kingdom—everywhere it is obvious that the power of the
Spirit is seldom known.

Endless discussions and efforts are made to lift our churches
to a higher level and to convince people to accept the truth
of God's Word. But there has not yet been, on the part of the
church as a whole, anything like the intense and sorrowful confession that, as churches and as Christians, we have grieved the
Spirit of God. Our calling is to honor Him and to prove by His
presence in our lives that Christ is indeed Lord.

The Source of Spiritual Blessings

In the epistle to the Ephesians, the Holy Spirit takes an
important place. Paul must have had some reason for saturating
the letter with the truth of the Spirit's presence and work. The
epistle to the Colossians was written about the same time, and
it carries the same theme. Yet there is one very marked difference. In Colossians the Holy Spirit is mentioned only once, but
in Ephesians He is mentioned twelve times. Paul felt the need to
express a system of truth in which the presence and power of
the Holy Spirit is evident in the life of the Christian.

Let us make certain that when we think of the Holy Spirit,
we mean what God means. He means the Holy Spirit, God the
Spirit, God the Holy One, God in His holiness living within us. In

Him we have the whole God, not only His power, but the living God Himself. We need to allow our whole selves—spirit, soul, and body—to be possessed and controlled by Him. As we think of what God in the Spirit is willing to do in us, we will realize that only we can keep Him from doing His work in us. We must get rid of ourselves, lose our lives, and die with Christ. Our new nature made alive in Him will be the fit vessel for all the blessing the Spirit will bring.

Chapter 20

———◆◆———

Giving God the Glory

*Now unto him that is able to do exceeding abundantly
above all that we ask or think, according to the power
that worketh in us, unto him be glory.*
—Ephesians 3:20–21

*I*n any discussion on Paul's letter to the Ephesians, we should
emphasize the power of God and the place it is meant to take
in the life of the Christian. All that we have learned about the
Holy Spirit cannot have its full effect in our lives without a complete surrender to the almighty working of God's power. Believers need to have an intense, personal, and abiding faith that
God's power must be known and honored as the secret of living
according to the New Testament standard. God will enlighten
us by His Spirit that we may know the greatness of His power
within us.

Paul gave special emphasis to the thought that our salvation is the result of the direct working of God's almighty power.
He spoke of *"the purpose of him who worketh all things after
the counsel of his own will"* (Eph. 1:11). God does this, not only
with regard to the great work of deliverance in Christ, but also in
every detail in the daily life of the Christian. We think of Him as

the omnipotent One, able to work mightily when He chooses. But the words suggest something far greater. God works every moment, not only in nature with its every leaf and flower, but in His children, too. He provides all that they need for carrying out His blessed will.

Power Working in You

Nothing less than the power of the Father's might that raised Christ from the dead can meet the daily needs of your soul and accomplish what God longs to see in you. The Holy Spirit gives you spiritual insight into the greatness of His power and enables you to know that God is working in you. Then He will be able to do for you what He has not yet done.

The Christian strives after the life that the Word puts before him. He prays that God would aid him in his weakness, but he fails to understand that only the greatness of God's power in him can do the work. *"The weakness of God is stronger than men"* (1 Cor. 1:25). The strength of God is found only in the consciousness of utter weakness.

This was the mark of the working of the might of His power in Christ. Our Lord died, sinking down into absolute weakness, without a vestige of the power of thought or will. He yielded Himself to the Father, and God's power raised Him out of absolute weakness to the place of power on the throne. Only the teaching of the Holy Spirit can enable us to know the greatness of God's power working in us.

As this thought masters us, we will understand the standard of the life Paul put before us. By divine power, God will work in us to give us the courage to see and live a life pleasing to Him in every way.

Paul spoke of the grace of God given to him *"by the effectual working of his power"* (Eph. 3:7). He experienced and counted on this direct working of God for all the grace he needed for his ministry. He said in Colossians, *"I also labour, striving according to his working, which worketh in me mightily"* (Col. 1:29).

The man who believes in the working of God's power will cease seeking strength in himself. His whole attitude will be that of simple dependence and perfect trust in God.

God's Almighty Power

The more we strive to take in these thoughts, the better we will understand why Paul again returned to the working of God's almighty power. In chapter one he spoke of the Spirit's enlightenment to show us that the power that raised Christ is needed to work in us in every moment of our spiritual life. In chapter three he went further and prayed that the greatness of God's power according to the riches of His glory may be given to us as an actual strengthening with might by His Spirit in the inner man. Take time and think what that means! The whole spiritual life can be permanently quickened with divine power. Then the indwelling of Christ in the heart will become a divine reality.

The church has almost lost the concept of the indwelling of Christ as a continual experience. Before this can become part of our living faith and experience, we must see the greatness of God's power that raised Christ from the dead as part of the inheritance of every Christian. The Holy Spirit is the pledge of our inheritance.

Paul realized the importance of the divine power as the one condition of the full spiritual life. The doxology he added gives God glory just for this one thing: that He is able to do *"exceeding abundantly above all that we ask or think"* (Eph. 3:20). Other attributes of God—His love, His righteousness, His holiness—give us reasons to bless His name. But as the groundwork of all, His almighty power must be our only confidence in all that He is to do in us in carrying out His purpose.

Let us worship and adore Him. Every thought of what is to be done in us, in the church, and in the world is summed up in the promise that He is *"able to do exceeding abundantly above all that we ask or think, according to the power that worketh in us"* (v. 20).

Paul closed his instruction in the epistle with the conclusion: *"Finally, my brethren, be strong in the Lord, and in the power of his might"* (Eph. 6:10). He used the same thought in Ephesians 1:19, *"according to the working of his mighty power,"* and in Ephesians 3:16, *"to be strengthened with might by his Spirit in the inner man."*

This power and strength was meant to be the standard of devotion in those Christians in Ephesus. It will become the standard of our devotion when we learn to cast all our weakness at His feet and believe with childlike assurance in the greatness of His power toward us. We will then be prepared to experience a life strong in the Lord and in the power of His might.

Book Three

———◆·◆———

Covenants and Blessings

Contents

———————◆————————

Introduction

*I*t is often said that the great aim of the preacher should be to translate Scripture truth from its Jewish form into the language and thought of today. He should make it intelligible and acceptable to ordinary Christians. It is feared that the experiment will do more harm than good. In the course of the translation, the power of the original message is lost. The scholar who trusts translations will never become a master of the language he wants to learn. A race of Christians will arise who will be strangers to the language of God's Word and the God who spoke it. In the wording of some Scripture translations, much of Scripture truth will be lost. For the true Christian life, nothing is as healthy and invigorating as having each man come and study for himself the very words the Holy Spirit has spoken.

One of the words of Scripture that is almost obsolete is the word *covenant*. There was a time when it was the keynote of theology and the basis for the Christian life of strong, holy men. We know how in Scotland it entered deep into the national life and thought. It made mighty men, men to whom God and His promise and power were wonderfully real. It still brings strength and purpose to those who take the trouble to bring all their life under the control of the inspiring assurance that they are living in covenant with God. He has faithfully sworn to fulfill in them every promise He has given.

This book is a humble attempt to show exactly which blessings God has covenanted to us. It gives His assurance that the covenant must, can, and will be fulfilled. It also shows how we can approach God and the conditions for receiving the full, continual experience of the covenant blessings. I am confident that if I can lead anyone to listen to what God has to say about His covenant, and to deal with Him as a covenant God, it will bring them strength and joy.

Not long ago I received a letter from one of my correspondents with the following passage in it: "I think you will excuse and understand me when I say there is one further note of power I would like to have introduced in your next book on intercession. God has been giving me some direct teaching this winter about the place the new covenant is to have in intercessory prayer.

"I know you believe in the covenant and the covenant rights we have because of it. Have you followed out your views of the covenant as they bear upon this subject of intercession? Am I wrong in coming to the conclusion that we may come boldly into God's presence and not only ask for, but claim, a covenant right through Christ Jesus to all the spiritual searching, cleansing, knowledge, and power promised in the three great covenant promises?

"If you take the covenant and speak about it as God enables you to speak, I think that would be the quickest way for the Lord to make His church wake up to the power He has put in our hands in giving us a covenant. I would be so glad if you told God's people that they have a covenant."

Though this letter was not the occasion of the writing of the book, and our covenant rights have been considered in a far wider aspect than their relationship to prayer, I, too, am persuaded that nothing will help us more in our work of intercession than the entrance into what it means to have a covenant God.

My one great desire has been to ask Christians whether they are really seeking to find out exactly what God wants them to be and is willing to make them. It is only then that their faith can ever truly see, accept, or enjoy what God calls

"His salvation." As long as we expect God to do for us only what we ask or think, we limit Him. When we believe that His thoughts are as high above our thoughts as the heavens are above the earth, and wait on Him as God to do to us according to His Word, we will be prepared to live the truly supernatural, heavenly life the Holy Spirit can work in us—the true Christ life.

May God lead every reader into the secret of His presence and show him His covenant.

—ANDREW MURRAY

Chapter 1

---◆◆---

A Covenant God

*Know therefore that the L*ord *thy God,*
he is God, the faithful God, which keepeth
covenant and mercy with them that love him
and keep his commandments.
—Deuteronomy 7:9

*M*en know the advantages of making covenants. A covenant has often been of unspeakable value as an end to hatred or uncertainty, as an agreement of services rendered, as an assurance of good quality and honesty, and as a basis for confidence and friendship.

God's Covenant

In His infinite descent to our human weakness and need, God's pledge of faithfulness goes beyond the ways of men. He gives us perfect confidence in Him and the full assurance of all that He, in His infinite riches and power, has promised to do. He has consented to bind Himself by covenant, as if He could not be trusted. Blessed is the man who truly knows God as his covenant God and knows what the covenant promises him. What unwavering confidence of expectation it secures. All its terms will be fulfilled. What a claim and hold it gives him on the covenant-keeping God Himself.

To the many who have never thought much about the covenant, it would mean the transformation of their whole lives to have a true, living faith. The full knowledge of what God wants to do, the assurance that it will be done, and the being drawn to God Himself in personal surrender makes the covenant the very gate of heaven. May the Holy Spirit give us some vision of its glory.

When God created man in His image and likeness, it was so that he would have a life as similar to God's as possible. This occurred by God Himself living and working in man. For this, man was to yield himself in loving dependence to the wonderful glory of being the recipient, bearer, and manifestation of a divine life. The one secret of man's happiness was a trustful surrender of his whole being to the willing and the working of God. When sin entered, this relationship to God was destroyed. When man disobeyed, he feared God and fled from Him. He no longer knew, loved, or trusted God.

Getting Man to Believe

Man could not save himself from the power of sin. If his redemption was to be accomplished, God had to do it all. If God was to do it in harmony with the law of man's nature, man must be brought to desire it, yield to it, and entrust himself to God. All God wanted man to do was to believe in Him. What a man believes moves and rules his whole being. It enters into him and becomes part of his very life. Salvation could only be by faith. God restored the life man had lost. In faith, man yielded himself to God's work and will.

The first great work of God was to get man to believe. This work cost God more care, time, and patience than we can conceive. All the dealings with individual men and with the people of Israel had this one purpose—to teach men to trust Him. Where He found faith He could do anything. Nothing dishonored and grieved Him so much as unbelief. Unbelief was the root of disobedience and every sin. It made it impossible for God to do His work. The one thing God sought to waken in men, by promise, mercy, and judgment, was faith.

The main way God's patient grace awakened and strengthened faith was the covenant. In more than one way, God sought to effect this by His covenant. First of all, His covenant was always a revelation of His purpose. It showed, in definite promise, that God was willing to work in those with whom the covenant was made. It was a divine pattern of the work God intended to do in their behalf so that they might know what to desire and expect. It was a pattern so their faith could nourish itself with the very things, though as yet unseen, which it was working out.

Then, the covenant was meant to be a security and guarantee. It was to be as simple, plain, and humanlike as the divine glory could make it. The very things that God had promised would be brought to pass and worked out in those with whom He had entered into covenant. Amid all delay, disappointment, and apparent failure of the divine promises, the covenant was to be the anchor of the soul, pledging the divine truthfulness, faithfulness, and unchangeableness for the certain performance of what had been promised. So the covenant was, above all, to give man a hold upon God, as the covenant-keeping God. It was to link him to God in expectation and hope. It was to cause him to make God alone the portion and the strength of his soul.

Unbelief Holds Us Back

If only we knew how much God wants us to trust Him and how surely His every promise will be fulfilled for those who do so! If only we knew that it is our unbelief that prevents us from entering into the possession of God's promises! Because we do not, God cannot do His mighty works in us, for us, and through us. One of the surest remedies for our unbelief—the divinely chosen cure for it—is the covenant into which God has entered with us. The whole dispensation of the Spirit, the whole economy of grace in Christ Jesus, the whole of our spiritual lives, and the whole of the health, growth, and strength of the church has been laid down, provided for, and secured in the new covenant. It is a great shame that the covenant and its wonderful promises are so little thought of. Its plea for an abounding, unhesitating confidence in God is so little understood. Its claim to the faithfulness of the omnipotent God is rarely tested. No wonder the Christian life misses the joy, holiness, and heavenly quality that God meant and so clearly promises that it should have.

Take God's Promises

Let us listen to God's Word, which calls us to know, worship, and trust our covenant-keeping God. Maybe we will find what we have been looking for: the deep, full experience of all that God's grace can do in us. In the text Moses said, *"Know therefore that the LORD thy God, he is God, the faithful God, which keepeth covenant and mercy with them that love him."* Notice what God says in Isaiah.

> *The mountains shall depart, and the hills be removed; but my kindness shall not depart from thee, neither shall the covenant of my peace be removed, saith the LORD that hath mercy on thee.* (Isa. 54:10)

The fulfillment of every covenant promise is surer than any mountain. In Jeremiah God speaks of the new covenant,

> *And I will make an everlasting covenant with them, that I will not turn away from them, to do them good; but I will put my fear in their hearts, that they shall not depart from me.* (Jer. 32:40)

The covenant secures that God will not turn from us nor will we depart from Him. He undertakes both for Himself and us.

Let us earnestly ask whether the lack in our Christian life, especially in our faith, is due to neglect of the covenant. We have not worshipped nor trusted the covenant-keeping God. Our souls have not done what God called us to—to take hold of

His covenant; to remember the covenant. No wonder our faith has failed and comes short of the blessing. God could not fulfill His promises in us.

If we begin to examine the terms of the covenant as the deed of our inheritance and the riches we are to possess even here on earth, we will be different. If we will think of the certainty of their fulfillment and turn to the God who has promised to do it all for us, our lives will be different from what they have been. They can and will be all that God desires to make them.

We Need More of God

The greatest lack of our faith is that we need more of God. We accept salvation as His gift, but often do not know that the main blessing of salvation is to prepare us for and bring us back to that close fellowship with God for which we were created. All that God has ever done for His people in making a covenant was to bring them to Himself and to teach them to trust in Him, delight in Him, and be one with Him. It cannot be otherwise.

If God is the very fountain of goodness and glory, beauty and blessedness, the more we can have of His presence, conform to His will, engage in His service, and have Him ruling and working in us, the happier we will be. Only a true, good Christian life, which brings us nearer to God every day, makes us give up everything to have more of Him. No obedience can be too strict, no dependence too absolute, no submission too complete, no confidence too implicit to a person who is learning to count God his highest good and exceeding joy.

God's one objective in entering into covenant with us is to draw us to Himself. He wants to make us entirely dependent on Him, to bring us into the right position and attitude so He can fill us with Himself, His love, and His blessedness. Let us study the new covenant. God is at this moment living and walking with us. Let us go to God with the honest purpose and surrender to know what He wants to be in us, and to have us be to Him. The new covenant will become one of the windows of heaven through which we see into the face and very heart of God.

Chapter 2

———————◆◆◆———————

The Two Covenants

*It is written, that Abraham had two sons, the one
by a bondmaid, the other by a freewoman.
But he who was of the bondmaid was born
after the flesh; but he of the freewoman
was by promise. Which things are an allegory:
for these are the two covenants.*
—Galatians 4:22–24

*T*here are two covenants: the old covenant and the new covenant. God speaks of this very distinctly in Jeremiah where He says,

> *Behold, the days come...that I will make a new covenant with the house of Israel...not according to the covenant that I made with their fathers.* (Jer. 31:31–32)

This passage is quoted in Hebrews, with the addition: *"In that he saith, A new covenant, he hath made the first old"* (Heb. 8:13). Our Lord spoke of the new covenant in His blood. In His dealings with His people and in working out His great redemption, it has pleased God that there are two covenants.

Why Two Covenants?

It has pleased Him for good and wise reasons that made it necessary that it should be so. The clearer our insight into the reasons and the divine reasonableness of there being two covenants and their relationship to each other, the more we can understand what the new covenant means to us.

The covenants indicate two stages in God's dealing with man. There are two ways of serving God: an elementary one of preparation and promise, and a more advanced one of fulfillment and possession. As the true excellency of the second is revealed to us, we can spiritually enter into what God has prepared for us. Let us try to understand why there should have been two.

The reason is found in the fact that in all fellowship between God and man, there are two parties. Each of them must have the opportunity to demonstrate what his part is in the covenant. In the old covenant, man had the opportunity to prove what he could do. This was done with the aid of all the means of grace God could bestow. That covenant ended in man proving his own unfaithfulness and failure. In the new covenant, God proves what He can do with man, unfaithful and weak as he is, when He is allowed and trusted to do all the work. The old covenant was dependent on man's obedience, which he could and did break. (See Jeremiah 31:32.) The new covenant was one that God has promised will never be broken. He Himself keeps it and ensures our keeping it, thus making it an everlasting covenant.

The Problem

Let us look a little deeper. The relationship of God to fallen man in covenant is the same as it was with unfallen man to Creator. What was that relationship? God planned to make man in His own image and likeness. The ultimate glory of God is that He has life in Himself. He is independent of all else and owes what He is to Himself alone. If man was to be the image and likeness of God in more than just name, he had to have the power of free will and self-determination.

This free will was the problem God had to solve in man's creation in His image. Man was to be a being made by God, yet he was to be, as far as could be, self-made like God. In all God's treatment of man, these two factors were always to be taken into account. God would always take the initiative and be the Source of life to man. Man was always supposed to be the recipient and, at the same time, the executive of the life God bestowed.

When man fell, through sin, and God entered into a covenant of salvation, these two sides of the relationship still had to be kept intact. God would always be the first and man the second. Yet man, made in God's image, would always have the time and opportunity to appropriate or reject what God gave. He had the opportunity to prove how far he could help himself and be self-made. His absolute dependence on God was not to be forced on him. If it was really to be a thing of moral worth and true blessedness, it must be his deliberate, voluntary choice.

This is the reason why there was a first and second covenant. In the first, man's desires and efforts would be fully awakened. He would be given time to prove what his human nature, aided by outward instruction, miracles, and grace, could accomplish. When his hopeless captivity under the power of sin had been discovered, the new covenant came. In it God revealed how man's true liberty from sin and self, his true nobility and godliness, was to be found in absolute dependence on God. It was found in God's being and doing all within him.

In the very nature of things there was no other possible way for God to deal with a being whom He had endowed with the godlike power of a will. All the weight this reason has in God's dealing with His people as a whole is equally as important in dealing with the individual. The two covenants represent two stages of God's education of man and of man's seeking after

God. The progress and transition from the one to the other is not merely chronological or historical. It is also organic and spiritual.

The Transition

In greater or lesser degree the transition from the old covenant to the new covenant is seen in every member of the body, as well as in the body as a whole. Under the old covenant there were men in whom the powers of the coming redemption worked mightily. In the new covenant there are men in whom the spirit of the old still makes itself manifest. The New Testament proves, in some of its most important epistles, especially those to the Galatians, Romans, and Hebrews, how it is still possible to be held fast in the bondage of the old covenant.

This is the teaching of the passage from which our text is taken. Ishmael and Isaac are both found in Abraham's home. One was born of a slave, the other of a free woman. One was after the flesh and will of man, the other through the promise and power of God. One was to be cast out; the other was to be heir of all.

It was a picture held up to the Galatians of the life they were leading as they trusted the flesh. It made a fair show and yet proved—by their being held captive to sin—to be, not of the free but of the bondwoman. Only through faith in the promise and mighty quickening power of God could any of them be made truly free and stand in the freedom with which Christ has made us free.

We Need the New Covenant Spirit

As we proceed to study the covenants and their blessings in the light of this and other Scriptures, we will see how they are the divine revelation of two systems of worship. Each has its spirit or life principle ruling every man who professes to be a Christian. We will see how the one great cause of the weakness in so many Christians is that the old covenant spirit of bondage still rules their lives. We will see that nothing but spiritual insight, with wholehearted acceptance and a living experience of all the new covenant pledges that God will work in us, can possibly prepare us for walking as God wants us to. This truth of there being two stages in our service of God, two degrees of nearness in our worship, is typified by many things in the old covenant worship. Perhaps nowhere is it clearer than in the difference between the Holy Place and the Most Holy Place in the temple, with the veil separating them. The priests could always enter into the former to draw near to God, yet they could not come too near. The veil kept them at a distance. To enter within the Most Holy Place was death.

Once a year the high priest could enter as a promise of the time when the veil would be taken away and full access to dwell in God's presence would be given to His people. At Christ's death the veil of the temple was torn, and His blood gives us boldness and power to enter into the Holiest of All. We can live there day by day in the immediate presence of God. It is by the Holy Spirit, who came from that Holiest of All where Christ had entered, that we can have the power to live and walk with the consciousness of God's presence in us. The Holy Spirit is to bring us life and make us one with God.

The types of the two covenants, the spirit of bondage and the spirit of liberty were not only in Abraham's home. They also existed in God's home in the temple. The priests did not have the liberty of access into the Father's presence. Two classes of Christians are found not only among the Galatians but also throughout the church. Some are content with the double life, half flesh and half spirit, half self-effort and half grace. Others are not content and are seeking with their whole hearts to know fully what deliverance from sin and the abiding full power for a walk in God's presence is. God help us to be satisfied with nothing less. (See Note A on the Second Blessing.)

Chapter 3

—◆—

The First Covenant

Now therefore, if ye will obey my voice indeed, and keep my covenant, then ye shall be a peculiar treasure unto me.
—Exodus 19:5

He declared unto you his covenant, which he commanded you to perform, even ten commandments.
—Deuteronomy 4:13

If ye hearken to these judgments, and keep, and do them, that the LORD thy God shall keep unto thee the covenant.
—Deuteronomy 7:12

I will make a new covenant with the house of Israel, and with the house of Judah: not according to the covenant that I made with their fathers...which my covenant they brake.
—Jeremiah 31:31–32

We have seen that the reason there are two covenants is the necessity of giving the divine and the human will their due place in the working out of man's destiny. God always takes the initiative. Man must then have the opportunity to do his part and prove either what he can do or needs to have done for him. The old covenant was absolutely indispensable to awaken man's desires, call forth his efforts, deepen the sense of dependence on God, convince of his sin and weakness, and prepare him to feel the need of Christ's salvation. In the language of Paul,

> *We were kept under the law, shut up unto the faith which should afterwards be revealed. Wherefore the law was our schoolmaster to bring us unto Christ.* (Gal. 3:23–24)

Characteristics of the Old Covenant

To understand the old covenant, we must always remember its two great characteristics. First, it was of divine appointment, filled with much true blessing, and absolutely indispensable for the working out of God's purposes. Second, it was only provisional and preparatory to something higher and, therefore, absolutely insufficient for giving the full salvation man needs if his heart or the heart of God is to be satisfied.

Note the terms of this first covenant. *"If ye will obey my voice indeed, and keep my covenant, then ye shall be...unto me...an holy nation"* (Exod. 19:5–6). Or, as it is expressed in Jeremiah 7:23, *"Obey my voice, and I will be your God."* Obedience, especially in the book of Deuteronomy, is the condition: *"A blessing, if ye obey"* (Deut. 11:27). Some ask how God could make a covenant that He knew man could not keep.

The answer to this reveals the whole nature and purpose of the covenant. All education, divine or human, deals with its pupils on the principle that faithfulness in little things is essential to the attainment of greater things. In taking Israel into His training, God dealt with them as men in whom, with all the ruin sin had brought, there was still a conscience to judge good and evil. There was a heart capable of being stirred to long after God and a will to choose the good—to choose God Himself.

Before Christ and His salvation could be revealed, understood, and truly appreciated, these faculties of man had to be awakened and strengthened.

The Law

The law took men into its training and sought to make the very best that could be made of them by external instruction. Provision had been made in the law for a symbolic atonement and pardon. In all God's revelation of Himself through priest, prophet, and king, and in His intervention in providence and grace, everything possible was done to touch and win the heart of His people. He did all He could to emphasize the appeal of their self-interest or their gratitude, their fear or their love.

Its work did not lack fruit. Under the law, administered by the grace that always accompanied it, a number of men whose great mark was the fear of God and a desire to walk blameless in all His commandments were trained. Yet as a whole, Scripture represents the old covenant as a failure. The law had promised life, but it could not give it. (See Deuteronomy 4:1, Galatians 3:21.) The real purpose God gave it was the very opposite. He meant it as *"a ministration of death"* (2 Cor. 3:7). He gave it to convince man of his sin and awaken the confession of his frailty and his need of a new covenant and a true redemption.

It is in this view that Scripture uses such strong expressions, such as these: *"By the law is the knowledge of sin"* (Rom. 3:20). *"The law saith...that every mouth may be stopped, and all the world may become guilty before God"* (v. 19). *"The law worketh wrath"* (Rom. 4:15). *"The law entered, that the offence might abound"* (Rom. 5:20). *"That sin by the commandment might become exceeding sinful"* (Rom. 7:13). *"As many as are of the works of the law are under the curse"* (Gal. 3:10). *"We were kept under the law, shut up unto the faith which should afterwards be revealed"* (v. 23). *"Wherefore the law was our schoolmaster to bring us unto Christ, that we might be justified by faith"* (v. 24).

The Work of the Law

The great work of the law was to reveal what sin is. Its hatefulness is accursed of God. Its misery works temporal and eternal ruin. Its power binds man in hopeless slavery. The only hope of deliverance is divine intervention.

In studying the old covenant, we should always keep in mind the twofold aspect under which Scripture represents it. It was God's grace that gave Israel the law and made the law work out its purpose in individual believers and in the people as a whole. The entire old covenant was an elementary school of grace to prepare man for the fullness of grace and truth in Christ Jesus. A name is generally given to an object according to its main feature. So the old covenant is called a ministration of condemnation and death, not because there was no grace in it, but because the law with its curse was the predominating element.

We find the combination of the two aspects with special clearness in Paul's epistles. He spoke of all who are of the works of the law as *"under the curse"* (Gal. 3:10). Then almost immediately, he spoke of the law as being our schoolmaster unto Christ into whose charge we had been given until the time appointed by the Father. The old covenant is absolutely indispensable for the preparation it had to do. It was utterly insufficient to work a true and full redemption for us.

Sin versus Holiness

God teaches us two great lessons by the old covenant. The one is the lesson of sin; the other, the lesson of holiness.

The old covenant attains its objective only as it brings men to a sense of their utter sinfulness and hopeless inability to deliver themselves. As long as they have not learned this, no offer of the new covenant life can lay hold of them. As long as an intense longing for deliverance from sin has not taken place, they will naturally fall back into the power of the law and flesh. The holiness that the new covenant offers will terrify rather than attract them. The life in the spirit of bondage appears to allow for sin because obedience is declared to be impossible.

The other is the lesson of holiness. In the new covenant the triune God promises to do everything. He undertakes to give and keep the new heart, give His own Spirit in it, and give the will and power to obey and do His will. As the one demand of the first covenant was the sense of sin, one great demand of the new covenant is faith that the need of holiness created by the discipline of God's law will be met in a divine, supernatural way. The law cannot work out its purpose, except to bring a man to lie guilty and helpless before the holiness of God. There the new covenant finds him and reveals God, in His grace, accepting and making him a partaker of His holiness.

Live a New Covenant Life

This book is written with a very practical purpose. Its objective is to help believers know that wonderful new covenant of grace that God has made with them. It was written to lead them into the living, daily enjoyment of the blessed life that the new covenant secures for them. The practical lesson taught by the fact that the one special work of the first covenant, to convince of sin, is just what many Christians need. Without it the new covenant could not come. At conversion they were convicted of sin by the Holy Spirit. But this mainly referred to the guilt of sin, and, in some degree, to its hatefulness.

A real knowledge of the power of sin, and their entire and utter inability to cast it out or work in themselves what is good, is what they did not learn at once. Until they have learned this, they cannot fully enter into the blessing of the new covenant. When a man sees that, just as he cannot raise himself from the dead, he cannot make or keep his own soul alive, then he becomes capable of appreciating the New Testament promise. Then he is made willing to wait on God to do all in him.

Do you feel that you are not fully living in the new covenant and its blessings? Do you feel there is still some of the old covenant spirit of bondage in you? Come and let the old covenant finish its work in you. Accept its teaching that all your efforts are failures. Just as you were content at conversion to fall down as a condemned, death-deserving sinner, be content now to come before God in the confession that, as His redeemed child, you still feel yourself utterly unable to do and be what He asks of you. Begin to ask whether the new covenant does not have a provision you have never yet understood for meeting your weakness and giving you the strength to do what is well pleasing to God. You will find the wonderful answer in the assurance that God, by His Holy Spirit, undertakes to work everything in you.

Chapter 4

———————◆◄———————

The New Covenant

*But this shall be the covenant that I will make with the house of
Israel; After those days, saith the LORD, I will put my law in their
inward parts, and write it in their hearts; and will be their God,
and they shall be my people. And they shall teach no more
every man his neighbour, and every man his brother, saying,
Know the LORD: for they shall all know me, from the least of
them unto the greatest of them, saith the LORD. for I will forgive
their iniquity, and I will remember their sin no more.*
—Jeremiah 31:33–34

*B*ecause of the wonderful clearness with which he announced
the coming Redeemer, both in His humiliation and suffering and in the glory of the kingdom He was to establish, Isaiah
has often been called the evangelical prophet. Yet it was given
to Jeremiah, in the above passage, and to Ezekiel, in the parallel
one (see Ezekiel 37), to foretell what would actually result from
the Redeemer's work. He also described the essential character of the salvation God was to effect. God's plan is revealed in
words that the author of Hebrews 8 took as the divinely inspired
revelation of what the new covenant, of which Christ is the
Mediator, is.

The New Covenant Blessings

We are shown what He will do in us to make us prepared and worthy to be the people of whom He is God. Through the entire old covenant there was always one problem. Man's heart was not right with God. In the new covenant the evil is remedied. Its central promise is a heart delighting in God's law and capable of knowing and holding fellowship with Him. Let us observe the fourfold blessing that is mentioned.

1. *"I will put my law in their inward parts, and write it in their hearts."* Let us understand this well. In our inward parts, our hearts, there are no separate rooms where the law can be put while the rest of the heart is given to other things. The heart is a unity. The inward parts and the heart are not like a house that can be filled with things of an entirely different nature from that of which the walls are made—void of any living, organic connection. No, the inward part, the heart, is the disposition, love, will, and the life.

Nothing can be put into the heart, especially by God, without entering, taking possession, securing its affection, and controlling its being. This is what God undertakes to do in the power of His divine life and operation. He breathes the very spirit of His law into and through the whole inward being. *"I will put it into their inward parts, and write it in their hearts."* At Sinai the tables of the covenant, with the law written on them, were of stone as a lasting substance.

It is easy to understand what that means. The stone was wholly set apart for this one thing—to carry and show this divine writing. The writing and the stone were inseparably connected. Likewise, the heart in which God gets His way and writes His law in power lives wholly to carry that writing. It is unchangeably identified with it. Thus God can realize His purpose in creation and have His child of one mind and spirit with Himself, delighting in doing His will.

When the old covenant with the law written on stone had done its work in the discovering and condemning, the new covenant would give in its stead a life of obedience and true holiness of heart. The whole of the covenant blessing centers in this—the heart being made right and equipped to know God. *"And I will give them an heart to know me, that I am the* Lord: *and they shall be my people, and I will be their God: for they shall return unto me with their whole heart"* (Jer. 24:7).

2. *"They shall be my people, and I will be their God."* Do not take these words lightly. They occur most often in Jeremiah and Ezekiel in connection with the promise of the everlasting covenant. They express the very highest experience of the covenant relationship. It is only when His people learn to love and obey His law, when their hearts and lives are wholly devoted to Him and His will, that He can be the inconceivable blessing that these words express, *"I will be* [your] *God."* All I am and have as God will be yours. I will be to you all you need or wish for in a God. In the fullest meaning of the word, I, the Omnipresent, will be ever-present with you in all My grace and love. I, the Almighty One, will work each moment in you by My mighty power. I, the Thrice Holy One, will reveal My sanctifying life within you. I will be your God.

And you will be My people, saved, blessed, ruled, guided, and provided for by Me. You will be known and seen to be the people of the Holy One, the God of glory. Let us give our hearts time to meditate and wait for the Holy Spirit to work in us all that these words mean.

3. *"And they shall teach no more every man his neighbour, and every man his brother, saying, Know the* Lord: *for they shall all know me, from the least of them unto the greatest of them, saith the* Lord." Individual, personal fellowship with God, for the weakest and the least, is the wonderful privilege of every member of the new covenant. Each one will know the Lord. That does not mean the knowledge of the mind, which is not the equal privilege of all and in itself may hinder the fellowship more than help it. We will know the Lord with the knowledge that means appropriation and assimilation and that is eternal life.

As the Son knew the Father because He was one with Him and dwelt in Him, the child of God will receive, by the Holy Spirit, that spiritual illumination that will make God the One he knows best. Thus it will be because he loves Him most and lives in Him. The promise, *"They shall be all taught of God"* (John 6:45), will be fulfilled by the Holy Spirit's teaching. God will speak to each one from His Word what he needs to know.

4. *"For I will forgive their iniquity, and I will remember their sin no more."* The word *"for"* shows that this is the reason for all that precedes. Because the blood of this new covenant was of such infinite worth and its Mediator and High Priest in heaven of such divine power, there is promised such a divine blotting out of sin that God cannot remember it. It is this entire blotting out of sin that cleanses and sets us free from its power.

Thus God can write His law in our hearts and show Himself in power as our God. By His Spirit He can reveal to us His deep things—the deep mystery of Himself and His love. The atonement and redemption of Jesus Christ (brought about without us and for us) has removed every obstacle and made it fit for God. It also made us fit so that the law in the heart, the claim on our God, and the knowledge of Him should now be our daily life and our eternal portion. Here we now have the divine summary of the new covenant inheritance. The last-named blessing, the pardon of sin, is the root of it all. The second, having God as our God, and the third, the divine teaching, are the fruit. The tree that grows on this root and bears such fruit is what is named first—the law in the heart. (See Note B.)

The Heart

The central demand of the old covenant, *"Obey my voice, and I will be your God"* (Jer. 7:23), has now been met. With the law written on the heart, He can be our God, and we will be His people. Perfect harmony with God's will and holiness in heart and life is the only thing that can satisfy God's heart or ours. This is what the new covenant gives in divine power. *"I will give them an heart to know me...and they shall be my people, and I will be their God: for they shall return to me with their whole heart"* (Jer. 24:7). The new covenant life hinges on the state of the new heart given by God.

Why, if all this is meant to be literally and exactly true of God's people, do we see and experience so little of this life? There is only one answer—our unbelief! We have already spoken of the relationship of God and man in creation. Sin destroyed the perfection that God intended in His relationship with man. The new covenant is meant to make this perfect relationship possible and real again. However, God will not force His law into the heart. He can fulfill His purpose only as the heart is willing and accepts His offer. In the new covenant all is by faith. Let us turn away from what human wisdom and experience says and ask God to teach us what His covenant and its blessings mean. If we persevere in this prayer in a humble and teachable spirit, we can certainly count on its promise, *"They shall teach no more every man his neighbour..., saying, Know the Lord: for they shall all know me."* The teaching of God Himself, by the Holy Spirit, to make us understand what He says in His Word, is our covenant right. Let us count on it.

It is only by a God-given faith that we can appropriate these God-given promises. It is only by God-given teaching and inward illumination that we can see their meaning and believe them. When God teaches us the meaning of His promises in hearts yielded to His Holy Spirit, then we can believe and receive them in a power that makes them a reality in our lives.

Let God Do the Work

Is it really possible, amid the wear and tear of daily life, to walk in the experience of these blessings? Are they really meant for all God's children?

Let us, instead, ask the question, "Is it possible for God to do what He has promised?" One part of the promise we believe—the complete and perfect pardon of sin. Why should we not believe the other part—the law written on the heart and the direct, divine fellowship and teaching?

We have been so accustomed to separating what God has joined together: the objective, outward work of His Son and the subjective, inward work of His Spirit. Therefore, we consider the glory of the new covenant above the old to consist chiefly in the redeeming work of Christ for us and no equally in the sanctifying work of the Spirit in us. Because of this ignorance and unbelief of the indwelling of the Holy Spirit as the power through whom God fulfills the new covenant promises, we do not really expect them to be made true to us.

Let us turn our hearts away from all past experience of failure, caused by nothing but unbelief. Let us admit fully and heartily what failure has taught us—the absolute impossibility of even a regenerate man walking in God's law in his own strength at the same time. Then let us turn our hearts quietly and trustfully to our covenant God. Let us hear what He says He will do for us and believe Him. Let us rest on His unchangeable faithfulness, the surety of the covenant, and on His almighty power and the Holy Spirit working in us. Let us give ourselves to Him as our God. He will prove that what He has done for us in Christ is no more wonderful than what He will do in us every day by the Spirit of Christ.

Chapter 5

The Covenants in
Christian Experience

These [women] *are the two covenants; the one from the mount Sinai, which gendereth to bondage, which is Agar. For this Agar...answereth to Jerusalem which now is, and is in bondage with her children. But Jerusalem which is above is free, which is the mother of us all....So then, brethren, we are not children of the bondwoman, but of the free. Stand fast therefore in the liberty wherewith Christ hath made us free, and be not entangled again with the yoke of bondage.*
—Galatians 4:24–26, 31; 5:1

The house of Abraham was the church of God at that time. The division in his house—one son, born after the flesh; the other, after the promise—was a divinely ordained manifestation of the division that would exist down through the ages. This division was between the children of the bondwoman, who served God in the spirit of bondage, and those who were children of the free, who served Him in the Spirit of His Son. The passage teaches us what the whole epistle confirms. The Galatians had become entangled in a yoke of bondage and were not standing fast in the freedom that Christ brings.

Instead of living in the new covenant—the Jerusalem that is from above and the liberty that the Holy Spirit gives—their whole walk proved that, though Christians, they were of the old covenant, which brings forth children of bondage. The passage teaches us the great truth that is of the utmost consequence for us to understand thoroughly. A man with a measure of the knowledge and experience of the grace of God may prove, by a legal spirit, that he is yet under the old covenant. It will also show us, with wonderful clearness, the characteristics of the absence of the true new covenant life.

The Old Contrasted with the New

A careful study of the epistle shows us that the difference between the two covenants is seen in three things. The law and its works is contrasted with the hearing of faith. The flesh and its religion is contrasted with the flesh crucified. The inability to do good is contrasted with a walk in the liberty and power of the Spirit. May the Holy Spirit reveal this twofold life to us.

The Law

We find the first contrast in Paul's words, *"Received ye the Spirit by the works of the law, or by the hearing of faith?"* (Gal. 3:2). These Galatians had certainly been born into the new covenant. They had received the Holy Spirit. But they had been led away by Jewish teachers, and though they had been justified by faith, they were seeking to be sanctified by works. They were looking for the maintenance and growth of their Christian life in the observance of the law. They had not understood that the progress of the divine life is by faith alone. Day by day it receives its strength from Christ alone. In Jesus Christ nothing avails but faith working by love.

Almost every believer makes the same mistake as the Galatian Christians. Very few learn at conversion that it is only by faith that we stand, walk, and live. They have no idea of the meaning of Paul's teaching about being dead to the law and freed from the law—the freedom with which Christ makes us free. *"If ye be led of the Spirit, ye are not under the law"* (Gal. 5:18).

Regarding the law as a divine ordinance for our direction, they consider themselves prepared and equipped by conversion to take up the fulfillment of the law as a natural duty. They do not know that in the new covenant the law written in the heart needs an unceasing faith in a divine power to enable them by a divine power to keep it. They cannot understand that it is not to the law but to a living Person that we are now bound. Our obedience and holiness are possible only by the unceasing faith in His power ever working in us. It is only when this is seen that we are truly prepared to live in the new covenant.

The Flesh

The second word that reveals the old covenant spirit is the word *flesh*. Its contrast is the flesh crucified. Paul asked, *"Are ye so foolish? having begun in the Spirit, are ye now made perfect by the flesh?"* (Gal. 3:3). Flesh means our sinful, human nature. At his conversion the Christian generally has no conception of the terrible evil of his nature and the subtlety with which it offers itself to take part in the service of God.

Man's nature may be very willing and diligent in God's service for a time. It may devise numerous observances for making His worship pleasing and attractive. Yet this may be making only a fair show in the flesh, glorying in the flesh and in man's will and man's efforts. The power of the religious flesh is one of the great marks of the old covenant religion. It misses the deep humility and spirituality of the true worship of God—a heart and life entirely dependent on Him.

The proof that our faith is very much like that of the religious flesh is that the sinful flesh will flourish along with it. It was so with the Galatians. While they were making a fair show in the flesh and glorying in it, their daily lives were full of bitterness, envy, hatred, and other sins. They were biting and devouring one another. Religious flesh and sinful flesh are one. No wonder that, in many Christians, temper, selfishness, and worldliness are so often found side by side. The faith of the flesh cannot conquer sin.

What a contrast to the faith of the new covenant! What is the place of the flesh there? *"They that are Christ's have crucified the flesh with the affections and lusts"* (Gal. 5:24). Scripture speaks of the will of the flesh, the mind of the flesh, and the lust of the flesh. The true believer has seen that this is to be condemned and crucified in Christ. He has given it over to the death. He accepts the cross, with its bearing of the curse and its redemption from it, as his entrance into life. He also glories in it as his only power to daily overcome the flesh and the world.

"I am crucified with Christ" (Gal. 2:20). *"But God forbid that I should glory, save in the cross of our Lord Jesus Christ, by whom the world is crucified unto me, and I unto the world"* (Gal. 6:14). Just as nothing less than Christ's death was needed to inaugurate the new covenant and the resurrection life, there is no entrance into true new covenant life except by partaking of that death.

The Inability to Do Good

"Fallen from grace" (Gal. 5:4). This is a third word that describes the condition of the Galatians. Paul was not speaking of a final falling away here, for he still addressed them as Christians. But they had wandered from that walk in the way of enabling and sanctifying grace where a Christian gains victory over sin.

As long as grace is principally connected with pardon and the entrance to the Christian life, the flesh is the only power in which to serve and work. But when we know what exceeding abundance of grace has been provided and how *"God is able to make all grace abound toward you; that ye...may abound to every good work"* (2 Cor. 9:8), we know that it is by faith and grace that we stand a single moment or take a single step.

The contrast to this life of failure is found in this one word, the *"Spirit." "If ye be led of the Spirit, ye are not under the law"* (Gal. 5:18), with its demand on your own strength. *"Walk in the Spirit, and ye shall not"*—a definite promise—*"fulfil the lust of the flesh"* (v. 16). The Spirit gives liberty from the law, the flesh, and from sin. *"The fruit of the Spirit is love, joy, peace"* (v. 22). The Spirit is the center and the sum of the new covenant promise, *"I will put my spirit within you, and cause you to walk in my statutes, and ye shall keep my judgments"* (Ezek. 36:27). The Spirit is the power of the supernatural life of true obedience and holiness.

What course would the Galatians have taken if they had accepted this teaching of Paul? As they heard his question, *"Now, after that ye have known God,...how turn ye again to the weak and beggarly elements, whereunto ye desire again to be in bondage?"* (Gal. 4:9), they understood that there was only one course. Nothing else could help them except to turn back to the path they had left. At the point where they had left it, they could enter again.

This turning away from the old covenant legal spirit and renewing the surrender to the Mediator of the new covenant could be the act of a moment—one single step. As the light of the new covenant promise dawns upon you and you see how Christ is all—faith all, the Holy Spirit in the heart all, and the faithfulness of a covenant-keeping God all in all—you will feel you have one thing to do. In utter weakness you must yield yourself to God. In simple faith you must count on Him to perform what He has spoken. In Christian experience there may still be the old covenant life of bondage and failure. In Christian experience there may be a life that gives in entirely to the new covenant grace and spirit. When a Christian receives the true vision of what the new covenant means, a faith that rests entirely on the Mediator of the new covenant can immediately enter the life that the covenant secures.

The Reason for Failure

I beg all believers who sincerely want to know what the grace of God can work in them to carefully study the question of whether the reason for our failure is our being in bondage to the old covenant. They should also study whether a clear insight into the possibility of an entire change in our relationship to God is not what is needed to give us the help we seek.

We may be seeking growth in a more diligent use of the means of grace and a more earnest striving to live in accordance with God's will and yet fail. The reason is that there is a secret root of evil that must be removed. That root is the spirit of bondage, the legal spirit of self-effort, that hinders the humble faith that knows that God will work out all and yields to Him to do it. That spirit can be found amid great zeal for God's service and very earnest prayer for His grace. It does not enjoy the rest of faith and cannot overcome sin because it does not stand in the liberty with which Christ has made us free. It does not know that *"where the Spirit of the Lord is, there is liberty"* (2 Cor. 3:17). There the soul can say, *"The law of the Spirit of life in Christ Jesus hath made me free from the law of sin and death"* (Rom. 8:2).

Once we admit that are there failings in our lives and also that something radically wrong can be changed, we will turn with new interest, deeper confession of ignorance and weakness, and hope that looks to God alone for teaching and strength. We will find that in the new covenant there is an actual provision for every need.

Chapter 6

————◆————

The Everlasting Covenant

*They shall be my people, and I will be their God....And I will
make an everlasting covenant with them, that I will not turn
away from them, to do them good; but I will put my fear in
their hearts, that they shall not depart from me.*
—Jeremiah 32:38, 40

*A new heart also will I give you, and a new spirit will I put
within you: and I will take away the stony heart out of your
flesh, and I will give you an heart of flesh. And I will put my
spirit within you, and cause you to walk in my statutes, and
ye shall keep my judgments, and do them....Moreover I will
make a covenant of peace with them; it shall be an everlasting
covenant with them.*
Ezekiel 36:26–27; 37:26

W e have already heard about the institution of the new covenant. Listen to further teaching we have concerning it in
Jeremiah and Ezekiel where God speaks of it as an everlasting
covenant.

In every covenant there are two parties. The very foundation of a covenant rests on the thought that each party is to be

faithful to the part it has undertaken to perform. Unfaithfulness on either side breaks the covenant.

It was so with the old covenant. God had said to Israel, *"Obey my voice,...and I will be your God"* (Jer. 11:4). These simple words contained the whole covenant. When Israel disobeyed, the covenant was broken. The question of Israel's being able or unable to obey was not taken into consideration. Disobedience forfeited the privileges of the covenant.

Securing Obedience

If a new and better covenant were to be made, this was the one thing to be provided for. No new covenant could be beneficial unless provision was made for securing obedience. There must be obedience. God as Creator could never take His creatures into His favor and fellowship unless they obeyed Him. That would have been an impossibility. If the new covenant is to be an everlasting covenant, never to be broken, it must make sufficient provision for securing the obedience of the covenant people.

That this provision has been made is the glory of the new covenant. The new covenant, which no human thought could have devised or implemented, was an undertaking in which God's infinite condescension, power, and faithfulness were wonderfully exhibited. By a supernatural mystery of divine wisdom and grace, the new covenant provides a guarantee not only for God's faithfulness, but for man's, too! There is no other way than by God Himself undertaking to secure man's part as well as His own. Try to understand this.

Because this essential part of the new covenant so exceeds and confounds all human thought of what a covenant means, Christians throughout history have been unable to see and believe what the new covenant really means. They understood that human unfaithfulness was a factor to be permanently dealt with as something utterly unconquerable and incurable. The possibility of a life of obedience, with the witness from within of a good conscience and of God's pleasure, was not to be expected. Therefore, they sought to stir the mind to its utmost by arguments and motives. They never realized how the Holy Spirit is to be the unceasing, universal, all-sufficient Worker of everything that has to be done by the Christian. Let us earnestly ask God to reveal, by the Holy Spirit, the wonderful life of the new covenant that He has prepared for those who love Him. All depends upon our knowledge of what God will work in us.

God's Covenant Promises

Listen to what God says in Jeremiah about the two parts of His everlasting covenant shortly after He had announced the new covenant and further explained it. The central thought, that the heart is to be put right, is repeated and confirmed here: *"I will make an everlasting covenant with them, that I will not turn away from them, to do them good."* That is, God will be unchangeably faithful. He will not turn from us. *"But I will put my fear into their hearts, that they shall not depart from me."* This is the second half; Israel will be unchangeably faithful, too. Because God will so put His fear in their hearts, they will not depart from Him. As little as God will turn from them, will they depart from Him! As faithfully as He undertakes for the fulfillment of His part, He will undertake for the fulfillment of their part, that they will not depart from Him!

Listen to God's Word in Ezekiel, in regard to one of the terms of His covenant of peace, His everlasting covenant. *"And I will put my spirit within you, and cause you to walk in my statutes, and ye shall keep my judgments, and do them."* In the old covenant we have nothing of this sort. On the contrary, from the story of the golden calf and the breaking of the tables of the covenant onward, we have the sad fact of continual departure from God.

We find God longing for what He would so willingly have seen, but it was not to be found. *"O that there were such an heart in them, that they would fear me, and keep all my commandments always"* (Deut. 5:29). We find throughout the book of Deuteronomy that Moses distinctly prophesied their forsaking of God with the terrible curses and dispersion that would come upon them.

It is only in the close of Moses' threatening that he gave the promise of the new time that would come.

And the LORD *thy God will circumcise thine heart, and the heart of thy seed, to love the* LORD *thy God with all thine heart, and with all thy soul, that thou mayest live.*
(Deut. 30:6)

The entire old covenant was dependent on man's faithfulness. *"The* LORD *thy God...keepeth covenant and mercy with them that...keep his commandments"* (Deut. 7:9). God's keeping the covenant would mean very little if man did not keep it. Nothing could help man until the *"if ye shall diligently keep"* (Deut. 11:22) of the law was replaced by the word of promise, *"I will put my spirit within you,...and ye shall keep my judgments, and do them."*

The Heart of Man

The one supreme difference of the new covenant for which the Mediator, the Blood, and the Spirit were given was a heart filled with His fear and love, cleaving to Him and not departing from Him. The one fruit God sought and engaged to bring forth was this: a heart in which His Spirit and His law dwells and a heart that delights to do His will.

Here is the innermost secret of the new covenant. It deals with the heart of man in a way of divine power. It not only appeals to the heart by every motive of fear, love, duty, or gratitude, as the law did, but it also reveals God Himself cleansing our hearts and making them new, changing them from stony hearts into hearts of flesh, and making them tender, living, loving hearts. He puts His Spirit within and, by His almighty power and love, breathes and works in us to make the promise true, *"I will...cause you to walk in my statutes, and ye shall keep my judgments."* A heart in perfect harmony with Himself, a life and walk in His way—this is what God has engaged in covenant to work in us. He undertakes for our part in the covenant as much as for His own.

This is nothing but the restoration of the original relationship between God and the man He had made in His likeness. Man was on earth to be the very image of God because God was to live and work all in him. Man was to find his glory and blessedness in owing all to God. This is the exceeding glory of the new covenant: that, by the Holy Spirit, God could again be the indwelling life of His people. Thus He can make the promise a reality, *"I will...cause you to walk in my statutes."*

With God's presence secured to us, His fear put into our hearts by His Spirit, and our hearts thus responding to His holy presence, we can and will walk in His statutes and keep His judgments.

Don't Limit God

Israel's great sin under the old covenant by which they greatly grieved Him was this: *"They...limited the Holy One of Israel"* (Ps. 78:41). Under the new covenant there is still the danger of this sin. It makes it impossible for God to fulfill His promises. Above everything, let us seek the Holy Spirit's teaching to show us exactly what God has established the new covenant for. In this way we will honor Him by believing all that His love has prepared for us.

If we ask for the cause of the unbelief that prevents the fulfillment of the promise, we will find that we do not have to look far. In most cases, it is the lack of desire for the promised blessing. The intensity of their desire for their needed healing made all who came to Jesus ready and glad to believe in His Word. Where the law has done its full work and where the actual desire to be freed from every sin is strong and masters the heart, the presence of the new covenant, when it is really understood, comes like bread to a starving man.

The subtle belief that it is impossible to be kept from sinning destroys the power of accepting the promises of the everlasting Old Testament promise. God's Word, *"I will put my fear in their hearts, that they shall not depart from me,"* and, *"I will put my spirit within you,...and ye shall keep my judgment,"* is understood in some feeble sense according to our experience and not according to what the Word and God means. The soul settles into a despair of self-contentment that says it can never be otherwise. It makes true conviction for sin impossible.

Let me speak to every reader who would gladly believe all that God says. Cherish every whisper of the conscience and the Spirit that convicts of sin. Whatever it is, a hasty temper, a sharp word, an unloving or impatient thought, anything of selfishness or self-will, cherish that which condemns it in you as part of the schooling that is to bring you to Christ and the full possession of His salvation. The new covenant is meant to meet the need for the power of not sinning that the old could not give. Come with that need. It will prepare and open your heart for all the everlasting covenant provides.

Chapter 7

————————◆◆————————

A Ministration of the Spirit

*Ye are manifestly declared to be the epistle of Christ ministered
by us, written not with ink, but with the Spirit of the living God;
not in tables of stone, but in fleshly tables of the heart....Our
sufficiency is of God; who also hath made us able ministers
of the new testament; not of the letter, but of the spirit: for
the letter killeth, but the spirit giveth life. But if the ministration
of death, written and engraven in stones, was glorious,...how
shall not the ministration of the spirit be rather glorious? For
if the ministration of condemnation be glory, much more doth
the ministration of righteousness exceed in glory.*
—2 Corinthians 3:3, 5–9

*I*n this wonderful chapter Paul reminded the Corinthians of
the chief characteristics of his ministry among them. He contrasted it as a ministry of the new covenant and the whole dispensation of which it is part with that of the old. The old was
written on stone; the new, on the heart. The old could be written in ink and was in the letter that killed. The new, of the Spirit,
makes alive. The old was a ministration of condemnation and
death. The new was of righteousness and life. The old had its
glory, for it was of divine appointment and brought its divine
blessing. But it was a glory that passed away.

With the old there was the veil on the heart. In the new the veil is taken away from the face and the heart. The Spirit of the Lord gives liberty. Reflecting with unveiled faces the glory of the Lord, we are changed from glory to glory, into the same image by the Spirit of the Lord. The glory that excels proved its power in this. It not only marked the dispensation on its divine side but exerted its power in the hearts and lives of its subjects, so that it was seen in them, as they were changed by the Spirit into Christ's image, from glory to glory.

Think for a moment about the contrast. The old covenant was of the letter that killed. The law came with its literal instruction. It sought by the knowledge it gave of God's will to appeal to man's fear, love, and his natural powers of mind, conscience, and will. It spoke to him as if he could obey, so that it could convince him of what he did not know: that he could not obey. So it fulfilled its mission. *"The commandment, which was ordained to life, I found to be unto death"* (Rom. 7:10).

The Work of the Spirit

In the new, however, everything was different. Instead of the letter, the Spirit that gives life breathes the very life of God into us. Instead of a law engraved in stone, the law written in the heart is worked into the heart's affection and powers, making it one with them. Instead of the vain attempt to work inward from without, the Spirit and the law are put into the inward parts to work outward in life and walk.

This passage brings the distinctive blessing of the new covenant into view. In working out our salvation, God bestowed two wonderful gifts on us. We read,

> *God sent forth his Son...to redeem them that were under the law, that we might receive the adoption of sons. And because ye are sons, God hath sent forth the Spirit of his Son into your hearts, crying, Abba, Father.* (Gal. 4:4–6)

Here we have the two parts of God's work in salvation.

The more objective part He did so that we might become His children. He sent forth His Son. The more subjective part He did so that we might live as His children. He sent forth the Spirit of His Son into our hearts. In the former we have the external manifestation of the work of redemption. In the other, we have its inward appropriation, the former for the sake of the latter. These two halves form one great whole and cannot be separated.

In the promises of the new covenant, found in Jeremiah and Ezekiel as well as in our text and many other passages of Scripture, it is evident that God's great objective in salvation is to acquire possession of the heart. The heart is the real life. With the heart a man loves, wills, and acts. The heart makes the man. God made man's heart for His own dwelling so that in it He might reveal His love and glory. God sent Christ to accomplish a redemption by which man's heart could be won back to Him. Nothing but that could satisfy God.

That is what is accomplished when the Holy Spirit makes the heart of His child what it should be. The whole work of Christ's redemption—His atonement, victory, exaltation, intercession, and His glory at the right hand of God—are only preparatory to the major triumph of His grace: the renewal of the heart to be the temple of God. Through Christ, God gives the Holy Spirit to glorify Him in the heart, by working there all that He has done and is doing for the soul.

New Covenant Promises

In a great deal of our spiritual teaching, the fear that we detract from Christ's honor is taught as the reason for giving His work for us, on the cross or in heaven, a greater prominence than His work in our hearts by the Holy Spirit. The result has been that the indwelling of the Holy Spirit and His mighty work as the life of the heart are known or experienced very little. If we look carefully at what the new covenant promises mean, we will see how the sending *"forth the Spirit of his Son into* [our] *hearts"* (Gal. 4:6) is the consummation and crown of

Christ's redeeming work. Let us think of what these promises imply.

In the old covenant, man failed in what he had to do. In the new, God does everything in him. The old could only convict of sin. The new puts it away and cleanses the heart from its filthiness. In the old, it was the heart that was wrong. For the new, a new heart is provided into which God puts His fear, His law, and His love. The old demanded but failed to secure obedience. In the new, God causes us to walk in His judgments.

The new prepares man for true holiness. It is a true fulfillment of the law of loving God with our whole hearts and our neighbors as ourselves. It is a walk truly pleasing to God. The new changes a man from glory to glory after the image of Christ, all because the Spirit of God's Son is given to the heart. The old gave no power. In the new, all is by the Spirit, the mighty power of God. As complete as the reign and power of Christ on the throne of heaven is, so is His dominion on the throne of the heart by His Holy Spirit given to us. (See Note C.) As we bring all these traits of the new covenant life together and look at the heart of God's child as the object of this mighty redemption, we will begin to understand what it guarantees us and what we are to expect from our covenant God. We will see what the glory of the ministration of the Spirit consists of. God can fill our hearts with His love and make it His abode.

We Need the Spirit

We are accustomed to saying that the worth of the Son of God, who came to die for us, is the measure of the worth of the soul in God's sight and the greatness of the work that had to be done to save it. Let us also see that the divine glory of the Holy Spirit is the measure of God's longing to have our hearts wholly for Himself, the glory of the work that is to be formed within us, and of the power by which that work will be accomplished.

We will see that the glory of the ministration of the Spirit is no other than the glory of the Lord. This is true not only in heaven but also here on earth, resting on us, dwelling in us, and changing us into the same image from glory to glory. The inconceivable glory of our exalted Lord in heaven has its counterpart here on earth in the exceeding glory of the Holy Spirit. He glorifies Him in us and lays His glory on us as He changes us into His likeness.

The new covenant has no power to save and bless except as it is a ministration of the Spirit. That Spirit works in lesser or greater degree as He is neglected and grieved or yielded to and trusted. Let us honor Him and give Him His place as the Spirit of the new covenant by expecting and accepting all He waits to do for us. He is the great gift of the covenant. His coming from heaven was the proof that the Mediator of the covenant was on the throne in glory and could now make us partakers of the heavenly life. He is the only Teacher of what the covenant means. Dwelling in our hearts, He awakens the thought and desire for what God has prepared for us. He is the Spirit of faith who enables us to believe the otherwise incomprehensible blessing and power in which the new covenant works and claims it as our own. He is the Spirit of grace and of power by whom the obedience of the covenant and the fellowship with God can be maintained without interruption. He is the Possessor, Bearer, and Communicator of all the covenant promises. He is the Revealer and Glorifier of Jesus, its Mediator and Surety. To fully believe in the Holy Spirit as the present, abiding, and all-comprehending gift of the new covenant has been an entrance into its fullness of blessing to many people.

Child of God, begin at once to give the Holy Spirit the place in your life that He has in God's plan. Be still before God and believe that He is in you. Ask the Father to work in you through Him. Regard yourself, spirit as well as body, with holy reverence as His temple. Let the consciousness of His holy presence and working fill you with holy calm and fear. Be sure that all God calls you to be, Christ through His Spirit will work in you.

Chapter 8

——————◆——————

The Transition

Now the God of peace, that brought again from the dead our Lord Jesus, that great shepherd of the sheep, through the blood of the everlasting covenant, make you perfect in every good work to do his will, working in you that which is wellpleasing in his sight, through Jesus Christ.
—Hebrews 13:20–21

*T*he transition from the old covenant to the new was not slow or gradual, but by a tremendous crisis. Nothing less than the death of Christ could close the old. Nothing less than His resurrection from the dead, through the blood of the everlasting covenant, could open the new. The path of preparation that led to the crisis was long and slow. The rending of the veil that symbolized the end of the old worship was the work of a moment. By His death, once and for all, Christ's work as Fulfiller of law and prophets was finished forever. By His resurrection in the power of an endless life, the covenant of life was ushered in.

Characteristics of the Covenants

These events have an infinite significance in revealing the character of the covenants they are related to. The death of Christ shows the true nature of the old covenant. It is elsewhere called *"a ministration of death"* (2 Cor. 3:7). It brought nothing but death. It ended in death. Only by death could the life that had been lived under it be brought to an end. The new was to be a covenant of life. It had its birth in the omnipotent resurrection power that brought Christ from the dead.

Its one mark and blessing is that all it gives comes not only as a promise, but as an experience in the power of an endless life. The death reveals the utter ineffectiveness and insufficiency of the old. The life brings near and imparts to us forever all that the new has to offer. An insight into the completeness of the transition, as seen in Christ, prepares us for understanding the reality of the change in our life. *"Like as Christ was raised up from the dead by the glory of the Father, even so we also should walk in newness of life"* (Rom. 6:4).

The complete difference between the life in the old and the new is remarkably illustrated in Hebrews 9:16. After having said that a death for the redemption of transgression had to take place before the new covenant could be established, the writer added, *"Where a testament is, there must also of necessity be the death of the testator"* (Heb. 9:16). Before any heir can obtain the legacy, its first owner, the testator, must have died. The old proprietorship, the old life, must disappear entirely before the new heir, the new life, can enter into the inheritance. Nothing but death can work the transference of the property. It is also true with Christ, the old and the new covenant life, and our own deliverance from the old and our entrance into the new. Having been made dead to the law by the body of Christ, we have been discharged from the law. We have died to that which bound us—here is the completeness of the deliverance from Christ's side. *"That we should serve"*—here is the completeness of the change in our experience—*"in newness of spirit, and not in the oldness of the letter"* (Rom. 7:6).

A Ministration of Death

The transition, if it is to be real and whole, must take place by a death. As it is with Christ the Mediator of the covenant, so it also must be with His people, the heirs of the covenant. In Him we are dead to sin and the law. Just as Adam died to God and we inherit a nature dead in sin to God and His kingdom, so in Christ we died to sin and inherit a nature dead to sin and its dominion. When the Holy Spirit reveals and makes real this death to sin and the law as the one condition of a life yielded to God, the transition from the old to the new covenant can be fully realized in us.

The old was meant to be a *"ministration of death"* (2 Cor. 3:7). Until it has completely done its work in us, there is no complete discharge from its power. Man must see that self is incurably evil and must die. He must give self utterly to death as he sinks before God in complete weakness and surrenders to His working. He must consent to death with Christ on the cross and in faith accept it as his only deliverance. He alone is prepared to be led by the Holy Spirit into the full enjoyment of the new covenant life. He will learn to understand how completely death makes an end to all self-effort. He will discover how, as he lives in Christ to God, everything from now on is to be the work of God Himself.

See how beautifully our text brings out this truth. Just as much as Christ's resurrection out of death was the work of God Himself, our life is to be entirely God's own work, too. The experience of what the new covenant life is to bring in us should be as direct and wonderful as Christ's transition from death to life.

Notice the subject of the two verses. In verse 20 we have what God has done in raising Christ from the dead. In verse 21 we have what God is to do in us, working in us what is pleasing to Him.

> *Now the God of peace, that brought again from the dead our Lord Jesus, that great shepherd of the sheep,...make you perfect in every good work to do his will, working in you that which is wellpleasing in his sight, through Jesus Christ.*

We have the name of our Lord Jesus mentioned twice. In the first case it refers to what God has done to Christ for us, raising Him. In the second case it refers to what God is doing through Christ in us, working His pleasure in us.

From Death to Life

Because it is the same God continuing in us the work He began in Christ, it is in us just what it was in Christ. In Christ's death we see Him in utter submission allowing and counting on God to work all and give Him life. God worked out the wonderful transition. In us we see the same thing. It is only as we also give ourselves to that death, cease entirely from self and its works, and lie as in the grave waiting for God to work all, that the God of resurrection life can work in us all His good pleasure.

It was *"through the blood of the everlasting covenant,"* with its atonement for sin and its destruction of sin's power, that God effected that resurrection. It is through that same blood that we are redeemed, freed from the power of sin, and made partakers of Christ's resurrection life. The more we study the new covenant, the more we will see that its one aim is to restore man, out of the Fall, to the life in God for which he was created. First, it does this by delivering him from the power of sin in Christ's death. Then it takes possession of his heart and his life for God to work all in him by the Holy Spirit. The whole argument of the epistle to the Hebrews concerning the old and new covenants is summed up here in these concluding verses. Just as He raised Christ from the dead, the God of the everlasting covenant can and will now make you perfect in every good thing to do His will. He will work in you that which is wellpleasing in His sight through Jesus Christ.

Your doing His will is the purpose of creation and redemption. God's working all in you is what redemption has made possible. The old covenant of law, effort, and failure has ended in condemnation and death. The new covenant is coming to give, in all whom the law has slain and brought to bow in their utter failure, the law written on the heart, the Spirit dwelling there, and God working all, both to will and to do through Jesus Christ.

God Working All in All

We need a divine revelation that the transition from Christ's death in its humility to His life in God's power is the image, pledge, and power of our transition out of the old covenant into the new, with God working in us all in all! The transition from old to new, as effected in Christ, was sudden. Is it also in the believer? Not always. It depends on a revelation in us. There have been cases in which a believer, sighing and struggling against the yoke of bondage, has in one moment seen the complete salvation the new covenant brings to the heart and the inner life through the ministration of the Spirit. By faith he has entered at once into his rest. There have been other cases in which, as gradually as the dawn of day, the light of God has touched the heart. God's offer of entrance into the enjoyment of our new covenant privileges is always urgent and immediate. Every believer is a child of the new covenant and heir to all its promises. The death and resurrection of Christ gives him full right to immediate possession. God longs to bring us into the land of promise. Let us not fail because of unbelief.

May God reveal to us the difference between the two lives under the old and the new. In the resurrection power of the new, God works all in us. In the power of the transition secured for us in death with Christ, there is life in Him. May He teach us at once to trust Christ Jesus for a full participation in all that the new covenant secures.

There may be someone who can hardly believe that such a mighty change in his life is within his reach. Yet he would gladly know what he is to do if there is to be any hope of his attaining it. I have just said, the death of the testator gives the heir immediate right to the inheritance. Yet the heir, if he is a minor, does not enter into the possession. A term of years ends the stage of minority on earth, and he is no longer under guardians.

In the spiritual life the state of being a pupil ends, not with the expiration of years, but the moment the minor proves his fitness for being made free from the law by accepting the liberty there is in Christ Jesus. The transition, as with the Old Testament and with Christ and with the disciples, comes when the time is fulfilled and all things are now ready.

What is one to do to be made ready? Accept your death to sin in Christ and act it out. Acknowledge the sentence of death on everything that is of nature. Take and keep the place before God of utter unworthiness and helplessness. Fall down before Him in humility, meekness, patience, and resignation to His will and mercy. Fix your heart on the great and mighty God. In His grace He will work in you above what you can ask or think and will make you a monument of His mercy.

Believe that every blessing of the covenant of grace is yours. By the death of the Testator, you are entitled to it all. Act on that faith, knowing that all is yours. The new heart is yours, the law written in the heart is yours, and the Holy Spirit, the seal of the covenant, is yours. Act on the faith and count on God as faithful, able, and so loving to reveal and make true in you all the power and glory of His everlasting covenant.

Chapter 9

———————◆——————

The Blood of the Covenant

Behold the blood of the covenant, which the LORD
hath made with you.
—Exodus 24:8

This cup is the new testament in my blood.
—1 Corinthians 11:25

The blood of the covenant, wherewith he was sanctified.
—Hebrews 10:29

The blood of the everlasting covenant.
—Hebrews 13:20

*T*he blood is one of the strangest, deepest, mightiest, and
most heavenly of the thoughts of God. It lies at the very root
of both covenants, but especially of the new covenant. The difference between the two covenants is the difference between
the blood of beasts and the blood of the Lamb of God! The
power of the new covenant has no lesser measure than the
worth of the blood of the Son of God!

Your Christian experience should know no standard of
peace with God, purity from sin, and power over the world than

the blood of Christ can give! If we want to truly and fully enter into all the new covenant is meant to be to us, let us ask God to reveal the worth and power of the blood of the covenant—the precious blood of Christ!

A Blood Sacrifice

The first covenant was also brought in with blood. There could be no covenant of friendship between a holy God and sinful men without atonement and reconciliation. There could be no atonement without death as the penalty of sin. God said, *"I have given it to you upon the altar to make an atonement for your souls: for it is the blood that maketh an atonement for the soul"* (Lev. 17:11). The blood shed in death meant the death of a sacrifice slain for the sin of man. The blood sprinkled on the altar meant that God accepted this vicarious death as atonement for the sin. There is no forgiveness, no covenant, without bloodshed.

All this was but a type and shadow of what was one day to become a mysterious reality. No thought of man or angel could have conceived what now passes all understanding—the eternal Son of God took flesh and blood and shed that blood as the blood of the new covenant. He did this not merely to ratify it but to open the way for it and to make it possible. Even more, He did it to be, in time and eternity, the living power by which entrance into the covenant was to be obtained and all life in it be secured.

Until we learn to form an expectation of life in the new covenant, according to the inconceivable worth and power of the blood of God's Son, we can never have an insight into the entirely supernatural and heavenly life that a child of God may live. Let us think for a moment about the threefold light in which Scripture teaches us to regard it.

The Blood of the New Covenant

In Hebrews 9:15 we read,

And for this cause he [Christ] *is the mediator of the new testament, that by means of death, for the redemption of the transgressions that were under the first testament, they which are called might receive the promise of eternal inheritance.*

The sins of the ages of the first covenant, which had only figuratively been atoned for, had accumulated before God. A death was needed for the redemption of these sins. In that death and bloodshed by the Lamb of God not only were these atoned for, but the power of all sin was broken forever.

The blood of the new covenant is redemption blood, a purchase price and ransom from the power of sin and the law. In any purchase made on earth, the transference of property from the old owner to the new is complete. Though its worth may be so great and the hold on it so strong, if the price is paid, it is gone forever from him who owned it. The hold sin had on us was terrible. No one can realize its legitimate claim on us under God's law or its awful tyrant power in enslaving us.

But the blood of God's Son has been paid.

Ye were not redeemed with corruptible things, as silver and gold, from your vain conversation received by tradition from your fathers; but with the precious blood of Christ, as of a lamb without blemish and without spot.
(1 Pet. 1:18–19)

We have been rescued, ransomed, and redeemed entirely and eternally out of our old natural lives of being under the power of sin.

Sin does not have the slightest claim on us or the slightest power over us except as our ignorance, unbelief, or half-heartedness allows it to have dominion. Our new covenant birthright is to stand in the freedom with which Christ has made us free. Until the soul sees, accepts, desires, and claims the redemption and liberty that the blood of the Son of God has for its purchase price, measure, and security, it can never fully live the new covenant life.

The blood shed for our redemption is as wonderful as the blood sprinkling for our cleansing. Here is another one of the spiritual mysteries of the new covenant, which loses its power when understood in human wisdom instead of the ministering of the Spirit of life. When Scripture speaks of *"having our hearts sprinkled from an evil conscience"* (Heb. 10:22), of our singing here on earth, *"unto him that...washed us from our sins in his own blood"* (Rev. 1:5), it brings this mighty, quickening blood of the Lamb into direct contact with our hearts.

It gives the assurance that the infinite worth of that blood in its divine, sin-cleansing power can keep us clean in our walk in the sight and light of God. As this blood of the new covenant is known, trusted, waited for, and received from God in its divine, mighty operation in the heart, we will begin to believe that the blessed promise of a new covenant life and walk can be fulfilled.

There is one more thing Scripture teaches concerning this blood of the new covenant. When the Jews contrasted Moses with our Lord Jesus, He said, *"Except ye eat the flesh of the Son of man, and drink his blood, ye have no life in you....He that eateth my flesh, and drinketh my blood, dwelleth in me, and I in him"* (John 6:53, 56). As if the redeeming, sprinkling, washing, and sanctifying do not sufficiently express the intense inwardness of its action and power to permeate our whole being, the drinking of this precious blood is declared to be indispensable to having life. If we move deep into the Spirit and power of the new covenant, let us by the Holy Spirit drink deep of this cup— the cup of the new covenant in His blood.

Cleansing Blood

Because of sin there could be no covenant between man and God without blood and no new covenant without the blood of the Son of God. The cleansing of sins was the first condition in making a covenant and the first condition of entrance into it. It has been found that a deeper appropriation of the blessings of the covenant must be preceded by a new and deeper cleansing from sin. In Ezekiel 36:25 we know that the words about God's causing us to walk in His statutes are preceded by, *"From all your filthiness, and from all your idols, will I cleanse you."*

> *Neither shall they defile themselves any more with...any of their transgressions: but I...will cleanse them: so shall they be my people, and I will be their God....Moreover I will make a covenant of peace with them; it shall be an everlasting covenant with them.* (Ezek. 37:23, 26)

The confession, casting away, and cleansing of sin in the blood are the indispensable, all-sufficient preparation for a life in everlasting covenant with God. Many people feel they do not understand or realize this wonderful power of the blood. Thought and prayer do not appear to bring the light they seek. The blood of Christ is a divine mystery that passes all thought. Like every spiritual and heavenly blessing, this also needs to be imparted to us by the Holy Spirit. It was through the eternal Spirit that Christ offered the sacrifice in which the blood was shed.

Prepared for the Spirit

The blood had the life of Christ and the life of the Spirit in it. The outpouring of the blood for us was to prepare the way for the outpouring of the Spirit on us. It is the Holy Spirit alone who can minister the blood of the everlasting covenant in power. Just as He leads the soul to the initial faith in the pardon that blood has purchased and the peace it gives, He further leads to the knowledge and experience of its cleansing power. Here again, by a faith in a heavenly power, which the soul does not fully understand and cannot define, the action that it knows is an operation of God's mighty power and effects a cleansing that gives a clean heart. This clean heart is known and accepted by the same faith, apart from signs or feelings, from sense or reason. It is experienced in joy and fellowship with God. Let us believe in the blood of the everlasting covenant and the cleansing the Holy Spirit ministers. Let us believe in the ministry of the

Holy Spirit until our whole lives in the new covenant become entirely His work to the glory of the Father and of Christ.

The blood of the covenant, mystery of mysteries! Grace above all grace! O mighty power of God, open the way into the holiest, into our hearts, and into the new covenant where the Holy One and our hearts meet! Let us ask God, by His Holy Spirit, to teach us what the blood of the covenant means and works. The transition from the death of the old covenant to the life of the new was, in Christ, *"through the blood of the everlasting covenant."* It will not be otherwise for us.

Chapter 10

———◆———

Jesus, Mediator of the New Covenant

I...give thee for a covenant of the people.
—Isaiah 42:6

*The Lord, whom ye seek, shall suddenly come to his temple,
even the messenger of the covenant, whom ye delight in.*
—Malachi 3:1

Jesus [was] *made a surety of a better testament.*
—Hebrews 7:22

*He is the mediator of a better covenant,
which was established upon better promises....
He is the mediator of the new testament.*
—Hebrews 8:6; 9:15

*H*ere we have four titles given to our Lord Jesus in connection with the new covenant. He is Himself called a covenant. The union between God and man, at which the covenant aims, was worked out in Him personally. In Him the reconciliation between the human and divine was perfectly effected. In Him His people find the covenant with all its blessings. He is all that God has to give and is the assurance that it is given. He is called the Messenger of the covenant because He came to establish and proclaim it. He is the Surety of the covenant not only because He paid our debt, but also because He is surety to us for God, that God will fulfill His part. And He is surety for us with God that we will fulfill our part. Finally, He is Mediator of the covenant. As the covenant was established in His atoning blood, is administered and applied by Him, is entered in alone by faith in Him, so it is known only through the power of His resurrection life and His never-ceasing intercession. All these names point to the one truth that in the new covenant Christ is all in all.

Entering into the Blessings

The subject is so large that it would be impossible to enter into all the various aspects of this precious truth. Christ's work in atonement and intercession, His bestowal of pardon and the Holy Spirit, and His daily communication of grace and strength are truths that lie at the very foundation of the faith of Christians. We do not need to speak about them here. What especially needs to be made clear is how, by faith in Christ as the Mediator of the new covenant, we actually have access to and enter into the enjoyment of all its promised blessings. We have already seen in studying the new covenant how all these blessings culminate in one thing. The heart of man is to be put right. This is the only possible way for him to live in the favor of God and for God's love to find its satisfaction in him. He is to fear God, love God with all his strength, obey God, and keep all His statutes.

All that Christ did and does has this for its aim. All the higher blessings of peace and fellowship flow from this. In this, God's saving power and love find the highest proof of their triumph over sin. Nothing reveals the grace of God, the power of Jesus

Christ, the reality of salvation, and the blessedness of the new covenant as the heart of a believer where sin once abounded and where grace now abounds more exceedingly within it.

I do not know how I can better illustrate the glory of our blessed Lord Jesus as He accomplishes the real objective of His redeeming work and takes entire possession of the heart He has bought, won, and cleansed as a dwelling for His Father than by pointing out the place He takes and the work He does in a soul. This soul is being led out of the old covenant bondage with its failure into the real experience of the promise and power of the new covenant and its blessings. (See Note D.)

Attaining the Blessings

In studying the work of the Mediator in an individual, we can form a truer conception of the real glory and greatness of the work He actually accomplishes than when we merely think of the work He has done for all. It is in the application of the redemption in the life here on earth where sin abounded that its power is seen. Let us see how the entrance into the new covenant blessing is attained.

The first step toward it in one who has been truly converted and assured of his acceptance with God is the sense of sin. He sees that the new covenant promises are not made true in his experience. Not only is there indwelling sin but also temper, self-will, worldliness, and other known transgressions of God's law. The obedience to which God calls and will fit him; the life of abiding in Christ's love, which is his privilege; the power for a holy walk, wellpleasing to God—in all this his conscience condemns him. It is in this conviction of sin that any thought or desire of the full new covenant blessing must have its beginning.

The thought that obedience is impossible and nothing but a life of failure and self-condemnation is possible has brought about a secret despair of deliverance or a contentment with our present state. In this state it is vain to speak of God's promise or power. The heart does not respond. It knows well enough that the liberty spoken about is a dream. Where the dissatisfaction with our state has worked a longing for something better, the heart is open to receive the message. The new covenant is meant to be the deliverance from the power of sin. A keen longing for this is the indispensable proposition for entering fully into the covenant.

Now comes the second step. The mind is directed to the literal meaning of the terms of the new covenant in its promises of cleansing from sin, a heart filled with God's fear and law, and a power to keep God's commands and never depart from Him. The eye is fixed on Jesus, the Surety of the covenant, who will Himself make it all true. As witnesses declare how, after years of bondage, all this has been fulfilled in them, the longing begins to grow into a hope. They inquire about what is needed to enter this blessed life.

Another step follows. The heart-searching question is asked: are we willing to give up every evil habit, all our own self-will, all that is of the world, and surrender ourselves to be wholly and exclusively for Jesus? God cannot take complete possession of a man, bless him so wonderfully, and work in him so mightily unless He has him completely and wholly for Himself. Happy is the man who is ready for any sacrifice.

The last step is the simplest and yet often the most difficult. Here we need to know Jesus as Mediator of the covenant. As we hear of the life of holiness, obedience, and victory over sin, which the covenant promises, and realize that it will be to us according to our faith, our hearts often fail because of fear. I am willing, but do I have the power to make and maintain this full surrender? Do I have the power and strong faith to grasp and hold this offered blessing so that it will be and continue to be mine? How such questions perplex the soul until it finds the answer to them in the one word, *Jesus*! He will bestow the power to make the surrender and to believe.

This is as surely and exclusively His work as atonement and intercession are His alone. As sure as it was His to win and ascend to the throne, it is His to prove His dominion in the individual soul. He, the Living One, is in divine power to work and maintain the life of communion and victory within us. He is the Mediator and Surety of the covenant. He is the God-man who has undertaken not only for all that God requires but for all that we need as well.

Claiming the Promises

When this is seen, the believer learns that here, just as at conversion, it is all by faith. With the eyes fixed on some promise of the new covenant, we need now to turn from self and anything it could or needs to do, let go of self, and fall into the arms of Jesus. He is the Mediator of the new covenant. He leads us into it.

With the assurance that Jesus and every new covenant blessing is already ours because we are God's children, we must claim God's promises. With the desire to appropriate and enjoy what we have allowed to lie unused, we must ask God's guidance. With the faith that Jesus gives us the needed strength to claim and accept our heritage as a present possession, the will boldly dares to do the deed and take the heavenly gift. This gift is a life in Christ according to the better promises. By faith in Jesus you have seen and received Him as the Mediator of the new covenant both in heaven and in your heart. He is the Mediator who makes it true between God and you as your experience.

Sometimes the fear has been expressed that, if we urgently seek the work the Spirit does in the heart, we may be drawn away from trusting in what He has done and is doing by what we are experiencing of its working. The answer is simple. It is with the heart alone that Christ truly can be known or honored. The work of grace and the saving power of Christ is to be done and displayed in the heart. It is in the heart alone that the Holy Spirit has His sphere of work. There He is to work Christ's likeness. It is there alone He can glorify Christ.

The Spirit can glorify Christ only by revealing His saving power in us. If we were to speak of what we are to do in cleansing our hearts and keeping them right, the fear would be well-grounded. But the new covenant calls us to the very opposite. What it tells us of the Atonement and righteousness of God it has won for us will be our only glory even amid the highest holiness of heaven. Christ's work of holiness here in the heart can only deepen the consciousness of that righteousness as our only plea. The sanctification of the Spirit, as the fulfillment of the new covenant promises, is a taking of the things of Christ and revealing and imparting them to us.

The deeper our entrance into and possession of the new covenant gift of a new heart, the fuller our knowledge and love of Him who is its Mediator will be, and the more we will glory in Him alone. The covenant deals with the heart so that Christ may be found there and dwell there by faith. As we look at the heart, not in the light of feeling or experience but in the light of the faith of God's covenant, we will learn to think and speak of it as God does. We will begin to know what it is. There Christ manifests Himself and He and the Father come to make their abode.

Chapter 11

———————◆———————

Jesus, Surety of the Better Covenant

And inasmuch as not without an oath he was made priest:..
By so much was Jesus made a surety of a better testament....
Wherefore he is able also to save them to the uttermost
that come unto God by him, seeing he ever liveth to make
intercession for them.
—Hebrews 7:20, 22, 25

A surety is one who stands good for another so that a certain engagement will be faithfully performed. Jesus is the Surety of the new covenant. He stands as surety with us for God so that God's part in the covenant will faithfully be performed, and He stands as surety with God for us so that our part will also be faithfully performed.

Jesus as Surety

If we are to live in covenant with God, everything depends on our knowing correctly what Jesus secures to us. The more we know and trust Him, the more assured our faith will be that its every promise will be fulfilled. We will be assured that a life of faithful keeping of God's covenant is indeed possible because

Jesus is the Surety of the covenant. He makes God's faithfulness and ours equally sure.

We read that it was because His priesthood was confirmed by the oath of God that He became the Surety of a much better covenant. The oath of God gives us the security that His surety will secure all the better promises. The meaning and infinite value of God's oath has been explained in the previous chapter.

> *An oath for confirmation is to them* [to men] *an end of all strife. Wherein God, willing more abundantly to show unto the heirs of promise the immutability of His counsel, confirmed it by an oath: that by two immutable things, in which it was impossible for God to lie, we might have a strong consolation.* (Heb. 6:16–18)

We have a covenant with certain definite promises, and we have Jesus as the Surety of that covenant. We also have perfect confidence in the unchangeableness of the counsel and promise of the living God coming in between with an oath. Can we not see that the one thing God aims at in this covenant and asks with regard to it is an absolute confidence that He is going to do all He has promised however difficult or wonderful it may appear?

His oath is an end to all fear or doubt. Let no one think of understanding the covenant, judging or saying what may be expected from it, much less experiencing its blessings, until he meets God with an Abraham-like faith. Be fully assured that what He has promised He is able to perform. The covenant is a sealed mystery, except to the soul who is going without reserve to trust God and abandon itself to His Word and work.

Our passage tells us about the work of Christ, the Surety of the better covenant. Because of this priesthood confirmed by oath, He is able to completely save those who draw near to God through Him. He can do this because *"he ever liveth to make intercession for them"* (Heb. 7:25). As the Surety of the covenant, He is ceaselessly engaged in watching their needs, presenting them to the Father, receiving His answer, and imparting its blessing.

It is because of this never-ceasing mediation, receiving and transmitting from God to us the gifts and powers of the heavenly world, that He is able to save completely. Because of this He is able to work and maintain in us a salvation as complete as God is willing it should be and as complete as the better covenant has assured us it will be in the better promises on which it was established. These promises are expounded (see Hebrews 8:7–13) as being none other than those of the new covenant of Jeremiah, with the law written in the heart by the Spirit of God as our experience of the power of that salvation.

Christ, Our Assurance

Jesus, the Surety of a better covenant, is to be our assurance that everything connected with the covenant is unchangeably and eternally sure. Jesus is the keynote of all our fellowship with God, all our prayers and desires, and all our life and walk. With full assurance of faith and hope, we can look for every word of the covenant to be made fully true to us by God's own power. Let us look at some of these things we are to be fully assured of if we are to breathe the spirit of children of the new covenant.

There is the love of God. The very thought of a covenant is an alliance of friendship. It is a means of assuring us of His love, drawing us close to His heart of love, getting our hearts under the power of His love and filled with it. It is because God loves us with an infinite love, wants us to know it, and to give it complete liberty to bestow itself on us, and bless us, that the new covenant has been made and God's own Son been made its Surety.

This love of God is an infinite divine energy doing its utmost to fill the soul with itself and its blessedness. God's Son is the Messenger of this love. He is the Surety of the covenant in which God reveals it to us. Let us learn that the chief need in studying the covenant, keeping it, and seeking and claiming its blessings is the exercise of a strong, confident assurance in God's love.

Then there is the assurance of the sufficiency of Christ's finished redemption. All that was needed to put away sin and free us entirely and forever from its power has been accomplished by Christ. His blood, death, resurrection, and ascension have taken us out of the power of the world and transplanted us into a new life in the power of the heavenly world. All this is divine reality. Christ is our Surety that the divine righteousness, acceptance, and all-sufficient grace and strength are always ours. He is our Surety that all these can and will be communicated to us in unbroken continuance.

It is also true with the assurance of what is needed on our part to enter into this life in the new covenant. We shrink back either from the surrender of all because we do not know whether we have the power to let it go or from the faith because we fear ours will never be as strong or bold to take and hold all that is offered to us in this wonderful covenant. Jesus is the Surety of a better covenant. The better consists in this very thing, that it undertakes to provide the children of the covenant with the very dispositions they need to accept and enjoy it.

A Heart Surrendered to God

We have seen how the heart is the central object of the covenant promise. Jesus is the Surety of a heart circumcised to love God completely and into which God's law and fear have been put so that it will not depart from Him. Let us repeat: the one thing God asks of us and has given the covenant and its Surety to secure—the confident trust that all will be done in us that is needed—is what we dare not withhold.

I think some of us are beginning to see what our great mistake has been. We have thought and spoken great things of what Christ did on the cross and does on the throne as covenant Surety, but we have stopped there. We have not expected Him to do great things in our hearts. Yet it is there, in our hearts, that the consummation of the work on the cross and the throne takes place. In the heart the new covenant has its full triumph. The Surety is to be known not by what the mind can think of Him in heaven, but by what He does to make Himself known in the heart. There is the place where His love triumphs and is enthroned.

Let us believe and receive Him with the heart as the covenant Surety. With every desire we entertain in connection with it, every duty it calls us to, and every promise it holds out, let us look to Jesus, under God's oath the Surety of the covenant. Let us believe that by the Holy Spirit the heart is His home and throne. If we have not done it yet, in a definite act of faith, let us throw ourselves utterly on Him for our entire new covenant life and walk. No surety was ever so faithful to his undertaking as Jesus will be to His on our behalf, in our hearts.

Offer Yourself in Weakness

In spite of the strong confidence and consolation the oath of God and the Surety of the covenant gives, there are some still looking wistfully at this blessed life. They are still afraid to trust themselves to this wondrous grace. They have a conception of faith as something great and mighty, and they know and feel that theirs is not such. So their feebleness remains an insurmountable barrier to their inheriting the promise. Let me say it again: brother and sister, the act of faith by which you accept and enter this life in the new covenant is not commonly an act of power. It is often of weakness, fear, and much trembling.

Even in the midst of this feebleness, it is not an act in your strength. Rather, it is a secret and perhaps unfelt strength that Jesus, the Surety of the covenant, gives you. God has made Him Surety with the purpose of inspiring us with courage and confidence. He longs and delights to bring you into the covenant. Why not bow before Him and say meekly: He does hear prayer. He brings souls into the covenant. He enables a soul to believe. I can trust Him confidently.

Begin to quietly believe that there is an almighty Lord, given by the Father, to do everything needed to make all covenant grace wholly true in you. Bow low and look up out of your humble estate to your glorified Lord. Maintain your confidence that a soul who, in its nothingness, trusts in Him will receive more than it can ask or think.

Believer, come and truly be a believer. Believe that God is showing you how completely the Lord Jesus wants to have you and your life for Himself and how He is willing to take total charge of you and work all in you. Believe how entirely you can even now commit your trust, surrender, and faithfulness to the covenant, with all you are and are to be, to Him who is your Blessed Surety. If you believe, you will see the glory of God.

In a sense and measure and power that surpasses knowledge, Jesus Christ is Himself all that God can either ask or give. He is all that God wants to see in us. *"He that believeth on me...out of his belly shall flow rivers of living water"* (John 7:38).

Chapter 12

---◆◆---

The Book of the Covenant

*And he [Moses] took the book of the covenant, and read in the audience of the people: and they said, All that the L*ORD *hath said will we do, and be obedient. And Moses took the blood, and sprinkled it on the people, and said, Behold the blood of the covenant, which the L*ORD *hath made with you concerning all these words.*
—Exodus 24:7–8

*H*ere is a new aspect of God's blessed Book. Before Moses sprinkled the blood, he read the Book of the covenant and obtained the people's acceptance of it. When he had sprinkled it he said, *"Behold the blood of the covenant, which the L*ORD *hath made with you concerning all these words."* The Book contained all the conditions of the covenant. Only through the Book could they know all that God asked of them and all that they might ask of Him. Let us consider what new light can be thrown upon the covenant and the Book by the one thought that the Bible is the Book of the covenant. The first thought suggested will be this: the spirit of our life and experience as it lives either in the old or new covenant will be in nothing more manifest than in our dealings with the Book. The old as well as the new had a Book. Our Bible contains both. The new was enfolded in the old. The old is unfolded in the new. It is possible to read the old in the spirit of the new. It is possible to read the new as well as the old in the spirit of the old.

The Spirit of the Old Covenant

We can clearly see this spirit of the old in Israel when the covenant was made. At once they were ready to promise, *"All that the Lord hath said will we do, and be obedient."* There was so little sense of their own sinfulness or the holiness and glory of God that, with perfect self-confidence, they considered themselves able to undertake and keep the covenant. They understood little of the meaning of the blood with which they were sprinkled or of the death and redemption of which it was the symbol. In their own strength and power of the flesh, they were ready to undertake to serve God.

It is just this spirit in which many Christians regard the Bible. It is a system of laws, a course of instruction to direct us in the way God would have us go. All He asks of us is that we do our utmost in seeking to fulfill them. We cannot do more. This we are sincerely ready to do. They know little or nothing of what death through which the covenant is established means. They know little of what life from the dead is through which a man can walk in covenant with the God of heaven.

This self-confident spirit in Israel is explained by what had previously happened. When God came down on Mount Sinai in thunder and lightning to give the law, the Israelites were greatly afraid. *"They said unto Moses, Speak thou with us, and we will hear: but let not God speak with us, lest we die"* (Exod. 20:19). They thought it was simply a matter of hearing and knowing. They thought they could certainly obey. They did not know that it is only the presence, nearness, and the power of God humbling us and making us afraid that can conquer the power of sin. Only this can give the power to obey.

It is so much easier to receive the instruction from man and live than to wait and hear the voice of God and die to all our own strength and goodness. Is it any wonder that many Christians seek to live in daily contact with Him and without the faith that it is only His presence that can keep from sin? Their faith is a matter of outward instruction from man. Waiting to hear God's voice that they may obey Him and death to the flesh and the world that comes with a close walk with God are unknown. They may be faithful and diligent in the study of their Bible, in reading or hearing Bible teaching, but they do not seek to have as much fellowship with the covenant God as possible. It is fellowship that makes the Christian life possible.

The Book of the New Covenant

If you want to be delivered from all this, learn to read the Book of the new covenant in the new covenant Spirit. One of the very first articles of the new covenant refers to this matter. When God says, *"I will put my law in their inward parts, and write it in their hearts"* (Jer. 31:33), He promises that the words of His Holy Book will no longer be mere outward teaching. What they command will be our very disposition and delight worked in us as a birth and life by the Holy Spirit. Every word of the new covenant then becomes a divine assurance of what can be obtained by the Holy Spirit's working. The soul learns to see that the letter kills and the flesh profits nothing.

The study, knowledge of, and delight in Bible words and thoughts cannot profit except as the Holy Spirit is waited on to make them life. The acceptance of Holy Scripture in the letter and in the human understanding and reception of it is as fruitless as Israel's was at Sinai. But, as the Word of God, spoken by the living God through the Spirit into the heart that waits on Him, it is found to be quick and powerful. It is a word that works effectually in those who believe, placing within the heart the actual possession of the very grace of which the Word has spoken.

The new covenant is a ministry of the Spirit. All its teaching is meant to be teaching by the Holy Spirit. The two most remarkable chapters in the Bible on the preaching of the Gospel are those in which Paul expounded the secret of his teaching. (See 1 Corinthians 2; 2 Corinthians 3.) Every minister ought to see whether he can pass his examination in them. They tell us that in the new covenant the Holy Spirit is everything. It was the Holy Spirit entering the heart, writing, revealing, and impressing upon it God's law and truth that could work true obedience. No excellency of speech or human wisdom can profit. God must reveal to the preacher and hearer by His Holy Spirit the things He has prepared for us.

The Work of the Spirit

What is true of the preacher is equally true of the hearer. One of the great reasons that so many Christians never come out of the old covenant—never even know they are in it and have to come out of it—is that there is so much head knowledge, yet they lack the power of the Spirit in the heart. It is only when preachers, hearers, and readers believe that the Book of the new covenant needs the Spirit of the new covenant to explain and apply it that the Word of God can do its work.

Learn the double lesson. What God has joined together, let no man put asunder. The Bible is the Book of the new covenant. And the Holy Spirit is the only minister of what belongs to the covenant. Do not expect to understand or profit by your Bible knowledge without continually seeking the teaching of the Holy Spirit. Beware that your earnest Bible study, excellent books, or beloved teachers do not take the place of the Holy Spirit!

Pray daily, perseveringly, and believingly for His teaching. He will write the Word in your heart.

The Bible is the Book of the new covenant. Ask the Holy Spirit especially to reveal the new covenant in it to you. It is inconceivable what loss today's church is suffering because so few believers truly live as its heirs and in the true knowledge and enjoyment of its promises.

Ask God, in humble faith, to give you in all your Bible reading the spirit of wisdom and revelation and enlightened eyes of your heart, to know what promises the covenant reveals. Ask God to reveal the divine security in Jesus, the Surety of the covenant, that every promise will be fulfilled in you in divine power. Ask Him to reveal the intimate fellowship to which it admits you with the God of the covenant. Humbly waiting for and listening to the ministry of the Spirit will make the Book of the covenant shine with new light—even the light of God's countenance and a full salvation.

Unbroken Fellowship

All this especially applies to the knowledge of what the new covenant is actually meant to work. Amid all we hear, read, and understand of the different promises of the new covenant, it is quite possible that we have never had that heavenly vision of it as a whole. With its overmastering power it compels acceptance. Hear once again what it really is. The obedience and fellowship with God is now brought within our reach and offered us.

Our Father tells us in the Book of the new covenant that He now expects us to live in full, unbroken obedience and communion with Him. He tells us that by the mighty power of His Son and Spirit He Himself will work this in us. Everything has been arranged for it. He tells us that a life of unbroken obedience is possible because Christ, the Mediator, will live in us and enable us each moment to live in Him. He tells us that all He wants is the surrender of faith and the yielding of ourselves to Him to do His work.

Let us look and see this holy life, with all its powers and blessings, coming down from God in heaven, in the Son and His Spirit. Let us believe that the Holy Spirit can give us a vision of it, as a prepared gift to be bestowed in living power and take possession of us. Let us look upward and inward in the faith of the Son and the Spirit. God will show us that every word written in the Book of the covenant is not only true but that it can be made spirit and truth within us and in our daily lives. This certainly can be.

Chapter 13

———◆———

New Covenant Obedience

Now therefore, if ye will obey my voice indeed, and keep my covenant, then ye shall be...an holy nation.
—Exodus 19:5–6

And the Lord thy God will circumcise thine heart, and the heart of thy seed, to love the Lord thy God with all thine heart, and with all thy soul....And thou shalt return and obey the voice of the Lord, and do all his commandments.
—Deuteronomy 30:6, 8

And I will put my spirit within you, and cause you to walk in my statutes, and ye shall keep my judgments.
—Ezekiel 36:27

*I*n making the new covenant, God very definitely said, *"Not according to the covenant that I made with their fathers"* (Heb. 8:9). We have learned the fault with that covenant. It made God's favor dependent on the obedience of the people. *"Obey my voice, and I will be your God"* (Jer. 7:23). We have learned how the new covenant remedied the defect. God Himself provided for the obedience. It changes "If ye *'keep my* *judgments'"* into *"I will put my Spirit within you,...and ye shall keep."* Instead of the covenant and its fulfillment depending on man's obedience, God undertakes to ensure the obedience. The old covenant proved the need and pointed out the path of holiness. The new inspires the love and gives the power of holiness.

In connection with this change, a serious and dangerous mistake is often made. Because the new covenant obedience no longer occupies the place it had in the old and free grace has replaced it, justifying the ungodly and bestowing gifts on the rebellious, many are under the impression that obedience is no longer as indispensable as it was then. The error is a terrible one.

Obedience Is Still Essential

The whole old covenant was meant to teach the lesson of the absolute, indispensable necessity of obedience for a life in God's favor. The new covenant comes, not to provide a substitute for that obedience in faith, but through faith to secure the obedience by giving a heart that delights in it and has the power for it. Men abuse the free grace when they rest content with grace without the obedience it is meant for.

They boast of the higher privileges of the new covenant, while its chief blessings, the power of a holy life, a heart delighting in God's law, and a life in which God causes and enables us by His indwelling Spirit to keep His commandments, is neglected. If there is one thing we need to know well, it is the place obedience takes in the new covenant.

Let our first thought be, "Obedience is essential." The thought of obedience lies at the very root of the relationship of a creature to his God and God admitting the creature to His fellowship. It is the only thing God spoke of in Paradise when *"the Lord God commanded the man"* not to eat of the forbidden fruit (Gen. 2:16). In Christ's great salvation it is the power that redeemed us. *"By the obedience of one shall many be made righteous"* (Rom. 5:19).

In the promise of the new covenant, it takes the first place. God arranges to circumcise the hearts of His people—in the putting off of the body of the flesh in the circumcision of Christ—to love God with all their hearts and obey His commandments. The crowning gift of Christ's exaltation was the Holy Spirit to bring salvation to us as an inward thing. The first covenant demanded obedience and failed because it could not find it. The new covenant was expressly made to provide for obedience. Obedience is essential to a life in the full enjoyment of the new covenant blessing.

Obedience Overcomes Unbelief

It is this indispensable necessity of obedience that explains why so often the entrance into the full enjoyment of the new covenant has depended on a single act of surrender. There was some evil or doubtful habit in the life, or the conscience often said that it was not in perfect accord with God's perfect will. Attempts were made to push aside the troublesome suggestion. Unbelief said it would be impossible to overcome the habit and maintain the promise of obedience to the Voice within.

In the meantime, all our prayers seemed to be of no avail. It was as if faith could not lay hold of the blessing that was in full sight until the soul finally consented to regard this little thing as the test of its surrender to obey in everything. It was a test of its faith that in everything the Surety of the covenant would give power to maintain the obedience. With the evil or doubtful thing given up, a good conscience restored, and the heart's confidence before God assured, the soul could receive and possess what it sought. Obedience is essential.

Obedience is possible. The thought of a demand that man cannot possibly give up cuts at the very root of true hope and strength. The secret thought that no man can obey God throws thousands back into the old covenant life and into a false peace that God does not expect more than that we do our best. Obedience is possible; the entire new covenant promises and secures this.

Simply understand what obedience means. The renewed man still has the flesh with its evil nature out of which involuntary evil thoughts and dispositions arise. These may be found in a truly obedient man. Obedience deals with doing what is known to be God's will as taught by the Word, the Holy Spirit, and conscience. When George Müller spoke of the great happiness he had for more than sixty years in God's service, he attributed it to two things. First, he had loved God's Word, and then "he had maintained a good conscience, not willfully going on in a course he knew to be contrary to the mind of God."

When the full revelation of God broke on Gerhard Tersteggen, he wrote, "I promise, with Thy help and power, rather to give up the last drop of my blood, than knowingly and willingly in my heart or my life be untrue and disobedient to Thee." Such obedience is an attainable degree of grace.

Obedience is possible. When the law is written in the heart, the heart is circumcised to love the Lord with all our hearts and to obey Him. When the love of God is shed abroad in the heart, it means that the love of God's law and Himself has now become the moving power of our lives. This love is no vague sentiment in man's imagination of something that exists in heaven. It is a living, mighty power of God in the heart, working effectually according to His working, which works mightily in us. A life of obedience is possible.

This obedience is of faith. *"By faith Abraham...obeyed"* (Heb. 11:8). By faith the promises of the covenant, the presence of the Surety of the covenant, the hidden inworking of the Holy Spirit, and the love of God in His infinite desire and power to make true in us all His love and promises must live in us. Faith can bring them near and make us live in the very midst of them.

Christ and His wonderful redemption do not need to remain at a distance from us in heaven but can become our continual experience. However cold or feeble we may feel, faith knows that the new heart is in us. The love of God's law is our very nature, and the teaching and power of the Spirit are within us.

Such faith knows it can obey. Let us hear the voice of our Savior, the Surety of the covenant, as He says with a deeper, fuller meaning than when He was on earth: *"Only believe"* (Mark 5:36). *"If thou canst believe, all things are possible to him that believeth"* (Mark 9:23).

Last of all, let us understand that obedience is a joy and a delight. Do not regard it as a requirement for the joy and blessing of the new covenant. Regard it, in its very nature, as part of that blessedness. To have the voice of God teaching and guiding you, be united to God in willing what He wills, working out what He works in you by His Spirit, doing His holy will, and pleasing Him. All this is joy unspeakable and full of glory.

New Covenant Obedience

To a healthy man it is a delight to walk or work, to put forth his strength and conquer difficulties. To a sick man it is bondage and weariness. The old covenant demanded obedience with an unrelenting "must" and the threat that followed it. The new covenant changes the "must" to "can" and "may."

Ask God by the Holy Spirit to show you how you have been *"created in Christ Jesus unto good works"* (Eph. 2:10). Ask how, as fitted as a vine is for bearing grapes, your new nature is perfectly prepared for every good work. Ask Him to show you that He means obedience to be possible and also the most delightful, attractive gift He has to bestow. It is the entrance into His love and all its blessedness.

In the new covenant the most important thing is not the wonderful treasure of strength and grace it contains nor the divine security that the treasure can never fail. But it is that the living God gives Himself, makes Himself known, and takes possession of us as our God. Man was created for this. For this He was redeemed. So that it may be our actual experience, the Holy Spirit has been given and is dwelling in us. Obedience is the blessed link between what God has already worked in us and what He waits to work. Let us seek to walk before Him in the consciousness that we are one of those who live in noble, holy consciousness. My one work is to obey God.

Why do so many believers see so little of the beauty of this new covenant life with its power of holy, joyful obedience? *"Their eyes were holden that they should not know him"* (Luke 24:16).

The Lord was with the disciples, but their hearts were blind. It is still this way. Like Elisha's servant, all heaven is around them, and they do not know it. Nothing will help but the prayer, *"Lord, I pray thee, open his eyes, that he may see"* (2 Kings 6:17). Lord, is there someone reading this who needs just one touch to see it all? Give that touch!

Listen, friends. Your Father loves you with an infinite love and longs to make you His holy, happy, obedient children. Hear His message. He has an entirely different life for you than what you are living. He gives a life in which His grace will actually work in you every moment all He asks you to be. He brings a life of simple, childlike obedience, doing for the day just what the Father shows you to be His will. He offers a life in which the abiding love of your Father, the abiding presence of your Savior, and the joy of the Holy Spirit can keep and make you glad and strong.

This is His message. This life is for you. Do not be afraid to accept this life. Give yourself to it and its entire obedience. In Christ it is possible. It is sure.

Brothers and sisters, just look heavenward and ask the Father, by the Holy Spirit, to show you the beautiful heavenly life. Ask and expect it. Keep your eyes fixed upon it. The great blessing of the new covenant is obedience. It is the wonderful power to will and do as God wills. It is the entrance to every other blessing. It is paradise restored and heaven opened—the creature honoring his Creator and the Creator delighting in His creature. It is the child glorifying the Father and the Father glorifying the child as He changes him from glory to glory into the likeness of His Son.

Chapter 14

─────◆─────

A Covenant of Grace

Sin shall not have dominion over you: for ye are not under the law, but under grace.
—Romans 6:14

*T*he phrase, "covenant of grace," though not found in Scripture, is the correct expression of the truth it abundantly teaches. The contrast between the two covenants is none other than that of law and grace. Grace is the great characteristic of the new covenant. *"The law entered, that the offence might abound. But where sin abounded, grace did much more abound"* (Rom. 5:20). To bring the Romans entirely away from under the old covenant and teach them their place in the new, Paul wrote, *"Ye are not under the law, but under grace."*

He assured them that if they believe this and live in it, their experience would confirm God's promise: *"Sin shall not have dominion over you."* What the law could not do—give deliverance from the power of sin over us—grace would effect. The new covenant was entirely a covenant of grace. It had its origin in the wonderful grace of God. It was meant to be a manifestation of the riches and the glory of that grace. Of and by grace working in us, all its promises can be fulfilled and experienced.

The Abundance of Grace

The word *grace* is used in two senses. First it is the gracious disposition in God that moves Him to love us freely without our merit and bestow all His blessings upon us. Then it also means the power that this grace bestows upon us to work in us. The redeeming work of Christ and the righteousness He won for us together with the work of the Spirit in us as the power of the new life are spoken of as *grace*. It includes all that Christ has done and still does, all He has and gives, and all He is for us and in us. John said, *"We beheld his glory, the glory as of the only begotten of the Father, full of grace and truth"* (John 1:14). The law was given by Moses. Grace and truth came by Jesus Christ. *"And of his fullness have all we received, and grace for grace"* (v. 16). What the law demands, grace supplies.

The contrast that John pointed out was expounded by Paul. *"The law entered, that the offence might abound"* (Rom. 5:20) and the way be more exceedingly prepared for the abounding of grace. The law points the way but gives no strength to walk in it. It demands but makes no provision for its demands being met. The law burdens, condemns, and slays. It can awaken desire but not satisfy it. It can rouse to effort but not secure success. It can appeal to motives but gives no inward power beyond what man himself has. So, while warring against sin, it became its very ally in giving the sinner over to a hopeless condemnation. *"The strength of sin is the law"* (1 Cor. 15:56).

To deliver us from the bondage and dominion of sin, grace came by Jesus Christ. Its work is twofold. Its exceeding abundance is seen in the free, full pardon of all transgression, the bestowal of a perfect righteousness, and the acceptance into God's favor and friendship. *"In whom we have redemption through his blood, the forgiveness of sins, according to the riches of his grace"* (Eph. 1:7). It is not only at conversion when we are admitted into God's favor, but throughout our lives, that we owe everything to grace, and grace alone. The thought of merit and work and worthiness is forever excluded.

The exceeding abundance of grace is equally seen in the work that the Holy Spirit maintains every moment within us. We have found that the central blessing of the new covenant, flowing from Christ's redemption and the pardon of our sins, is the new heart in which God's law, fear, and love have been put. It is in the fulfillment of this promise, in the maintenance of the heart in a state of meekness for God's indwelling, that the glory of grace is especially seen. In the very nature of things this must be so.

Grace Reigns in the Heart

Paul wrote, *"Where sin abounded, grace did much more abound"* (Rom. 5:20). And where, as far as I was concerned, did sin abound? All the sin in earth and hell could not harm me if it were not present in my heart. There it has exercised its terrible dominion. There the exceeding abundance of grace must be proved if it is to benefit me. All grace in heart and heaven could not help me. It is only in the heart that it can be received, known, and enjoyed.

"Where sin abounded," in the heart, *"grace did much more abound:....As sin hath reigned unto death,"* working its destruction in the heart and life, *"even so might grace reign"* in the heart *"through righteousness unto eternal life by Jesus Christ our Lord"* (vv. 20–21). As has been said before, *"They which receive abundance of grace...shall reign in life by one, Jesus Christ"* (v. 17).

Scripture speaks wondrous things about this reign in the heart. Paul spoke of the grace that prepared him for his work, of *"the gift of the grace of God given unto me by the effectual working of his power"* (Eph. 3:7).

> *The grace of our Lord was exceeding abundant with faith and love.* (1 Tim. 1:14)

> *His grace which was bestowed upon me was not in vain; but I labored more abundantly than they all: yet not I, but the grace of God which was with me.* (1 Cor. 15:10)

*He said unto me, My grace is sufficient for thee: for my
strength is made perfect in weakness.* (2 Cor. 12:9)

He spoke in the same way about grace as working in the
life of believers when he exhorted them to *"be strong in the
grace that is in Christ Jesus"* (2 Tim. 2:1). He told us of *"the grace
of God"* (2 Cor. 8:1) exhibited in the liberality of the Macedo-
nian Christians and *"the exceeding grace of God"* (2 Cor. 9:14) in
the Corinthians. He encouraged them, *"God is able to make all
grace abound toward you; that ye...may abound to every good
work"* (v. 8).

Grace is not only the power that moves the heart of God
in its compassion toward us, when He acquits and accepts the
sinner and makes him a child. It is also the power that moves
the heart of the saint and provides it each moment with just the
disposition and the power that it needs to love God and do His
will.

Sanctifying Grace

It is impossible to speak of the wonderful, free, sufficient
grace that pardons without speaking of the grace that sanctifies.
We are just as dependent on the latter as the former. We can do
as little to the one as the other. The grace that works in us must
exclusively do all in and through us as the grace that pardons
does all for us. In both cases everything is by faith alone. Not to
comprehend this brings a double danger.

On the one hand, people think that grace cannot be more
exalted than in the bestowal of pardon on the vile and unworthy. A secret feeling arises that if God is magnified by our sins
more than anything else, we must not expect to be freed from
them in this life. With many this cuts at the root of the life of
true holiness. On the other hand, from not knowing that grace
always and alone does all the work in our sanctification and
fruitbearing, men are thrown on their own efforts. Their life
remains one of feebleness and bondage under the law, and they
never yield themselves to let grace do all it would.

Let us listen to what God's Word says.

By grace are ye saved through faith;...not of works, lest any man should boast. For we are his workmanship, created in Christ Jesus unto good works, which God hath before ordained that we should walk in them. (Eph. 2:8–10)

Grace stands in contrast to our own good works not only before conversion but after conversion, too. We are created in Christ Jesus for good works, which God had prepared for us. Grace alone can work them in us and work them out through us. The work of grace is not only the commencement but also the continuance of the Christian life.

"And if by grace, then is it no more of works: otherwise grace is no more grace. But if it be of works, then is it no more grace: otherwise work is no more work" (Rom. 11:6). As we see that grace literally and absolutely does all in us, so that all our actions are the showing forth of grace in us, we will consent to live the life of faith in which every moment, everything is expected from God. It is only then that we will experience that sin will ever for a moment have dominion over us.

"Ye are not under the law, but under grace" (Rom. 6:14). There are three possible lives: one entirely under the law; one entirely under grace; and one a mixed life that is partly law and partly grace. It is against this last that Paul warned the Romans. It is this that is so common and works such ruin among Christians. Let us find out whether this is our position and the cause of our low state. Let us ask God to open our eyes by the Holy Spirit to see that in the new covenant everything—every movement, every moment of our Christian life—is of abounding grace working mightily. Let us believe that our covenant God waits to cause all grace to abound toward us. Let us begin to live the life of faith that depends on, trusts in, looks to, and ever waits for God, through Jesus Christ by the Holy Spirit, to work in us that which is pleasing in His sight.

Grace to you and peace be multiplied.

Chapter 15

An Everlasting Priesthood

That my covenant might be with Levi, saith the LORD of hosts. My covenant was with him of life and peace; and I gave them to him for the fear wherewith he feared me, and was afraid before my name. The law of truth was in his mouth, and iniquity was not found in his lips: he walked with me in peace and equity, and did turn many away from iniquity.
—Malachi 2:4–6

God meant Israel to be a nation of priests. In the first making of the covenant, this was distinctly stipulated. *"If ye will obey my voice indeed, and keep my covenant,...ye shall be unto me a kingdom of priests"* (Exod. 19:5–6). They were to be the stewards of the oracles of God and the channels through whom God's knowledge and blessing were to be communicated to the world. In them all nations were to be blessed.

Within the people of Israel, one tribe was especially set apart to embody and emphasize the priestly idea. The firstborn sons of the entire nation were to have been the priests. But to secure a more complete separation from the rest of the people and the entire giving up of any share in their possessions and pursuits, God chose one tribe to be exclusively devoted to the work of proving what constitutes the spirit and power of priesthood. Just as the priesthood of the entire nation was part of God's covenant with them, so the special calling of Levi is spoken of as God's covenant of life and peace being with Him. It is the covenant of an everlasting priesthood. All this was to be a picture to help them and us to understand the priesthood of His own blessed Son, the Mediator of the new covenant.

The Call to Priesthood

Like Israel, under the new covenant all God's people are a royal priesthood. The right of free and full access to God—the duty and power of mediating for our fellowmen and being God's channel of blessing to them—is the inalienable birthright of every believer. Because of the feebleness of many of God's children and their ignorance of the mighty grace of the new covenant, they are utterly unable to exercise their priestly functions. To make up for this lack of service, through the exceeding riches of His grace and the power He gives men to become His followers, God still allows and invites those redeemed ones who are willing to offer their lives to this blessed ministry.

To the one who accepts the call, the new covenant brings in special measure what God has said: *"My covenant was with him of life and peace"* (Mal. 2:5). It becomes to him *"the covenant of an everlasting priesthood"* (Num. 25:13). As the covenant of Levi's priesthood issued and culminated in Christ's, ours issues from that again and receives from it its blessing to dispense to the world.

Conditions of Priesthood

To those who desire to know the conditions on which the covenant of an everlasting priesthood can be received and carried out, a study of the conditions on which Levi received the priesthood will be most instructive. Not only are we told that God chose that tribe but what there was in that tribe that especially prepared it for the work. Our text says,

My covenant was with him of life and peace; and I gave them to him for the fear wherewith he feared me, and was afraid before my name.

The reference is to what took place at Sinai when Israel had made the golden calf.

Moses called all who were on the Lord's side and who were ready to avenge the dishonor done to God to come to him. The tribe of Levi did so, and at his bidding took their swords and slew three thousand of the idolatrous people. (See Exodus 32:26–29.) In the blessing with which Moses blessed the tribes before his death, their absolute devotion to God, without considering relative or friend, is mentioned as the proof of their readiness for God's service.

Let thy Thummin and thy Urim be with thy holy one...who said unto his father and to his mother, I have not seen him; neither did he acknowledge his brethren, nor knew his own children: for they have observed thy word, and kept thy covenant. (Deut. 33:8–9)

The same principle is strikingly illustrated in the story of Aaron's grandson, Phinehas, where, in his zeal for God, he executed judgment on disobedience to God's command. The words are most suggestive.

And the LORD spake unto Moses, saying, Phinehas, the son of Eleazer, the son of Aaron the priest, hath turned my wrath away from the children of Israel, while he was zealous for my sake among them, that I consumed not the children of Israel in my jealousy. Wherefore say, Behold, I give unto him my covenant of peace: and he shall have it, and his seed after him, even the covenant of an everlasting priesthood; because he was zealous for his God, and made an atonement for the children of Israel. (Num. 25:10–13)

The gate into the covenant of an everlasting priesthood is to be jealous with God's jealousy, to be jealous for God's honor and rise up against sin. It is the secret of being entrusted by God with the sacred work of teaching His people, burning incense before Him, and turning many from iniquity (See Deuteronomy 33:10; Malachi 2:6.)

Even the new covenant is in danger of being abused—by seeking our own happiness or holiness more than the honor of God or the deliverance of men. Even where these are not entirely neglected, they do not always take the place they are meant to have. They must have the first place that makes everything, even the dearest and best, secondary and subordinate to the work of helping and blessing men. The school of training for the priestly office is a reckless disregard of everything that would interfere with God's will and commands, a being jealous with God's jealousy against sin, and witnessing and fighting against it at any sacrifice.

We Need Men of God!

This is what the world needs today. It needs men of God in whom the fire of God burns. It needs men who can stand, speak, and act in power on behalf of a God who, amid His own people, is dishonored by the worship of the golden calf. God often disapproves of a religion even where the people still profess to be in covenant with God. *"Consecrate yourselves to day to the LORD, even every man upon his...brother"* (Exod. 32:29). This call of Moses is also needed today. To each one who responds there is the reward of the priesthood.

All who want to know fully what the new covenant means should remember God's covenant of life and peace with Levi. Accept the holy calling to be an intercessor and burn incense before the Lord continually. Live, work, pray, and believe as one whom God has sought and found to stand in the gap before Him. The new covenant was dedicated by a sacrifice and a death.

Consider this sacrifice as your most wonderful privilege and your fullest entrance into the covenant life as you reflect the glory of the Lord and are changed into the same image from glory to glory. As you are led by the Spirit of the Lord, let the Spirit of that sacrifice and death be the moving power in all your priestly functions. Sacrifice yourself. Live and die for your fellowmen.

The Call to Intercessory Prayer

One of the great objectives with which God has made a covenant with us is to awaken strong confidence in Himself and His faithfulness to His promise. One of the purposes that He has in waking and strengthening the faith in us is that He may use us as His channels of blessing to the world. In the work of saving men, He wants intercessory prayer to take the first place. He wants us to come to Him to receive from Him in heaven the spiritual life and power that can flow out from us to them.

He knows how difficult and hopeless it is in many cases to deal with sinners. He knows that it is no light thing for us to believe that in answer to our prayers the mighty power of God will move to save those around us. He knows that it needs strong faith to persevere patiently in prayer in cases in which the answer is long delayed and every year appears farther off than ever. So He undertakes, in our own experience, to prove what faith in His divine power can do. It brings down all the blessings of the new covenant on us, so that we may be able to confidently expect what we ask for others.

In our priestly life there is still another aspect. The priests had no inheritance with their brethren. The Lord God was their inheritance. They had access to His dwelling and presence so that they might intercede there for others and then testify what God is and wills. Their personal privilege and experience prepared them for their work. If we want to intercede in power, we should live in the full realization of new covenant life. It gives us more than liberty and confidence with God and the power to persevere. It also gives us power with men so we can testify to and prove what God has done to us. Here is the full glory of the new covenant. Like Christ, its Mediator, we have the fire of divine love dwelling in us and consuming us in the service of men. The chief glory of the new covenant to each of us should be that it is the covenant of an everlasting priesthood.

Chapter 16

———— ◆ ————

The Ministry of the New Covenant

Ye are our epistle written in our hearts, known and read of all men: forasmuch as ye are manifestly declared to be the epistle of Christ ministered by us, written not with ink, but with the Spirit of the living God; not in tables of stone, but in fleshly tables of the heart. And such trust have we through Christ to Godward: not that we are sufficient of ourselves to think any thing as of ourselves; but our sufficiency is of God; who also hath made us able ministers of the new testament; not of the letter, but of the spirit: for the letter killeth, but the spirit giveth life.
—2 Corinthians 3:2–6

We have seen that the new covenant is a ministry of the Spirit that ministers all its grace and blessing in divine power and life. He does this through men who are called ministers of a new covenant or ministers of the Spirit. The divine ministry of the covenant to men and the earthly ministry of God's servants are equal in the power of the Holy Spirit. The ministry of the new covenant has its glory and fruits in this: it is all to be a demonstration of the Spirit and of power.

What a contrast this is to the old covenant. Moses had received the glory of God shining upon him but had to put a veil over his face. Israel was incapable of looking at it. In hearing and reading Moses, there was a veil on their hearts. From Moses they could receive knowledge, thoughts, and desires. The power of God's Spirit to enable them to see the glory of what God speaks was not yet given.

Ministers of the Spirit

This is the exceeding glory of the new covenant. It is a ministry of the Spirit. Its ministers have their sufficiency from God, who makes them ministers of the Spirit and makes them able to speak the words of God in the Spirit. Then they are written in the heart, and the hearers become legible, living epistles of Christ showing the law written in their hearts and lives.

The ministry of the Spirit! What a glory there is in it! What a responsibility it brings! What a sufficiency of grace is provided for it! What a privilege to be a minister of the Spirit!

Thousands throughout Christendom are called ministers of the Gospel. What an inconceivable influence they exert for life or death over the millions who depend on them for their knowledge and participation of the Christian life. What a power there would be if all these were ministers of the Spirit! Let us study the Word until we see what God meant the ministry to be and learn to take our part in praying and laboring to have it be nothing less. God has made us ministers of the Spirit. The first thought is that a minister of the new covenant must be someone who is personally possessed by the Holy Spirit. There is a twofold work of the Spirit. One, it gives a holy disposition and character. Second, it qualifies and empowers a person for work. The former must always come first. The promise of Christ to His disciples—that they should receive the Holy Spirit for their service—was very definitely given to those who had followed and loved Him and kept His commandments.

It is not enough that a man has been born of the Spirit. If he is to be a "sufficient minister" of the new covenant, he must know what it is to be led by the Spirit, walk in the Spirit, and say, *"The law of the Spirit of life in Christ Jesus hath made me free from the law of sin and death"* (Rom. 8:2). If you wanted to learn Greek or Hebrew, would you accept a professor who hardly knows the basics of these languages?

How to Minister in the Spirit

How can a man be a minister of the new covenant, which is so entirely a ministry of the Spirit, unless he knows by experience what it is to live in the Spirit? The minister must, before everything, be a personal proof and witness of the truth and power of God in the fulfillment of what the new covenant promises. Ministers are to be chosen men. They should be the best specimens and examples of what the Holy Spirit can do to sanctify a man, and by the working of God's power in him fit him for His service.

God has made us ministers of the Spirit. Next to this thought of being personally possessed by the Spirit comes the truth that all their work in the ministry can be done in the power of the Spirit. What an unspeakably precious assurance! Christ sends them to do a heavenly work—His work—and be instruments in His hands by which He works. He clothes them with a heavenly power. Their calling is to preach *"the gospel unto you with the Holy Ghost sent down from heaven"* (1 Pet. 1:12).

As far as feelings are concerned, they may have to say like Paul, *"I was with you in weakness, and in fear, and in much trembling"* (1 Cor. 2:3). That does not prevent their adding—in fact, it may just be the secret of their being able to add, *"My preaching was...in demonstration of the Spirit and of power"* (v. 4). If a man is to be a minister of the new covenant, a messenger and a teacher of its true blessing to lead God's children to live in it, nothing less will do than a full experience of its power in himself, as the Spirit ministers it.

Whether in his feeding on God's Word himself or his seeking in it for God's message for his people, whether in secret or intercessory prayer or in private fellowship with souls or public teaching, he is to wait upon, receive, and yield to the energizing of the Holy Spirit. It is the mighty power of God working with him. This is his sufficiency for the work. Every day he may claim afresh and receive the anointing with fresh oil, the new inbreathing from Christ of His own Spirit and life.

God has made us ministers of the Spirit. There is still something that is no less important. The minister of the Spirit must especially see to it that he leads others to the Holy Spirit. Many will say, "If he is led of the Spirit in teaching, is that not enough?" No. People may become too dependent on him. They may take his Scripture teaching at second hand. And while there is power and blessing in his ministry, he may have reason to wonder why the results are not more definitely spiritual and permanent. The reason is simple.

The new covenant is this: *"They shall not teach every man his...brother, saying, Know the Lord: for all shall know me, from the least to the greatest"* (Heb. 8:11). The Father wants every child, from the least, to live in continual, personal fellowship with Himself. This cannot be, except as he is taught and helped to know and wait on the Holy Spirit. Bible study, prayer, faith, love, and obedience—the whole daily walk—must be taught as entirely dependent on the teaching and working of the indwelling Spirit.

Qualities of a Minister

The minister of the Spirit definitely and perseveringly points away from himself toward the Spirit. This is what John the Baptist did. He was filled with the Holy Spirit from his birth but sent men away from himself to Christ, to be baptized by Him with the Spirit. Christ did the same. In His farewell discourse He called His disciples to turn from His personal instruction to the inward teaching of the Holy Spirit, who would dwell in them and guide them into the truth and power of all He had taught them.

Nothing is so needed in the church today as this. All its feebleness, formalities, worldliness, lack of holiness, personal devotion to Christ, and enthusiasm for His cause and kingdom is due to one thing. The Holy Spirit is not known, honored, and yielded to as the only, all-sufficient Source of a holy life. The new covenant is not known as a ministry of the Spirit in the heart of every believer. The one needful thing for the church is the Holy Spirit in His power dwelling and ruling in the lives of God's saints.

One of the main ways to achieve this indwelling is for the ministers of the Spirit to live in the enjoyment and power of this great gift. They must persistently labor to bring their brethren into the possession of their birthright, which is the Holy Spirit in the heart, maintaining, in divine power, an unceasing communion with the Son and Father. The ministry of the Spirit makes the Spirit's ministry possible and effectual. The ministry of the Spirit also makes the ministration of the Spirit a reality in the life of the church.

We know how dependent the church is on its ministry. The converse is no less true. Ministers are dependent on the church. They are its children. They breathe its atmosphere. They share its health or sickness. They are dependent on its fellowship and intercession. None of us should think that all that the new covenant calls us to is to see that we personally accept and rejoice in its blessings. No, God wants everyone who enters into it to know that its privileges are for all His children.

There is no more effectual way of doing this than thinking about the ministry of the church. Compare the ministry around you with its pattern in God's Word. (See especially 1 Corinthians 2; 2 Corinthians 3.) Join with others who know how the new covenant is nothing if it is not a ministration of the Spirit. Cry to God for a spiritual ministry. Ask the leading of God the Holy Spirit to teach you what can be done and what you can do to have the ministry of your church become a truly spiritual one. Human condemnation will do as little good as human approval.

As the supreme place of the Holy Spirit, as the Representative and Revealer of the Father and Son is made clear to us, the one desire of our hearts and our continual prayer will be that God would so reveal to all the ministers of His Word their heavenly calling. Then they may, above everything, seek this one thing—to be sufficient ministers of the new covenant, not of the letter, but of the Spirit.

Chapter 17

———◆———

His Holy Covenant

To remember his holy covenant...grant unto us,
that we being delivered out of the hand
of our enemies might serve him without fear,
in holiness and righteousness before him,
all the days of our life.
—Luke 1:72–75

When Zacharias was filled with the Holy Spirit and prophesied, he spoke of God's visiting and redeeming His people
as a remembering of His holy covenant. He speaks of the blessings of that covenant, not in words that had been used before,
but in what is manifestly a divine revelation to him by the Holy
Spirit. He gathers up all the former promises in these words,
*"That we...might serve him without fear, in holiness and righ-
teousness before him, all the days of our life."* Holiness in life
and service is to be the great gift of the covenant of God's holiness. As we have seen before, the old covenant proclaimed and
demanded holiness. The new provides it. Holiness of heart and
life is its great gift.

God's Holiness

There is no attribute of God so difficult to define, so peculiarly a matter of divine revelation, so mysterious, incomprehensible, and inconceivably glorious, as His holiness. It is this holiness by which He is especially worshipped in His majesty on the throne of heaven. (See Isaiah 6:3; Revelation 4:8; 15:3–4.) It unites His righteousness that judges and condemns with His love that saves and blesses. As the Holy One He is a consuming fire (Isa. 10:17). As the Holy One He loves to dwell among His people (Isa. 12:6). As the Holy One He is at an infinite distance from us. As the Holy One He comes inconceivably near and makes us one with and like Himself. The one purpose of His holy covenant is to make us holy as He is holy.

As the Holy One He says, *"Be ye holy; for I am holy"* (1 Pet. 1:16); *"I am the Lord which* [sanctifies] *you"* (Lev. 22:32). The highest conceivable summit of blessedness is our being partakers of the divine nature, of the divine holiness.

We Are Holy

This is the great blessing Christ, the Mediator of the new covenant, brings. He has been made unto us *"righteousness, and sanctification"* (1 Cor. 1:30)—righteousness as a preparation for sanctification or holiness. He prayed to the Father, *"Sanctify them...for their sakes I sanctify myself, that they also might be sanctified through the truth"* (John 17:17, 19). Saints, in Him we are sanctified, holy ones. We have *"put on the new man, which after God is created in righteousness and true holiness"* (Eph. 4:24). Holiness is our very nature.

We are holy in Christ. As we believe it, receive it, yield ourselves to the truth, and draw closer to God to have the holiness drawn forth and revealed in fellowship with Him, we will know how divinely true it is.

It is for this the Holy Spirit has been given in our hearts. He is the Spirit of holiness. His every work is in the power of holiness. Paul said, *"God hath from the beginning chosen you to salvation through sanctification of the Spirit and belief of the truth"* (2 Thess. 2:13). As simple and entire as our dependence on the Word of truth is, as the external means, our confidence must be in the hidden power for holiness that the working of the Spirit brings.

The connection between God's electing purpose and the working of the Spirit is clearly spoken of in Peter, *"Elect...through sanctification of the Spirit, unto obedience"* (1 Pet. 1:2). The Holy Spirit is the Spirit of the life of Christ. As we know, honor, and trust Him, we will learn and experience that in the new covenant the holiness of the Holy Spirit is our covenant right. We will be assured that, as God has promised, He will work it in us, so that we *"might serve him without fear, in holiness and righteousness before him, all the days of our life."* With a treasure of holiness in Christ and the very Spirit of holiness in our hearts, we can live holy lives if we believe Him *"which worketh in you both to will and to do of his good pleasure"* (Phil. 2:13).

New Covenant Holiness

What new meaning is given to the teaching of the New Testament in the light of this covenant promise! The Blessed Son and the Holy Spirit work it out in us. Take the first epistle Paul ever wrote. It was directed to men who only a few months previously had been turned from idols to serve the living God and wait for His Son from heaven. The words he spoke in regard to the holiness they might aim at and expect, because God was going to work it in them, are so grand that many Christians pass them by as practically unintelligible. *"The Lord make you to increase and abound in love...to the end he may stablish your hearts unblameable in holiness...at the coming of our Lord Jesus Christ with all his saints"* (1 Thess. 3:12–13). That promises unblameable holiness—and a heart unblameable in holiness—and we are established in all this by God Himself.

Paul might respond to the question, "Who has believed our report?" by saying, *"Ye are witnesses,...how holily and justly and unblameably we behaved ourselves"* (1 Thess. 2:10).

He assured them that what God has done for him, He will also do for them. He will give them hearts that are unblameable in holiness. The church believes so little in the mighty power of God and the truth of His holy covenant that the grace of such heart-holiness is hardly spoken of. The verse is often quoted in connection with *"the coming of our Lord Jesus Christ with all His saints,"* but its real point and glory is that when He comes, we may meet Him with hearts established *"unblameable in holiness"* by God Himself. This is not proclaimed or expected.

Take another verse in the epistle also spoken to these young converts in reference to the coming of our Lord. Some think that to speak much of the coming of the Lord will make us holy. How little it has done this in so many cases. It is the new covenant holiness, worked in us by God Himself, believed in and waited for from Him, that can make our waiting differ from the carnal expectations of the Jews or the disciples.

Listen: *"The very God of peace"*—that is the keynote of the new covenant; what you can never do, God will work in you. *"Sanctify you wholly"*—this you may ask and expect—*"and I pray God your whole spirit and soul and body be preserved blameless unto the coming of our Lord Jesus Christ"* (1 Thess. 5:23). And now, as if to meet the doubt that will arise, *"Faithful is he that calleth you, who also will do it"* (v. 24). Again, it is the secret of the new covenant—what has not entered into the heart of man—God will work in them that wait for Him. Until the church awakens to see and believe that our holiness is to be the immediate, almighty working of the Three-in-One God in us and that our Christianity must be an unceasing dependence to receive it directly from Himself, these promises remain a sealed book.

Now, let us return to the prophecy of the Holy Spirit by Zacharias, of God's remembering the covenant of His holiness, to make us holy, to establish our hearts unblameable in holiness that we should serve Him *"in holiness and righteousness."* Note how every word is significant.

To *"grant unto us."* It is to be a gift from above. The promise given with the covenant was, *"I the LORD have spoken it, and I will do it"* (Ezek. 36:36). We need to ask God to show us what He will do. When our faith expects all from Him, the blessing will be found.

Zacharias had just said before, "[God] *hath raised up an horn of salvation for us...that we should be saved from our enemies, and from the hand of all that hate us"* (Luke 1:69, 71). Only free people can serve a holy God or be holy. It is only as the teaching of Romans 6–8 is experienced that I can expect God to do His mighty work in me. I need to know that I am *"freed from sin"* (Rom. 6:7), and that *"the Spirit of life in Christ Jesus hath made me free from the law of sin and death"* (Rom. 8:2).

"Might serve him." God's servant does not serve Him by spending all his time getting himself ready for work but in doing work. The holy covenant sets us free and empowers us with divine grace so that God can have us for His work. It is the same work Christ began, and we now carry it on.

"Without fear." We must have childlike confidence and boldness before God and men. It is freedom from fear in every difficulty because we have learned that God works all in us, so we can trust Him to work all for us and through us.

"Before him." We have His continued, unceasing presence all day as the unceasing security of our obedience and fearlessness. It is the never-failing secret of our being sanctified wholly.

"All the days." Not only all the day for one day, but for every day, because Jesus is a High Priest in the power of an endless life. The mighty operation of God as promised in the covenant is as unchanging as God is Himself.

Can you not begin to see that God's Word appears to mean more than you have ever conceived of or expected? It is only when you begin to say, "Glory to Him who *'is able to do exceeding abundantly above all that we ask or think'* (Eph. 3:20)," that you will really come to the place of helplessness and dependence where God can work. You must expect God's almighty, supernatural, altogether immeasurable power and grace to work out the new covenant life in you and make you holy.

Friends, believe that God's Word is true, and say with Zacharias,

> *Blessed be the Lord God of Israel; for he hath visited and redeemed his people...to remember his holy covenant...that he would grant unto us, that we being delivered out of the hand of our enemies might serve him without fear, in holiness and righteousness before him, all the days of our life.*
> (Luke 1:68, 72, 74–75)

Chapter 18

———◆———

Entering the Covenant
with All the Heart

*And they entered into a covenant to seek the LORD God of their
fathers with all their heart and with all their soul.*
—2 Chronicles 15:12

*The LORD thy God will circumcise thine heart, and the heart of
thy seed, to love the LORD thy God with all thine heart, and with
all thy soul.*
—Deuteronomy 30:6

*And I will give them an heart to know me, that I am the LORD:
and they shall be my people, and I will be their God: for they
shall return unto me with their whole heart.*
—Jeremiah 24:7

*I will make an everlasting covenant with them, that I will not
turn away from them, to do them good; but I will put my fear
in their hearts, that they shall not depart from me. Yea, I will
rejoice over them to do them good...with my whole heart and
with my whole soul.*
—Jeremiah 32:40–41

Covenants and Blessings

*I*n the days of Asa, Hezekiah, and Josiah, we read about Israel entering into a covenant with their whole heart, *"to perform the words of this covenant that were written in this book"* (2 Kings 23:3). Of Asa's day we read, *"They sware unto the L*ord*....And all Judah rejoiced at the oath: for they had sworn with all their heart, and sought him with their whole desire; and he was found of them"* (2 Chron. 15:14–15).

Wholeheartedness is the secret of our entering the covenant and finding God in it. Wholeheartedness is the secret of joy in Christianity—a full entrance into all the blessedness the covenant brings. God rejoices over His people to do them good, with His whole heart and His whole soul. We need our whole hearts and our whole souls to enter into and enjoy this joy of God in doing us good with His whole heart and His whole soul. With what measure we give, it will be measured unto us again.

Love God with All Your Heart

If we have at all understood the teaching of God's Word in regard to the new covenant, we know what it reveals about the two parties who meet in it. On God's side there is the promise to do for us and in us all that we need to serve and enjoy Him. With His whole heart, He will rejoice in doing us good. He will be our God, doing for us all that a God can do, giving Himself as God to be wholly ours. On our side there is the prospect of our being able, in the power of what He engages to do, to return unto Him with our whole hearts; to love Him with all our hearts and all our strength.

The first and great commandment, the only possible terms on which God can fully reveal Himself or give Himself to His creature to enjoy, is, *"Thou shalt love the Lord thy God with all thy heart"* (Matt. 22:37). That law is unchangeable. The new covenant comes and brings us the grace to obey by lifting us into the love of God. It calls on us in the faith of that grace to rise and be of good courage. With our whole hearts we must yield ourselves to the God of the covenant and life in His service.

How should I speak of wholeheartedness in the love and service of God and its imperative necessity? It is the one unalterable condition of true communion with God, of which nothing can supply the need. How can I speak of its infinite reasonableness? Such a God, who is the very Fountain of all that is loving and lovely, of all that is good and blessed, the all-glorious God! Surely there cannot for a moment be a thought of anything else being His due or of our consenting to offer Him anything less than the love of the whole heart. How can I speak of its unspeakable blessedness? To love Him with the whole heart is the only possible way of receiving His great love into our hearts and rejoicing in it. We must yield ourselves to that great love and allow God Himself, just as an earthly love enters into us and makes us glad, to give us the taste and joy of the heavenly quality of that love.

How can I speak of its terrible lack? Where will I find words to open the eyes and reach the heart? How can I show how almost universal the lack of true wholeheartedness in the faith and love of God is? It is lacking in our seeking to love Him with the whole heart and in our giving up everything to possess Him, please Him, and be wholly possessed of Him.

The Certainty of Wholeheartedness

And then what of the blessed certainty of its attainability? The covenant has provided for it. The triune God will work it by taking possession of the heart and dwelling there. The blessed Mediator of the covenant undertakes for all we have to do. His constraining love shed abroad in our hearts by the Holy Spirit can bring and maintain it. Yes, how will I speak of all this?

Have we not said enough already? We need something more than words and thoughts. What we need is to quietly turn to the Holy Spirit who dwells in us. With faith in the light and strength our Lord gives through Him, we need to accept and act out what God tells about the heart He has placed within us. We must yield to the wholeheartedness He works. Surely the new heart given to us with which to love God, and which has God's

Spirit in it, is wholly for God. Let our faith accept and rejoice in the wondrous gift and not be afraid to say, "I will love you, O Lord, with my whole heart." Just think for a moment what it means that God has given us such a heart.

We know what God's giving means. His giving depends on our taking. He does not force spiritual possessions on us. He promises and gives in such measure as desire and faith are ready to receive. He gives in divine power. As faith trusts and yields itself to that power, the gift becomes consciously and wholly our possession.

God's spiritual gifts are not recognized by sense or reason.

Eye hath not seen, nor ear heard, neither have entered into the heart of man, the things which God hath prepared for them that love him. But God hath revealed them unto us by his Spirit....Now we have received...the spirit which is of God; that we might know the things that are freely given to us of God. (1 Cor. 2:9–10, 12)

It is as you yield yourself to be led and taught by the Spirit that your faith will be able, despite all lack of feeling, to rejoice in the possession of the new heart and all that is given with it.

Then, this divine giving is continuous. I bestow a gift on a man. He takes it, and I never see him again. So God gives temporal gifts to men, and they never think of Him. But spiritual gifts are only to be received and enjoyed in unceasing communication with God Himself. The new heart is not a power I have in myself, like the natural endowments of thinking or loving. No, it is only in unceasing dependence on and close contact with God that the heavenly gift of a new heart can be maintained uninjured and day by day become stronger. It is only in God's immediate presence and in unceasing, direct dependence on Him that spiritual endowments are preserved.

Then, further, spiritual gifts can be enjoyed only by acting them out in faith. None of the graces of the Christian life, such as love, meekness, or boldness, can be felt or known, much less strengthened, until we begin to exercise them. We must not wait to feel them or feel the strength for them. We must practice them in the obedience of the faith that they are given and hidden within us. Whatever we read of the new heart and of all God has given into it in the new covenant must be boldly believed and carried out in action.

All this is especially true of wholeheartedness and loving God with all our hearts. You may at first be very ignorant of all it implies. God has planted the new heart in the midst of the flesh. The animating principle of the flesh—self—has to be denied, kept crucified, and be mortified by the Holy Spirit. God has placed you in the midst of a world from which you are to come out and be entirely separate. God has given you your work in His kingdom, for which He asks all your interest, time, and strength.

Give God Your Whole Heart

In all these three respects you need wholeheartedness to enable you to make the sacrifices that may be required. If you take the ordinary standard of Christian life around you, you will find that wholeheartedness and intense devotion to God and His service are hardly thought of. How to make the best of both worlds, innocently to enjoy as much as possible of this present life, is the ruling principle. As a natural consequence, the present world secures the larger share of interest. To please self is considered legitimate, and the Christlike life of not pleasing self has little place. Wholeheartedness will lead and enable you to accept Christ's command and sell all for the pearl of great price. At first you may be afraid of what it may involve. Do not hesitate to speak these words frequently in the ear of your Father: "with my whole heart." You may count on the Holy Spirit to open up its meaning, show you to what service or sacrifice God calls you in it, increase its power, reveal its blessedness, and make it the very spirit of your life of devotion to your covenant God.

And now, who is ready to enter into this new and everlasting covenant with his whole heart? Each of us should do it.

Begin very humbly by asking God to give you, by the Spirit who dwells in you, the vision of the heavenly life and whole-hearted love and obedience as it has actually been prepared for you in Christ. It is an existing reality, a spiritual endowment out of the life of God that can come upon you. It is secured for you in the covenant and in Christ Jesus, its Surety. Ask earnestly, definitely, believingly, that God will reveal this to you. Do not rest until you know fully what your Father means you to be and has provided for your being. When you begin to see why the new covenant was given, what it promises, and how divinely certain its promises are, offer yourself to God unreservedly to be taken up into it. If He will take you in, offer to love Him with your whole heart and obey Him with all your strength. Do not hold back or be afraid.

God has sworn to do you good with His whole heart. Do not hesitate to say that you now wholeheartedly enter into this covenant in which He promises to cause you to turn to Him and love Him with your whole heart. If there is any fear, just ask again, believing for a vision of the covenant life. God swears to do you good with His whole heart. He undertakes to make and enable you to love and obey Him with your whole heart. The vision of this life will make you bold to say, "Into this covenant of a wholehearted love in God and in me I now enter with my whole heart."

Let us close with this one thought. A redeeming God, rejoicing with His whole heart and soul to do us good and work in us all that is wellpleasing in His sight, this is the one side. This is the God of the covenant. Look at Him. Believe Him. Worship Him. Wait on Him until the fire begins to burn and your heart is drawn out with all its might to love this God. Then there is the other side. A redeemed soul, rejoicing with all its heart and soul in the love of this God, entering into the covenant of wholehearted love and venturing to say to Him, "With my whole heart I love You, God, my exceeding joy." These are the children of the covenant.

Reader, do not rest until you have entered in, through the beautiful gate, through Christ the door, into the temple of love— the heart of God.

Note A

---◆---

The Second Blessing

*I*n the life of the believer there sometimes comes a crisis, as clearly marked as his conversion, in which he passes out of a life of continual feebleness and failure into one of strength, victory, and abiding rest. The transition has been called the Second Blessing. Many have objected to the phrase because they think it is unscriptural or tends to make a general rule for everyone when it was only a method of experience in some.

Others have used it to help clearly express in human words what ought to be taught to believers as a possible deliverance from the ordinary life of the Christian, to one of abiding fellowship with God and entire devotion to His service. It is my belief that the words express a scriptural truth and may help believers in clearly putting before them what they can expect from God. Let me try to clarify how I think we ought to understand it.

Victory over Sin

I have connected the expression with the two covenants. Why did God make two covenants—not one or three? Because there were two parties concerned. In the first covenant, man was to prove what he could do and what he was. In the second, God would show what He would do. The former was the time of needed preparation. The latter was the time of divine fulfillment. The same necessity as there was for this in the whole of mankind exists in the individual, too.

Conversion makes a sinner a child of God, full of ignorance and weakness, without any conception of what the whole-hearted devotion that God asks of him is or the full possession God is ready to take of him. In some cases the transition from the elementary stage is by a gradual growth and enlightenment. But experience teaches that in the great majority of cases this healthy growth is not found.

To those who have never found the secret of victory over sin and perfect rest in God and have despaired of ever finding it because of their failure, it has often been a wonderful help to learn that by a single, decisive step, they can have a right relationship to Christ, His Spirit, and His strength. It is possible to enter into an entirely new life.

Confess Your Sin

What is needed to help a person to take that step is very simple. He must see and confess the sin of the life he is living that is not in harmony with God's will. He must see and believe in the life that Scripture holds out and that Christ Jesus promises to work and maintain in him. As he sees that his failure has been due to his striving in his own strength and believes that our Lord Jesus will actually work all in him in divine power, he takes courage and dares to surrender himself to Christ anew. Confessing and giving up all that is of self and sin and yielding himself wholly to Christ and His service, he believes and receives a new power to live his life by the faith of the Son of God. The change is in many cases as clear, marked, and as wonderful as conversion. For lack of a better name, that of a "Second Blessing" came most naturally.

Once we see how greatly this change is needed in the life of most Christians and how entirely it rests on faith in Christ and His power as revealed in the Word, all doubt of its scriptural validity will be removed. Once its truth is seen, we will be surprised to find how throughout Scripture and in history and teaching we find what illustrates and confirms it.

Take the twofold passage of Israel through water, first out of Egypt and then into Canaan. The wilderness journey was the result of unbelief and disobedience. It was allowed by God to humble, prove, and show them what was in their hearts. When this purpose had been accomplished, a second blessing led them through Jordan, as mightily into Canaan as the first had brought them through the Red Sea out of Egypt.

Or take the Holy Place and the Holiest of All as types of life in the two covenants and equally in the two stages of Christian experience. In the former there is very real access to God and fellowship with Him, but it is always with a veil between. In the latter there is the full access into the immediate presence of God and the full experience of the power of the heavenly life. As the eyes are opened to see how terribly the average Christian life falls short of God's purpose and how truly the mingled life can be expelled by the power of a new revelation of what God waits to do, the verses of Scripture will shine with new meaning.

Surrender to the Spirit

Look at the teachings of the New Testament. In Romans, Paul contrasted the life of the Christian under the law with that under grace—the spirit of bondage with the Spirit of adoption. What does this mean but that Christians may still live under the law and its bondage. They need to come out of this into the full life of grace and liberty through the Holy Spirit. When they first see the difference, nothing is needed but the surrender of faith to accept and experience what grace will do by the Holy Spirit. Paul wrote to the Corinthians of some being carnal and still babes walking as men after the flesh. Others are spiritual, with spiritual discernment and character. To the Galatians, he spoke of the liberty with which Christ, by the Spirit, makes free from the law. He contrasted this with those who sought to perfect in the flesh what was begun in the Spirit and who gloried in the flesh. All these teachings call believers to recognize the danger of the carnal, divided life and to come at once to the life of faith, the life in the Spirit, which alone is according to God's will.

How sad that the church of the present day often makes the same mistakes about living a carnal, divided life. Conversion is only the gate that leads into the path of life. Within that gate there is still great danger of mistaking the path, turning aside, or turning back. Where this has taken place, we are called at once with our whole hearts to turn and give ourselves to nothing less than all that Christ is willing to work in us.

Many have always thought that conversion must be slow, gradual, and uncertain because they take only man's powers into account and cannot understand how it can be sudden and final. Many fail to see how the revelation of the true life of holiness and the entrance into it by faith out of a life of self-effort and failure can be immediate and permanent. They look at man's efforts too much and do not know how the second blessing is nothing more nor less than a new vision of what Christ is willing to work in us. It is the surrender of faith that yields all to Him.

I hope that what I have written in this book may help some to see that the Second Blessing is just what they need. It is what God by His Spirit will work in them. It is nothing but the acceptance of Christ in all His saving power as our strength and life. It will bring them into and prepare them for that full life in the new covenant in which God works all in all.

Let me close this note with a quotation from the introduction I wrote to the book *Dying to Self: A Golden Dialogue* by William Law.

> A great deal has been said against the use of the terms, the *Higher Life* and the *Second Blessing*. In the writings of William Law, one finds nothing of such language, but his book is full of the deep truth of which they are the, perhaps defective, expression. The points on which so much stress is laid in what is called Keswick teaching stand prominently out in his whole argument. The following truths are

common to both: the low state of the average life of believers, the cause of all failure as coming from self-confidence, the need of an entire surrender of the whole being to the operation of God, the call to turn to Christ as the One and Sure Deliverer from the power of self, the Divine certainty of a better life for all who will in self-despair trust Christ for it, and the heavenly joy of a life in which the Spirit of love fills the heart. What makes Law's putting of the truth of special value is the way in which he shows how humility and utter self-despair, with the resignation to God's mighty working in simple faith, is the infallible way to be delivered from self, and have the Spirit of Love born in the heart.

Note B

The Law Written in the Heart

*T*he thought of the law written in the heart sometimes causes difficulty and discouragement because believers do not see or feel anything corresponding to it. An illustration may help this difficulty. There are fluids you can write with so that nothing is visible, either at once or later, unless the writing is exposed to the sun or the action of some chemical. The writing is there, but the person who is ignorant of the process cannot believe it is there and does not know how to make it readable. The man of faith who knows of the process realizes it is there even though he does not see it.

The Lord in the Heart

It is also true with the new heart. God has put His law into it. Blessed are the people in whose heart is God's law. (See Isaiah 51:7.) But it is there invisibly. He takes God's promise in faith and knows that it is in his own heart. As long as there is no clear faith on this point, all attempts to find it or fulfill that law will be vain. But when by simple faith the promise is held fast, the first step is taken to realize it. The soul is then prepared to receive instruction as to what the writing of the law in the heart means.

First, it means that God has implanted in the new heart a love of God's law and a readiness to do all His will. You may not feel this disposition there, but it is there. God has put it there. Believe this and be assured that there is a divine nature in you that says, and therefore you do not hesitate to say, *"I delight to do thy will, O my God"* (Ps. 40:8). In the name of God, and in faith, say it.

This writing of the law also means that in planting this principle in you, God has taken all that you know of His will already and inspired that new heart with the readiness to obey it. It may be written there with invisible writing, and you are not conscious of it. That does not matter. Here you have to deal with a divine and hidden work of the Holy Spirit. Do not be afraid to say, "Oh, how I love Your law!" God has put the love of it into your new heart. He has taken away the stony heart; you have to live by the new heart.

The next thing implied in this writing of the law is that you have accepted all God's will, even what you do not know yet, as the delight of your heart. In giving yourself up to God, you gave yourself wholly to His will. That was the one condition to your entering the covenant. Covenant grace will now teach you to know and strengthen you to do all your Father would have you do.

We Need More Faith

The entire life in the new covenant is a life of faith. Faith accepts every promise of the covenant, is certain that it is being fulfilled, and looks confidently to the God of the covenant to do His work. Faith believes implicitly in the new heart with the law written in it because it believes in the promise and in the God who gave and fulfills the promise.

It may be well to add here that the same truth holds true of all the promises concerning the new heart. They must be accepted and acted on by faith. When we read, *"The love of God is shed abroad in our hearts by the Holy Ghost"* (Rom. 5:5), *"Christ may dwell in your hearts,"* (Eph. 3:17), *"Love one another with a pure heart fervently,"* (1 Pet. 1:22), and *"[God] stablish your hearts unblameable in holiness"* (1 Thess. 3:13), we must, with the eye of faith, regard these spiritual realities as actually existing within us.

In His hidden, unseen way God is working them there. We know—not by sight or feeling but by faith in the living God and His Word—that they are an inspiration for the dispositions and inclinations of the new heart. We are to act in this faith, knowing that we have the power to love, obey, and be holy. The new covenant gives us a God who works all in us. Faith in Him gives us the assurance above and beyond all feeling that God is doing His blessed work. If we ask what we are to think of all there is within us that contradicts this faith, let us remember what Scripture teaches. We sometimes speak of an old and new heart. Scripture does not do this. It speaks of the old, stony heart being taken away. The heart, with its will, disposition, and affections, is being made new with a divine newness. This new heart is placed in the midst of what Scripture calls the flesh, where no good thing dwells. (See Romans 7:18.)

We will find it a great advantage to adhere as closely as possible to scriptural language. It will help our faith greatly to use the very words God by His Holy Spirit uses to teach us. It will also clear our view for knowing what to think of the sin that remains in us if we think of it and deal with it in the light of God's truth. Every evil desire and affection comes from the flesh, man's sinful natural life. It owes its power to our ignorance of its nature and our trusting to its help and strength to cast out its evil. I have already pointed out how sinful flesh and religious flesh are one and how all failure in our Christian walk is due to a secret trust in ourselves.

Renounce the Flesh

As we accept and make use of what God says of the flesh, we will realize that it is the source of all evil in us. We will say of its temptations, "It is no more I, but sin that dwells in me." (See Romans 7:17, 20.) We will maintain our integrity as we maintain a good conscience that condemns us for nothing knowingly done against God's will. We will be strong in the faith of the Holy Spirit, who dwells in the new heart to strengthen us so that we *"shall not fulfil the lusts of the flesh"* (Gal. 5:16).

I conclude with an extract of an address given by Rev. F. Webster at Keswick in confirmation of what I have just said:

"Put ye on the Lord Jesus Christ, and make not provision for the flesh, to fulfil the lusts thereof" (Rom. 13:14). *"Make not provision for the flesh."* The flesh is there, you know. To deny or ignore the existence of an enemy is to give him a great chance against you; and the flesh is in the believer to the very end. It is a force of evil to be reckoned with continually. It is an evil force inside a man, and yet, thank God, a force that can be so dealt with by the power of God that it will have no power to defile the heart or deflect the will. The flesh is in you, but your heart may be kept clean moment by moment in spite of the existence of evil in your fallen nature. Every avenue, every opening that leads into the heart, and every thought, desire, purpose, and imagination of your being may be closed against the flesh so that there will be no opening to come in and defile the heart or deflect the will from the will of God.

You say that is a very high standard, but it is the Word of God. There is to be no secret sympathy with sin. Although the flesh is there, you are to make it no excuse for sins. You are not to say, "I am naturally irritable, anxious, jealous, and I cannot help letting these things crop up; they come from within." Yes, they come from within, but there does not have to be any provision or opening in your heart for these things to enter. Your heart can be barricaded with an impassable barrier against these things. *"Make not provision for the flesh."* Not only should the front door be barred and bolted so that you do not invite them to come in, but the side and back door should be closed, too. You can be so Christ-possessed and Christ-enclosed that you will positively hate everything that is of the flesh.

"Make not provision for the flesh." The only way to do this is to *"put ye on the Lord Jesus Christ"* (Rom. 13:14). I spoke of the heart being so barricaded that there could be no entrance to it. The flesh should never be able to defile it or deflect the will from the will of God. How can that be done? By putting on the Lord Jesus Christ. It has been such a blessing to me just to learn that one secret, the positive side of deliverance—putting on the Lord Jesus Christ.

Note C

George Müller's Second Conversion

*I*n the life of George Müller of Bristol, there was a memorable time, four years after his conversion, that he often spoke about as his entrance into the true Christian life.

Full Surrender

In an address given to ministers and workers after his ninetieth birthday, he spoke the following of it himself:

That leads to another thought: the full surrender of the heart to God. I was converted in November 1825, but I only came into the full surrender of the heart four years later in July 1829. The love of money, the love of place, the love of position, the love of worldly pleasures and engagements were gone. God alone became my portion. I found my all in Him; I wanted nothing else. And by the grace of God this has remained and has made me an exceedingly happy man. It led me to care only about the things of God. I ask affectionately, brethren, have you fully surrendered your heart to God, or is there this or that thing with which you are taken up irrespective of God? I read a little of the Scriptures before but preferred other books. Since that time the revelation He has made of Himself has become unspeakably blessed to me, and I can say from my heart, God is an infinitely lovely Being. Oh! Do not be satisfied until in your inmost soul you can say, "God is an infinitely lovely Being!"

The account he gives in his journal of this change is as follows. He speaks of one whom he had heard preach at Teignmouth where he had gone for the sake of his health.

Though I did not like all he said, I saw a gravity and solemnity in him different from the rest. Through the instrumentality of this brother, the Lord gave me a great blessing that I will thank Him for throughout eternity.

God then began to show me that the Word of God alone is to be our standard of judgment in spiritual things. It can be explained only by the Holy Spirit. In our day as well as in former times, He is the Teacher of His people. I had not experimentally understood the office of the Holy Spirit before that time. Before I had not seen that the Holy Spirit alone can teach us about our state by nature, show us our need of a Savior, enable us to believe in Christ, explain to us the Scriptures, help us in preaching, etc.

It was my beginning to understand this point in particular that had a great effect on me. The Lord enabled me to put it to the test of experience by laying aside commentaries and almost every other book and simply reading the Word of God and studying it. The result was that the first evening I shut myself into my room to give myself to prayer and meditation over the Scriptures, I learned more in a few hours than I had previously done during a period of several months. But the particular difference was that I received real strength in my soul in doing so.

In addition to this, it pleased the Lord to lead me to see a higher standard of devotedness than I had seen before. He led me, in a measure, to see what is my glory in this world, even to be despised, poor, and mean with Christ....I returned to London much better in body. And in regard to my soul, the change was so great that it was like a second conversion.

The Word Is Essential Reading

In another passage he wrote,

I fell into the snare that so many young believers fall into. The reading of religious books is preferred to the Scriptures. Now the scriptural way of reasoning would have been this: God Himself has condescended to become an author, and I am ignorant of that precious Book that His Holy Spirit has caused to be written. Therefore, I ought to read this Book of books again very earnestly, prayerfully, and with much meditation.

Instead of acting this way and being led by my ignorance of the Word to study it more, my difficulty of understanding it made me careless in reading it. Then, like many believers, for the first four years of my Christian life, I practically preferred the works of uninspired men to the oracles of the living God. The consequence was that I remained a babe both in knowledge and grace. I say in knowledge for all true knowledge must be derived by the Spirit from the Word. This lack of knowledge kept me back from walking steadily in the ways of God.

It is the truth that makes us free by delivering us from the slavery of the lusts of the flesh, the lusts of the eyes, and the pride of life. The Word, the experience of the saints, and also my own experience most decidedly proves it. For when it pleased the Lord in August 1829 to bring me really to the Scriptures, my life and walk became very different.

If any one would ask me how he may read the Scriptures most profitably, I would answer him:

1. Above all he must seek to have it settled in his own mind that God alone, by the Holy Spirit, can teach him. Therefore, since God will be sought for all blessings, it

becomes him to seek God's blessing prior to reading, and also while reading.

2. He should also have it settled in his mind that though the Holy Spirit is the best and sufficient Teacher, yet He does not always teach immediately when we desire it. Therefore, we may have to ask Him again and again for the explanation of certain passages. But He will surely teach us if we will seek for light prayerfully, patiently, and for the glory of God.

Let us look at one more passage from an address given on his ninetieth birthday.

For sixty-nine years and ten months he had been a very happy man. He attributed that to two things. He had maintained a good conscience, not willfully going on in a course he knew to be contrary to the mind of God. He did not, of course, mean that he was perfect. He was poor, weak, and sinful. Secondly, he attributed it to his love of Holy Scripture. Lately his practice had been to read through the Scriptures four times every year with meditation and application to his own heart. That day he was a greater lover of God's Word than he was sixty-six years ago. It was this, and maintaining a good conscience, that had given him peace and joy in the Holy Ghost all these years.

The Spirit Brings Power

In connection with what has been said about the new covenant being a work of the Spirit, this narrative is most helpful. It shows us how George Müller's power lay in God's revealing to him the work of the Holy Spirit. He wrote that up to the time of that change he had "not experimentally understood the office of the Holy Spirit." We speak much of George Müller's power in prayer. It is important to remember that that power was entirely due to his love of and faith in God's Word.

But it is still more important to notice that his power to believe God's Word so fully was entirely due to his having learned to know the Holy Spirit as his Teacher. When the words of God are explained to us and made living within us by the Holy Spirit, they have a power to awaken faith that they otherwise do not have. The Word then brings us into contact with God, comes to us directly from God, and binds our whole lives to Him.

When the Holy Spirit feeds us on the Word, our whole lives come under His power and the fruit is seen not only in the power of prayer but in the power of obedience. Notice how Müller tells us this. The two secrets of his great happiness were his great love for God's Word and his ever maintaining a good conscience, not knowingly doing anything against the will of God. In giving himself to the teaching of the Holy Spirit, he made a full surrender of his entire heart to God to be ruled by the Word. He gave himself to obey that Word in everything.

He believed that the Holy Spirit gave the grace to obey, and so he was able to maintain a walk free from knowingly transgressing God's law. This is a point he always insisted on. He wrote the following in regard to a life of dependence on God. "It will not do—it is not possible—to live in sin and at the same time, by communion with God, to draw down from heaven everything one needs for the life that now is."

Again, speaking of the strengthening of faith he said,

> It is of the utmost importance that we seek to maintain an upright heart and a good conscience. Therefore do not knowingly and habitually indulge in those things that are contrary to the mind of God. All my confidence in God, all my leaning upon Him in the hour of trial, will be gone if I have a guilty conscience, and do not seek to put away this guilty conscience, but still continue to do things that are contrary to His mind.

A careful reading of this testimony will show us how the chief points insisted upon in connection with the second blessing are all found here. There is a full surrender of the heart to be taught and led alone by the Spirit of God. There is the higher standard of holiness that is set up at once. There is the tender desire to offend God in nothing but to have a good conscience at all times that testifies that we are pleasing to God. And there is the faith that where the Holy Spirit reveals the will of God to us in the Word, He gives sufficient strength for doing it. "The particular difference," he said about reading with faith in the Holy Spirit's teaching, "was that I received real strength in my soul in doing so."

Everything centers in this, that we believe in the new covenant and its promises as a work of the Spirit. That belief may come suddenly to some, as it did to George Müller, or it may dawn upon others by degrees. All must say to God that they are ready to put their whole hearts and lives under the rule of the Holy Spirit dwelling in them, teaching them by the Word, and strengthening them by His grace. He enables us to live pleasing to God.

Note D

———————◆◆◆———————

Canon Battersby

I do not know whether I can find a better illustration of the place Christ, the Mediator of the covenant, takes in leading into its full blessing than that of the founder of the Keswick Convention, the late Canon Battersby.

It was at the Oxford Convention in 1873 that he witnessed to having received a new and distinct blessing to which he had been a stranger before. For more than twenty-five years, he had been very diligent as a minister of the Gospel and, as appears from his journals, most faithful in seeking to maintain a close walk with God. But he was always disturbed by the consciousness of being overcome by sin. As far back as 1853 he had written,

> I feel again how very far I am from habitually enjoying that peace, love, and joy that Christ promises. I must confess that I do not have it, and that very ungentle, unchristian tempers often strive within me for the mastery.

The Rest of Faith

In 1873 when he read what was being published of the Higher Life, the effect made him utterly dissatisfied with himself and his state. There were difficulties he could not quite understand in that teaching, but he felt that he must either reach forward to better things, nothing less than redemption from *all* iniquity, or fall back more and more into worldliness and sin. At Oxford he heard an address on the rest of faith. It opened his eyes to the truth that a believer who really longs for deliverance from sin must simply take Christ at His word. He must believe, without relying on his feelings, on Him to do His work of cleansing and keeping of the soul. He wrote,

> I thought of the sufficiency of Jesus, and said, "I will rest in Him," and I did rest in Him. I was afraid that it would be a passing emotion. But I found that a presence of Jesus was graciously manifested to me in a way I did not know before, and that I did abide in Him. I do not want to rest in these emotions, but just believe and cling to Christ as my all.

He was a man with a very reserved nature, but he felt it his duty before the close of the conference to publicly confess his past shortcomings and openly testify to his having entered upon a new and definite experience.

In a paper written not long after this, he explained the steps that led to this experience. First, there is a clear view of the possibilities of Christian attainment—a life in word and action, habitually governed by the Spirit, in constant communion with God, and continual victory over sin through abiding in Christ. Then, there must be the deliberate purpose of the will for a full renunciation of all the idols of the flesh or spirit and a will-surrender to Christ. Then comes the last and important step. We must look up to and wait for our ascended Lord for all we need to enable us to do this.

Faith Centers in Christ

A careful reading of this very brief statement will prove how everything centers in Christ. The surrender for a life of continual communion and victory is to be given up to Christ. The strength for that life is to be in Him and from Him by faith in Him. And the power to make the full surrender and rest in Him is to be waited for from Him alone.

In June 1875, the first Keswick Convention was held. The newspaper reporting it stated:

> Many everywhere are thirsting that they may be brought to enjoy more of the divine presence in their daily lives, and a fuller manifestation of the Holy Spirit's power, whether in subduing the lusts of the flesh or in enabling them to offer more effective service to God. It is certainly God's will that His children should be satisfied in regard to these longings. There are those who can testify that He has satisfied them and does satisfy them with daily fresh manifestations of His grace and power.

The results of the very first convention were so blessed that after its close Battersby wrote,

> There is a very remarkable resemblance in the testimonies I have since received as to the nature of the blessing obtained, and the ability given to make a full surrender to the Lord and the consequent experience of an abiding peace far exceeding anything previously experienced.

Through all, the chief thought was Christ first drawing and enabling the soul to rest in Him, and then meeting it with the fulfillment of its desire—the abiding experience of His power to keep it in victory over sin and in communion with God.

What was the fruit of this new experience? Eight years later Canon Battersby spoke,

> It is now eight years since I knew this blessing as my own. I cannot say that I have never for a moment ceased to trust the Lord to keep me. But I can say that as long as I have trusted Him, He has kept me. He has been faithful.

Note E

---◆---

Nothing of Myself

O ne would think that no words could make it plainer than the words of the covenant—that the one difference between old and new is that in the latter everything is to be done by God Himself. Yet believers and even teachers do not take it in. Even those who do understand find it difficult to live it out. Our whole beings are so blinded to our true relationship to God. His inconceivable, omnipresent omnipotence working in us every moment is so far beyond the reach of human conception that our little hearts cannot rise to the reality of His infinite love making itself one with us. We fail to conceive how He delights to dwell in us and to work all in us that has to be done there. When we think we have accepted the truth, we find it is only a thought. We are such strangers to the knowledge of what God really is, as the actual life by which His creatures live. *"In Him we live, and move, and have our being"* (Acts 17:28).

And the knowledge of the triune God is especially too high for us. It is beyond our comprehension to understand that wonderful, most real, and most practical indwelling that enabled the Son to become incarnate and the Holy Spirit to be sent into our hearts. Only they who confess their ignorance and wait very humbly and persistently on our blessed God to teach us by His Holy Spirit what that all-working indwelling is can hope to have it revealed to them.

Christ Depends on the Father

In preparing a series of Bible lessons for our Students' Association here, I made a study of the gospel of John and the life of our Lord that is set forth there. I cannot say how deeply I have been impressed with the profound secret of His life on earth— His dependence on the Father. It has come to me like a new revelation. Twelve times or more He uses the words *not* and *nothing* of Himself. *"Not my will"* (Luke 22:42). *"Not mine own glory"* (John 8:50). *"I speak not of myself"* (John 14:10). *"I do nothing of myself"* (John 8:28).

Just think a moment what this means in connection with what He tells us of His life in the Father. *"As the Father hath life in himself; so hath he given to the Son to have life in himself"* (John 5:26). *"That all men should honour the Son, even as they honour the Father"* (v. 23). And yet this Son, who has life in Himself even as the Father has, immediately adds: *"I can of mine own self do nothing"* (v. 30). We would think that with this life in Himself He would have the power of independent action as the Father has. But no. *"The Son can do nothing of himself, but what he seeth the Father do"* (v. 19).

The chief mark of this divine life He has in Himself is evidently unceasing dependence, continually receiving from the Father what He had to speak or do. "Nothing of Myself" is manifestly as true of Him as it ever could be of the weakest or most sinful man. The life of the Father dwelling in Christ, and Christ in the Father, meant that just as truly as when He was begotten of the Father, He received divine life and glory from Him. Thus the continuation of that life came only by an eternal process of giving and receiving, as absolute as is the eternal generation itself. The more closely we study this truth and Christ's life in the light of it, the more we are compelled to say that the deepest root of Christ's relationship to the Father, the secret of His glorifying the Father, was this: He allowed God to do all in Him. He received and worked out only what God worked in Him. His whole attitude was that of the open ear, the servant spirit, and the childlike dependence that waited for all on God.

Christ Gives His Life to Us

The infinite importance of this truth in the Christian life is easily felt. The life Christ lived in the Father is the life He imparts to us. We are to abide in Him and He in us, even as He is in the Father and the Father is in Him. If the secret of His abiding in the Father is this unceasing self-denial—"[I] *can do nothing of myself*" (John 5:19)—this life of most entire and absolute dependence and waiting upon God should be the most marked feature of our Christian life. It must be the first and all-pervading disposition we seek to maintain.

In his writings, William Law especially insisted upon this in his striking repetition of the call to die to self in order to have the birth of divine love in our souls. We must sink down in humility, meekness, patience, and resignation to God. I think that all who enter into this advice will feel the new point given by remembering how entire self-renunciation was not only one of the many virtues in the character of Christ, but the first essential one. Without this self-denial, God could have worked nothing in Him; through this self-denial, God worked all.

Let us make Christ's words our own. "[I] *can do nothing of* [myself]" (John 5:19). Take them as the keynote of a single day. Look up and see the infinite God waiting to do everything as soon as we are ready to give up all to Him and receive all from Him. Bow down in humble worship and wait for the Holy Spirit to work some measure of the mind of Christ in you. Do not be disconcerted if you do not learn the lesson at once. The God of love is waiting to do everything in the one who is willing to be nothing. At moments the teaching appears dangerous; at other times, terribly difficult. The blessed Son of God teaches it to us. This was His whole life: I can do nothing of Myself. He is our life. He will work it in us. And when, as the Lamb of God, He begets His disposition in us, we will be prepared for Him to shine in us in His heavenly glory.

"Nothing of himself"—these words spoken nearly two thousand years ago, coming out of the inmost depths of the heart of

the Son of God—are a seed in which the power of the eternal life is hidden. Take it straight from the heart of Christ and hide it in your heart. Meditate on it until it reveals the beauty of His divine meekness and humility and explains how all the power and glory of God could work in Him. Believe in it as containing the very life and disposition that you need. Believe in Christ whose Spirit dwells in the seed to make it true in you.

Begin in single acts of self-emptying to offer it to God as the one desire of your heart. Count on God accepting them and meeting them with His grace to make the acts into habits and the habits into dispositions. And you can depend on it. There is nothing that will lift you so near to God, nothing that will unite you closer to Christ, nothing that will prepare you for the abiding presence and power of God working in you, as the death to self that is found in the simple words *nothing of myself.*

This truth is one of the keys to the new covenant life. As I believe that God is actually to work all in me, I will see that the one thing that is hindering me is my doing something of myself. As I am willing to learn from Christ by the Holy Spirit to say truly, "Nothing of myself," I will have the true preparation to receive all God has engaged to work and the power to confidently expect it. I will learn that the whole secret of the new covenant is just one thing: God works all! The seal of the covenant stands sure. *"I the Lord have spoken it, and will do it"* (Ezek. 22:14).

Note F

———————◆———————

The Whole Heart

*L*et me give some of the principal passages in which the words "the whole heart" and "all the heart" are used. A careful study of them will show how wholehearted love and service is what God has always asked, because He can, in the very nature of things, ask nothing less. The prayerful and believing acceptance of the words will waken the assurance that such wholehearted love and service is exactly the blessing the new covenant was meant to make possible. That assurance will prepare us for turning to the omnipotence of God to work in us what may have hitherto appeared beyond our reach.

Hear, first, God's word in Deuteronomy 30:6: *"The Lord thy God will circumcise thine heart, to love the Lord thy God with all thine heart and with all thy soul."* (See also verses 9–10.)

Take these words as the expression of God's will concerning His people, and concerning yourself; ask if you could wish to give God anything less. Take this verse as the divine promise of the new covenant—that He will circumcise, will so cleanse the heart to love Him with a wholehearted love, that obedience is within your reach. Now will you not vow afresh to keep this, His first and great commandment?

Listen to Joshua:

*Take diligent heed...to love the L*ORD *your God, and to walk in all his ways, and to keep his commandments, and to cleave unto him, and to serve him with all your heart and with all your soul.* (Josh. 22:5)

Listen to Samuel: *"Turn not aside from following the L*ORD, *but serve the L*ORD *with all your heart....Only fear the L*ORD, *and serve him in truth with all your heart"* (1 Sam. 12:20, 24).

Hear Solomon in his temple prayer: *"If they...return unto thee with all their heart, and with all their soul,...hear thou their prayer"* (1 Kings 8:47–49).

Oh, that all would ask God to give them, by the Holy Spirit, a simple vision of Himself—claiming, giving, accepting, blessing, and delighting in the love and service of the whole heart—the sacrifice of the whole burnt offering. Surely they would fall down and join the ranks of those who have given it; and refuse to think of anything as religious life, worship, or service, except the things in which their whole hearts went out to God. Shall we not begin asking more earnestly than ever, as often as we see men engaged in their earthly pursuits in search of money, pleasure, fame, or power, with their whole hearts, Is this the spirit in which Christians consider that God must be served? Is this the spirit in which I serve Him? Is not this the one thing needful in our religion?

Now, just a few words more from the prophets about the new time, the great change that can come into our lives. Let my reader not be weary of reading carefully these divine words: they contain the secret, the seed, the living power of a complete transition out of a life in the bondage of halfhearted service, to the glorious liberty of the children of God.

I will give them one heart...that they may fear me for ever. And I will make an everlasting covenant with them, that I will not turn away from them, to do them good; but I will put my fear in their hearts, that they shall not depart from me. Yea, I will rejoice over them to do them good...with my whole heart and my whole soul. (Jer. 32:39–41)

It is to be all God's doing. And He is to do it with His whole heart and His whole soul. It is the vision of this God with His whole heart loving us, longing and delighting to fulfill His promise, and make us wholly His own, that we need. This vision makes it impossible not to love Him with our whole hearts.

Now one word from our Lord Jesus: *"Thou shalt love the Lord thy God with all thy heart"* (Matt. 22:37). This is the first and great commandment. This is the sum of that law He came to fulfill for us and in us, came to enable us to fulfill.

> *For what the law could not do, in that it was weak through the flesh, God sending his own Son...condemned sin in the flesh: that the righteousness of the law metright be fulfilled in us, who walk...after the Spirit.* (Rom. 8:3–4)

Book Four

———— ◆ ————

Divine Healing

Contents

Preface

———◆———

*T*he publication of this work may be regarded as a testimony of my faith in divine healing. After being stopped for more than two years in the exercise of my ministry, I was healed by the mercy of God in answer to the prayer of those who see in Him *"the Lord that healeth thee"* (Exod. 15:26).

This healing, granted to faith, has been the source of rich spiritual blessing to me. I have clearly seen that the church possesses in Jesus, our divine Healer, an inestimable treasure, which it does not yet know how to appreciate. I have been convinced anew of what the Word of God teaches us in this matter, and of what the Lord expects of us. I am sure that if Christians learned to realize, in a practical sense, the presence of the Lord who heals in their everyday lives, their spiritual lives would thereby be developed and sanctified.

I can, therefore, no longer keep silent. This series of meditations is published to show, according to the Word of God, that *"the prayer of faith"* (James 5:15) is the means appointed by God for the cure of the sick. My purpose is to show that this truth is in perfect accord with Holy Scripture, and that the study of this truth is essential for everyone who desires to see the Lord manifest His power and His glory in the midst of His children.

—Andrew Murray

Chapter 1

———————————◆◄———————————

Pardon and Healing

But that ye may know that the Son of man hath power
on earth to forgive sins, (then saith he to the sick of the palsy,)
Arise, take up thy bed, and go unto thine house.
—Matthew 9:6

*M*an is a combination of opposing natures; he is at the same time spirit and matter, heaven and earth, soul and body. For this reason, on one side he is the son of God, and on the other he is doomed to destruction because of the Fall. Sin in his soul and sickness in his body bear witness to the right that death has over him. It is this twofold nature that has been redeemed by divine grace. When the psalmist called upon all that was within him to bless the Lord for His benefits, he cried, *"Bless the Lord, O my soul,…who forgiveth all thine iniquities; who healeth all thy diseases"* (Ps. 103:2–3). When Isaiah foretold the deliverance of his people, he added, *"The inhabitant shall not say, I am sick: the people that dwell therein shall be forgiven their iniquity"* (Isa. 33:24).

This prediction was accomplished beyond all anticipation when Jesus the Redeemer came down to this earth. How numerous were the healings brought about by Him who had come to establish on earth the kingdom of heaven! By His own acts and afterward by the commands that He left for His disciples, He showed us clearly that the preaching of the Gospel and the healing of the sick went together in the salvation that He came to bring. Both are given as evidence of His mission as the Messiah: *"The blind receive their sight, and the lame walk,...and the poor have the gospel preached to them"* (Matt. 11:5). Jesus, who took upon Himself the soul and body of man, delivers both in equal measure from the consequences of sin.

Healing for Body and Soul

This truth is nowhere more evident or better demonstrated than in the healing of the paralytic. The Lord Jesus began by saying to him, *"Thy sins be forgiven thee"* (Matt. 9:5), after which He added, *"Arise, take up thy bed, and go."* The pardon of sin and the healing of sickness complete one another, for in the eyes of God, who sees our entire natures, sin and sickness are as closely united as the body and the soul.

With us, sin belongs to the spiritual domain; we recognize that sin is under God's just displeasure, and that it is justly condemned by Him. Sickness, on the contrary, seems only a part of the present condition of our natures, having nothing to do with God's condemnation and His righteousness. Some go so far as to say that sickness is a proof of the love and grace of God.

But neither the Scripture nor Jesus Christ Himself ever speaks of sickness in this light, nor do they ever present sickness as a blessing, as proof of God's love that should be borne with patience. The Lord spoke to the disciples of various sufferings that they would have to bear, but when He spoke of sickness, it was always as an evil caused by sin and Satan, from which we should be delivered. Very solemnly, He declared that every disciple of His would have to bear his cross (Matt. 16:24), but He never taught one sick person to resign himself to being sick.

Everywhere, Jesus healed the sick; everywhere, He dealt with healing as one of the graces belonging to the kingdom of heaven. Sin in the soul and sickness in the body both bear witness to the power of Satan, and *"the Son of God was manifested, that he might destroy the works of the devil"* (1 John 3:8).

Jesus came to deliver men from sin and sickness so that He might make known the love of the Father. In His actions, in His teaching of the disciples, and in the work of the apostles, pardon and healing were always found together. Their appearance depended on the development, or the faith, of those to whom they spoke. Sometimes healing prepared the way for the acceptance of forgiveness; sometimes forgiveness preceded healing, which, coming afterward, sealed it.

In the early part of His ministry, Jesus cured many of the sick, finding them eager to believe in the possibility of their healing. In this way, He sought to influence hearts to receive Him as One who could also pardon sin. When He saw that the paralytic could receive pardon at once, He pardoned him, because that was of the greatest importance. Then came the healing, which put a seal on the pardon he had been given.

We see, in the accounts given in the Gospels, that it was more difficult for the Jews at that time to believe in the pardon of their sins than in divine healing. Now, it is just the opposite. The Christian church has heard so much preaching about the forgiveness of sins that the thirsty soul easily receives this message of grace. But it is not the same with divine healing, which is rarely mentioned. Believers who have experienced it are not many.

Healing is not always given in this day, as it was in those times, to the multitudes whom Christ healed without any previous conversion. In order to receive healing, it is usually necessary to begin by confessing sin and desiring to live a holy life. This is without doubt the reason people find it more difficult to believe in healing than in forgiveness. This is also why those who receive healing receive at the same time new spiritual blessings; they feel more closely united to the Lord Jesus and learn to love and serve Him better. Unbelief may attempt to separate these two gifts, but they are always united in Christ. He is always the same Savior both of the soul and of the body, equally ready to grant pardon and healing. The redeemed may always cry, *"Bless the LORD, O my soul,...who forgiveth all thine iniquities; who healeth all thy diseases"* (Ps. 103:2–3).

Chapter 2

---◆---

Because of Your Unbelief

*Then came the disciples to Jesus apart, and said, Why
could not we cast him out? And Jesus said unto them,
Because of your unbelief: for verily I say unto you, If ye
have faith as a grain of mustard seed, ye shall say unto this
mountain, Remove hence to yonder place; and it shall remove;
and nothing shall be impossible unto you.*
—Matthew 17:19–20

When the Lord Jesus sent His disciples into different parts of
Palestine, He endued them with a double power, to cast
out unclean spirits and to heal all sickness and all infirmity. (See
Matthew 10:1.) He did the same for the seventy who came back
to Him with joy, saying, *"Lord, even the devils are subject unto
us through thy name"* (Luke 10:17). On the day of the Trans-
figuration, while the Lord was still on the mountain, a father
brought his son who was possessed with a demon to His disciples, beseeching them to cast out the evil spirit, but they could
not.

After Jesus had cured the child, the disciples asked why
they had been unable to do it themselves, as they had in other
cases. He answered them, *"Because of your unbelief."* It was

their unbelief, and not the will of God, that had been the cause of their defeat.

Is Divine Healing for Today?

In our day, divine healing is very little believed in because it has almost entirely disappeared from the Christian church. One may ask the reason, and here are the two answers that have been given. The greater number think that miracles—the gift of healing included—should be limited to the time of the early church, that their purpose was to establish the foundation of Christianity, but that, from that time, circumstances have changed.

Other believers say unhesitatingly that if the church has lost these gifts, it is its own fault. It is because the church has become worldly that the Spirit acts so feebly in it. It is because it has not remained in a direct and habitual relationship with the full power of the unseen world. But if men and women would spring up in the church, living the life of faith and of the Holy Spirit, entirely consecrated to their God, it would see again the manifestation of the same gifts as in former times.

Which of these two opinions coincides with the Word of God? Is it by the will of God that the *"gifts of healing"* (1 Cor. 12:9) have been suppressed, or is it man who is responsible for the lack of healings? Is it the will of God that miracles should not take place? If this is so, will He no longer give the faith that produces them? Or again, is it the church that has been guilty of lacking faith?

The Bible does not authorize us, either by the words of the Lord or His apostles, to believe that the gifts of healing were granted only to the early church. On the contrary, the promise that Jesus made to the apostles shortly before His ascension, when He gave them instructions concerning their mission, appears to be applicable to all times. (See Mark 16:15–18.) Paul placed the gift of healing among the operations of the Holy Spirit. James gave a precise command on this matter without any restriction of time. (See James 5:14–15.) The entire Scriptures declare that these graces will be granted according to the measure of the Spirit and of faith.

It is also alleged that at the outset of each new dispensation God works miracles, and that it is His ordinary course of action. But it is nothing of the kind. Think of the people of God in the former dispensation, in the time of Abraham, all through the life of Moses, in the Exodus from Egypt, under Joshua, in the time of the Judges and of Samuel, under the reign of David and other godly kings up to Daniel's time. During more than a thousand years, miracles took place.

It is said that miracles were much more necessary in the early days of Christianity than later. But what about the power of heathenism even in this day, wherever the Gospel seeks to combat it? It is impossible to conclude that miracles would have been more necessary for the heathen in Ephesus (see Acts 19:11–12) than for the heathen scattered throughout the world today. Ignorance and unbelief reign even in the midst of Christian nations.

Are we not driven to say that there is a need for manifest acts of the power of God to sustain the testimony of believers and to prove that God is with them? Besides, among believers themselves, how much doubt and how much weakness there is! How their faith needs to be awakened and stimulated by some evidence of the presence of the Lord in their midst! One part of our being consists of flesh and blood; it is therefore in our flesh and blood that God wills to manifest His presence.

Unbelief Hinders Healing

In order to prove that it is the church's unbelief that has lost the gift of healing, let us see what the Bible says about it. Does it not often put us on our guard against unbelief, against all that can estrange and turn us from our God? The history of the church shows us the necessity of these warnings. It furnishes us with numerous examples of backward steps—of world-pleasing—in which faith was weakened to the same extent that the spirit of the world took the upper hand. Faith is possible only to those who live in the spiritual world.

Until the third century, healings by faith in Christ were numerous, but in the centuries following, they became more infrequent. Do we not know from the Bible that it is always unbelief that hinders the mighty working of God? Oh, that we could learn to believe in the promise of God! God does not go back on His promises.

Jesus still heals both soul and body. Even now, salvation offers us healing and holiness, and the Holy Spirit is always ready to give us some manifestations of His power. When we ask why this divine power is not seen more often, He answers us, *"Because of your unbelief."* The more we allow ourselves to personally experience sanctification by faith, the more we also experience healing by faith. These two doctrines work together. The more the Spirit of God lives and acts in the souls of believers, the more miracles He will work in the body. By this, the world will recognize what redemption means.

Chapter 3

---◆---

Jesus and the Doctors

And a certain woman, which had an issue of blood twelve years, and had suffered many things of many physicians, and had spent all that she had, and was nothing bettered, but rather grew worse, When she had heard of Jesus, came in the press behind, and touched his garment. For she said, If I may touch but his clothes, I shall be whole. And straightway the fountain of her blood was dried up; and she felt in her body that she was healed of that plague. And Jesus, immediately knowing in himself that virtue had gone out of him, turned him about in the press, and said, Who touched my clothes?...The woman...came and fell down before him, and told him all the truth. And he said unto her, Daughter, thy faith hath made thee whole; go in peace, and be whole of thy plague.
—Mark 5:25–30, 33–34

We may be thankful to God for giving us doctors. Their vocation is one of the most noble, for a large number of them truly seek to do—with love and compassion—all they can to alleviate the suffering that burdens humanity as a result of sin. There are even some who are zealous servants of Jesus Christ, seeking also the good of their patients' souls. Nevertheless, it is

Jesus Himself who is always the first, the best, and the greatest Physician.

Jesus heals diseases for which earthly physicians can do nothing, for the Father gave Him this power when He charged Him with the work of our redemption. Jesus, in taking our human body upon Himself, delivered it from the dominion of sin and Satan. He has made our bodies temples of the Holy Spirit, and members of His own body (1 Cor. 6:15, 19). Even in our day, how many have been given up by the doctors as incurable? How many cases of cancer, infection, paralysis, heart disease, blindness, and deafness have been healed by Him? Is it not then astonishing that so small a number of the sick come to Him?

Jesus' method is quite different from that of earthly physicians. They seek to serve God in making use of remedies that are found in the natural world, according to the natural properties of each, while the healing that proceeds from Jesus is of a totally different order. It is by divine power—the power of the Holy Spirit—that Jesus heals. The difference between these two ways of healing is very striking.

In order to understand it better, consider this example: here is a physician who is an unbeliever, but extremely clever in his profession. Many sick people owe their healing to him. God gives this result by means of the prescribed remedies and the physician's knowledge of them. Here is another physician who is a believer, and who prays God's blessing on the remedies that he employs. In this case also, a large number are healed, but in neither case does the healing bring with it any spiritual blessing. They will be preoccupied, even the believing among them, with the remedies that they use much more than with what the Lord may be doing with them. In some instances, their healing may be more hurtful than beneficial to their spiritual lives. On the other hand, when it is Jesus alone to whom the sick person applies for healing, he learns to rely no longer on remedies alone, but to put himself into direct contact with Christ's love and His almightiness. In order to obtain such healing, he must begin by confessing and renouncing his sins, and exercising a living faith. Then, healing will come directly from the Lord, who takes possession of the sick body. It thus becomes a blessing for the soul as well as for the body.

"But is it not God who has given medical treatments to man?" it is asked. "Doesn't their power come from Him?" Without a doubt it does. But on the other hand, is it not God who has given us His Son with all power to heal? Will we ignore spiritual means as we follow the way of natural law—as do those who do not yet know Christ or those whose faith is still too weak to abandon themselves to His almightiness? Or, rather, will we choose the way of faith, receiving healing from the Lord and from the Holy Spirit, seeing therein the result and the proof of our redemption?

The healing that is brought about by our Lord Jesus brings with it and leaves behind it more real blessing than the healing that is obtained through physicians' means alone. Healing that relies only on human means has been a misfortune to the spiritual lives of more persons than one. Although thoughts of the Lord may cross the sick man's mind while he's still on his sick-bed, once he has been healed, he finds himself far from the Lord.

Additional Blessings Come When Christ Heals

It is not that way when it is Jesus who heals. Healing is granted after confession of sin; therefore, it brings the sufferer nearer to Jesus, and it establishes a new link between him and the Lord. It causes him to experience Christ's love and power; it begins within him a new life of faith and holiness. When the woman who had touched the hem of Christ's garment felt that she was healed, she learned something of what divine love means. She went away, possessing the words, *"Daughter, thy faith hath made thee whole; go in peace."*

Oh, you who are suffering from some sickness, know that Jesus, the sovereign Healer, is yet in our midst. He is close to us, and He is giving many new proofs of His presence to His church.

Are you ready to break with the world, to abandon yourself to Him with faith and confidence? Then fear not.

Remember that divine healing is a part of the life of faith. If nobody around you can help you in prayer, if no elder is at hand to pray the prayer of faith, do not be afraid to go to the Lord yourself in the silence of solitude, like the woman who touched the hem of His garment. Commit the care of your body to Him. Become quiet before Him, and like the poor woman, say, "I will be healed." Perhaps it may take some time to break the chains of your unbelief, but assuredly no one who waits on Him will be ashamed (Ps. 25:3).

Chapter 4

———◆———

Health and Salvation by the Name of Jesus

*And his name through faith in his name hath made
this man strong, whom ye see and know: yea,
the faith which is by him hath given him this perfect
soundness in the presence of you all.*
—Acts 3:16

*Be it known unto you all, and to all the people of
Israel, that by the name of Jesus Christ of Nazareth,
whom ye crucified, whom God raised from the dead, even
by him doth this man stand here before you whole....
Neither is there salvation in any other: for there is
none other name under heaven given among men,
whereby we must be saved.*
—Acts 4:10, 12

After Pentecost, the paralytic was healed through Peter and
John at the gate of the temple. It was *"in the name of Jesus
Christ of Nazareth"* (Acts 3:6) that they said to him, *"Rise up
and walk"* (v. 6). As soon as the people in their amazement ran

together to them, Peter declared that it was the name of Jesus that had so completely healed the man.

As a result of this miracle and of Peter's discourse, many people who had heard the Word believed (Acts 4:4). The next day, Peter repeated these words before the Sanhedrin: *"By the name of Jesus Christ of Nazareth...doth this man stand here before you whole"*; and then he added, *"There is none other name under heaven...whereby we must be saved."* This statement of Peter declares to us that the name of Jesus both heals and saves. We have here a teaching of the highest importance for divine healing.

We see that healing and health form part of Christ's salvation. Peter clearly stated this in his discourse to the Sanhedrin where, having spoken of healing, he immediately went on to speak of salvation by Christ. (See Acts 4:10, 12.) In heaven, even our bodies will have their part in salvation. Salvation will not be complete for us until our bodies enjoy the full redemption of Christ. Shouldn't we believe in this work of redemption here below? Even here on earth, the health of our bodies is a fruit of the salvation that Jesus has acquired for us.

Health and Salvation Are Obtained by Faith in Christ

We also see that health, as well as salvation, is to be obtained by faith. The tendency of man by nature is to bring about his own salvation by his works, and it is only with difficulty that he comes to receive it by faith. But when it is a question of the healing of the body, he has still more difficulty in seizing it. He finally accepts salvation because by no other means can he open the door of heaven. But it is much easier for him to accept well-known remedies for his body. Why, then, should he seek divine healing?

Happy is he who comes to understand that it is the will of God to heal, to manifest the power of Jesus, and to reveal to us His fatherly love. It is also His will that we exercise and confirm our faith, to make us prove the power of redemption in the body as well as in the soul. The body is part of our being. Even the body has been saved by Christ. Therefore, it is in our bodies that our Father wills to manifest the power of redemption, and to let men see that Jesus lives. Oh, let us believe in the name of Jesus! Was it not in the name of Jesus that perfect health was given to the crippled man? And were not the words *"Thy faith hath made thee whole"* (Mark 5:34) pronounced when the woman with the issue of blood was healed? Let us seek, then, to obtain divine healing.

Wherever the Spirit acts with power, He works divine healings. If ever there was an abundance of miracles, it was at Pentecost, for then the word of the apostles worked mightily, and the pouring out of the Holy Spirit was great. Well, it is precisely because the Spirit acted powerfully that His working was so visible in the body. If divine healing is seen but rarely in our day, we can attribute it to no other cause than that the Spirit does not act with power. The unbelief of worldlings and the lack of zeal among believers stop His working. The healings that God is giving here and there are the initial signs of all the spiritual graces that are promised to us, and it is only the Holy Spirit who reveals the almightiness of the name of Jesus to operate such healings. Let us pray earnestly for the Holy Spirit, let us place ourselves unreservedly under His direction, and let us seek to be firm in our faith in the name of Jesus, whether for preaching salvation or for the work of healing.

God grants healing to glorify the name of Jesus. Let us seek to be healed by Jesus, so that His name may be glorified. It is sad to see how little the power of His name is recognized, how little it is used in preaching and prayer. Treasures of divine grace—of which Christians deprive themselves by their lack of faith and zeal—are hidden in the name of Jesus.

It is the will of God to glorify His Son in the church, and He will do it wherever He finds faith. Whether among believers or among the heathen, He is ready with virtue from on high to awaken consciences and to bring hearts to obedience. God is ready to manifest the power of His Son, and to do it in striking ways in bodies as well as in souls. Let us believe it for ourselves; let us believe it for others, for the circle of believers around us, and also for the church in the whole world. Let us give ourselves to believe with firm faith in the power of the name of Jesus. Let us ask great things in His name, counting on His promise, and we will see that God still does wonders by the name of His holy Son.

Chapter 5

───◆───

Not by Our Own Power

And when Peter saw it, he answered unto the people,
Ye men of Israel, why marvel ye at this? or why look
ye so earnestly on us, as though by our own power
or holiness we had made this man to walk?
—Acts 3:12

A s soon as the crippled man had been healed at the gate of
the temple, the people ran together to Peter and John. Peter,
seeing this miracle was attributed to their power and holiness,
lost no time in setting them right by telling them that all the glory
of this miracle belonged to Jesus, and that it is He in whom we
must believe.

Peter and John were undoubtedly full of faith and of holiness; they may have been the holiest and most zealous servants
of God in their time. Otherwise, God might not have chosen
them as instruments in this case of healing. But they knew
that their holiness of life was not of themselves, that it was of
God through the Holy Spirit. They thought so little of themselves
that they ignored their own holiness and knew only one thing—
that all power belonged to their Master. They hastened, then, to
declare that in this act of healing, their efforts counted for nothing; it was the work of the Lord alone! This is the purpose of

divine healing: to be a proof of the power of Jesus, to be a witness in the eyes of men of what He is, proclaiming His divine intervention and attracting hearts to Him. Those whom the Lord uses in helping others should remember Peter's words: "[Not] *by our own power or holiness."*

The Glory Belongs to the Lord

It is necessary to insist on this because of the tendency of believers to think the contrary. Those who have recovered their health in answer to *"the prayer of faith"* (James 5:15) and *"the effectual fervent prayer of a righteous man"* (v. 16) are in danger of being too much occupied with the human instrument that God is pleased to employ, and to think that the power lies in man's piety.

Doubtless the prayer of faith is the result of real godliness, but those who possess it will be the first to acknowledge that it does not come from themselves, nor from any efforts of their own. They fear to rob the Lord of the least particle of the glory that belongs to Him. They know that if they do so, they will compel Him to withdraw His grace from them. It is their great desire to see the souls that God has blessed through them enter into a direct and increasingly intimate communion with the Lord Jesus Christ Himself since that is the result that their healing should produce. Thus they insist that it is not caused by their own power or holiness.

Such testimony on their part is necessary to reply to the erroneous accusations of unbelievers. The church of Christ needs to hear clearly announced that it is because of her worldliness and unbelief that she has lost these spiritual gifts of healing (1 Cor. 12:9), and that the Lord restores those gifts to those who, with faith and obedience, have consecrated their lives to Him. This grace cannot reappear, however, without being preceded by a renewal of faith and of holiness. But then, says the world, and with it a large number of Christians, "You are laying claim to the possession of a higher order of faith and holiness; you consider yourselves holier than others." To such accusations, this word of Peter is the only reply before God and before man, confirmed by a life of deep and real humility: "[Not] *by our own power or holiness.*" "*Not unto us, O LORD, not unto us, but unto thy name give glory, for thy mercy, and for thy truth's sake*" (Ps. 115:1).

Such a testimony is necessary also in view of our own hearts and the wiles of Satan. As long as, through the church's unfaithfulness, the gifts of healing are but rarely given, those children of God who do receive these gifts are in danger of taking pride in them, imagining that they are somehow special. Satan does not forget to persecute them by such insinuations, and woe unto them if they listen to him. They should be made aware of his devices. Then, they need to pray continually to the Lord to keep them in humility, the true means of obtaining continually more grace. If they persevere in humility, they will recognize that the more God makes use of them, the more they will be penetrated with the conviction that it is God alone who works by them, and that all the glory belongs to Him. "*Not I, but the grace of God which was with me*" (1 Cor. 15:10)—such is their watchword.

Finally, this testimony is useful for the weaker ones who long for salvation and who desire to receive Christ as their Healer. They hear of full consecration and entire obedience, but they form a false idea of it. They think they must attain such a high degree of knowledge and of perfection that they become discouraged. Remember this: it is not by our own power or holiness that we obtain grace, but by a faith quite simple—a childlike faith—that knows that it has no power or holiness of its own, and that commits itself completely to Him. He is faithful, and His almightiness can fulfill His promise. Oh, let us not seek to do or to be anything of ourselves! It is only as we feel our own powerlessness, and expect everything from God and His Word, that we realize the glorious way in which the Lord heals sickness by faith in His name.

Chapter 6

According to the Measure of Faith

And Jesus said unto the centurion, Go thy way;
and as thou hast believed, so be it done unto thee.
And his servant was healed in the selfsame hour.
—Matthew 8:13

*T*his passage of Scripture brings us one of the principal laws of the kingdom of heaven. In order to understand God's ways with His people and our relationship with the Lord, it is necessary to understand this law thoroughly and not to deviate from it. Not only does God give or withhold His grace according to the faith or unbelief of each, but also it is granted in greater or lesser measure in proportion to the faith that receives it. Therefore, He can bless us only to the extent to which each believer yields himself up to His divine working and opens all his heart to Him. Faith in God is nothing less than the full opening of the heart to receive everything from God. Therefore, man can receive divine grace only according to his faith. This applies as much to divine healing as to any other grace of God.

This truth is confirmed by the spiritual blessings that may result from sickness. Two questions are often asked. First, is it not God's will that His children should sometimes remain in a prolonged state of sickness? Second, since it is recognized that divine healing brings with it greater spiritual blessing than the sickness itself, why does God allow some of His children to remain sick for many years, and while in this condition, still bless them in communion with Himself? The answer to these two questions is that God gives to His children according to their faith.

We have already had occasion to remark that in the same degree to which the church has become worldly, its faith in divine healing has diminished, until at last it has almost disappeared. Believers do not seem to be aware that they may ask God for the healing of their sicknesses, and that, through their healing, they may be sanctified and equipped for His service. They have come to seek only submission to His will and to regard sickness as a means to be separate from the world. In such conditions, the Lord gives them what they ask. He would have been willing to give them much more—to grant them healing in answer to the prayer of faith—but they lacked the faith to receive it.

God always meets His children where they are, however weak they may be. The sick ones, therefore, who have desired to be submissive to His will at all costs will enjoy a deep inner communion with Him. But they might have been able to receive healing, in addition, as a proof that God accepted their submission. If this has not happened, it is because faith has failed them to ask for it.

"As thou hast believed, so be it done unto thee." These words give the reply to yet another question: how can you say that divine healing brings so much spiritual blessing with it, when one sees that the greater number of those who were healed by the Lord Jesus received nothing more than a deliverance from their present sufferings, without giving any proof that they were also spiritually blessed? Here again, as they believed, so was it done unto them.

A good number of sick people, having witnessed the healing of others, gained just enough confidence in Jesus to be healed. Jesus granted them their requests, without adding other blessings for their souls. Before His ascension, the Lord did not have as free an entrance as He now has into the hearts of men, because *"the Holy Ghost was not yet given"* (John 7:39). The healing of the sick was then hardly more than a blessing for the body. It was only later, with the dispensation of the Spirit, that the conviction and confession of sin have become, for the believer, the first grace to be received, the essential condition for obtaining healing. Paul told us this in his epistle to the Corinthians, and James in his to the twelve tribes scattered abroad. (See 1 Corinthians 11:31–32; James 5:16.) Thus, the degree of spiritual grace that it is possible for us to receive depends on the amount of our faith, whether it be for its external manifestation or for its influence on our inner lives.

We commend, then, to every suffering one who is looking for healing and seeking to know Jesus as his divine Healer, not to let himself be hindered by his unbelief and not to doubt the promises of God. Be strong in faith, giving glory to God as is His due. *"As thou hast believed, so be it done unto thee."* If with all your heart you trust in the living God, you will be abundantly blessed. Do not doubt it.

Faith's part is to grasp that which appears impossible or strange to human eyes. Let us be willing to be considered fools for Christ's sake (1 Cor. 4:10). Let us not fear to be considered weak-minded in the eyes of the world and of uninformed Christians because, on the authority of the Word of God, we believe what others cannot yet admit. Do not, then, let yourself be discouraged in your expectation, even though God should delay to answer you, or your sickness should seem to worsen.

Place your feet firmly on the immovable rock of God's own Word. Pray to the Lord to manifest His almightiness in your body because you are one of the members of His body (see 1 Corinthians 12:12–13) and *"the temple of the Holy Spirit"* (1 Cor. 6:19). Persevere in believing in Him with the firm assurance that He has undertaken for you, that He has made Himself responsible for your body, and that His healing power will glorify Him in you even as it heals you.

Chapter 7

———◆◆———

The Way of Faith

And straightway the father of the child cried out, and said with tears, Lord, I believe; help thou mine unbelief.
—Mark 9:24

*T*hese words have been a help and strength to thousands of souls in their pursuit of salvation and the gifts of God. Notice that it is in relation to an afflicted child that they were said, as the child's father fought the fight of faith and sought healing from the Lord Jesus. In them, we see that in one and the same soul a struggle between faith and unbelief can occur. It is not without a struggle that we come to believe in Jesus and in His complete power to heal the sick. In this truth, we find the necessary encouragement for realizing the Savior's power.

I speak here especially to sufferers who do not doubt the power or the will of the Lord Jesus to heal in this day, but who lack the boldness to accept healing for themselves. They believe in the divine power of Christ; they believe in His goodwill to heal; they believe, either from the Scriptures or from present-day healings, that the Lord can help even them, but they shrink back from accepting healing. They cannot say with faith, "The Lord has heard me. I know that He is healing me."

Take notice, first, that without faith no one can be healed. When the father of the afflicted child said to Jesus, *"If thou canst do any thing, have compassion on us, and help us"* (Mark 9:22), Jesus replied, *"If thou canst believe"* (v. 23). Jesus had the power to heal, and He was ready to do it, but He cast responsibility on the man. *"If thou canst believe, all things are possible to him that believeth"* (v. 23).

In order to obtain your healing from Jesus, it is not enough to pray. Prayer without faith is powerless. It is *"the prayer of faith"* (James 5:15) that saves the sick. If you have already asked for healing from the Lord, or if others have asked it for you, you must, before you are conscious of any change, be able to say with faith, "On the authority of God's Word, I have the assurance that He hears me and that I am healed." To have faith means to surrender your body absolutely into the Lord's hands, and to leave yourself entirely to Him. Faith receives healing as a spiritual grace that proceeds from the Lord, even while there is no conscious change in the body. Faith can glorify God and say, *"Bless the LORD, O my soul,...who healeth all* [my] *diseases"* (Ps. 103:2–3). The Lord requires this faith so that He may heal.

But how is such faith to be obtained? Tell God of the unbelief that you find in your heart, and count on Him for deliverance from it. Faith is not money by which your healing can be purchased from the Lord. It is He who desires to awaken and develop in you the necessary faith. "Help my unbelief," cried the father of the child. It was his ardent desire that his faith should not come short.

Confess to the Lord all the difficulty you have in believing Him on the ground of His Word. Tell Him you want to be rid of this unbelief, that you bring it to Him with a will to listen only to His Word. Do not lose time in deploring your unbelief, but look to Jesus. The light of His countenance will enable you to find the power to believe in Him (Ps. 43:3). He calls on you to trust in Him. Listen to Him and, by His grace, faith will triumph in you. Say to Him, "Lord, I am still aware of the unbelief that is in me. I find it difficult to believe that I am assured of my healing just because I possess Him who works it in me. Nevertheless, I want to conquer this unbelief. You, Lord, will give me the victory. I desire to believe, I will believe, and by Your grace, I can believe. Yes, Lord, I believe, for You help me with my unbelief." It is when we are in intimate communion with the Lord, and when our hearts respond to His, that unbelief is overcome and conquered.

It is necessary to testify to the faith one has. Believe what the Lord says to you and believe, above all, who He is. Lean completely on His promises. *"The prayer of faith shall save the sick"* (James 5:15). *"I am the Lord that healeth thee"* (Exod. 15:26). Look to Jesus, who *"bare our sicknesses"* (Matt. 8:17) and who healed all who came to Him. Count on the Holy Spirit to manifest the presence of Jesus in your heart, and to work the power of His grace in your body. Praise the Lord without waiting to feel better or to have more faith. Praise Him, and say with David, *"O Lord, my God, I cried unto thee, and thou hast healed me"* (Ps. 30:2).

Divine healing is a spiritual grace that can be received only spiritually and by faith before its effect is felt on the body. Accept it, then, and give glory to God. When the Lord Jesus had commanded the unclean spirit to come out of the child, many of the onlookers believed the child had died. If, therefore, your sickness does not yield at once, or if Satan and your own unbelief attempt to get the upper hand, do not heed them. Cling closely to Jesus, your Healer, and He will surely heal you.

Chapter 8

———— ►◆◄ ————

Your Body Is the Temple
of the Holy Spirit

*Know ye not that your bodies are the members of Christ?
shall I then take the members of Christ, and make them the
members of an harlot? God forbid....What? know ye not that
your body is the temple of the Holy Ghost which is in you,
which ye have of God, and ye are not your own? For ye
are bought with a price: therefore glorify God in your body,
and in your spirit, which are God's.*
—1 Corinthians 6:15, 19–20

*T*he Bible teaches us that the body of Christ is the company
of the faithful. These words are generally taken in their spiritual sense, but the Bible asks us specifically whether we know
that our bodies are the members of Christ. In the same way,
when the Bible speaks of the indwelling of the Holy Spirit or of
Christ, we limit His presence to the spiritual part of our being.
Nevertheless, the Bible says expressly, *"Know ye not that your
body is the temple of the Holy Ghost?"* The church needs to
understand that the body also has part in the redemption that
is by Christ, by which it ought to be brought back to its original
destiny, to be the dwelling place of the Holy Spirit, to serve

as His instrument, and to be sanctified by His presence. The church must also recognize the place that divine healing has in the Bible and in the counsels of God.

The account of creation tells us that man is composed of three parts. God first formed the body from the dust of the earth, after which He breathed into it *"the breath of life"* (Gen. 2:7). He caused His own life, His Spirit, to enter into it. By this union of Spirit with matter, the man became *"a living soul"* (v. 7). The soul, which is essentially the man, finds its place between the body and the spirit; it is the link that binds them together. By the body, the soul finds itself in relation to the external world; by the spirit, it relates with the invisible world and with God. By means of the soul, the spirit can subject the body to the action of the heavenly powers and, thus, spiritualize it; by means of the soul, the body also can act on the spirit and attract it earthward. The soul, subject to the solicitations of both spirit and body, is in a position to choose between the voice of God, speaking to the spirit, or the voice of the world, speaking through the senses.

This union of spirit and body forms a combination that is unique in the creation. It makes man the jewel of God's work. Other creatures had existed already. Some were like angels—all spirit, without any material body. Others, like the animals, were only flesh, possessing a body animated with a living soul, but devoid of spirit. Man was destined to show that the material body, governed by the spirit, was capable of being transformed by the power of the Spirit of God, and of being thus led to participate in heavenly glory.

We know what sin and Satan have done with this possibility of gradual transformation. By means of the body, the spirit was tempted and seduced; it became a slave of the senses. We know also what God has done to destroy the work of Satan and to accomplish the purpose of creation. *"The Son of God was manifested, that he might destroy the works of the devil"* (1 John 3:8). God prepared a body for His Son (Heb. 10:5). *"The Word was made flesh"* (John 1:14). *"In him dwelleth all the fulness of the Godhead bodily"* (Col. 2:9). *"Who his own self bare our sins in his own body on the tree"* (1 Pet. 2:24). And now Jesus, raised up from the dead with a body as free from sin as His spirit and His soul, communicates to our bodies the virtue of His glorified body. The Lord's Supper is *"the communion of the body of Christ"* (1 Cor. 10:16), and our bodies are *"the members of Christ"* (1 Cor. 6:15).

Faith puts us in possession of everything that the death of Christ and His resurrection obtained for us. It is not only in our spirits and our souls that the life of the risen Jesus manifests its presence here below, but also in our bodies, according to our faith.

"Know ye not that your body is the temple of the Holy Ghost?" Many believers imagine that the Holy Spirit comes to dwell in our bodies as one dwells in a house. This comparison is not a good one. I can dwell in a house without its becoming part of my being. I may leave it without suffering; no vital union exists between my house and me. It is not this way with the presence of our souls and spirits in our bodies.

The life of a plant lives and animates every part of it. In the same way, our souls are not limited to dwell in a certain part of the body—the heart or the head, for instance. It penetrates throughout, even to the ends of the lowest members. The life of the soul pervades the whole body; the life throughout proves the presence of the soul. Similarly, the Holy Spirit comes to dwell in our bodies. He penetrates them entirely. He animates and possesses us infinitely more than we can imagine.

In the same way that the Holy Spirit brings to our souls and spirits the life of Jesus—His holiness, His joy, His strength—He comes also to impart to the sick body all the vigorous vitality of Christ as soon as the hand of faith is stretched out to receive it. When the body is fully subjected to Christ, crucified with Him, renouncing all self-will and independence, desiring nothing but to be the Lord's temple, it is then that the Holy Spirit manifests the power of the risen Savior in the body. Only then can we glorify God in our bodies, leaving Him full freedom to manifest His power in us, to show that He knows how to set His temple free from the domination of sickness, sin, and Satan.

Chapter 9

————◆————

The Body for the Lord

Meats for the belly, and the belly for meats: but God shall destroy both it and them. Now the body is not for fornication, but for the Lord; and the Lord for the body.
—1 Corinthians 6:13

One of the most knowledgeable theologians has said that the redemption and glorification of the body is the end of the ways of God. As we have already seen, this is indeed what God has accomplished in creating man. It is this that makes the inhabitants of heaven wonder and admire when they contemplate the glory of the Son. Clothed with a glorified human body, Jesus has taken His place forever on the throne of God, to share His glory. It is this that God has willed. It shall be recognized in that day when regenerated humanity, forming the body of Christ, shall be truly and visibly the temple of the living God (1 Cor. 6:19). All creation in the new heavens and the new earth will share the glory of the children of God. The material body will then be wholly sanctified and glorified by the Spirit. This body, thus spiritualized, will be the highest glory of the Lord Jesus Christ and of His redeemed.

It is in anticipation of this new condition of things that the Lord attaches a great importance to the indwelling and sanctification of our bodies, here on earth, by His Spirit. This truth is so little understood by believers that they seek the power of the Holy Spirit in their bodies even less. Many of them, believing that this body belongs to them, use it as it pleases them. Not understanding how much the sanctification of the soul and spirit depends on the body, they do not grasp the meaning of the words, "The body is for the Lord," in such a way as to receive them in obedience.

"The body is...for the Lord." What does this mean? The apostle had just said, *"Meats for the belly, and the belly for meats: but God shall destroy both it and them."* Eating and drinking afford the Christian an opportunity of carrying out this truth: *"The body is...for the Lord."* He must indeed learn to eat and drink to the glory of God. By eating, sin and the Fall came about. It was also through eating that the devil sought to tempt our Lord. Thus Jesus Himself sanctified His body in eating only according to the will of His Father. (See Matthew 4:4.) Many believers fail to watch over their bodies, to observe a holy sobriety through the fear of rendering it unfit for the service of God. Eating and drinking should never impede communion with God. On the contrary, they should help us maintain the body in its normal condition.

The apostle spoke also of fornication, this sin that defiles the body, and that is in direct opposition to the words, *"The body is...for the Lord."* It is not simply sexual promiscuity outside the married state, but all voluptuousness, all lack of sobriety regarding sensual pleasure is condemned in these words: *"Your body is the temple of the Holy Ghost"* (1 Cor. 6:19). In the same way, all that goes to maintain the body—to clothe it, strengthen it, give it rest or enjoyment—should be placed under the control of the Holy Spirit. Just as, under the old covenant, the temple was constructed solely for God and for His service, even so our bodies have been created for the Lord and for Him alone.

One of the chief benefits, then, of divine healing is to teach us that our bodies ought to be set free from the yoke of our own wills to become the Lord's property. God does not grant healing in response to our prayers until He has attained the end for which He has permitted the sickness. He wills that this discipline brings us into a more intimate communion with Him. He wants us to understand that we have regarded our bodies as our own property, while they actually belong to the Lord, and that the Holy Spirit seeks to sanctify all their actions. He leads us to understand that if we yield our bodies unreservedly to the influence of the Holy Spirit, we will experience His power in us, and He will heal us by bringing into our bodies the very life of Jesus. He leads us, in short, to say with full conviction, *"The body is...for the Lord."*

There are believers who seek holiness, but only for the soul and spirit. In their ignorance, they forget that the body and all its systems—and even the hands, the ears, the eyes, and the mouth—are called to testify directly to the presence and the grace of God in them. They have not sufficiently taken in these words: *"Your bodies are the members of Christ"* (v. 15). *"If ye through the Spirit do mortify the deeds of the body, ye shall live"* (Rom. 8:13). *"And the very God of peace sanctify you wholly; and I pray God your whole spirit and soul and body be preserved blameless unto the coming of our Lord Jesus Christ"* (1 Thess. 5:23).

Oh, what a renewing takes place in us when, by His own touch, the Lord heals our bodies, when He takes possession of them, and when, by His Spirit, He becomes life and health to them! It is with an indescribable consciousness of holiness, of fear, and of joy that the believer can then offer his body a living sacrifice to receive healing, and to have for his motto these words: *"The body is...for the Lord."*

Chapter 10

————◆————

The Lord for the Body

*Meats for the belly, and the belly for meats: but God shall
destroy both it and them. Now the body is not for fornication,
but for the Lord; and the Lord for the body.*
—1 Corinthians 6:13

There is reciprocity in God's relationship with man. What God has been for me, I ought, in turn, to be for Him. And what I am for Him, He desires to be for me. If, in His love, He gives Himself fully to me, it is in order that I may lovingly give myself fully to Him. In the measure in which I really surrender myself to Him, in that measure, also, He gives Himself back to me. God thus leads the believer to understand that this abandonment of Himself is for our bodies.

The more our lives bear witness that our bodies are for the Lord, the more we experience that *"the Lord* [is] *for the body."* In saying, *"The body is...for the Lord,"* we express the desire to regard our bodies as wholly consecrated, offered in sacrifice to the Lord, and sanctified by Him. In saying, *"The Lord* [is] *for the body,"* we express the precious certainty that our offering has been accepted. We show we believe that, by His Spirit, the Lord will impart to our bodies His own strength and holiness, and that henceforth He will strengthen and keep us.

371

This is a matter of faith. Our bodies are material, weak, feeble, sinful, and mortal. Therefore, it is difficult to grasp the full meaning of the words, *"The Lord* [is] *for the body."* It is the Word of God that enables us to do so. The body was created by the Lord and for the Lord. Jesus took upon Him an earthly body. In His body, He bore our sins on the cross, and thereby set our bodies free from the power of sin. In Christ, the body has been raised again and seated on the throne of God. The body is the habitation of the Holy Spirit; it is called to eternal partnership in the glory of heaven. Therefore, with certainty, and in a wide and universal sense, we can say, "Yes, the Lord Jesus, our Savior, is for the body."

This truth has various applications. In the first place, it is a great help in practical holiness. More than one sin derives its strength from some physical tendency. The recovering alcoholic has a horror of intoxicating drinks, but his appetites can still be a snare to him, gaining victory over his new convictions. If, however, in the conflict, he gives his body with confidence to the Lord, all physical appetite, all desire to drink will be overcome.

Our tempers also often result from our physical constitutions. A nervous, irritable system produces words that are sharp, harsh, and unloving. But let the body, with this physical tendency, be taken to the Lord, and the Holy Spirit will overcome the risings of impatience and sanctify the body, rendering it blameless.

These words, *"The Lord* [is] *for the body,"* are applicable also to the physical strength that the Lord's service demands of us. When David cried, *"It is God that girdeth me with strength"* (Ps. 18:32), he meant physical strength, for he added, *"He maketh my feet like hinds' feet....A bow of steel is broken by mine arms"* (vv. 33–34). Again, these words, *"The LORD is the strength of my life"* (Ps. 27:1), do not refer only to the spiritual man, but to the entire man. Many believers have experienced that the promise, *"They that wait upon the LORD shall renew their strength"* (Isa. 40:31), touched their bodies, and that the Holy Spirit increased their physical strength.

Divine Healing

But it is especially in divine healing that we see the truth of these words: *"The Lord* [is] *for the body."* Yes, Jesus, the sovereign and merciful Healer, is always ready to save and cure. In Switzerland some years ago, there was a young girl near death from tuberculosis. The doctor had advised a milder climate, but she was too weak to take the journey. She learned that Jesus is the Healer of the sick and believed the good news. One night when she was thinking of this subject, it seemed to her that the body of the Lord drew near to her, and that she ought to take these words literally, "His body for our body." From this moment, she began to improve. Some time after, she began to hold Bible readings, and later on she became a zealous and much blessed worker for the Lord among women. She had learned to understand that *"the Lord* [is] *for the body."*

Dear sick one, the Lord has shown you by sickness what power sin has over the body. By your healing, He would like to show you the power of redemption of the body. He calls to show you what you have not understood until now, that *"the body is...for the Lord."* Therefore, give Him your body. Give it to Him with your sickness and your sin, which is the original source of sickness. Always believe that the Lord has taken charge of this body, and He will manifest with power that He really is the Lord, who is for the body. The Lord, who took an earthly body and regenerated it, sends us His divine strength from the highest heaven, where He is now clothed in His glorified body. He is willing thus to manifest His power in our bodies.

Chapter 11

———◆———

Do Not Consider Your Body

*I speak after the manner of men because of the infirmity
of your flesh: for as ye have yielded your members
servants to uncleanness and to iniquity unto iniquity, even
so now yield your members servants to righteousness
unto holiness. For when ye were the servants of sin,
ye were free from righteousness. What fruit had ye then
in those things whereof ye are now ashamed?
for the end of those things is death.*
—Romans 6:19–21

When God promised to give Abraham a son, the patriarch would never have been able to believe in this promise if he had considered his own body, already aged and worn out. But Abraham would see nothing but God and His promise. He looked to the power and faithfulness of God who guaranteed him the fulfillment of His promise.

This kind of faith enables us to lay hold of all the difference there is between the healing that is expected from earthly remedies alone and the healing that is looked for from God. When we use earthly remedies alone for healing, all the attention of the sick one is on the body. Divine healing, however, calls us to turn our attention away from the body, abandoning ourselves—soul and body—to the Lord's care, occupying ourselves with Him alone.

This truth also enables us to see the difference between the sickness retained for blessing and the healing received from the Lord. Some are afraid to take the promises in James 5:13–16 in their literal sense because they say sickness is more profitable to the soul than health. It is true that in the case of healing obtained by earthly remedies, many people would be more spiritually blessed in remaining ill than in recovering health, but it is quite otherwise when healing comes directly from the hand of God. In order for the child of God to receive divine healing, the following usually must take place: sin must be confessed and renounced, one must completely surrender to the Lord, self must be yielded up to be wholly in His hands, and one must firmly believe that Jesus desires to take charge of the body. Then, the healing becomes the beginning of a new life of intimate communion with the Lord.

Thus we learn to relinquish the ultimate care of our health entirely to Him. The smallest indication of the return of the sickness is regarded as a warning not to consider our bodies, but to be occupied with the Lord only.

What a contrast this is from the greater number of sick people who look for healing from earthly remedies alone. Some of them may have been sanctified by the sickness, having learned to lose sight of themselves. But how many more are there who are drawn by the sickness itself to be constantly occupied with themselves and with the condition of their bodies? What infinite care they exercise in observing the least symptom, favorable or unfavorable. What a constant preoccupation to them is their eating and drinking—the anxiety to avoid this or that. How much they are taken up with what they consider is due to them from others—whether they are sufficiently thought of, whether well enough nursed, whether visited often enough. How much time is thus devoted to considering the body and what it needs, rather than to the Lord and the relationship that

He seeks to establish with their souls. Oh, how many are they who, through sickness, are occupied almost exclusively with themselves!

All this is totally different when healing is sought for in faith from the loving God. Then the first thing to learn is to cease to be anxious about the state of your body. You have trusted it to the Lord, and He has taken the responsibility. If you do not see a rapid improvement immediately, but on the contrary the symptoms appear to be more serious, remember that you have entered on a path of faith, and therefore you should not consider the body, but cling only to the living God. The commandment of Christ, *"Take no thought...for your body"* (Matt. 6:25), appears here in a new light. When God told Abraham not to consider his own body, it was so that He could call him to the greatest exercise of faith there is—to see only God and His promise. Sustained by his faith, Abraham gave glory to God, convinced that God would do what He had promised.

Divine healing is a marvelous tie to bind us to the Lord. At first, one may fear to believe that the Lord will stretch forth His mighty hand and touch the body. But, in studying the Word of God, the soul takes courage and confidence. At last, one decides, saying, "I yield up my body into the hands of God, and I leave the care of it to Him." Then the body and its sensations are forgotten, and only the Lord and His promises are in view.

Dear reader, will you also enter this way of faith, very superior to that which is natural? Walk in the steps of Abraham. Learn from him not to consider your own body, and not to doubt through unbelief. To consider the body gives birth to doubts, while clinging to the promise of God and being occupied with Him alone gives entrance into the way of faith, the way of divine healing, which glorifies God.

Chapter 12

———————— ◆ ————————

Discipline and Sanctification

For whom the Lord loveth he chasteneth,...for our profit, that
we might be partakers of his holiness.
—Hebrews 12:6, 10

If a man...purge himself...he shall be a vessel
unto honour, sanctified, and meet for the master's use, and
prepared unto every good work.
—2 Timothy 2:21

To sanctify anything is to set it apart—to consecrate it—to God and to His service. The temple at Jerusalem was holy; that is to say, it was consecrated, dedicated to God to serve Him as a dwelling place. The vessels of the temple were holy because they were devoted to the service of the temple. The priests were holy, chosen to serve God and ready to work for Him. In the same way, the Christian ought also to be sanctified, at the Lord's disposal, ready to do every good work.

When the people of Israel went out of Egypt, the Lord reclaimed them for His service as a holy people. *"Let my people go, that they may serve me"* (Exod. 7:16), He said to Pharaoh.

Set free from their hard bondage, the children of Israel were debtors who immediately entered the service of God, becoming His happy servants. Their deliverance was the road that led to their sanctification.

Again in this day, God is forming a holy people for Himself, and Jesus sets us free so that we may join them. He *"gave himself for us, that he might redeem us from all iniquity, and purify unto himself a peculiar people, zealous of good works"* (Titus 2:14). It is the Lord who breaks the chains by which Satan tries to hold us in bondage. He wants us to be free, wholly free to serve Him. He wills to save us, to deliver both the soul and the body, so that each of the members of the body may be consecrated to Him and placed unreservedly at His disposal.

A large number of Christians do not yet understand all this. They cannot comprehend that the purpose of their deliverance is that they may be sanctified, prepared to serve their God. They make use of their lives and their bodies to obtain their own satisfaction; consequently, they do not feel at liberty to ask for healing with faith. It is to chasten them that the Lord permits Satan to inflict sickness on them, and by it keeps them chained and prisoners. God chastens us *"for our profit, that we may be partakers of his holiness,"* and that we may be sanctified, *"meet for the master's use."*

The discipline that sickness inflicts brings great blessings with it. It is a call to the sick one to reflect; it leads him to see that God is occupied with him and seeks to show him what there is that still separates him from the Master. God speaks to him, calling him to examine His ways, to acknowledge that he has lacked holiness, and that the purpose of the chastisement is to make him a partaker of His holiness. He awakens within him the desire to be enlightened by the Holy Spirit down to the inmost recesses of his heart, to get a clear idea of what his life has been up to the present time—a life of self-will, very unlike the holy life that God requires of him. He leads him to confess his sins, to entrust them to the Lord Jesus, to believe that the Savior can deliver him from them. He urges him to yield to Him, to consecrate his life to Him, to die to himself so that he may be able to live for God.

Sanctification is not something that you can accomplish yourself. It cannot even be produced by God in you as something that you can possess and contemplate yourself. No, it is the Holy Spirit, the Spirit of holiness alone, who can communicate His holiness to you and renew it continually. Therefore, it is by faith that you become partakers of His holiness. Jesus sanctifies you for God (1 Cor. 1:30), and the Holy Spirit imparts to you His holiness, which was manifested in His life on earth.

Surrender yourself to Him by faith, so that He may enable you to live that life from hour to hour. Believe that the Lord will, by His Spirit, lead you into, and keep you in, this life of holiness and of consecration to God's service. Live thus in the obedience of faith, always attentive to His voice and the guidance of His Spirit.

From the time that this fatherly discipline has led the sick one to a life of holiness, God has attained His purpose, and He will heal him who asks it in faith. Our earthly parents *"for a few days chastened us....No chastening for the present seemeth to be joyous, but grievous: nevertheless afterward it yieldeth the peaceable fruit of righteousness unto them which are exercised thereby"* (Heb. 12:10–11). Yes, it is when the believer realizes this *"peaceable fruit of righteousness"* that he is in a condition to be delivered from the chastisement.

Because believers still cannot understand that sanctification means an entire consecration to God, they cannot really believe that healing will quickly follow the sanctification of the sick one. Good health is too often for them only a matter of personal comfort and enjoyment that they may dispose of at their will. God cannot minister to this kind of selfishness. If they understood better that God requires His children to be *"sanctified, and meet for the master's use,"* they would not be surprised to see Him giving healing and renewed strength to those who have learned to place their entire bodies at His disposal, willing to be sanctified and employed in His service by the Holy Spirit. The Spirit of healing is also the Spirit of sanctification.

Chapter 13

———————◆———————

Sickness and Death

*Surely he shall deliver thee from the snare of the fowler,
and from the noisome pestilence....Thou shalt not be afraid for
the terror by night; nor for the arrow that flieth by day; nor for
the pestilence that walketh in darkness; nor for the destruction
that wasteth at noonday....With long life will I satisfy him, and
show him my salvation.*
—Psalm 91:3, 5–6, 16

*They shall still bring forth fruit in old age;
they shall be fat and flourishing.*
—Psalm 92:14

An objection is often made to the words of the apostle James, *"The prayer of faith shall save the sick"* (James 5:15), in this form: if we have the promise of being always healed in answer to prayer, how can it be possible to die? And some add, How can a sick person know whether God, who fixes the times of our lives, has not decided that we will die by such a sickness? In such a case, would not prayer be useless, and would it not be a sin to ask for healing?

380

Before replying, we would remark that this objection touches not only those who believe in Jesus as the Healer of the sick, but the Word of God itself, and the promise so clearly declared in the epistle of James and elsewhere. We are not at liberty to change or to limit the promises of God whenever they present some difficulty to us; neither can we insist that they be clearly explained to us before we bring ourselves to believe what they state. We begin by simply receiving them without resistance. Only then can the Spirit of God find us in the state of mind in which we can be taught and enlightened.

In the beginning, it will be difficult to completely understand a divine truth that has been neglected in the church for such a long time. It is only little by little that its importance and bearing are discerned. Gradually, as it revives, after it has been accepted by faith, the Holy Spirit will accompany it with new light. Let us remember that it is by the unbelief of the church that divine healing has left it. Faith in Bible truths should be made to depend on nothing but the Holy Spirit's enlightenment. *"There ariseth light in the darkness"* (Ps. 112:4) for the *"upright"* (v. 4)—for those who are ready to submit themselves to the Word of God.

It is easy to reply to the first objection. Scripture fixes seventy or eighty years as the ordinary measure of human life. The believer who receives Jesus as the Healer of the sick should be satisfied with this declaration of the Word of God. He will feel at liberty to *expect* a life of seventy or eighty years, but not necessarily longer. Besides, the man of faith places himself under the direction of the Spirit, which will enable him to discern the will of God regarding him, if something should prevent his attaining the age of seventy. Just as it is on earth, every rule in heaven has its exceptions.

We are sure according to the Word of God, whether by the words of Jesus or by those of James, that our heavenly Father wills to see His children in good health, so that they may labor in His service. For the same reason, He wills to set them free from sickness as soon as they have made a confession of sin and prayed with faith for their healing. For the believer who has walked with his Savior, full of the strength that comes from divine healing, and under the influence of the Holy Spirit, it is not necessary that when his time comes to die, he should die of sickness. The death of the believer, when the end of his life has come, is to fall asleep in Jesus Christ (1 Cor. 15:18). For him, death is only sleep after fatigue, the entering into rest.

The promise *"that it may be well with thee, and that thou mayest live long on the earth"* (Eph. 6:3) is addressed to us who live under the new covenant. The more the believer has learned to see the Savior as He who *"took our infirmities"* (Matt. 8:17), the more he has the liberty to claim the literal fulfillment of the promises: *"With long life will I satisfy him"*; *"They shall bring forth fruit in old age; they shall be fat and flourishing."*

The same text applies to the second objection. The sick one sees in God's Word that it is His will to heal His children after the confession of their sins, and in answer to the prayer of faith. It does not follow that they will be exempt from other trials. But as for sickness, they are healed of it because it attacks the body, which has become the dwelling place of the Holy Spirit. The sick one should then desire healing, so that the power of God may be made manifest in him, and that he may serve Him in accomplishing His will. In this, he clings to the revealed will of God. As for that which is not yet revealed, he knows that God will make known His mind to His servants who walk with Him.

Remember that faith is not a logical reasoning that obliges God to act according to His promises. It is, rather, the confident attitude of a child who honors his Father and counts on His love. He knows His Father fulfills His promises and is faithful to communicate the new strength that flows from redemption to the body as well as to the soul, until the moment of departure comes.

Chapter 14

The Holy Spirit—The Spirit of Healing

*Now there are diversities of gifts, but the same Spirit....To
another faith by the same Spirit; to another the gifts
of healing by the same Spirit;...but all these worketh
that one and the selfsame Spirit, dividing to every
man severally as he will.*
—1 Corinthians 12:4, 9, 11

What is it that distinguishes the children of God? What is
their glory? It is that God dwells in the midst of them and
reveals Himself to them in power. (See Exodus 33:16; 34:9–10.)
Under the new covenant, this dwelling of God in the believer is
even more manifest than in former times. God sends the Holy
Spirit to His church—the body of Christ—to act in it with power.
Its life and prosperity depend on Him. The Spirit must find unre-
served, full liberty in the church, so that it may be recognized as
the church of Christ, the Lord's body. In every age, the church
may look for manifestations of the Spirit, for they form our indis-
soluble unity: *"one body and one Spirit"* (Eph. 4:4).

The Spirit operates in various members of the church at different times. It is possible to be filled with the Spirit for one special work and not for another. There are also times in the history of the church when certain gifts of the Spirit are given with power, while at the same time ignorance or unbelief may hinder other gifts. Wherever the more abundant life of the Spirit is to be found, we may expect Him to manifest all His gifts.

The gift of healing is one of the most beautiful manifestations of the Spirit. It is recorded of Jesus, *"God anointed Jesus of Nazareth...who went about doing good, and healing all that were oppressed of the devil"* (Acts 10:38). The Holy Spirit in Him was a healing Spirit, and He was the same in the disciples after Pentecost. Thus the words of our text express what was the continuous experience of the early churches. (See Acts 3:7; 4:30; 5:12, 15–16; 6:8; 8:7; 9:41; 14:9–10; 16:18–19; 19:12; 28:8–9.) The abundant outpouring of the Spirit produced abundant healings. What a lesson for the church in our day!

Divine healing is the work of the Holy Spirit. Christ's redemption extends its powerful working to the body, and the Holy Spirit is in charge of transmitting it to us and maintaining it in us. Our bodies share in the benefit of the redemption, and even now we can receive the pledge of it by divine healing. It is Jesus who heals, Jesus who anoints and baptizes with the Holy Spirit, and Jesus who baptized His disciples with the same Spirit. It is He who sends us the Holy Spirit here on earth to take sickness away from us and to restore us to health.

Divine healing accompanies the sanctification by the Spirit. It is to make us holy that the Holy Spirit makes us partakers of Christ's redemption. Hence His name "Holy." Therefore, the healing that He works is an intrinsic part of His divine mission. He bestows this healing to lead the sick one to be converted and to believe (see Acts 4:29–30; 5:12, 14; 6:7–8; 8:6, 8; 9:42) or to confirm his faith if he is already converted. The Spirit constrains him thus to renounce sin and to consecrate himself entirely to God and to His service. (See 1 Corinthians 11:31; James 5:15–16; Hebrews 12:10.)

Divine Healing

Divine healing glorifies Jesus. It is God's will that His Son should be glorified, and the Holy Spirit does this when He comes to show us what the redemption of Christ does for us. The redemption of the mortal body appears almost more marvelous than that of the immortal soul. In these two ways, God wills to dwell in us through Christ, and thus to triumph over the flesh. As soon as our bodies become the temple of God through the Spirit, Jesus is glorified.

Divine healing takes place wherever the Spirit of God works in power. Examples of this are to be found in the lives of the Reformers, and in other people of God called to His service over the centuries. But there are even more promises accompanying the outpouring of the Holy Spirit that have not been fulfilled up to this time. Let us live in a holy expectation, praying for the Lord to accomplish them in us.

Chapter 15

Persevering Prayer

And he spake a parable unto them to this end, that men ought always to pray, and not to faint; saying, There was in a city a judge, which feared not God, neither regarded man: and there was a widow in that city; and she came unto him, saying, Avenge me of mine adversary. And he would not for a while: but afterward he said within himself, Though I fear not God, nor regard man; yet because this widow troubleth me, I will avenge her, lest by her continual coming she weary me. And the Lord said, Hear what the unjust judge saith. And shall not God avenge his own elect, which cry day and night unto him, though he bear long with them? I tell you that he will avenge them speedily. Nevertheless when the Son of man cometh, shall he find faith on the earth?
—Luke 18:1–8

*T*he necessity of praying with perseverance is the secret of all spiritual life. What a blessing to be able to ask the Lord for a particular answer until He gives it, knowing with certainty that it is His will to answer prayer! But what a mystery the call to persevere in prayer is for us—to knock in faith at His door, to remind Him of His promises, and to do so without wearying until He grants us our petition! That our prayers can obtain from the Lord something He would not otherwise give should prove that man has been created in the image of God, that man is God's friend, that man is God's fellow worker. The believers who together form the body of Christ partake of His intercessory work in this manner. It is to Christ's intercession that the Father responds and to which He grants His divine favors.

More than once the Bible explains to us the need for persevering prayer. There are many grounds for it, the chief of which is the justice of God. God has declared that sin must bear its consequences. Sin, therefore, has rights over a world that welcomes and remains enslaved by it. When the child of God seeks to quit this way of life, it is necessary that the justice of God consent to his request. Time is needed, however, for the privileges that Christ obtained for the believers to go into effect.

Besides this, the opposition of Satan, who always seeks to prevent the answer to prayer, is a reason for it. (See Daniel 10:12–13.) The only means by which this unseen enemy can be conquered is faith. Standing firmly on the promises of God, faith refuses to yield, continuing to pray and wait for the answer, even when it is delayed, knowing that the victory is sure. (See Ephesians 6:12–13.)

Finally, perseverance in prayer is necessary for ourselves. Delay in the answer is intended to prove and strengthen our faith. It ought to develop in us a steadfast faith that will no longer let go of the promises of God, but that renounces its own side of things to trust in God alone. It is then that God, seeing our faith, finds us ready to receive His favor and grants it to us. He will avenge speedily, even though He tarries. Yes, notwithstanding all the necessary delays, He will not make us wait a moment too long. If we cry to Him day and night, He will answer us speedily.

This perseverance in prayer will become easy for us, as soon as we fully understand what faith is. Jesus teaches us in these words: *"All things, whatsoever ye shall ask in prayer, believing, ye shall receive"* (Matt. 21:22). When the Word of God authorizes us to ask for anything, we should believe that we receive it at once. God gives it to us; this we know by faith. We can say, between God and us, that we have received it, although it might be only later that we are permitted to realize the effects here on earth. Before having seen or experienced anything tangible, faith rejoices in having received and perseveres in praying and waiting until the answer is manifested. Sometimes, it is useful to continue to pray, just to learn to count on the answer. After having believed that we are heard, it is good to persevere until it has become an accomplished fact.

This is of great importance in obtaining divine healing. Sometimes, it is true that healing is immediate and complete. But it may happen that we have to wait, even when a sick person has been able to ask for healing in faith. Sometimes, also, the first symptoms of healing are immediately obvious, but afterward, the following progress is slow and interrupted by times when it is arrested or when the evil returns. In either case, it is important, as much for the sick person as for those who pray with him, to believe in the effectiveness of persevering prayer, even though they may not understand the mystery of it. That which God appears at first to refuse, He grants later in response to the prayer of the woman from Canaan, to the prayer of the widow, and to that of the friend who knocks at midnight. (See Matthew 15:22–28; Luke 18:3–8; 11:5–8.) Without regarding either change or answer, faith that is grounded on the Word of God, and that continues to pray with importunity, ends by gaining the victory. *"Shall not God avenge his own elect which cry day and night unto him, though he bear long with them? I tell you that he will avenge them speedily."*

God's timing is perfect. He can delay anything as He sees necessary and then more speedily bring the answer at just the right moment. The same two abilities should belong to our faith. Let us grasp the grace that is promised to us, as if we had already received it, but wait with untiring patience for the answer that is slow to come. Such faith belongs to those who are living in Him. It is in order to produce this faith in us that sickness is sent to us, and that healing is granted to us, for such faith, above all, glorifies God.

Chapter 16

Let Him Who Is Healed Glorify God

And immediately he received his sight, and followed him,
glorifying God: and all the people, when they saw it, gave
praise unto God.
—Luke 18:43

And he leaping up stood, and walked, and entered
with them into the temple, walking, and leaping,
and praising God.
—Acts 3:8

_I_t is a prevalent idea that piety is easier in sickness than in health, and that silent suffering inclines the soul to seek the Lord more than the distractions of active life. For these reasons, sick people sometimes hesitate to ask for healing from the Lord. They believe the sickness may be more of a blessing to them spiritually than health. To think in this way is to ignore that healing and its fruits are divine. Although healing by earthly remedies alone may cause God to relax His hand, divine healing, on the contrary, binds us more closely to Him. Thus in our day, as in the time of the early ministry of Jesus Christ, the believer who has been healed by Him can glorify Him far better than the

389

one who remains sick. Sickness can glorify God only insofar as it manifests His power. (See John 9:3; 11:4.)

The sufferer who is led by his sufferings to give glory to God does it, so to speak, by constraint. If he had health and the liberty to choose, it is quite possible that his heart would turn back to the world. In such a case, the Lord must keep him where he is; his piety depends on his sickly condition. This is why the world supposes that Christianity is hardly effective anywhere but in sick rooms or on deathbeds. In order for the world to be convinced of the power of faith against temptation, it must see the healthy believer walking in calmness and holiness, even in the midst of work and active life. Although many sick people may have glorified God by their patience in suffering, He can be more glorified still by a health that He has sanctified.

Why then, we are asked, should those who have been healed in answer to the prayer of faith glorify the Lord more than those who have been healed through earthly remedies alone? Here is the reason: healing by means of remedies shows us the power of God in nature, but it does not bring us into living and direct contact with Him. Divine healing, however, is an act proceeding directly from God, relying on nothing but the Holy Spirit.

In this latter case, contact with God is what is essential, and it is for this reason that an examination of the conscience and the confession of sins should be the preparation for it (1 Cor. 11:30–32; James 5:15–16). One who is healed by divine intervention alone is called to consecrate himself anew and entirely to the Lord (1 Cor. 6:13, 19). All this depends on the act of faith that takes the Lord's promise, yields to Him, and never doubts that the Lord takes immediate possession of what is consecrated to Him. This is why the continuance of the health received depends on the holiness of the life of the believer, and the obedience to always seek the pleasure of the divine Healer (Exod. 15:26).

Health obtained under such conditions ensures spiritual blessings much greater than the mere restoration to health by ordinary means. When the Lord heals the body, it is so that He may take possession of it and make it a temple that He may dwell in. The joy that then fills the soul is indescribable. It is not only the joy of being healed, but it is also joy mingled with humility and a holy enthusiasm that realizes the touch of the Lord, receiving a new life from Him. In the exuberance of his joy, the healed one exalts the Lord, glorifies Him by word and deed, and consecrates all his life to God.

It is evident that these fruits of healing are not the same for everyone, and that sometimes backward steps are made. The life of the healed one joins with the life of believers around him. Their doubts and their inconsistencies may make his steps totter, although this generally results in a new beginning. Each day he discovers and recognizes afresh that his life is the Lord's life. He enters into a more intimate and more joyous communion with Him, learning to live in habitual dependence on Jesus and receiving from Him the strength that results from a more complete consecration.

Oh, what the church can become when it lives in this faith! When every sick person recognizes in sickness a call to be holy, and *expects* a manifestation of the Lord's presence, then healings will be multiplied. Each will produce a witness of the power of God, all ready to cry with the psalmist, *"Bless the Lord, O my soul,...who healeth all thy diseases"* (Ps. 103:2–3).

Chapter 17

———◆———

The Need of a Manifestation
of God's Power

And now, Lord, behold their threatenings: and grant unto thy
servants, that with all boldness they may speak thy word,
by stretching forth thine hand to heal, and that signs and
wonders may be done by the name of thy holy child Jesus.
And when they had prayed, the place was shaken where they
were assembled together; and they were all filled with the Holy
Ghost, and they spake the word of God with boldness.
—Acts 4:29–31

*I*s it permissible to ask the Lord, *"Grant unto thy servants, that*
with all boldness they may speak thy word, by stretching forth
thine hand to heal"? Let us look into this question.

The Word of God meets as many difficulties in our day as
then, and today's needs are equally pressing. Imagine the apostles in the midst of Jerusalem and her unbelief. The rulers of
the people were making threats, while the blinded multitude
were refusing to accept Jesus. The world is no longer as openly
hostile to the church because it has lost its fear of the church,
but its tolerance is more to be dreaded than its hatred. Apathy

is sometimes worse than violence. A Christianity of mere form, in the sleep of indifference, is just as inaccessible as an openly resisting Judaism. Even in the present day, God's servants need His power to be clearly evident among them, so that the Word can be preached with all boldness.

The help of God is as necessary now as it was then. The apostles knew very well that it was not the eloquence of their preaching that caused the truth to triumph. They were aware of their dependence on the Holy Spirit manifesting His presence by miracles. It was necessary for the living God to stretch forth His hand, so that there might be healings, miracles, and signs in the name of His holy Son Jesus. Only then could His servants rejoice. Strengthened by His presence, they could then speak His Word with boldness and teach the world to fear His name.

The divine promises should concern us today, also. The apostles counted on these words of the Lord before He ascended: *"Go ye into all the world, and preach the gospel to every creature....And these signs shall follow them that believe;...they shall lay hands on the sick, and they shall recover"* (Mark 16:15, 17–18). This charge indicates the divine vocation of the church. The promise that follows shows us what its armor is and proves to us that the Lord acts in agreement with the church. Because the apostles counted on this promise, they prayed for the Lord to grant them this proof of His presence. They had been filled with the Holy Spirit on the Day of Pentecost, but they still needed the supernatural signs that His power works.

The same promise is intended just as much for us. The command to preach the Gospel cannot be severed from the promise of divine healing with which it is accompanied. Nowhere is it found in the Bible that this promise was not for future times. In all ages, God's people greatly need to know that the Lord is with them and to possess the irrefutable proof of it. Therefore, this promise *is for us;* let us pray for its fulfillment.

Should we expect the same grace? We read in the book of Acts that when the apostles had prayed,

they were all filled with the Holy Ghost, and they spake the word of God with boldness....And by the hands of the apostles were many signs and wonders wrought among the people;...and believers were the more added to the Lord, multitudes both of men and women.
(Acts 4:31; 5:12, 14)

What joy and new strength God's people would receive today if the Lord would thus stretch forth His hand! Many tired and discouraged laborers grieve that they do not see more results from, and more blessings on, their labors. Their faith would be rejuvenated if signs of this kind would arise to prove that God is with them!

Many who are indifferent would be led to reflect, more than one doubter would regain confidence, and all unbelievers would be reduced to silence. The poor sinner would wake up if he saw with his own eyes what he could not comprehend by words only. He would be forced to acknowledge that the Christian's God is the living God who does wonders, the God of love who blesses!

Awake and put on your strength, church of Christ. Although, because of your unfaithfulness, you have lost the joy of seeing your preaching of the Word allied with the hand of the Lord stretched out to heal, the Lord is ready to grant you this grace again. Acknowledge that it is your own unbelief that has so long deprived you of it, and pray for pardon. Clothe yourself with the strength of prayer.

"Awake, awake, put on strength, O arm of the Lord; awake, as in the ancient days" (Isa. 51:9).

Chapter 18

---◆---

Sin and Sickness

The prayer of faith shall save the sick, and the Lord shall raise him up; and if he has committed sins, they shall be forgiven him. Confess your faults one to another, and pray one for another, that ye may be healed.
—James 5:15–16

*H*ere, as in other Scriptures, the pardon of sins and the healing of sickness are closely united. James declared that a pardon of sins would be granted with the healing. For this reason, he desired to see confession of sin accompanying the prayer that claims healing. We know that confession of sin is necessary to obtain the pardon of sin from God. It is equally necessary to obtain healing. Unconfessed sin presents an obstacle to the prayer of faith. It could even cause the sickness to reappear. When called to treat a patient, a physician should first diagnose the cause of the disease. If he succeeds, he stands a better chance of combating it. Our God also goes back to the primary cause of all sickness—sin. It is the patient's part to confess the sin, and it is God's part to grant the pardon that removes this first cause, so that healing can take place. When seeking healing by means of earthly remedies alone, find a clever physician and follow his prescriptions. But when seeking healing through the prayer of faith, you must also keep your eyes on the Lord, and be continuously conscious of how you stand with Him. James, therefore, was showing his readers a condition that was essential to the recovery of their health; namely, they must confess and forsake sin.

Sickness can be a consequence of sin. Often God permits sickness in order to show us our faults, chasten us, and purify us from them. Sickness is, I believe, a visible sign of God's judgment on sin. The one who is sick is not necessarily a greater sinner than another who is in health. On the contrary, it is often the holiest among the children of God whom He chastens, as we see from the example of Job. Sickness is also not always intended to check some fault that we can easily determine. Its main purpose is to draw the attention of the sick one to that which remains in him of the egotism of the *"old man"* (Rom. 6:6) and of all that hinders him from a life entirely consecrated to his God.

The first step that the sick one has to take in the path of divine healing will be, therefore, to let the Holy Spirit of God probe his heart and convict him of sin. This will be followed by humiliation, a decision to break with sin, and confession. To confess our sins is to lay them down before God and to subject them to His judgment, with the full intention of falling into them no more. A sincere confession will be followed by a new assurance of pardon.

"If he has committed sins, they shall be forgiven him." When we have confessed our sins, we must receive the promised pardon, believing that God gives it. Faith in God's pardon is often vague for a young Christian. Either he is uncertain about its meaning, or he has difficulty accepting it. But if he receives the pardon with confidence, in answer to the prayer of faith, it will bring him new life and strength. His soul will rest in the redemption of the blood of Christ, receiving the certainty from the Holy Spirit of his pardon. Therefore, nothing remains to hinder the Savior from filling him with His love and with His grace. God's

pardon brings with it a divine life that acts powerfully on him who receives it.

Once the soul has consented to make a sincere confession and has obtained pardon, it is ready to grasp God's promise of healing. Believing that the Lord will raise up His sick one is no longer difficult. It is when we keep far away from God that it is difficult to believe; confession and pardon bring us quite near to Him. As soon as the cause of the sickness has been removed, the sickness itself can be arrested. It now becomes easy for the sick one to believe that if the Lord subjected his body to the chastisement of sickness because of his sins, He now wills that this same body should be healed because the sin is pardoned. His presence is revealed; a ray of life—of His divine life—comes to quicken the body; and the sick one proves that as soon as he is no longer separated from the Lord, the prayer of faith does save the sick.

Chapter 19

———◆—◆———

Jesus Bore Our Sickness

*Surely he hath borne our griefs, and carried our sorrows:
yet we did esteem him stricken, smitten of God,
and afflicted….He shall see of the travail of his soul,
and shall be satisfied: by his knowledge shall my
righteous servant justify many; for he shall bear their
iniquities. Therefore will I divide him a portion with the
great, and he shall divide the spoil with the strong;
because…he bare the sin of many.*
—Isaiah 53:4, 11–12

Are you familiar with the beautiful fifty-third chapter of Isaiah, which has been called the fifth Gospel? Enlightened by the Spirit of God, Isaiah predicted the sufferings of the Lamb of God and described the divine grace that would result from them.

The words *to bear* had to appear in this prophecy. These words must accompany the mention of sin, whether as committed directly by the sinner, or as transmitted to a substitute. The transgressor, the priest, and the atoning victim must all bear the sin. In the same way, it is because the Lamb of God has borne our sins that God smote Him for the iniquity of us all. Sin was not found in Him, but it was put on Him; He took it voluntarily.

It is because He bore it, and, in bearing it, put an end to it, that He has the power to save us. *"My righteous servant* [shall] *justify many; for he shall bear their iniquities....He shall divide the spoil with the strong; because...he bare the sin of many."* It is, therefore, because our sins have been borne by Jesus Christ that we are delivered from them as soon as we believe this truth; consequently, we no longer have to bear them ourselves.

In Isaiah 53, the verb *to bear* occurs twice, but in relation to two different things. It is said not only that the Lord's righteous Servant bore our sins (v. 12), but also that He bore our griefs, or sicknesses (v. 4). Thus His bearing our sicknesses as well as our sins forms an integral part of the Redeemer's work. Although He was without sin, He has borne our sins and has done the same with our sicknesses.

The human part of Jesus could not be touched by sickness because it remained holy. We never find in the account of His life any mention of sickness. Although experiencing all our human weaknesses—hunger, thirst, fatigue, and sleep—because these things are not the consequence of sin, He still had no trace of sickness. Sickness had no hold on Him because He was without sin. He could, therefore, die only a violent death (and that only by His voluntary consent). Thus, it is not in Him, but *on Him* that we see sickness as well as sin. He took them on Himself and bore them of His own free will. By bearing them, He triumphed over them and has acquired the right of delivering His children from them.

Sin had attacked and ruined the soul and body equally. Jesus came to save both. Having taken sickness as well as sin on Himself, He is in a position to set us free from the one as well as the other. In order for Him to accomplish this double deliverance, He expects only one thing from us: our faith.

As soon as a sick believer understands the meaning of the words, "Jesus has borne my sins," he is not afraid to say, "I no longer need to bear my sins." In the same way, as soon as he fully believes that Jesus has borne our sicknesses, he is not afraid to say, "I no longer need to bear my sickness." Jesus, in bearing sin, bore sickness also. He has made payment for both, and He delivers us from both.

I witnessed the blessed influence this truth exercised one day. A sick woman had spent almost seven years in bed. A sufferer from tuberculosis, epilepsy, and other sicknesses, she had been assured that no hope of a cure remained for her. In a half-fainting condition, she was carried into the room where the late Mr. W. E. Boardman was holding a Sunday evening service for the sick, and she was laid on the sofa. She was not conscious enough to remember anything of what took place until she heard the words, *"Himself took our infirmities and bare our sicknesses"* (Matt. 8:17). She then seemed to hear the words, "If He has borne your sicknesses, why then bear them yourself? Get up."

"But," she thought, "if I attempt to get up, and fall on the ground, what will they think of me?"

But the inward voice began again, "If He has borne my sins, why should I have to bear them?" To the astonishment of all who were present, she rose, and, although still feeble, sat down in a chair by the table. From that moment, her healing made rapid progress. At the end of a few weeks, she no longer had the appearance of an invalid. Soon she was so strong that she could spend many hours a day in visiting the poor. With what joy and love she could then speak of Him who was *"the strength of* [her] *life"* (Ps. 27:1)! She had believed that Jesus had borne her sicknesses as well as her sins, and her faith remained firm. It is thus that Jesus reveals Himself as a perfect Savior to all those who will trust themselves unreservedly to Him.

Chapter 20

————◆—————

Is Sickness a Chastisement?

For this cause many are weak and sickly among you,
and many sleep. For if we would judge ourselves,
we should not be judged. But when we are judged,
we are chastened of the Lord, that we should not
be condemned with the world.
—1 Corinthians 11:30–32

*I*n writing to the Corinthians, the apostle Paul had to reprove them for the manner in which they observed the Lord's Supper, which had caused them to be chastised by God. Here we see sickness as a judgment of God, a chastisement for sin. Paul saw it as such, and added that it was in order to prevent them from falling more deeply into sin—to prevent them from being *"condemned with the world"*—that they were thus afflicted. He warned them that if they would rather be neither judged nor chastened by the Lord, they should examine themselves to discover the cause of their sickness and condemn their own sins. The Lord would then no longer need to exercise severity. Is it not evident that in this instance sickness is a judgment of God, a chastisement of sin, that we can avoid by examining and condemning ourselves?

Yes, sickness is—more often than we know—a chastisement for sin. God *"doth not afflict willingly nor grieve the children of men"* (Lam. 3:33). It is not without a cause that He allows us to be deprived of health. Perhaps it is to make us more aware of a particular sin from which we can repent. *"Sin no more, lest a worse thing come unto thee"* (John 5:14). Perhaps we have become entangled in pride and worldliness. Or it may be that self-confidence or caprice have entered our service for God.

It is, however, quite possible that the chastisement may not be directed against any particular sin. It may be the result of the sin that weighs upon the entire human race. In the case of the man born blind, the disciples asked the Lord, *"Who did sin, this man, or his parents, that he was born blind?"* (John 9:2), and Jesus answered, *"Neither hath this man sinned, nor his parents"* (v. 3). He does not say that sin and sickness are not related, but He teaches us not to accuse every sick person of sin.

In any case, sickness is always a discipline that ought to awaken our attention to sin and turn us from it. Therefore, a sick person should begin by judging himself (1 Cor. 11:31), by placing himself before his heavenly Father with a sincere desire to see anything that could have grieved Him or could have rendered the chastisement necessary. In so doing, he may count assuredly on the Holy Spirit's light to clearly show him his failure.

Let him be ready to renounce at once what he may discern, and to place himself at the Lord's disposal to serve Him with perfect obedience.

But do not let him imagine that he can conquer sin by his own efforts. No, that is impossible for him. He can, however, with all his power of will, join God in renouncing the sin, and then believe that he is accepted by Him. In so doing, he will be yielding himself, consecrating himself anew to God, willing to do only His holy will in all things.

Scripture assures us that if we thus examine ourselves, the Lord will not judge us. Our Father chastens His children only as far as it is necessary. God seeks to deliver us from sin and self.

As soon as we understand Him and break with these, sickness may cease; it has done its work.

We must find out what the sickness means and recognize it as a part of the discipline of God. One may recognize vaguely that he commits sins, without attempting to define them. Even if he does, he may not believe it is possible to give them up. And if he goes so far as to renounce them, he may fail to count on God to put an end to the chastisement, despite the glorious assurance that Paul's words give us.

Dear sick one, have you considered that your heavenly Father may disapprove of some hidden sin in your life? He would like your sickness to help you discover it, and His Holy Spirit will guide you in the search. Renounce what He may point out to you at once. Then not even the smallest shadow will remain between your Father and you. It is His will to pardon your sin and to heal your sickness.

In Jesus, we have both pardon and healing; they are two sides of His redemptive work. He is calling you to live a life of dependence on Him in a greater degree than you have before. Abandon yourself to Him in complete obedience, and follow His steps as a little child would imitate his father. With joy, your heavenly Father will deliver you from chastisement. He will reveal Himself to you as your Healer, bringing you nearer to Him by this new tie of His love. He will make you obedient and faithful in serving Him. If, as a wise and faithful Father, He has been obliged to chasten you, it is also as a Father that He wills your healing, and that He desires to bless and keep you henceforth.

Chapter 21

God's Prescription for the Sick

Is any sick among you? let him call for the elders of the church; and let them pray over him, anointing him with oil in the name of the Lord: and the prayer of faith shall save the sick, and the Lord shall raise him up; and if he have committed sins, they shall be forgiven him.
—James 5:14–15

James 5:14–15, above all other Scriptures, most clearly declares to the sick what they have to do in order to be healed. Sickness and its consequences abound in the world. What joy, then, for the believer to learn from the Word of God the way of healing for the sick! The Bible teaches us that it is the will of God to see His children in good health. The apostle James had no hesitation in saying that *"the prayer of faith shall save the sick, and the Lord shall raise him up."* May the Lord teach us to pay attention to and receive with simplicity what His Word tells us!

Notice, first, that James made a distinction between affliction, or suffering, and sickness. In the previous verse, he said, *"Is any among you afflicted? let him pray"* (v. 13). He did not specify what we should request in such a case; he definitely did not say to ask for deliverance from suffering. No, suffering that may arise from various exterior causes is the portion of every Christian. Let us therefore understand that James's objective was to lead the tried believer to ask for deliverance only with a spirit of submission to the will of God, and, above all, to ask also for the patience that he considered to be the privilege of the believer (James 1:2–4, 12; 5:7–8).

But in dealing with the words, *"Is any sick among you?"* James replied in quite another manner. He said with assurance that the sick one may ask for healing with confidence that he will obtain it, and the Lord will hear him. There is, therefore, a great difference between suffering and sickness. The Lord Jesus spoke of suffering as being necessary, as being willed and blessed by God, while He said that sickness ought to be cured. All other suffering comes to us from without and will cease only when Jesus triumphs over the sin and evil that are in the world. Sickness is an evil that is in the body itself, in this body saved by Christ, so that it may become the temple of the Holy Spirit. This body should, in my opinion, be healed as soon as the sick believer receives, by faith, the working of the Holy Spirit, the very life of Jesus in him.

What course did James instruct the sick to follow? Let him call for the elders of the church, and let the elders pray for him. In the time of James, there were physicians, but he did not tell the sick believer to turn to them. The elders then were the pastors and leaders of the churches, called to the ministry not because they had passed through schools of theology, but because they were filled with the Holy Spirit and were well-known for their piety and faith. Why should their presence be needed by the sick one? Couldn't he pray for himself? Couldn't his friends have prayed? Yes, but it is not so easy for everybody to exercise the faith that obtains healing. That is, without a doubt, one reason why James desired that men should be called whose faith was firm and sure.

Besides this, the elders were representatives of the church, of the collective body of Christ, for it is the communion of believers that invites the Spirit to act with power. In short, they should, after the pattern of the great Shepherd of the sheep, care for the flock as He does. They should identify themselves with the sick one, understand his trouble, receive from God the necessary discernment to instruct him, and encourage him to persevere in faith. It is, then, to the elders of the church that the healing of the sick is committed. And it is they, the servants of the God who pardons iniquities and heals diseases (Ps. 103:3), who are called to transmit to others the Lord's graces for soul and body.

Finally, there is a promise still more direct: that of healing. The apostle spoke of it as the certain consequence of the prayer of faith. *"The prayer of faith shall save the sick, and the Lord shall raise him up."* This promise ought to stimulate in every believer the desire and expectation of healing. As we receive these words with simplicity and as they are written, shouldn't we see in them an unlimited promise that offers healing to whoever will pray in faith? May the Lord teach us to study His Word with the faith of a truly believing heart!

Chapter 22

---◆---

The Lord Who Heals You

I will put none of these diseases upon thee,
which I have brought upon the Egyptians:
for I am the LORD that healeth thee.
—Exodus 15:26

*H*ow often have we read these words without daring to take
them for ourselves, and without expectation that the Lord
would fulfill them in us! We have seen in them that the people
of God ought to be exempt from the diseases inflicted upon the
Egyptians. But we believed that this promise applied only to the
Old Testament, and that, by the direct intervention of the
Lord, we who live under the New Testament cannot expect to
be kept from, or healed of, sickness. Because we were obliged
to recognize the superiority of the new covenant, we came, in
our ignorance, to assert that sickness often brings great blessings. Consequently, we believed God had done well to withdraw
what He had formerly promised, and to be no longer for us what
He was for Israel, *"the LORD that healeth thee."*

But in our day, we see the church awakening and acknowledging its mistake. It sees that it is under the new covenant that
the Lord Jesus acquired the title of Healer by all His miraculous

healings. The church is beginning to see that in charging His church to preach the Gospel to every creature, He has promised *"alway, even unto the end of the world"* (Matt. 28:20) to be with His church.

As the proof of His presence, His disciples should have the power to lay hands on the sick, who should then be healed. In the days of Pentecost, the miraculous outpouring of the Holy Spirit was accompanied by miraculous healings, which were evidence of the blessings brought about by the power from on high. (See Acts 3:16; 5:12; 9:40.) There is nothing in the Bible to make the church believe that the promise made to Israel has since been retracted, and it hears, from the mouth of the apostle James, this new promise: *"The prayer of faith shall save* [or heal] *the sick"* (James 5:15).

The church knows that unbelief has always *"limited* [or set boundaries around] *the Holy One of Israel"* (Ps. 78:41), and it asks itself if it is not this same unbelief that is hindering the manifestation of God's power to heal today. Who can doubt it? It is not God or His Word that are to blame here; it is our unbelief that impedes the miraculous power of the Lord and that holds Him back from healing as He did in the past.

Let our faith awaken. Let it recognize and adore in Christ the full power in Him who says, *"I am the Lord that healeth thee."* It is by the works of God that we can best understand what His Word tells us. The healings that, again, are responding to the prayer of faith confirm, by gloriously illustrating, the truth of His promise.

Let us learn to see, in the risen Jesus, the divine Healer, and let us receive Him as such. In order that I may recognize in Jesus my justification, my strength, and my wisdom, I must grasp, by faith, that He really is all these things to me. When the Bible tells me that Jesus is the sovereign Healer, I must take hold of this truth and say, "Yes, Lord, it is You who are my Healer."

And why may I hold Him as such? Because He gives Himself to me, making me *"planted together"* (Rom. 6:5) with Him. Inseparably united to Him, I thus possess His healing power.

His love is pleased to bestow His favors on His beloved, to communicate Himself with all His heart to all who desire to receive Him. Let us believe that He is ready to extend the treasure of blessing contained in the name, *"The Lord that healeth thee,"* to all who know and who can trust in this divine name. This is the treatment for the sick indicated by the law of His kingdom.

When I bring my sickness to the Lord, I do not depend on what I see, what I feel, or what I think, but on what He says. Even when everything appears contrary to the expected healing, even if it should not take place at the time or in the way that I had thought I should receive it, even when the symptoms seem only to be aggravated, my faith, strengthened by the very waiting, should cling immovably to this word that has gone out of the mouth of God: *"I am the Lord that healeth thee."*

God is always seeking to make us true believers. Healing and health are of little value if they do not glorify God and serve to unite us more closely with Him. Thus, in the matter of healing, our faith must always be put to the test. He who counts on the name of his God, who can hear Jesus saying to him, *"Said I not unto thee, that, if thou wouldest believe, thou shouldest see the glory of God?"* (John 11:40), will have the joy of receiving from God Himself the healing of the body, and of seeing it take place in a manner worthy of God, conformable to His promises. When we read these words, *"I am the Lord that healeth thee,"* let us not fear to answer eagerly, "Yes, Lord, You are the Lord who heals me."

Chapter 23

———◆———

Jesus Heals the Sick

*He...healed all that were sick: that it might be fulfilled which
was spoken by Esaias the prophet, saying, Himself took our
infirmities, and bare our sicknesses.*
—Matthew 8:16–17

*I*n a preceding chapter, we studied the words of the prophet
Isaiah. If you still have any doubt as to the interpretation that
has been given, I remind you of what the Holy Spirit caused the
evangelist Matthew to write. It is expressly said, regarding all the
sick ones whom Jesus healed, *"That it might be fulfilled which
was spoken by Esaias the prophet."* It was because Jesus had
taken our sicknesses on Himself that He could, that He ought
to, heal them. If He had not done so, one part of His work of
redemption would have remained powerless and fruitless.

The text of the Word of God is not generally understood in
this way. Often, it is the accepted view that the miraculous healings done by the Lord Jesus are to be considered only as the
proof of His mercy, or as being the symbol of spiritual graces.
They are not seen to be a necessary consequence of redemption, although that is what the Bible declares. The body and the
soul have been created to serve together as a habitation of God.

Divine Healing

The sickly condition of the body, as well as that of the soul, is a consequence of sin, and that is what Jesus came to bear, to atone for, and to conquer.

When the Lord Jesus was on earth, it was not in the character of the Son of God that He cured the sick, but as the Mediator who bore our sicknesses. This enables us to understand why Jesus gave so much time to His healing work, and why, also, the Bible evangelists speak of it in a manner so detailed.

Read, for example, what Matthew said about it,

Jesus went about all Galilee, teaching in their synagogues, and preaching the gospel of the kingdom, and healing all manner of sickness and all manner of disease among the people. And his fame went throughout all Syria: and they brought unto him all sick people that were taken with divers diseases and torments, and those which were possessed with devils, and those which were lunatic, and those that had the palsy; and he healed them.
(Matt. 4:23–24)

And Jesus went about all the cities and villages, teaching in their synagogues, and preaching the gospel of the kingdom, and healing every sickness and every disease among the people. (Matt. 9:35)

And when he had called unto him his twelve disciples, he gave them power against unclean spirits, to cast them out, and to heal all manner of sickness and all manner of disease. (Matt. 10:1)

Still in the gospel of Matthew, when the disciples of John the Baptist came to ask Jesus if He was the Messiah, so that He might prove it to them, He replied, *"The blind receive their sight, and the lame walk, the lepers are cleansed, and the deaf hear, the dead are raised up, and the poor have the gospel preached to them"* (Matt. 11:5). After the cure of the withered hand, and the opposition of the Pharisees who sought to destroy Him, we read that *"great multitudes followed him, and he healed them all"* (Matt. 12:15). Later, the crowd followed Him into a desert place, *"and Jesus went forth, and saw a great multitude, and was moved with compassion toward them, and he healed their sick"* (Matt. 14:14).

Further on in the passage we read,

> *They sent out into all that country round about, and brought unto him all that were diseased; and besought him that they might only touch the hem of his garment: and as many as touched were made perfectly whole.*
> (vv. 35–36)

It is said, also, of the sick who were among the multitudes that they *"cast them down at Jesus' feet; and he healed them"* (Matt. 15:30). Matthew added, *"Insomuch that the multitude wondered, when they saw the dumb to speak, the maimed to be whole, the lame to walk, and the blind to see: and they glorified the God of Israel"* (v. 31). Finally, when He came into the coasts of Judea beyond Jordan, *"Great multitudes followed him; and he healed them there"* (Matt. 19:2).

Let us add to these various texts those that give us in detail the account of healings worked by Jesus. These healings give us not only the proof of His power during His life here on earth, but also the continual result of His work of mercy and of love, the manifestation of His power of redemption, that delivers the soul and body from the dominion of sin.

Yes, that was in very deed the purpose of God. If, then, Jesus bore our sicknesses as an integral part of the redemption, if He has healed the sick *"that it might be fulfilled which was spoken by Esaias,"* and if His Savior-heart is always full of mercy and love, we can believe with certainty that to this very day it is the will of Jesus to heal the sick in answer to the prayer of faith.

Chapter 24

———————— ➤◆◄ ————————

Fervent and Effectual Prayer

Pray one for another, that ye may be healed. The
effectual fervent prayer of a righteous man availeth much.
Elias was a man subject to like passions as we are, and
he prayed earnestly that it might not rain: and it rained not
on the earth by the space of three years and six months.
And he prayed again, and the heaven gave rain,
and the earth brought forth her fruit.
—James 5:16–18

James knew that a faith that obtains healing is not the fruit of human nature; therefore, he added that the prayer must be *"fervent."* Only such prayer can be effective. In this James stood on the example of Elijah, a man of the same nature (subject to similar passions) as we are, drawing the inference that our prayer can and ought to be of the same nature as his. How, then, did Elijah pray? The answer will throw some light on what the prayer of faith should be.

Elijah received from God the promise that rain was about to fall on the earth (1 Kings 18:1), and he declared this to Ahab. Strong in the promise of his God, Elijah went atop Mount Carmel to pray (v. 42; James 5:18). He knew—he believed—that God's will was to send rain. Nevertheless, he had to pray, or the rain would not come. His prayer was no empty form; it was a real power, which was about to make itself felt in heaven. God willed that it would rain, but the rain would come only at Elijah's request, a request repeated with faith and perseverance until the appearance of the first cloud in the sky.

In order for the will of God to be accomplished, this will must, on one side, be expressed by a promise, and, on the other, be received and grasped by the believer who prays. He, therefore, must persevere in prayer to show God that his faith expects an answer, that it will not grow weary until it is obtained.

This is how prayer must be made for the sick. The promise of God, *"The Lord shall raise him up"* (James 5:15), must be rested on, and His will to heal recognized. Jesus Himself teaches us to pray with faith that counts on the answer of God. He says to us, *"What things soever ye desire, when ye pray, believe that ye receive them, and ye shall have them"* (Mark 11:24). After the prayer of faith, which receives what God has promised before it manifests itself, comes the prayer of perseverance, which does not lose sight of what has been asked until God has fulfilled His promise (1 Kings 18:43).

There may be some obstacle that hinders the fulfillment of the promise, whether on the side of God and His righteousness (Deut. 9:18), or on the side of Satan and his constant opposition to the plans of God. This obstacle may still impede the answer to the prayer (Dan. 10:12–13). It may be also that our faith is called to persevere until the answer comes. He who prays six times fervently and stops there, when he ought to have prayed seven times (see 2 Kings 13:18–19), deprives himself of the answer to his prayer.

Perseverance in prayer, a perseverance that strengthens the faith of the believer against everything that may seem opposed to the answer, is a real miracle. It is one of the impenetrable mysteries of the life of faith. Does it not say to us that the Savior's redeemed one is indeed His friend, a member of His body, and that the government of the world and the gifts of divine grace depend in some sense on his prayers? Prayer, therefore, is no vain form. It is the work of the Holy Spirit, who intercedes here on earth in us and by us. As such, it is as powerful and as indispensable as the work of the Son interceding for us before the throne of God.

It might seem strange that after having prayed with the certainty of being heard, and having seen therein the will of God, we would still need to continue in prayer. Nevertheless, it is so. In Gethsemane, Jesus prayed three times in succession. On Mount Carmel, Elijah prayed seven times. And we, if we believe the promise of God without doubting, will pray until we receive the answer. Both the importunate friend at midnight (Luke 11:5–8) and the widow who besieged the unjust judge (Luke 18:2–7) are examples of perseverance in seeking the end in view.

Let us learn from Elijah's prayer to humble ourselves and to recognize why the power of God cannot be manifested more in the church, whether in the healing of the sick, in conversion, or in sanctification. *"Ye have not, because ye ask not"* (James 4:2). It also teaches us patience. In the cases where healing is delayed, let us remember that obstacles may exist over which only perseverance in prayer can triumph. Faith that ceases to pray, or that is allowed to relax in its fervor, cannot take hold of what God has nevertheless given. Do not let your faith in the promises of Scripture be shaken by those things that are as yet beyond your reach. God's promise remains the same: *"The prayer of faith shall save the sick"* (James 5:15).

May the prayer of Elijah strengthen our faith. Let us remember that we have to imitate them who through faith and patience inherit the promises (Heb. 6:12). If we learn to persevere in prayer, its fruit will be always more abundant, always more evident. We will obtain, as Jesus obtained when He was on earth, healing of the sick, often immediate healing, which will bring glory to God.

Chapter 25

———————◄◆►———————

Intercessory Prayer

*Confess your faults one to another, and pray one for
another, that ye may be healed. The effectual fervent prayer of
a righteous man availeth much.*
—James 5:16

James began by speaking of the prayers of the elders of
the church; but here, he addressed all believers as he said,
"Pray one for another, that ye may be healed." Having already
spoken of confession and of pardon, he added, *"Confess your
faults one to another."*

This shows us that the prayer of faith that asks for healing is
not the prayer of one isolated believer, but that it ought to unite
the members of the body of Christ in the communion of the
Spirit. God certainly hears the prayers of each one of His children as soon as they are presented to Him with living faith, but
the sick one does not always possess such faith as this. In order
for the Holy Spirit to act with power, there must be a union of
several members of the body of Christ unitedly claiming His
presence. We need one as well as the other.

This dependence on our fellow believers should be exercised in two ways. First of all, we must confess our faults to any

whom we may have wronged and receive pardon from them. But besides this, one who is sick may see the cause of his sickness in a sin that he has committed and recognize it as a chastening of God. In such a case, he should acknowledge his sin before the elders, or brothers in Christ, who pray for him. This confession will enable them to pray with more light and more faith. Such confession will also be a touchstone that tests the sincerity of his repentance, for it is easier to confess our sins to God than to man. Before a man confesses, his humiliation needs to be real and his repentance sincere. The result will be a closer communion between the sick one and those who intercede for him, and their faith will be quickened anew.

"Pray one for another, that ye may be healed." Doesn't this clearly answer the frequently asked questions: What is the use in going to miracle-working evangelists in faraway places? Doesn't the Lord hear prayer in whatever place it is offered? Yes, without any doubt, wherever a prayer in living faith rises up to God, it finds Him ready to grant healing. But the church has so neglected to believe in this truth that it is a rare thing in the present day to find Christians capable of praying in this manner.

Thus, we cannot be too grateful to the Lord that He has inspired certain believers with the desire to consecrate their lives, in part, to testify to the truth of divine healing. Their words and their faith awaken faith in the hearts of many sick ones who, without their help, would never arrive at it. These are the very people who always say to everybody, "The Lord is to be found everywhere." Let Christians learn not to neglect the least part of the marvelous power of their God, and He will be able to manifest to all that He is always *"the Lord that healeth thee"* (Exod. 15:26). Let us take heed to obey the Word of God, to confess to one another, and to pray for one another that we may be healed.

James noted still another essential condition to successful prayer: it must be the prayer of the righteous. *"The effectual fervent prayer of a righteous man availeth much."* The Scriptures tell us that *"he that doeth righteousness is righteous, even as he*

[Jesus] *is righteous"* (1 John 3:7). James himself was surnamed "The Just" because of his piety and the tenderness of his conscience. Whether one is an elder or a simple believer, only after he is wholly surrendered to God and living in obedience to His will can he pray effectively for the brethren.

John made this point when he said, *"Whatsoever we ask, we receive of him, because we keep his commandments, and do those things that are pleasing in his sight"* (v. 22). It is, therefore, the prayer of one who lives in intimate communion with God that *"availeth much."* It is to such prayer that God will grant the answer that He would not be able to give to His children who do not live as close to Him.

We often hear these words quoted: *"The effectual fervent prayer of a righteous man availeth much,"* but very rarely is this passage taken in connection with its context or remembered that it is divine healing in particular that is in question here. May the Lord raise up in His church many of these righteous men, animated with living faith, whom He can use to glorify Jesus as the divine Healer of the sick!

Chapter 26

———————◆————

The Will of God

Thy will be done.
—Matthew 6:10

If the Lord will.
—James 4:15

*I*n days of sickness, when doctors and medicines fail, recourse is generally taken to such Scriptures as, *"Thy will be done,"* and, *"If the Lord will,"* but they may easily become a stumbling block in the way of divine healing. How can I know, it is asked, whether or not it is God's will that I remain ill? And as long as this is an open question, how can I pray for a healing with faith?

Here, truth and error seem to touch. It is, indeed, impossible to pray with faith when we are not sure that we are asking according to the will of God. "I can," one may say, "pray fervently in asking God to do the best for me, believing that He will cure me if it is possible." As long as one prays thus, one is praying with submission, but it is not the prayer of faith. That is possible only when we are certain that we are asking according to the will of God. The question then resolves itself into how we can know what the will of God is. It is a great mistake to think that the child of God cannot know His will about healing.

In order to know His divine will, we must be guided by the Word of God. It is His Word that promises us healing. The promise of James 5 is so absolute that it is impossible to deny it. This promise only confirms other passages, equally strong, that tell us that Jesus Christ has obtained for us the healing of our diseases because He has borne our sicknesses. According to this promise, we have the right to healing because it is a part of the salvation that we have in Christ. Therefore, we may expect it with certainty. Scripture tells us that sickness is, in God's hands, the means of chastening His children for their sins, but that this discipline ceases to be exercised as soon as His suffering child acknowledges and turns from the sin. Isn't it just as clear to say that God desires to make use of sickness only to bring back His children when they are straying?

Sick Christian, open your Bible, study it, and see in its pages that sickness is a warning to renounce sin. Whoever acknowledges and forsakes his sins finds pardon and healing in Jesus. Such is God's promise in His Word. If the Lord had some other arrangement in mind for His children whom He was about to call home to Him, He would make His will known to them. By the Holy Spirit, He would give them a desire to depart. In other special cases, He would awaken some particular conviction. As a general rule, however, the Word of God promises us healing in answer to the prayer of faith.

"Nevertheless," some might say, "is it not better in all things to leave it to the will of God?" They refer to those Christians who would have forced the hand of God with their prayers had they not added, "Thy will be done." Without that addition, they certainly would not have experienced blessing in the answer to their prayers. And these would say, "How do we know whether sickness would not be better for us than health?"

To begin with, this is no case of "forcing the hand of God," since it is His Word that tells us that it is His will to heal us. *"The prayer of faith shall save the sick"* (James 5:15). God wills that the health of the soul should have a blessed influence on the health of the body, that the presence of Jesus in the soul should have its confirmation in the good condition of the body. And when you know that this is His will, you cannot say truthfully that you are leaving all things to Him. It is not leaving it to Him when you make use of all possible remedies to be healed, instead of resting on His promise. Your submission is nothing else than spiritual sloth in view of what God commands you to do.

As to knowing whether sickness is better than health, we do not hesitate to reply that the return to health, which is the fruit of giving up sin, of consecration to God, and of an ultimate communion with God, is infinitely better than sickness. *"This is the will of God, even your sanctification"* (1 Thess. 4:3), and it is by healing that God confirms the reality of this. When Jesus comes to take possession of our bodies and cures them miraculously, it follows that the health received must be maintained from day to day by an uninterrupted communion with Him. This experience of the Savior's power and love comes as a result that is far superior to any that sickness has to offer. Undoubtedly, sickness may teach us submission, but healing received directly from God makes us better acquainted with our Lord and teaches us to confide in Him more deeply. Besides, it prepares the believer to accomplish the service of God in a far better way.

Sick Christian, if you would really seek to know what the will of God is in this thing, do not let yourself be influenced by the opinions of others, nor by your own former prejudices, but listen to and study what the Word of God has to say. Examine whether it does indeed tell you that divine healing is a part of the redemption of Jesus, and that God wills that every believer should have the right to claim it. See whether it promises that the prayer of every child of God for healing will be heard, and whether health restored by the power of the Holy Spirit manifests the glory of God in the eyes of the church and of the world. Ask these things of the Word; it will answer you. According to the will of God, sickness is a discipline occasioned by sin (or shortcoming), and healing, granted to the prayer of faith, bears witness to His grace that pardons, sanctifies, and takes away sin.

Chapter 27

Obedience and Health

There he made for them a statute and an ordinance,
and there he proved them, and said, If thou wilt diligently
hearken to the voice of the Lord thy God, and wilt do that which
is right in his sight, and wilt give ear to his commandments,
and keep all his statutes, I will put none of these diseases
upon thee, which I have brought upon the Egyptians:
for I am the Lord that healeth thee.
—Exodus 15:25–26

*I*srael was just released from the yoke of Egypt when their
faith was put to the test in the desert by the waters of Marah.
It was after the Lord had sweetened the bitter waters that He
promised He would not put on the children of Israel any of
the diseases that He had brought upon the Egyptians, as long
as the Israelites would obey Him. They would be exposed to
other trials. They might sometimes suffer the need of bread
and of water, or they would have to contend with mighty foes
and encounter great dangers. All these things might come upon
them in spite of their obedience, but sickness would not touch
them. In a world still under the power of Satan, they might be a
target for attacks coming from without, but their bodies would

not be oppressed with sickness, for God had delivered them from it. Had He not said, *"If thou wilt diligently hearken to the voice of the LORD thy God,...I will put none of these diseases upon thee, which I have brought upon the Egyptians: for I am the LORD that healeth thee"*? Elsewhere He said, *"Ye shall serve the LORD your God,...and I will take sickness away from the midst of thee"* (Exod. 23:25). (See also Leviticus 7:12–16; 26:14–16; 28:15–61.)

This calls our attention to a truth of the greatest importance: the intimate relationship that exists between obedience and health; and between sanctification, which is the health of the soul, and divine healing, which ensures the health of the body. Both are comprised in the salvation that comes from God. It is noteworthy that in several languages these three words—*salvation, healing,* and *sanctification*—are derived from the same root and present the same fundamental thought. (For instance, the German *heil,* salvation; *heilung,* healing; *heilichung,* sanctification.) Salvation is the redemption that the Savior has obtained for us; health is the salvation of the body, which also comes to us from the divine Healer; and, sanctification reminds us that true salvation and true health consist in being holy as God is holy. Thus it is in giving health to the body and sanctification to the soul that Jesus is really the Savior of His people. Our text clearly declares the relationship that exists between holiness of life and the healing of the body. The expressions that bear this out seem to be purposely multiplied: *"If thou wilt diligently hearken..., and wilt do that which is right..., and wilt give ear..., and keep all his statutes, I will put none of these diseases upon thee."*

Here we have the key to all true obedience and holiness. We often think we know the will of God well as it is revealed in His Word, but why doesn't this knowledge inspire obedience? It is because in order to obey, we must begin by listening. *"If thou wilt diligently hearken to the voice of the LORD thy God,...and wilt give ear."* As long as the will of God reaches me through the voice of a man, or through the reading of a book, it will have little power with me. But if I enter into direct communion with God and listen to His voice, His commandment is quickened with living power to accomplish its purpose.

Christ is the living Word, and the Holy Spirit is His voice. Listening to His voice means to renounce all our own will and wisdom, to close our ears to every other voice so as to expect no other direction but that of the Holy Spirit. One who is redeemed is like a servant or child who needs to be directed; he knows that he belongs entirely to God, and that all his being—spirit, soul, and body—ought to glorify God.

But he is equally conscious that this is above his strength, and that he needs to receive, hour by hour, the direction he needs. He knows, also, that the divine commandment, as long as it is a dead letter to him, cannot impart to him strength and wisdom, and that it is only as he attentively gives ear that he will obtain the desired strength. Therefore, he listens and learns to observe the laws of God. This life of attention and action, of renouncement and of crucifixion, constitutes a holy life. The Lord first brings it to us in the form of sickness, making us understand what we are lacking. He then shows us by our healing, which calls the soul to a life of continual attention to the voice of God.

Most Christians see nothing more in divine healing than a temporal blessing for the body, while in the promise of our holy God, its end is to make us holy. The call to holiness sounds stronger and clearer daily in the church. More and more believers are coming to understand that God wants them to be like Christ. The Lord is beginning, again, to make use of His healing virtue, seeking thereby to show us that, in our own day, the Holy One of Israel is still *"the LORD that healeth thee,"* and that it is His will to keep His people both in health of body and in obedience.

Let him who looks for healing from the Lord receive it with joy. It is not a legal obedience that is required of him, an obedience depending on his own strength. No, God asks of him, on the contrary, the abandonment of a little child, the attention that listens and consents to be led. This is what God expects of him. The healing of the body will respond to this childlike faith. The Lord will reveal Himself to him as the mighty Savior who heals the body and sanctifies the soul.

Chapter 28

---◆---

Job's Sickness and Healing

*So went Satan forth from the presence of the LORD,
and smote Job with sore boils from the sole of his foot
unto his crown.*
—Job 2:7

*T*he veil that hides the unseen world from us is lifted for a
moment in the mysterious history of Job, revealing heaven
and hell occupied with God's servants on earth. We see in it the
temptations peculiar to sickness, and how Satan makes use of
them to dispute with God and to seek the perdition of the soul
of man. God, on the other hand, seeks to sanctify it by the very
same trial. In the case of Job, we see, in God's light, where sickness comes from, what result it should have, and how it is possible to be delivered from it.

Where does sickness come from—from God or from Satan?
Opinions on this point differ vastly. Some hold that it is sent from
God; others see it as the work of the wicked one. Both are in
error, as long as they hold their view to the exclusion of that held
by the other party, while both are in the right if they admit that
there are two sides to this question. Let us say, then, that sickness comes from Satan, but that it cannot exist without the per-
mission of God. On the other hand, the power of Satan is that of

an oppressor, who has no right to attack man, but whose claims on man are legitimate in that God decrees that he who yields himself to Satan places himself under his domination.

Satan is the prince of the kingdom of darkness and of sin; sickness is the consequence of sin. This constitutes the right of Satan over the body of sinful man. He is the prince of this world, so recognized by God, until such time as he shall be legally conquered and dethroned. Consequently, he has a certain power over all those who remain down here under his jurisdiction. He then torments men with sickness and seeks thereby to turn them from God and to work their ruin.

But, we would hasten to say, the power of Satan is far from being almighty; it can do nothing without God's authorization. God permits him to do everything he does in tempting men, even believers, but it is in order that the trial may bring forth in them the fruit of holiness. It is also said that Satan has the power of death (Heb. 2:14), that he is everywhere that death reigns. Nevertheless, he has no power to decide as to the death of God's servants without the express will of God. It is the same with sickness. Because of sin, sickness is the work of Satan. But since supreme direction of this world belongs to God, it can also be regarded as the work of God. All who are acquainted with the book of Job know how very clearly this point is brought out there.

What should result from sickness? The result will be good or evil, depending on whether God or Satan has the victory in us. Under Satan's influence, a sick person sinks always deeper into sin. He does not recognize sin to be the cause of the chastisement, and he occupies himself exclusively with himself and with his suffering. He desires nothing but to be healed, without dreaming of a desire for deliverance from sin.

But wherever God gains the victory, sickness leads the sufferer to renounce himself and to abandon himself to God. The history of Job illustrates this. His friends accused him, unjustly, of having committed sins of exceptional gravity, which caused his terrible suffering. This was, however, not the case, since God

Himself had borne him witness that he was *"a perfect and an upright man, one that feareth God, and escheweth evil"* (Job 2:3).

But in defending himself, Job went too far. Instead of humbling himself in abasement before the Lord and recognizing his hidden sins, he attempted in all self-righteousness to justify himself. It was not until the Lord appeared to him that he came to say, *"I abhor myself, and repent in dust and ashes"* (Job 42:6). To him, sickness became a "signal" blessing in bringing him to know God in quite a new way, and to humble himself more than ever before Him. This is the blessing that God desires that we, too, may receive whenever He permits Satan to strike us with sickness, and this end is attained by all sufferers who abandon themselves unreservedly to Him.

How are we to be delivered from sickness? A father never prolongs the chastisement of his child beyond the time necessary. God, also, who has His purpose in permitting sickness, will not prolong the chastisement longer than is necessary to attain His end. As soon as Job had understood Him, from the time that he condemned himself and repented in dust and ashes, through paying attention to what God had revealed to him of Himself, the chastisement was at an end. God Himself delivered Job from Satan's hand and healed him of his sickness.

If only the sick in our day understood that God has a distinct purpose in permitting their chastisement, and that as soon as it is attained—as soon as the Holy Spirit leads them to confess and forsake their sins and to consecrate themselves entirely to the service of the Lord—the chastisement will no longer be needed. The Lord can and will deliver them! God makes use of Satan as a wise government makes use of a jailer. He leaves His children in his power for the given time only. After that, His good will is to associate us with Christ, who has conquered Satan, withdrawing us from his domination by bearing our sins and our sicknesses for us.

Chapter 29

————————◄•◆•►————————

The Prayer of Faith

The prayer of faith shall save the sick,
and the Lord shall raise him up.
—James 5:15

" The prayer of faith"! Only once does this expression occur in the Bible, and it relates to the healing of the sick. The church has adopted this expression but hardly ever uses the prayer of faith, except to obtain other graces. According to Scripture, it is especially intended for the healing of the sick.

Did the apostle expect healing through the prayer of faith alone, or should it be accompanied by the use of remedies? This is generally the question that is raised. It is easily decided, if we take into consideration the power of the church's spiritual life in the early ages. This includes the gifts of healing bestowed on the apostles by the Lord, and augmented by the subsequent outpouring of the Holy Spirit. (See Acts 4:30; 5:15–16.) What Paul said of *"these gifts of healing by the same Spirit"* (1 Cor. 12:9), James insisted on when he recalled Elijah's prayer and God's wonderful answer (James 5:17–18). All this clearly shows that the believer is to look for healing in response to the prayer of faith. Although God may use human remedies to aid in the healing, we must always remember that it is He who accomplishes the act.

Another question will arise: does the use of remedies exclude the prayer of faith? To this, we believe our reply should be no, for the experience of a large number of believers testifies that, in answer to their prayers, God has often blessed the use of remedies and made them a means of healing.

We come here to a third question: what is the method to follow in order to prove with the greatest certainty, and according to the will of God, the effectiveness of the prayer of faith? Is it, according to James, in setting aside all remedies or in using remedies as believers do for the most part? In a word, is it with or without remedies that the prayer of faith best obtains the grace of God? Which of these two methods will be most directly to the glory of God and for blessing to the sick one? Is it not perfectly simple to reply that if the prescription and the promise in James apply to believers of our time, the blessing today will be just the same as it was then? It will apply to believers in all areas, if they expect healing by the direct intervention of the Lord Himself, without using any remedies. It is, in fact, in this sense that Scripture always speaks of powerful faith and of the prayer of faith.

Both the laws of nature and the witness of Scripture show us that God often makes use of intermediary agencies to manifest His glory. Under the power of the Fall and the control of our senses, our tendency is to attach more importance to the remedies than to the direct action of God. It often happens that we are so preoccupied with the remedies that we turn away from God. Thus the laws and the properties of nature, which were destined to bring us back to God, have the contrary effect.

This is why, when the Lord called Abraham to be the father of His chosen people, He did not follow the laws of nature. (See Romans 4:17–21.) God desired to form for Himself a people of faith, who lived more in the unseen than in the tangible world. In order to lead them into this life, it was necessary to take away their confidence in ordinary means. We see, therefore, that it was not by natural ways that God led Abraham, Jacob, Moses, Joshua, Gideon, the Judges, David, and many other kings of Israel. His objective was to teach them by this to confide only in Him, to know Him as He is: *"Thou art the God that doest wonders"* (Ps. 77:14).

God wills to act in a similar way with us. When we seek to walk according to His prescription in James 5, abandoning the *"things which are seen"* (2 Cor. 4:18) to grasp God's promise—the desired healing—directly from Him, we discover how much importance we have attached to earthly remedies. Undoubtedly, there are Christians who can make use of remedies without damage to their spiritual lives, but the larger number of them are apt to count much more on the remedies than on the power of God. God's desire is to lead His children into a more intimate communion with Christ, and this is just what does happen, when, by faith, we commit ourselves to Him as our sovereign Healer. When one is led by God to renounce remedies, his faith my be strengthened in an extraordinary manner. Healing then becomes a source of innumerable spiritual blessings. What faith can accomplish becomes more real to us. A new tie is established between God and the believer, commencing in him a life of confidence and dependence. The body and the soul are placed equally under the power of the Holy Spirit. Thus, the prayer of faith, which saves the sick, leads us to a life of faith, strengthened by the assurance that God manifests His presence in our earthly lives.

Chapter 30

---◆--

Anointing in the Name of the Lord

*Is any sick among you? let him call for the elders
of the church; and let them pray over him,
anointing him with oil in the name of the Lord.*
—James 5:14

James's instruction to anoint the sick person with oil in the name of the Lord has given rise to controversy. Some have sought to infer that James mentioned anointing with oil as a remedy to be employed, and that to anoint in the name of the Lord simply meant to rub the patient with oil. But since this prescription is made for all kinds of sickness, oil would have to possess a miraculous healing power. Let us see what the Scriptures tell us about anointing with oil, and what sense it attaches to the two words, *anointing* and *oil*.

It was the custom of the people in the East to anoint themselves with oil when they came out of the bath; it was most refreshing in a hot climate. We see, also, that all those who were called to the special service of God were to be anointed with oil, as a token of their consecration to God, and of the grace that they would receive from Him to fulfill their vocation. Thus the oil that was used to anoint the priests and the tabernacle was looked upon as *"most holy"* (Exod. 30:29). Wherever the Bible speaks of anointing with oil, it is an emblem of holiness and consecration. Nowhere in the Bible do we find any proof that oil was used as a medicine.

Anointing with oil is mentioned once in connection with sickness, but its place there was evidently as a religious ceremony and not as a medicine. In Mark 6:13, we read that the Twelve *"cast out many devils, and anointed with oil many that were sick, and healed them."* Here the healing of the sick runs parallel with the casting out of devils: both are the result of miraculous power. Such was the kind of mission that Jesus commanded His disciples when He sent them two by two: *"He gave them power against unclean spirits, to cast them out, and to heal all manner of sickness and all manner of disease"* (Matt. 10:1). Thus, it was the same power that permitted them either to cast out devils or to heal the sick.

But let us seek to discover what was symbolized by the anointing administered by the Twelve. In the Old Testament, oil was the symbol of the gift of the Holy Spirit: *"The Spirit of the Lord God is upon me; because the Lord hath anointed me"* (Isa. 61:1). It is said of the Lord Jesus in the New Testament, *"God anointed Jesus of Nazareth with the Holy Ghost and with power"* (Acts 10:38), and it is said of believers, *"Ye have an unction* [anointing] *from the Holy One"* (1 John 2:20). Sometimes man feels the need of a visible sign, appealing to his senses, that may come to his aid to sustain his faith and enable him to grasp the spiritual meaning. The anointing, therefore, should symbolize to the sick one the action of the Holy Spirit who gives the healing.

Do we then need the anointing as well as the prayer of faith? The Word of God prescribes it. In order to follow God's Word, most of those who pray for healing receive the anointing. This is not so much because they regard it as indispensable, but to show that they are ready to submit to the Word of God in all things. In the last promise made by the Lord Jesus, He ordains the laying on of hands, not the anointing, to accompany the communication of healing virtue (Mark 16:18). When Paul circumcised Timothy and took upon himself a special vow, it was to prove that he had no objection to observe the institutions of the old covenant as long as the liberty of the Gospel did not thereby suffer loss. In the same way, James, the head of the church of Jerusalem, faithful in preserving as far as possible the institutions of his fathers, continued the system of the Holy Spirit. And we also should regard it, not as a remedy, but as a pledge of the mighty virtue of the Holy Spirit, as a means of strengthening faith, a point of contact and of communion between the sick one and the members of the church who are called to anoint him with oil.

"I am the LORD that healeth thee" (Exod. 15:26).

Chapter 31

———————◆◆◆———————

Full Salvation—Our High Privilege

Son, thou art ever with me, and all that I have is thine.
—Luke 15:31

We may talk a great deal about the father's love for the Prodigal Son, but when we think of the way he treated the elder brother, it brings to our hearts a truer sense of the wonderful love of the father.

I suppose that many readers of this book have "full salvation"; but perhaps more than half of you do not. You may not even understand the expression. Well, the great objective of this book is to bring you to see that full salvation is waiting for you now, and that God wants you to experience it. If you feel you do not have it, I wish to show you how wrong it is to be without it, and then to show you how to come out of that wrong life and into the right one. May all who do not have the experience pray very humbly, "Oh, my Father, bring me into the full enjoyment of Your full salvation."

In the parable that Jesus told in Luke 15:11–32, the elder son was always with his father and had two privileges: unceasing fellowship and unlimited partnership. But he was worse than the Prodigal Son, for, though he was always at home, he had never known, enjoyed, or understood these privileges. All this fullness of fellowship had been waiting for and offered to him, but he had not received it. While the Prodigal Son was away from home in the far country, his elder brother was far from the *enjoyment of* home, even while he was at home.

Full salvation includes unceasing fellowship: *"Ever with me."* An earthly father loves his child and delights to make his child happy. *"God is love"* (1 John 4:8), and He delights to pour out His own nature on His people. Many people talk about God hiding His face, but there are only two things that ever caused God to do so: sin and unbelief. Nothing else can. It is the very nature of the sun to shine, and it can't help shining on and on. *"God is love,"* and, speaking with all reverence, He can't help loving. We see His goodness toward the ungodly and His compassion on the erring. His fatherly love is manifested toward all His children.

"But," you say, "is it possible always to be happy and dwelling with God?" Yes, certainly, and there are many Scripture promises that speak to this point. Look at the epistle to the Hebrews, where we read of the *"boldness to enter into the holiest"* (Heb. 10:19). How often, too, did David speak of hiding *"in the secret of his tabernacle"* (Ps. 27:5) and dwelling *"under the shadow of the Almighty"* (Ps. 91:1)?

My message is that the Lord your God desires to have you living continually in the light of His countenance. Are your business, your temper, and your circumstances stronger than God? If you come and ask God to shine through them and onto you, you will see and prove that He can do it, and that you as a believer may walk all day long, every day, in the light of His love. That is "full salvation." "Ever with Thee"; I never knew it, Lord, and so I did not enjoy it, but I do now.

Full salvation includes unlimited partnership: *"All that I have is thine."* The elder son complained of the father's gracious reception of the Prodigal—of all the feasting and rejoicing over his return—while he, the elder brother, had never been given a lamb to enjoy in feasting with his friends. The father, in the tenderness of his love, answered him, "Son, you were always in my house; you had only to ask, and you would have been given everything you desired and required." And that is what our Father says to all His children.

But you are saying, "I am so weak; I cannot conquer my sins; I can't manage to keep right; I can't do anything." No, you cannot, but God can. For so long, He has been saying to you, "All that I have is yours. I have given it to you in Christ. All the Spirit's power and wisdom, all the riches of Christ, all the love of the Father—there is nothing that I have that is not yours. I am God who will love, keep, and bless you."

Thus God speaks, but it seems all a dream to some. Why are you so poor? God's Word is sure, and does He not promise all this? In John 14–16, He tells us that we may have wonderful answers to prayer if we come in Jesus' name and abide in Him. Do we really believe that it is possible for a Christian to live such a life?

Now, we have looked at this great privilege, which is for everyone, so we move on to consider the poverty of many of God's dear children. It is nothing short of starvation. The elder son—the child of a rich man—living in utter poverty! He never had a fatted calf, while all that was his father's was his—just exactly the state of many children of God! The way He wants us to live is in the fullest fellowship of all His blessings, yet what a contrast!

Ask some if their lives are full of joy; why, they don't even believe it is possible to be always happy and holy. "How could we survive like this in business?" they say, imagining the life of fullest blessing possible to be one of sighing and sadness and sorrow.

I asked a dear devoted Christian woman how she was doing. She answered that she experienced life as sometimes light and sometimes dark, arguing that, since this resembled nature, the kingdom of grace must be similar. So she willingly accepted a wretched experience. But I don't read in the Bible that there is to be any night or darkness in the believer's experience. On the contrary, I read, *"Thy sun shall no more go down"* (Isa. 60:20). Yet there are many who actually believe that there is nothing this good for them.

Again, nothing can hide God from us but sin and unbelief. If you are in spiritual poverty, with no joy and no experience of victory over sin, why is it so? You say, "I'm too weak; I must fall." But the Scriptures say that He is *"able to keep you from falling* [stumbling]" (Jude 24). A minister once told me that, although God is able, the verse does not say He is willing to do it. God does not mock us, beloved. If He says He is *"able,"* then it is a proof of His willingness to do it. Let us believe God's Word and examine our own experience in the light of it.

Again, are you working and bearing much fruit for God, and do people by your life see and say, "God is with that man, keeping him humble, pure, and heavenly minded"? Or are they forced to confess that you are just a very ordinary Christian, easily provoked, worldly, and not heavenly minded? That is not the life God wants us to live. We have a rich Father, and as no true earthly father would like to see his child in rags, or without shoes and proper clothing, neither does our God. He wishes to fill up our lives with the richest and choicest blessings.

How many Sunday school teachers there are who teach and teach, hoping for the conversion of their students, yet they can't say God uses them in the conversion of any of them. They enjoy no close fellowship with God, no victory over sin, no power to convince the world. To which class do you belong, the poverty level or the fully saved? Confess it today.

These two sons represent two classes of Christians: the Prodigal, who is away and backslidden; and the elder son, who is out of full fellowship with God. They were both poor. The elder son needed as great a change as the Prodigal. He needed to repent, confess, and claim his full privileges as a son. So should all low-level Christians repent, confess, and claim full salvation. Both of you, come today and say, "Father, I have sinned."

Now, ask why your experience is so much different than it should be. Ask yourself why you are not enjoying the full blessing. God's Word promises it, others speak of it, and some are actually living in it. Oh, ask the reason. Come to God and say, "Why is it that I never live the life You want me to live?"

You will find the answer in our story. Just like the elder son, you have an unchildlike spirit and don't really know your Father. If you knew the real character of your Father, your life would be all right. You have, as it were, said, "I never got a calf to enjoy; my Father is rich, but He never gives. I have prayed quite enough, but God does not answer me. I hear other people say that God fills and satisfies them, but He never does that for me."

A dear minister once told me than an abundant life was not for everybody, that it was of God's sovereignty to give this to whomever He pleased. Friends, there is no doubt as to God's sovereignty. He dispenses His gifts as He will. We are not all Pauls or Peters; places at the right and left hand of God are prepared for whomever He will. But this is not a matter of divine sovereignty; it is a question of a child's heritage. The Father's love offers to give to every child His full salvation in actual experience.

Now look at an earthly father. His children are of various ages, but all have equal right to the joy of their father's countenance. True, he gives to his son of twenty years more money than to the son of five, and he has more to speak of to the boy of fifteen than to the child of three. But his love toward them is all the same, and in their privileges as children, they are all alike. Likewise, God's love to His dear children is all the same.

Do not try to throw the blame on God, but say, "I have harbored bad thoughts about You, O God, and I have sinned. As a father, I have done for my children what I did not believe God was able and willing to do for me, and I have been lacking in childlike faith." Oh, believe in the love, the willingness, and the power of God to give you full salvation, and a change will surely come.

Now, let us consider the way of restoration, how to get out of this negative experience. The Prodigal Son repented, and so must those children of God who have been living within sight of, but not enjoying, His promises. Conversion is generally sudden, and a long repentance is usually a long impenitence.

Many in the church of Christ think it must take a long time to receive full salvation. Yes, it will take a long time if you do it yourself—indeed, you probably never will receive it. But if you come and trust God, it can be done in a moment. By God's grace, give yourself up to Him. Don't say, "What's the use? It will do no good." Put yourself, just as you are, in sin and weakness, into the bosom of your Father. God will deliver you, and you will find that it is only one step out of the darkness into the light. Say, "Father, what a wretch I have been, to live with You and yet not believe Your love for me!"

I come today with a call to repent, addressed not to the unsaved, but to those who know what it is to be pardoned. Have you not sinned in the cold thoughts you have had of God, and is there not a longing, a thirsting, and a hungering after something better? Come, then; repent, and believe that God can simply blot out the sin of your unbelief. Do you believe it? Oh, do not dishonor God by unbelief, but come today and confidently claim full salvation. Then trust in Him to keep you. This seems difficult to some, but there is no difficulty about it. God will shine His light on you always, saying, *"Son, thou art ever with me."* All you have to do is dwell in and walk in that light.

I began by saying there are two classes of Christians: those who enjoy full salvation, and those who do not understand it. Well, if it is not clear to you, ask God to make it clear. But if you do understand it, remember, it is a definite act. Just let yourself go into the arms of God. Hear Him say, "Everything is yours." Then you will say, "Praise God, I believe, I accept, I give myself to Him, and I believe God gives Himself now to me!"

Chapter 32

━━━━━◆━━━━━

You Are the Branches

Ye are the branches.
—John 15:5

What a simple thing it is to be a branch—the branch of a tree, or the branch of a vine! The branch grows out of the vine, or out of the tree, and there it lives and in due time bears fruit. It has no responsibility except receiving sap and nourishment from the root and stem.

If we only realized that our relationship to Jesus Christ, by way of the Holy Spirit, is like this, our lives would become heavenly! Instead of soul-weariness or exhaustion, our work would be a new experience, linking us to Jesus as nothing else can.

Is it not often true that our work comes between us and Jesus? What folly it is to allow the very work He has to do in me, and I for Him, to separate me from Christ. Many workers have complained that they have too much work and not enough time for close communion with Jesus, that their usual work weakens their inclination for prayer, and that even spending too much time with people clouds their spiritual lives. What a sad thought that the bearing of fruit should separate the branch from the vine! That must be because we have looked at our work as something other than the branch bearing fruit. May God deliver us from every false thought about the Christian life.

Now, just a few thoughts about this blessed branch-life. In the first place, it is a life of absolute dependence. The branch has nothing; it depends on the vine for everything. That phrase, *absolute dependence,* is one of the most solemn and precious phrases. A great German theologian wrote two large volumes some years ago to show that the whole of Calvin's theology is summed up in that one principle of absolute dependence on God, and he was right. If you can learn every moment of the day to depend on God, everything will turn out right. You will get the higher life if you depend absolutely on God.

I must understand, when I have to work, when I have to preach a sermon, or when I have to address a Bible class or go out and visit the poor, that all the responsibility of the work is His. That is exactly what Christ wants you to understand. Christ desires that the very foundation of all your work should be this simple, blessed consciousness: Christ must care for everything.

And how does He fulfill the trust of that dependence? He does it by sending down the Holy Spirit, not only now and then as a special gift, but hourly, daily, unceasingly, the living connection between the vine and the branches is maintained. The sap does not flow for a time, then stop, and then flow again. Rather, from moment to moment the sap flows from the vine to the branches. And just like this, my Lord Jesus wants me to take that blessed position as His worker. Morning by morning, day by day, hour by hour, and step by step, I must abide in Him in the simple, utter helplessness of one who knows nothing, and is nothing, and can do nothing.

Absolute dependence on God is the secret of all power in work. The branch has nothing but what it gets from the vine, and you and I can have nothing but what we get from Jesus.

The life of the branch is not only a life of entire dependence, but of deep restfulness. If that little branch could talk to us, we could ask it, "Branch of the vine, how can I be a true branch of the living Vine?"

The little branch would answer, "I hear that you are wise, and I know that you can do a great many wonderful things. You have much strength and wisdom given to you, but I have one lesson for you. With all your hurry and effort in Christ's work, you never prosper. The first thing you need is to come and rest in your Lord Jesus. That is what I do.

"Since I grew out of that vine, I have spent years and years doing nothing but resting in the vine. When spring came, I had no anxious thought or care. The vine began to pour its sap into me and produced the bud and leaf. When the summer came, I had no care. I trusted the vine to bring moisture to keep me fresh in the great heat. At harvest time, when the owner came to pluck the grapes, I had no care. If the grapes were not good, the owner never blamed the branch; the blame was always on the vine. If you desire to be a true branch of Christ, the living Vine, just rest on Him. Let Christ bear the responsibility."

You say, "Won't that make me slothful?" I tell you it will not. No one who learns to rest on the living Christ can become slothful, for the closer your contact with Christ, the more the Spirit of His zeal and love will fill you. A man sometimes tries and tries to be dependent on Christ. But by worrying about this absolute dependence, he tries and he cannot get it. Instead of worrying, he should sink down into entire restfulness every day.

Rest in Christ, who can give wisdom and strength. That restfulness will often prove to be the very best part of your Christian witness. You can plead with people, and you can argue. All they will know is that a man is arguing and striving with them. This is what happens when two men deal with each other, without Christ. But if you will let the deep rest of God come over you— the rest in Christ Jesus, the peace and holiness of heaven—that restfulness will bring a blessing to your heart, even more than the words you speak.

Furthermore, the branch teaches a lesson of much fruitfulness. You know the Lord Jesus repeated the word *fruit* often in that parable; He spoke first of *"fruit"* (John 15:2), then of *"more fruit"* (v. 2), finally of *"much fruit"* (vv. 5, 8). Yes, you are ordained not only to bear fruit, but also to bear much fruit. *"Herein is my Father glorified, that ye bear much fruit"* (John 15:8). In the first place, Christ said, "I am the Vine, and My Father is the Husbandman who has charge of Me and you." He who will watch over the connection between Christ and the branches is God; and it is in the power of God, through Christ, that we are to bear fruit.

Oh, Christians, this world is perishing because of the lack of workers! And it needs more than workers. Some are saying, "We need not only more workers, but also workers with a new power, a different life, so that the workers will be able to bring more blessing."

What is missing is the close connection between the worker and the heavenly Vine. Christ, the heavenly Vine, has blessings that He could pour on tens of thousands who are perishing. Christ, the heavenly Vine, has the power to provide heavenly grapes. But *"ye are the branches,"* and you cannot bear heavenly fruit unless you are in close connection with Jesus Christ.

Do not confuse work and fruit. There is a good deal of work for Christ that is not the fruit of the heavenly Vine. Do not seek work only. Study this question of fruit-bearing. It is the very life, power, Spirit, and love within the heart of the Son of God; it means the heavenly Vine Himself coming into your heart and mine.

Stand in close connection with the heavenly Vine and say, "Lord Jesus, we ask for nothing less than the sap that flows through You, nothing less than the Spirit of Your divine life. Lord Jesus, let your Spirit flow through me in all my work for You."

Once again, the sap of the heavenly Vine is nothing but the Holy Spirit, and the Holy Spirit is nothing but the life of the heavenly Vine. What you must get from Christ is nothing less than a strong inflow of the Holy Spirit. You need it exceedingly, and you need nothing more. Remember this. Do not expect Christ to give a bit of strength here, a bit of blessing yonder, and a bit of help over there. As the vine does its work in giving its own unique sap to the branch, expect Christ to give His own Holy Spirit to your heart. Then you will bear much fruit. And if you have only begun to bear fruit and are listening to the words of Christ in the parable, *"more fruit," "much fruit,"* remember that in order for you to bear more fruit, you just require more of Jesus in your life and heart.

Keep in mind that the life of the branch is a life of close communion. Such communion can be described only by Christ's precious, inexhaustible word: *abiding.* Your life is to be an abiding life. Just like the branch in the vine, abide every minute of the day in the living Vine. The branches are in close communion—in unbroken communion—with the vine, from January to December.

You say you are too busy with other things. You may do ten hours of hard work daily, during which your brain has to be occupied with temporal things; God orders it so. But the abiding work is the work of the heart, not of the brain. It is the work of the heart clinging to and resting in Jesus, a work in which the Holy Spirit links us to Christ Jesus. Oh, believe that deeper down than the brain—deep down in the inner life—you can abide in Christ. Then every moment you are free, the awareness will come: "Blessed Jesus, I am still in You." If you will learn for a time to put aside other work and to get into this abiding contact with the heavenly Vine, you will find that fruit will come.

What is the application of this abiding communion to our everyday life? What does it mean? It means close fellowship with Christ in secret prayer. Many Christians have experienced a great inflow of heavenly joy and a great outflow of heavenly gladness that has, after a time, passed away. They have not understood that close, personal, actual communion with Christ is an absolute necessity for daily life. Take time to be alone with Christ. Nothing in heaven or earth can free you from the necessity for that, if you are to be a happy and holy Christian.

How many Christians look at it as a burden, a duty, and a difficulty to be alone with God! That is the great hindrance to our Christian life everywhere.

We need more quiet fellowship with God. You cannot be healthy branches—branches into which the heavenly sap can flow—unless you take plenty of time for communion with God. If you are not willing to sacrifice time to be alone with Him, giving Him time every day to work in you and to maintain the connection between you and Himself, He cannot give you that blessing of His unbroken fellowship. Jesus Christ asks you to live in close communion with Him. Let every heart say, "O Christ, it is this I long for; it is this I choose." And He will gladly give it to you.

The life of the branch is a life of entire surrender. *Entire surrender* is a great and solemn concept that is difficult to understand, yet the little branch preaches it. "Can you do anything, little branch, besides bearing grapes?" "No, nothing." "Are you fit for nothing?" "Fit for nothing!" The Bible says that a bit of vine cannot be used even as a pen; it is fit for nothing but to be burned. "And now, little branch, what do you understand about your relationship to the vine?" "My relationship is just this: I am entirely given up to the vine; it can give me as much or as little sap as it chooses. I am at its disposal, and the vine can do with me what it likes."

We need this entire surrender to the Lord Jesus Christ. One of the most difficult points to make clear, and one of the most important and necessary points to explain, is what this entire surrender is. It is an easy thing for a man or a number of men to offer themselves up to God for entire consecration, and to say, "Lord, it is my desire to give myself entirely to You." That is of great value, and often brings a very rich blessing. But the one question that should be studied quietly is, What is meant by entire surrender?

It means that, just as literally as Christ was given up entirely to God, I am given up entirely to Christ. Some think that it is too strong. Some think it can never be, but it is true. Just as completely as Christ gave up His life to do nothing but seek the Father's pleasure, depending on the Father absolutely, I am to do nothing but seek the pleasure of Christ.

Christ Jesus came to breathe His own Spirit into us, to make us find our very highest happiness in living entirely for God, just as He did. Fellow believers, if that is the case, then I ought to say, "Yes, as true as it is of that little branch of the vine, so by God's grace, I would have it be true of me. I desire to live day by day, allowing Christ to do with me what He will."

Here lies the terrible mistake of so much of our own religion. A man thinks, "I have my business, my family duties, and my responsibilities as a citizen, all of which I cannot change. Now, in addition to all this, I am to enlist in the service of God as something that will keep me from sin. May He help me to perform my duties properly!"

That is not right. When Christ came, He came and bought the sinner with His blood. If there were a slave market here and I were to buy a slave, I would take that slave away from his old surroundings, and he would live at my house as my personal property, where I could order him about all day long. If he were a faithful slave, he would live as having no will and no interests of his own, his one care being to promote the well-being and honor of his master. In like manner, I, who have been bought with the blood of Christ, have been bought to live every day with only one thought: how can I please my Master?

We find the Christian life so difficult because we seek God's blessing while we live in our own wills. We would much rather live the Christian life according to our own liking. We could make our own plans and choose our own work. Then we ask the Lord Jesus to come in and guard us against sin and see that we do not go too far wrong. We also ask Him for much of His blessing.

But our relationship to Jesus ought to be such that we are entirely at His disposal. Every day we should go to Him humbly and straightforwardly and say, "Lord, is there anything in me that is not according to Your will, that has not been ordered by You, or that is not entirely given up to You?" If we could then wait patiently, a relationship would spring up between us that was so close and so tender that we would be amazed at the distance in our previous relationship.

There are a great many difficulties with the question of holiness, and much disagreement about it. If only everyone could honestly long to be free from every sin. But our hearts often compromise by thinking, "We cannot be without sin. We must sin a little every day; we cannot help it." Instead, we must actually cry to God, "Lord, keep me from sin!" Give yourself utterly to Jesus, and ask Him to do His utmost for you in keeping you from sin.

In conclusion, let me gather everything together. Christ Jesus said, *"I am the vine, ye are the branches"* (John 15:5). In other words: "I, the living One who has so completely given Myself to you, am the Vine. You cannot trust Me too much. I am the almighty Worker, full of divine life and power."

Christians, you are the branches of the Lord Jesus Christ. Your heart may lack the consciousness of being a strong, healthy, fruit-bearing branch, closely linked with Jesus. If you are not living in Him as you should be, then listen to Him saying, "I am the Vine. I will receive you, and I will draw you to Myself. I will bless you and strengthen you. I will fill you with My Spirit. I, the Vine, have taken you to be My branches. I have given Myself utterly to you; children, give yourselves utterly to Me. I have surrendered Myself as God absolutely to you. I became Man and died for you so that I might be entirely yours. Come and surrender yourselves entirely to be Mine."

What will our answer be? Oh, let it be a prayer from the depths of our hearts, that the living Christ may take each one of us and link us closely to Himself. Let our prayer be that He, the living Vine, will link each of us to Himself in such a way that we will walk victoriously, with our hearts singing, "He is my Vine, and I am His branch. I want nothing more, now that I have the everlasting Vine." Then, when you get alone with Him, worship and adore Him, praise and trust Him, love Him and wait for His love. "You are my Vine, and I am Your branch. It is enough; my soul is satisfied. Glory to His blessed name!"

Book Five

———◆◆———

God's Plans for You

Contents

Preface

---◆---

*T*he purpose of this little book is first of all to remind all Christian workers of the greatness and the glory of the work in which God gives us a share. It is nothing less than that work of bringing people back to their God in which God finds His highest glory and blessedness. As we see that it is God's own work we have to work out, that He works it through us, that in our doing it His glory rests on us and we glorify Him, we will count it our joy to give ourselves to live only and wholly for it.

The aim of the book at the same time is to help those who complain, those who perhaps do not even know to complain, that they are apparently laboring in vain to find out what may be the cause of so much failure. God's work must be done in God's way and in God's power. It is spiritual work that is to be done by spiritual men in the power of the Spirit. The clearer our insight into and the more complete our submission to God's laws of work, the surer and the richer will be our joy and our reward in it.

Along with this point, I have had in view the great number of Christians who practically take no real part in the service of their Lord. They have never understood that the chief characteristic of the divine life in God and Christ is love and its work of blessing men.

The divine life in us can show itself in no other way. I have tried to show that it is God's will that every believer without exception, whatever his position in life may be, should give himself wholly to live and work for God.

I have also written in the hope that some who already have training in Christian life and work may find thoughts that will be of use to them in teaching the imperative duty, the urgent need, and the divine blessedness of a life given to God's service, and to waken within the consciousness of the power that works in them, even the Spirit and power of Christ Himself.

To the great host of workers in churches and chapels, in mission halls and open-air meetings, in Day and Sunday schools, in Endeavor Societies, in Young Men's and Young Women's and Students' Associations, and all the various forms of the ministry of love throughout the world, I lovingly offer these meditations with the fervent prayer that God, the Great Worker, may make us true fellow workers with Himself.

—ANDREW MURRAY

Chapter 1

———◆◆◆———

Waiting and Working

*But they that wait upon the LORD shall renew
their strength; they shall mount up with wings
as eagles; they shall run, and not be weary;
and they shall walk, and not faint.*
—Isaiah 40:31

*Neither hath the eye seen, O God, beside thee,
what he hath prepared for him that waiteth for him.*
—Isaiah 64:4

*T*he relationship between waiting and working is made clear in the above verses. We see that waiting brings the needed strength for working—preparing us for joyful and unwearied work. *"They that wait upon the LORD shall renew their strength; they shall mount up with wings as eagles; they shall run, and not be weary; and they shall walk, and not faint."* Waiting on God has its value in this: it makes us strong to do His work. The second verse reveals the secret of this strength: *"Neither hath the eye seen…what he hath prepared for him that waiteth for him."* The waiting on God secures the working of God for us and in us, out of which our work must spring. These two passages teach the great lesson that waiting on God lies at the root of all true working for God. Our great need is to hold the two sides of this truth in perfect harmony.

There are some who say they wait upon God, but they do not work for Him. There may be various reasons for this. They confuse true waiting on God (living in direct communication with Him) with the lazy, helpless waiting that excuses itself from all work. Some wait on God as one of the highest exercises of the Christian life, yet they have never understood that the root of all true waiting must be surrender and readiness to be completely equipped for God's use in serving men.

Others are ready to work as well as wait, but they are looking for some great inflow of the Spirit's power to enable them to do mighty works, while they forget that as believers they already have the Spirit of Christ dwelling in them. They forget that more grace is given only to those who are faithful in the little (see Luke 16:10), and that it is only in working that we can be taught by the Spirit how to do the greater works.

All Christians need to learn that waiting has working for its objective. It is only in working that waiting can attain its full perfection and blessedness. It is as we elevate working for God to its true place, as the highest exercise of spiritual privilege and power, that the absolute need and the divine blessing of waiting on God can be fully known.

On the other hand, there are many who work for God but know little of what it is to wait on Him. They have been led to take up Christian work under the impulse of natural or spiritual feeling or the urging of a pastor. However, they do so with very little sense of what a holy thing it is to work for God. They do not know that God's work can be done only in God's strength, by God Himself working in us.

The Son of God could do nothing of Himself (John 8:28). The Father in Him did the work as He lived in continual dependence before Him. Many have never learned that the believer can do nothing unless God works in him. They do not understand that it is only in utter weakness that we depend upon Him, so that His power can rest on us. They have no conception of a continual waiting on God as being one of the first and essential conditions of successful work. Christ's church and the world are sufferers today, not only because so many of its members are not working for God, but also because so much working for God is done without waiting on God.

Among the members of the body of Christ, there is a great diversity of gifts and operations. Some who are confined to their homes because of sickness or other duties may have more time for waiting on God. Others, who are overworked, find it very difficult to make time and be quiet before the Lord. These may mutually supply each other's lack.

Let those who have time for waiting on God definitely link themselves to some who are working. Let those who are working seek the help of those to whom the special ministry of waiting on God has been entrusted. Thus will the unity and health of the church be maintained. Those who wait will know that the outcome will be power for work. Those who work will realize their only strength is the grace obtained by waiting. Thus will God work for His church that waits on Him.

Let us pray as we proceed in these meditations on working for God that the Holy Spirit will show us how sacred and urgent our calling is to work, and how absolute our dependence is upon God's strength to work in us. May we also learn how sure it is that those who wait on Him will renew their strength. Then we will find waiting on God and working for God to be inseparably one.

- It is only as God works for me and in me that I can work for Him.
- All His work for me is through His life in me.
- If I wait on Him, He will most surely work.
- All His working for me, and my waiting on Him, has but one aim: to equip me for His work of saving lost souls.

Chapter 2

———— ◆ ————

Good Works: The Light of the World

Ye are the light of the world....Let your light so shine
before men, that they may see your good works,
and glorify your Father which is in heaven.
—Matthew 5:14, 16

A light is meant for those in darkness to see. Just as the sun lights up the darkness of this world, a lamp is hung in a room to give it light. The church of Christ is the light of men, but the god of this world has blinded their eyes. (See 2 Corinthians 4:4.) Therefore, Christ's disciples are to shine into the darkness and give light. In the same way that the rays of light stream forth from the sun and scatter that light all about, the light of the good works of believers streams out to conquer the surrounding darkness of its ignorance of God and alienation from Him.

What a high and holy place is thus given to our good works! What power is attributed to them! How much depends on them! They are not only the light, health, and joy of our own lives, but also the means of bringing lost souls *"out of darkness into his marvellous light"* (1 Pet. 2:9). They not only bless men, but they also glorify God in leading men to know Him as the Author of the grace seen in His children. Study the teaching of Scripture in regard to good works, especially all work done directly for God and His kingdom. Listen to what these words of the Master have to teach us.

The aim of good works is that God may be glorified. You remember how our Lord said to the Father, *"I have glorified thee on the earth: I have finished the work which thou gavest me to do"* (John 17:4). More than once we read of how the people glorified God because of His miracles. It was because what He had done was manifested by a divine power. Thus it is when our good works are something more than the ordinary virtues of refined men and bear the imprint of God upon them that men will glorify God. They must be the good works of which the Sermon on the Mount (see Matthew 5:1–7:29) is the embodiment—a life of God's children doing more than others to help those in need, while, at the same time, they seek to be perfect as their Father in heaven is perfect. When Christians glorify God and reflect His love, they help prepare the unsaved for conversion. The works prepare the way for the testimony and demonstrate the reality of the divine truth that is taught.

The whole world was made for the glory of God. Christ came to redeem us from sin and bring us back to serve and glorify Him. Believers are placed in the world with this one purpose: that they may win others to God by the light of their good works. As truly as the light of the sun is meant to light up the world, the good works of God's children are meant to be the light of those who do not know or love God. We must clearly understand that good works bear the mark of something heavenly and divine and have the power of God in them.

The power is in good works. These words are written of Christ: *"In him was life; and the life was the light of men"* (John 1:4). The divine life gave out a divine light. And Christ said about His disciples, *"He that followeth me shall not walk in darkness, but shall have the light of life"* (John 8:12). Christ is our life and light. The deepest meaning of *"Let your light so shine"* is, let Christ, who dwells in you, be seen by everyone you meet. And because Christ in you is your light, your humble works can carry with them a power of divine conviction. The divine power working in you will be the same power working in those who see your works. Give way to the life and light of Christ dwelling in you, and people will glorify your Father who is in heaven for what they see in your good works.

There is an urgent need for good works in believers. As it is necessary that the sun shines every day, it is even more necessary that every believer lets his light shine before men. We have been created anew in Christ for this: to hold forth the Word of Life as lights in the world. Christ needs you urgently to let His light shine through you. The unsaved around you need your light if they are to find their way to God. God needs you to let His glory be seen through you. Just as a lamp functions to light up a room, every believer should function to light up the world.

Let us study what working for God is, and what good works are as part of this. We will then desire to follow Christ fully and have the light of life shine into our hearts and lives and then, from us, shine out to the world.

- *"Ye are the light of the world."* These words express the calling of the church as a whole. The fulfillment of this duty will depend upon the faithfulness with which each individual member loves and lives for those around him.
- In all our efforts to awaken the church to evangelize the world, our first aim must be to raise the standard of life for the individual believer concerning this teaching: as truly as a candle exists with the objective of giving light in the darkness, the one objective of your existence is to be a light to men.
- Pray that God by His Holy Spirit will reveal to you that you have nothing to live for but to let the light and love of God shine upon souls.

Chapter 3

"Son, Go Work"

Son, go work to day in my vineyard.
—Matthew 21:28

The father had two sons. To each he gave the command to go and work in his vineyard. The one went; the other did not. God has given the command and the power to every child of His to work in His vineyard, with the world as the field. Because the majority of God's children are not working for Him, the world is perishing.

Of all the mysteries that surround us in the world, one of the strangest and most incomprehensible is that, after hundreds of years, the very name of Jesus is still unknown to so many.

Consider what this means. To restore the ruin sin had caused, God, the almighty Creator, actually sent His own Son to the world to tell men of His love and to bring them His life and salvation. When Christ made His disciples partakers of that salvation, and the unspeakable joy it brings, He emphasized that they should make it known to others and be the lights of the world. He spoke of all who would come to Him through their witness. He left the world with the specific instruction to carry the Gospel to all men and teach all nations to practice all that He had commanded.

He also gave the definite assurance that all power for this work was in Him. By the power of His Holy Spirit, He would enable His people to be witnesses to the ends of the earth. And what do we see now? Many have yet to hear the name of Jesus, and many act as though they had never heard of Him!

Consider again what this means. All these dying millions have a right to come to the knowledge of Christ. Their salvation depends on their knowing Him. He could change their lives from sin and unhappiness to holy obedience and heavenly joy. Christ has a right to them. It would make His heart glad to have them come and be blessed in Him. Service to God is the connecting link. And yet, what His people do is nothing compared to what needs to be done, to what could be done, to what ought to be done.

What a revelation of the state of the church! The great majority of those who are counted as believers are doing nothing toward making Christ known to their fellowmen. There are those who are entirely in Christ's service, but they are not free to conquer the world because they are occupied with teaching and helping weak Christians! And so, with a finished salvation, a loving Redeemer, and a church set apart to spread the Gospel, many are still perishing!

There can be nothing of greater importance to the church than to consider what can be done to awaken believers to a sense of their holy calling and to make them see that *to work for God,* they must offer themselves as instruments *through whom God can do His work.* Two complaints that are continually heard are a lack of enthusiasm for God's kingdom in the majority of Christians and the vain attempts to awaken an interest in missions. Nothing less is needed than a revival that would raise the average Christian to an entirely new type of devotion. No true change can come until the truth is preached and accepted. The law of the kingdom is this: every believer is to live wholly for God's service and work.

The father who called his sons to go work in his vineyard did not leave it to their choice to do as much or as little as they chose. They lived in his home. They were his children; he counted on what they would give him—their time and strength. God expects this of His children. Until it is understood that each child of God is to give His whole heart to his Father's interest and work as a worker for God, the evangelization of the world cannot be accomplished. Listen carefully and the Father will say to you, *"Go work to day in my vineyard."*

- Why is it that stirring appeals on behalf of missions often have so little permanent result? It is because the command is brought to those who have not learned that absolute devotion and immediate obedience to the Lord are the essence of true salvation.

- Once Christians see and confess their lack of interest in missions, they will be taking the first step to renewing their desire to live completely for God. Every missionary meeting will be a consecration meeting to seek and surrender to the Holy Spirit's power.

- The average standard of holiness and devotion can be no higher at home or in the church than it is in individual believers.

- Not everyone can go abroad or give his whole time to direct work; but everyone, whatever his calling or circumstances, can give his whole heart to live for the winning of souls and the spreading of the kingdom.

Chapter 4

———◆———

To Each One His Work

For the Son of man is as a man taking a far journey, who left his house, and gave authority to his servants, and to every man his work, and commanded the porter to watch.
—Mark 13:34

What I have said about the failure of the church to do the Master's work has often led me to ask, "What must be done to arouse the church to a right sense of its calling?" This book attempts to give the answer. Working for God must take a very different and much more definite place in our teaching and training of Christ's disciples than it has before.

In studying the question, I have been helped very much by the life and writings of a great educator, Edward Thring. The opening sentence of the preface to his biography states, "Edward Thring was unquestionably the most original and striking figure in the schoolmaster world of his time in England." Thring attributed his own power and success to the prominence he gave to a few simple principles, and the faithfulness with which he carried them out at any sacrifice. I have found them helpful regarding the work of preaching as well as teaching, and to present them will help to clarify some of the chief lessons this book is meant to teach.

The basic principle that distinguished Thring's teaching from what was current at the time was this: every boy in school, regardless of ability, must have the same attention. At Eton, where he was educated and was first in his class, he saw the evil of the opposite system. Leaving the majority neglected, the school kept its prestige by training a select number of men for the highest awards. He maintained that this was dishonest. There could be no truth in a school that did not care for all alike. Every boy had some gift. Every boy needed special attention. Every boy could, with care and patience, be equipped to know and fulfill his mission in life.

Apply this principle to the church. Every believer has the calling to live and work for the kingdom of his Lord. Every believer has an equal claim on the grace and power of the Holy Spirit, according to his gifts, to equip him for the work of God. And every believer has a right to be taught and helped by the church for the service our Lord expects of him. When every believer, even the weakest, is trained as a worker for God, the church can fulfill its mission. No one can be left out because the Master entrusted His work to all believers.

Another of Thring's principles was this: it is a law of nature that work is pleasure. Make it voluntary and not compulsory. Do not lead people blindly. Show them why they have to work, what its value will be, what interest can be awakened in it, and what pleasure may be found in it.

What a field is opened for the preacher of the Gospel taking charge of Christ's disciples! The preacher must clarify the greatness, the glory, the divine blessedness of the work to be done. The preacher must show the value in carrying out God's will and gaining His approval. The preacher must lead us in introducing the Savior to the unsaved. The preacher must lead us in developing the spiritual vigor, the nobility of character, the spirit of self-sacrifice that leads to the true bearing of Christ's image.

A third truth on which Thring particularly insisted was the need for inspiring the belief in the assurance of attaining the goal. That goal is not to gain extensive knowledge, but rather, to cultivate the power to learn: this alone is true education. As a learner's powers of observation grow under guidance and teaching, he finds within himself a source of power and pleasure he never knew before. He feels a new self beginning to live, and the world around him acquires a new meaning. As Thring stated, "He becomes conscious of an infinity of unsuspected glory in the midst of which we go about our daily tasks and becomes lord of an endless kingdom full of light and pleasure and power."

If this is the law and blessing of a true education, what light is shed on the calling of all teachers and leaders in Christ's church! The *know ye not*s of Scripture—that you are the temple of God (1 Cor. 3:16), that Christ is in you (2 Cor. 13:5), that the Holy Spirit dwells in you (1 Cor. 6:19)—acquire a new meaning. It tells us that the one thing that needs to be awakened in the hearts of Christians is the faith in *"the power that worketh in us"* (Eph. 3:20). As one comes to see the worth and the glory of the work to be done; as one believes in the possibility of his, too, being able to do that work well; as one learns to trust the very power and very Spirit of God working in him, he will, in the fullest sense, become conscious of a new life, with "an infinity of unsuspected glory in the midst of which we go about our daily tasks," and he will become "lord of an endless kingdom full of light and pleasure and power." This is the royal life to which God has called all His people. The true Christian is one who knows God's power working in himself, and finds it his true joy to have the very life of God flowing into him, through him, and out from him to those around.

- We must learn to believe in the value of every individual believer. As people are saved one by one, they must be trained one by one for work.
- We must believe that work for Christ can become as natural, as much an attraction and a pleasure, in the spiritual as in the natural world.

- We must believe and teach that every believer can become an effective worker in his area of work. Are you seeking to be filled with love for souls?

Chapter 5

To Each according to His Ability

*For the kingdom of heaven is as a man travelling into a far
country, who called his own servants, and delivered unto them
his goods. And unto one he gave five talents, to another two,
and to another one; to every man according to his several
ability; and straightway took his journey.*
—Matthew 25:14–15

*I*n the parable of the talents, we have an instructive summary
of our Lord's teaching in regard to the work He has given
to His servants to do. He tells us He is going to heaven and leaving His work on earth to the care of His church. He tells us He
is giving everyone something to do, however different the gifts
might be. He tells us He is expecting to get back His money with
interest. He tells us of the failure of him who received least and
what it was that led to that terrible neglect.

"[He] *called his own servants, and delivered unto them his
goods...; and straightway took his journey.*" This is literally what
our Lord did. He went to heaven, leaving His work along with all
His goods to the care of His church. His goods were the riches
of His grace, spiritual blessings in heavenly places, and His Word
and Spirit. He gave these to His servants to be used in carrying

out His work on earth. They were to continue the work He had begun.

Our Lord took His people into partnership with Himself and entrusted His work on earth entirely to their care. Their neglect would cause it to suffer. Their diligence would be His enrichment. Here we have the true basic principle of Christian service: Christ has made Himself dependent on the faithfulness of His people for the extension of His kingdom.

"Unto one he gave five talents, to another two, and to another one; to every man according to his several ability." Though there was a difference in the measure, everyone received a portion of the master's goods. It is in connection with the service we are to provide each other that we read, *"Unto every one of us is given grace according to the measure of the gift of Christ"* (Eph. 4:7). This truth, that every believer without exception has been set apart to take an active part in the work of winning the world for Christ, has almost been lost.

Christ was first a son, then a servant. Every believer is first a child of God, then a servant. It is the highest honor of a son to be a servant, to have the father's work entrusted to him. Neither the home nor the foreign missionary work of the church will ever be done right until every believer feels that the one purpose of his being in the world is to work for the kingdom. The first duty of the servants in the parable was to spend their lives in caring for their master's interests.

"After a long time the lord of those servants cometh, and reckoneth with them" (Matt. 25:19). Christ keeps watch over the work He has left to be done on earth. His kingdom and glory depend upon it. Not only will He hold us accountable when He comes again to judge, but He also comes unceasingly to ask His servants about their welfare and work. He comes to approve and encourage, to correct and warn. By His Word and Spirit, He questions whether we are using our talents diligently and whether we, as His devoted servants, are living only and entirely for His work. He finds some laboring diligently, and to them He

frequently says, *"Enter thou into the joy of thy lord"* (Matt. 25:21). He sees that others are discouraged, and He inspires them with new hope. He finds some working in their own strength. These He reprimands. Still others He finds sleeping or hiding their talents. To such His voice speaks in solemn warning, *"From him that hath not shall be taken away even that which he hath"* (v. 29). Christ's heart is in His work. Every day He watches over it with the keenest interest. Let us not disappoint Him or deceive ourselves.

"I was afraid, and went and hid thy talent in the earth" (v. 25). It is a deeply solemn lesson that the man with the one talent was the one to fail and be so severely punished. It calls the church to beware. By neglecting to teach the weaker ones that their service is needed also, the church lets their gifts lie unused. In teaching the great truth that every branch is to bear fruit, the church must lay special emphasis on the danger of thinking this is expected only of the strong and advanced Christian. When truth reigns in a school, the most backward pupils receive the same attention as the more clever pupils. Care must be taken that the weakest Christians receive special training, so that they, too, may joyfully have their share in the service of their Lord and all the blessedness it brings. If Christ's work is to be done, not one can be missed.

"Lord, I knew thee that thou art an hard man,...and I was afraid" (vv. 24–25). Failure in service is caused chiefly by wrong thoughts of God and looking upon His service as that of a hard master. If the church is to care for the weak ones who are apt to be discouraged, we must teach them what God says of the sufficiency of grace and the certainty of success. They must learn to believe that the power of the Holy Spirit within them equips them for the work to which God has called them. They must learn to understand that God Himself will strengthen the inner man with might by His Spirit (Eph. 3:16). They must be taught that work is joy, health, and strength. Unbelief lies at the root of laziness. Faith opens the eyes to see the blessedness of God's service, the sufficiency of His strength, and His rich rewards.

The church must awake to its calling to train the weakest of its members to know that Christ counts on every redeemed individual to live entirely for His work. This alone is true Christianity. This alone is full salvation.

Chapter 6

———— ►◆◄ ————

Life and Work

My meat is to do the will of him that sent me,
and to finish his work.
—John 4:34

I must work the works of him that sent me.
—John 9:4

I have glorified thee on the earth: I have finished the work
which thou gavest me to do. And now, O Father, glorify thou
me with thine own self.
—John 17:4–5

*C*arefully read these words of our Lord again, and see what divine glory there is in His work. In His work, Christ showed His own glory and the Father's glory. It was because of the work He had done, and because He had glorified the Father in it, that He claimed to share the glory of the Father in heaven. He performed the great works so that the Father might be glorified. Work is indeed the highest form of existence, the highest manifestation of the divine glory in the Father and in His Son.

What is true of God is true of men. Life is action and reveals itself in what it accomplishes. The bodily life, the intellectual, the moral, the spiritual life—individual, social, and national life— each of these is judged by its work. The character and quality of the work depend on the life: as the life, so the work. And, on the other hand, the life depends on the work. Without this there can be no full development and manifestation and perfecting of the life: as the work, so the life.

This is especially true of the spiritual life—the life of the Spirit in us. There may be a great deal of religious work that is the result of human will and effort. But there is little true worth and power because the divine life is weak. When the believer does not know that Christ is living in him and does not know the Spirit and power of God working in him, there may be much sincerity and diligence, with little that lasts for eternity. On the contrary, there may be much external weakness and apparent failure, yet results prove that the life is indeed of God.

The work depends upon the life, and the life depends on the work for its growth and perfection. All life has a destiny. It cannot accomplish its purpose without work. Life is perfected by work. The highest manifestation of its hidden nature and power comes out in its work. And so work is the great factor by which the hidden beauty and the divine possibilities of the Christian life are revealed. Work must not only be performed by the child of God for the result of being used as God's instrument, but also be given the same place it has in God Himself. As in the Father and the Son, and with the Holy Spirit dwelling in us, work is the highest manifestation of life.

Work must be restored to its right place in God's scheme of the Christian life as the highest form of existence. As God never ceases to perform His work of love and blessing in and through us, so our performing what He works in us is our highest proof of being created anew in His likeness.

Working for God must have much greater prominence given to it if God's purposes are to be carried out. Every believer must be taught that work is to be his highest glory as it is the only perfect manifestation and, therefore, the perfection of life in God throughout the world. We must ask if it is to be so in our own lives.

If our work is to be our highest glory, we must remember two things: first, it can come only by beginning to work. Those who have not had their attention directed to it cannot realize how great the temptation is to make work a matter of thought, prayer, and purpose, without its really being done. It is easier to hear than to think, easier to think than to speak, easier to speak than to act. We may listen and accept and admire God's will, and in our prayers profess our willingness to do it, and yet not actually do it. Let us take up our calling as God's workers and work hard for Him. Doing is the best teacher. If you want to know how to do a thing, begin to do it.

Then you will be able to understand the second aspect: there is sufficient grace in Christ for all the work you have to do. You will see with ever-increasing gladness how He, the Head, works all in you, the member. You will see how work for God may become your closest and fullest fellowship with Christ— your highest participation in the power of His risen and glorified life.

- Beware of separating life and work. The more work you have, the more your work appears to be a failure. The more unfit you feel for work, the more time and care you should take to have your inner life renewed in close fellowship with God.
- That *"Christ liveth in me"* (Gal. 2:20) is the secret of joy and hope, and also of power for work. Care for the life, and the life will care for the work. *"Be filled with the Holy Ghost"* (Acts 9:17).

Chapter 7

———◆———

The Father Abiding in Me Does the Work

But Jesus answered them,
My Father worketh hitherto, and I work.
—John 5:17

Believest thou not that I am in the Father,
and the Father in me? the words that I speak
unto you I speak not of myself: but the Father
that dwelleth in me, he doeth the works.
—John 14:10

Jesus Christ became man so that He might show us what a true man is. He became man to show us how God meant to live and work in man. And He became man to show us how we can find purpose in our lives and do our work in God. In words like those above, our Lord opens up the inner mystery of His life and reveals to us the nature and the deepest secret of His working. He did not come to the world to work instead of the Father. Christ's work was the fruit, the earthly reflection, of the Father's working. It was not as if Christ merely saw and copied what the

476

Father willed or did—*"the Father that dwelleth in me, he doeth the works."* Christ did all His work in the power of the Father who was living and working in Him. So complete and real was His dependence on the Father that, in explaining it to the Jews, He used such strong expressions as, *"The Son can do nothing of himself, but what he seeth the Father do"* (John 5:19), and, *"I can of mine own self do nothing"* (v. 30). What He said—*"For without me ye can do nothing"* (John 15:5)—is as true of us as it is true of Him. *"The Father that dwelleth in me, he doeth the works."*

Jesus Christ became man so that He might show us what true man is, what the true relationship between man and God is, and what the true way of serving God and doing His work is. When we are made new creatures in Christ Jesus (2 Cor. 5:17), the life we receive is the very life that was and is in Christ. It is only by studying His life on earth that we know how we are to live. *"As the living Father hath sent me, and I live by the Father: so he that eateth me, even he shall live by me"* (John 6:57).

Christ did not consider it a humiliation to be able to do nothing of Himself—to be always and absolutely dependent on the Father. He counted it His highest glory because all His works were the works of the all-glorious God in Him. When will we understand that to wait on God, to bow before Him in perfect helplessness and let Him work everything in us, is our true nobility and the secret of the highest activity? This alone is the true Christ-life, the true life of every child of God. As this life is understood and maintained, the power for work will grow because the soul is in the attitude in which God can work in us, as the God who *"is good unto them that wait for him"* (Lam. 3:25).

By ignoring or neglecting the great truths, there can be no true work for God. The explanation of the extensive complaint of so much Christian activity with so little genuine result is that God works in us, yes, but He cannot work fully in us unless we live in absolute dependence on Him. The revival that many are longing and praying for must begin with this: the return of Christian ministers and workers to their true place before God—in Christ. And, like Christ, we must completely depend and continually wait on God to work in us.

I invite all workers, young and old, successful or disappointed, full of hope or full of fear, to come and learn from our Lord Jesus the secret of true work for God: *"My Father worketh hitherto, and I work." "The Father that dwelleth in me, he doeth the works."* Divine Fatherhood means that God is all, gives all, and works all. Continually depend on the Father, and receive, moment by moment, all the strength needed for His work. Try to grasp the great truth that because *"it is the same God which worketh all in all"* (1 Cor. 12:6), your one need is, in deep humility and weakness, to wait for and to trust in His working. From this, learn that God can work in us only as He dwells in us. *"The Father that dwelleth in me, he doeth the works."* Cultivate the holy sense of God's continual nearness and presence, of your being His temple, and of His dwelling in you. Offer yourself for Him to work in you all His good pleasure. You will find that work, instead of being a hindrance, can become your greatest incentive to a life of fellowship and childlike dependence.

At first it may appear as if the waiting for God to work will keep you back from your work. It may indeed—but only to bring the greater blessing, when you have learned the lesson of faith that believes on His working even when you do not feel it. You may have to do your work in weakness and fear and much trembling. You will know the merit of the power is of God and not of yourself. As you know yourself better and God better, you will be content that it should always be His strength made perfect in your weakness (2 Cor. 12:9).

- *"The Father that dwelleth in me, he doeth the works."* There is the same law for the Head and the member, for Christ and the believer. *"It is the same God which worketh all in all"* (1 Cor. 12:6).
- The Father worked in the Son while He was on earth, and now works through Him in heaven. It is as we believe in the

478

Father's working in Christ that we will do the greater works. (See John 14:10–12.)

- The indwelling and abiding God works in us. Allow God to live in you, and He will establish your good work.
- Pray much for grace to say, in the name of Jesus, *"The Father that dwelleth in me, he doeth the works."*

Chapter 8

———————◆◄———————

Greater Works

Verily, verily, I say unto you, He that believeth on me,
the works that I do shall he do also; and greater works
than these shall he do; because I go unto my Father.
And whatsoever ye shall ask in my name, that will I do,
that the Father may be glorified in the Son. If ye shall
ask any thing in my name, I will do it.
—John 14:12–14

*I*n John 14:10, which says, *"The Father that dwelleth in me,*
he doeth the works," Christ reveals the secret of all divine
service: man yielding himself for God to dwell and to work in
him. The law of God working in man remains unchanged when
Christ promises, *"He that believeth on me, the works that I do*
shall he do also." If Christ says, *"The Father that dwelleth in*
me, he doeth the works," how much more must *we* say it? With
Christ and with us, it is *"the same God which worketh all in all"*
(1 Cor. 12:6).

We are taught how this is to be in the words, *"He that*
believeth on me." That means not only that we must believe
Christ for salvation, as a Savior from sin, but there is much more.
In John 14:10–11 Christ said, *"The Father that dwelleth in me,*

he doeth the works. Believe me that I am in the Father, and the Father in me." We need to believe in Christ as the One in and through whom the Father unceasingly works. To believe in Christ is to receive Him into our hearts. When we see the Father working jointly with Christ, we know that to believe in Christ, and receive Him into our hearts, is to receive the Father dwelling in Him and working through Him. The works His disciples are to do cannot possibly be done in any other way than His own are done.

This becomes still clearer from what our Lord adds: "*And greater works than these shall he do; because I go unto my Father.*" It is clear what the greater works are. Three thousand were baptized by the disciples at Pentecost, and multitudes were added to the Lord afterward. Philip at Samaria, the men of Cyprus and Cyrene, Barnabas at Antioch, Paul in his travels—always many people were added to the Lord. Countless servants down to our day have, in the ingathering of souls, done these greater works in, for, with, and through Christ.

When the Lord says, "*Because I go unto my Father,*" He clearly reveals the reason that we are enabled to do these greater works. When He entered the glory of the Father, all power in heaven and on earth was given to Him as our Redeemer. The Father was to work through Him in a way more glorious than ever. He was then to work through His disciples. His own work on earth received power from the Father in heaven. So His people, in their weakness, would do works like His, and greater works in the same way, through power received from heaven. The law of the divine working is unchangeable: God's work can be done only by God Himself. It is as we see this in Christ and receive Him in this way, as the One in and through whom God works all, and yield ourselves completely to the Father working in Him and in us, that we will do greater works than He did.

The words that follow bring out still more strongly the great truths we have been learning, that it is our Lord Himself who will work all in us, even as the Father did in Him, and that our attitude is to be exactly what His was—one of entire receptivity and dependence. *"Greater works than these shall he do; because I go unto my Father. And whatsoever ye shall ask in my name, that will I do."* Christ connects the greater works the believer is to do with the promise that He will do whatever the believer asks. Prayer in the name of Jesus will be the expression of depending and waiting on Him for His working. He gives the promise: *"Whatsoever ye shall ask...that will I do,"* in you and through you. And when He adds, *"that the Father may be glorified in the Son,"* He reminds us how He had glorified the Father by yielding to Him as Father, to perform all His work in Himself as Son. In heaven Christ would still glorify the Father by receiving the power from the Father and by working in His disciples what the Father would. The believer, as Christ Himself, can give the Father no higher glory than yielding to Him to work all.

The believer can glorify the Father in no other way than by an absolute and unceasing dependence on the Son, in whom the Father works, to communicate and work in us all the Father's work. *"If ye shall ask any thing in my name, I will do it,"* and so, *"greater works than these shall he do."*

Let every believer strive to learn the blessed lesson—"I am to do the works I have seen Christ doing. I may do even greater works as I yield myself to Christ exalted on the throne in awesome power. I may count on Him working in me according to that power. I need the spirit of dependence and waiting, as well as prayer and faith, so that Christ abiding in me will do the works, even whatever I ask."

- How was Christ able to work the works of God? By God abiding in Him! How can I do the works of Christ? By Christ abiding in me!
- How can I do greater works than Christ? By believing not only in Christ, the Incarnate and Crucified, but also in Christ triumphant on the throne.

• In work everything depends, dear believer, on the life, the inner life, the divine life. Pray to realize that work is vain except when it is done in the power of the Holy Spirit dwelling in you.

Chapter 9

———◆◆◆———

Created in Christ Jesus
for Good Works

*For by grace are ye saved through faith; and that not of
yourselves: it is the gift of God: not of works, lest any
man should boast. For we are his workmanship, created
in Christ Jesus unto good works, which God hath before
ordained that we should walk in them.*
—Ephesians 2:8–10

We have been saved, not *by* works, but *for* good works. The difference is so great! The understanding of that difference is essential to the health of the Christian life. We are not saved *by* works that we have done. Yet we are saved *for* good works— the fruit and outcome of salvation, part of God's work in us, the one thing for which we have been created anew. Though our works are worthless in achieving salvation, their worth is infinite for which God has created and prepared us. We must seek to hold these two truths in the fullness of their spiritual meaning. The deeper our conviction that we have been saved, not by works, but by grace, the stronger the proof that we have been saved for good works.

"Not of works...for we are his workmanship." If works could have saved us, there was no need for our redemption. Because our works were all sinful and vain, God undertook to make us anew. We are now His workmanship, and all the good works we do are His workmanship, too. *"His workmanship, created in Jesus Christ."* So complete had been the ruin of sin that God had to do the work of creation over again in Jesus Christ. In Him, and particularly in His resurrection from the dead, God created us anew, after His own image, into the likeness of the life that Christ had lived. In the power of that life and resurrection, we are able, we are perfectly equipped, for doing good works.

The eye, because it was created for the light, is most perfectly adapted for its work. The branch of the vine, because it was created to bear grapes, does its work so naturally. We, who have been created in Jesus Christ for good works, may be assured that a divine capacity for good works is the very law of our being. If we simply know and believe in this our destiny, if we simply live our lives in Jesus Christ, as we were newly created in Him, we can and will be fruitful unto every good work.

"Created...unto good works, which God hath before ordained that we should walk in them." We have been prepared for the works, and the works prepared for us. To understand this, think of how God pre-appointed His servants of old—Moses and Joshua, Samuel and David, Peter and Paul—for the work He had for them, and preappointed equally the works He would have them do. The Father has prepared works for the humblest of His children as much as for those who are counted chief. God has a life-plan for each of His children, with work distributed according to the power and grace provided for the work. And so, just as the teaching salvation is *"not of works"* (Eph. 2:8) is clear, so is its blessed counterpart, "salvation is for good works" (see verse 10)—because God created us for them, and even prepared them for us.

The Scripture, therefore, confirms the double lesson this book desires to bring you: good works are God's design in the new life He has given you and ought to be your aim. As every human being was created for work and endowed with the necessary energy, man can live a true and healthy life only by working. Every believer, then, exists to do good works. In them his life will be perfected, his fellowmen will be blessed, and his Father in heaven will be glorified. We educate all our children with the thought that they must go out and work in the world. When will the church learn that its great work is to train every believer to take his share in *God's* great work and to abound in the good works for which he was created? We must each seek to take in the deep spiritual truth of the message, *"Created in Christ Jesus unto good works, which God hath before ordained,"* and joyfully take up the work awaiting us and do it eagerly.

Waiting on God is the one great thing needed on our part if we desire to do the good works God has prepared for us. We must take into our hearts the holy meaning of these words: we are God's workmanship, not by one act in the past, but in a continuous operation. We are created for good works, as the great means for glorifying God. The good works are prepared for each of us so that we might walk in them. Surrender to and dependence upon God's working is our one need. We must consider how our new creation for good works will become the habit of our souls and is all *in Christ Jesus,* and abiding *in Him,* believing *on Him,* and looking *for His strength alone.* Realizing that we are created for good works will reveal to us at once the divine command and the sufficient power to live a life in good works.

Let us pray for the Holy Spirit to work the Word into the very depths of our consciousness: created in Christ Jesus for good works! In the light of this revelation, we will learn what a glorious destiny, what an infinite obligation, what a perfect capacity is ours.

- Our creation in Adam was for good works. It resulted in entire failure. Our new creation in Christ is for good works again, but with this difference: perfect provision has been made for securing them.

- God has created us for good works. Let us pray for the Holy Spirit to show us and impart to us all that this means.
- If life in fellowship with God is true, the power for the work will be perfected. As the life, so the work.

Chapter 10

————————◆————————

Work, for It Is God Who Works in You

Work out your own salvation with fear and trembling.
For it is God which worketh in you both to will
and to do of his good pleasure.
—Philippians 2:12–13

*I*n the last chapter we saw what salvation is. It is our being
God's workmanship, created in Jesus Christ for good works.
The chapter concluded with one of its most important points:
there is a treasury of good works that God has prepared for us to
do. In the light of this thought, we get the true and full meaning
of the leading Scripture for this chapter. To work out your own
salvation, such as God meant it to be, is to walk in all the good
works that God has prepared for you. Study to know exactly
what the salvation is that God has prepared for you (all that He
has meant and made possible for you to be), and work it out
"with fear and trembling." Let the greatness of this divine and
most holy life hidden in Christ, your own weakness, and the terrible dangers and temptations confronting you, make you work
in fear and trembling.

And yet, that fear never needs to become unbelief; that trembling never needs to become discouragement, for it is God who works in you. Here is the secret of a power that is absolutely sufficient for everything we have to do, the perfect assurance that we can do all that God really means for us to do. God works in us both to will and to work. First, to will—He gives the insight into what is to be done, the desire that makes the work pleasure, the firm purpose of the will that masters the whole being and makes it ready and eager for action. And then, to work—He does not give us the will and then leave us unaided to work it out ourselves. The will may see and accept the work, yet lack the power to perform it. In the seventh chapter of Romans, we see that the new man delights in God's law, yet he is ill-equipped to obey it because of the war between the flesh and the Spirit. However, by *"the law of the Spirit of life in Christ Jesus"* (Rom. 8:2), man was set *"free from the law of sin and death"* (v. 2). Thus, the righteousness of the law could be fulfilled in Him as one who did not *"walk...after the flesh, but after the Spirit"* (v. 4).

One great reason why believers fail in their work is that they think since God has given them the will to do it, they will automatically work in the strength of that will. They have never learned the lesson that because God has created us in Christ Jesus for good works and has prepared the good works in which we are to walk, He must work them all in us Himself. They have never listened very long to the voice speaking, *"It is God which worketh in you."*

Here is one of the deepest, most spiritual, and most precious truths of Scripture—the unceasing operation of almighty God in our hearts and lives. In light of the very nature of God, as a spiritual being not confined to any place, but present everywhere, there can be no spiritual life unless it is supported by His personal indwelling.

Scripture states the deepest reason—He *"worketh all in all"* (1 Cor. 12:6). Not only *of* Him are all things as their first beginning, and *to* Him as their end, but also *through* Him, who alone maintains them.

The Father was the Source of all that Christ did. In the new man, created in Jesus Christ, the unceasing dependence on the Father is our highest privilege, our truest nobility. This is indeed fellowship with God—God Himself working in us to will and to do.

We must seek to learn the true secret of working for God. It is not, as many think, that we do our best, then leave God to do the rest. By no means. Rather, it is this: we know that God's working His salvation in us is the secret of our working it out—that salvation includes *every* work we have to do. The faith of God working in us is the measure of our fitness to work effectively. The promises, *"According to your faith be it unto you"* (Matt. 9:29), and, *"All things are possible to him that believeth"* (Mark 9:23), have their full application here. The deeper our faith in God's working in us, the more freely the power of God will work in us, and the truer and more fruitful our work will be.

Perhaps some Sunday school worker is reading this. Have you really believed that your only power to do God's work is as one who has been created in Jesus Christ for good works, as one in whom God Himself works to will and to work? Have you yielded yourself to wait for that working? Do you work because you know that God works in you? Do not say that these thoughts are too high. The work of leading young souls to Christ is too high for us, but if we live as little children in believing that God will work all in us, we will do His work in His strength. Pray much to learn and practice the lesson in all you do. Work, for God works in you.

- I think we begin to feel that the spiritual understanding of this great truth, "God works in you," is what all workers greatly need.
- The Holy Spirit is the mighty power of God, dwelling in believers for life and for work. Ask God to show you that, in all our service, our first care must be the daily renewing of the Holy Spirit.

- Obey the command to be filled with the Holy Spirit. Believe in His indwelling. Wait for His teaching. Yield to His leading. Pray for His mighty working. Live in the Spirit.
- What the mighty power of God works in us, we are surely able to do. Only give way to the power working in you.

Chapter 11

———————————◄◆►———————————

Faith Working by Love

For in Jesus Christ neither circumcision availeth any
thing, nor uncircumcision; but faith which worketh by
love....But by love serve one another. For all the law
is fulfilled in one word, even in this; Thou shalt love
thy neighbour as thyself.
—Galatians 5:6, 13–14

*I*n Jesus Christ no external privilege is an advantage. The Jew
might boast of his circumcision, the token of God's covenant.
The Gentile might boast of his uncircumcision, with an entrance
into the kingdom free from the Jewish laws. Neither was of use
in the kingdom of heaven—nothing but, as in Galatians 6:15, *"a*
new creature," in which *"old things are passed away...[and] all*
things are become new" (2 Cor. 5:17). Or, as our text describes
it, nothing but faith working by love, causing us to serve one
another in love.

What a perfect description of the new life! First, you have
faith, as the root, planted and rooted in Jesus Christ. Then, as
its aim, you have works as the fruit. And then, between the two,
as the tree, growing down into the root and bearing the fruit
upward, you have love, with the life-sap flowing through it by

which the root brings forth the fruit. We do not need to speak of faith here. We have seen how believing in Jesus does the greater works, and we have seen how faith in the new creation and in God working in us is the secret of all work. Nor do we need to speak here of works. This whole book aims at securing them in place in every heart and life just as they are in God's heart and in His Word.

We must especially study the great truth that all work is to be done in love. Faith cannot do its work except through love. No works can have any worth unless they come from love. Love alone is the sufficient strength for all the work we have to do.

The power for work is love. It was love that moved God to all His work in creation and redemption. It was love that enabled Christ as man to work and to suffer as He did. It is love that can inspire us with the power of a self-sacrifice that does not seek its own, but is ready to live and die for others. It is love that gives us the patience that refuses to give up on those who are unthankful or hardened. It is love that reaches and overcomes the most hopeless. Love is the power for work in ourselves and in those for whom we labor. Let us love as Christ loved us.

The power for love is faith. Faith roots its life in the life of Jesus Christ, which is all love. Faith knows, even when we cannot fully realize the wonderful gift that has been given into our hearts in the Holy Spirit's outpouring of God's love. A spring in the earth may often be hidden or stopped up. Until it is opened, the fountain cannot flow out. Faith knows that there is a fountain of love within that can spring up into eternal life and can flow out as *"rivers of living water"* (John 7:38). It assures us that we can love, that we have a divine power to love within us, as an inherent gift of our new nature.

The power to exercise and show love is work. There is no such thing as power apart from concrete realities. It acts only as it is exercised. Power at rest cannot be found or felt. This is particularly true of the Christian graces, hidden as they are amid the weakness of our human nature. It is only by *doing* that you know that you *have*. A grace must be performed before we can rejoice in its possession. This is the unspeakable blessedness of work. Working is so essential to a healthy Christian life because it wakes up and strengthens love, and it makes us partakers of its joy.

Faith works by love. In Jesus Christ few things are of as much value as this. Workers for God, believe this! Practice it. Thank God much for the fountain of eternal love opened within you. Pray fervently and frequently that God may strengthen you with might by the power of His Spirit in your inner man, so that, with Christ dwelling in you, you may be *"rooted and grounded in love"* (Eph. 3:17). Live your daily life, then, in your own home, in all your dealings with men, in all your work, as a life of divine love. The ways of love are so gentle and heavenly, you may not learn them all at once. But be of good courage; believe in the power that works in you, and yield yourself to the work of love. It will surely gain the victory.

Faith works by love. Let me press home this message, too, on those who have never thought of working for God. Come and listen.

You owe everything to God's love. The salvation you have received is all love. God's one desire is to fill you with His love for His own satisfaction, for your own happiness, for the saving of men. Now, I ask you, will you not accept God's wonderful offer to be filled with His love? Oh, come and give your heart and life to the joy and the service of His love! Believe that the fountain of love is within you. It will begin to flow as you make a channel for it by deeds of love. Whatever work for God you try to do, seek to put love into it. Pray for the spirit of love. Give yourself to live a life of love. Think how you can love those around you by praying for them, by serving them, by laboring for their temporal and spiritual welfare. Faith working by love in Jesus Christ is of great value.

- *"And now abideth faith, hope,* [love], *these three; but the greatest of these is* [love]*"* (1 Cor. 13:13). *"God is love"* (1 John 4:8). The most Godlike thing is love.

- Love is the nature of God. When it is *"shed abroad in our hearts by the Holy Ghost"* (Rom. 5:5), love becomes our new nature. Believe this, give yourself over to it, and act it out.
- Love is God's power to do His work. Love was Christ's power. To work for God, pray earnestly to be filled with love for souls!

Chapter 12

———————◆———————

Bearing Fruit in Every Good Work

That ye might walk worthy of the Lord unto all pleasing,
being fruitful in every good work, and increasing in
the knowledge of God; strengthened with all might,
according to his glorious power, unto all patience
and longsuffering with joyfulness.
—Colossians 1:10–11

*T*here is a difference between fruit and work. Fruit is that which comes spontaneously, without thought or will—the natural and necessary outcome of a healthy life. Work, on the contrary, is the product of effort guided by intelligent thought and will. In the Christian life, we have the two elements combined. All true work must be fruit, the growth and product of our inner lives, the operation of God's Spirit within us. And yet all fruit must be work, the result of our deliberate purpose and effort.

In the words *"being fruitful in every good work,"* we have the practical summing up of the truth taught in some previous chapters. Because God works by His life in us, the work we do is fruit. In having faith in His working, we desire to be used by Him and to bear fruit—work. The secret of all true work lies in the harmony between the perfect spontaneity that comes from God's life and Spirit animating us and our cooperation with Him as His intelligent fellow laborers.

In the words *"filled with the knowledge of his will in all wisdom and spiritual understanding"* (Col. 1:9), we have the human side, our need of knowledge and wisdom. In the words *"strengthened with all might, according to his glorious power,"* we have the divine side. God teaches and strengthens, and man learns to understand and patiently do His will. Such is the double life that will be fruitful in every good work.

It has been said of the Christian life that the natural man must first become spiritual, and then again the spiritual man must become natural. As the whole natural life becomes truly spiritual, all our work will partake of the nature of fruit, the outgrowth of the life of God within us. And as the spiritual again becomes perfectly natural to us, a second nature in which we are completely at home, all the fruit will bear the mark of true work, calling into full exercise every faculty of our being.

"Being fruitful in every good work" suggests again the great thought that as an apple tree or a vine is planted solely for its fruit, so the great purpose of our redemption is that God may have us for His work and service. It has been well said, "The end of man is an action and not a thought, though it were of the noblest." It is in his work that the nobility of man's nature as ruler of the world is proved. It is for good works that we have been created anew in Christ Jesus. It is when men see our good works that our Father in heaven will be glorified and have the honor that is His due His workmanship. In the parable of the vine, our Lord insisted on this. *"He that abideth in me, and I in him, the same bringeth forth much fruit"* (John 15:5). *"Herein is my Father glorified, that ye bear much fruit"* (v. 8). Few things give more honor to a farmer than to succeed in raising an abundant crop. Much fruit brings glory to God.

The great need is for every believer to be encouraged, helped, and even trained to aim at producing much fruit. A little strawberry plant may, in its measure, bear a more abundant crop than a large apple tree. The call to be fruitful in every good work is for every Christian without exception. The grace that is needed to do this is available to everyone. Every branch fruitful in every good work—this is an essential part of God's Gospel.

We must get a true impression of the two sides of the divine truth *"being fruitful in every good work."* God's first creation of life was in the vegetable kingdom. It was a life without anything of will or self-effort. All growth and fruit was simply His own direct work, the spontaneous outcome of His hidden working. There was progress in the creation of the animal kingdom. New elements were introduced—thought and will and work. In man these elements were united in perfect harmony. The absolute dependence of the grass and the lily on the God who clothes them with their beauty was to be the groundwork of our relationship.

Nature has nothing but what it receives from God. Our works are to be fruit, the product of a God-given power. But to this was added the true mark of our Godlikeness, the power of will and independent action—all fruit is to be our own work. As we grasp this concept, we will see how the most complete understanding of our having nothing in ourselves is consistent with the deepest sense of obligation and the strongest desire to exert our powers to the very utmost. We must study the lessons of the text as those who seek all their wisdom and strength from God alone. And we will boldly give ourselves, as those who are responsible for the use of that wisdom and strength, to the diligence, sacrifice, and effort needed for lives that will bear fruit in every good work.

- Much depends, for quality and quantity, on the healthy life of the tree. The life of God, of Jesus Christ, of His Spirit—the divine life in you—must be strong and sure.
- That life is love. Believe in it. Act it out. Have it replenished day by day out of the fullness that is in Christ.

- Let all your work be fruit. Let all your willing and working be inspired by the life of God. In this way you will *"walk worthy of the Lord unto all pleasing"* (Col. 1:10).

Chapter 13

—◆—

Always Abounding in the Work of the Lord

Therefore, my beloved brethren, be ye stedfast,
unmoveable, always abounding in the work of the Lord,
forasmuch as ye know that your labour is not
in vain in the Lord.
—1 Corinthians 15:58

*T*he fifteenth chapter of 1 Corinthians presents the divine revelation of the meaning of Christ's resurrection with all its blessings. It gives us a living Savior who revealed Himself from heaven to His disciples on earth and to Paul. It assures us of the complete deliverance from all sin. It is the pledge of His final victory over every enemy, when He gives up the kingdom to the Father, and God is all in all. It assures us of the resurrection of the body and our entrance to heavenly life. Paul had closed his argument with his triumphant appeal to death and sin and the law:

> *O death, where is thy sting? O grave, where is thy victory?*
> *The sting of death is sin; and the strength of sin is the law.*
> *But thanks be to God, which giveth us the victory through*
> *our Lord Jesus Christ.*   (1 Cor. 15:55–57)

Then, after fifty-seven verses of exultant teaching concerning the mystery and the glory of the resurrection life in our Lord and His people, there is one verse of practical application. *"Therefore, my beloved brethren, be ye stedfast, unmoveable, always abounding in the work of the Lord."* The faith in a risen, living Christ, and in all that His resurrection is to us in time and eternity, is to equip us for, and to prove itself in, abounding work for our Lord!

It cannot be otherwise. Christ's resurrection was His final victory over sin, death, and Satan. It was His entry to His work of giving the Spirit from heaven and extending His kingdom throughout the earth. Those who shared the resurrection joy at once received the direction to make known the joyful news. It was so with Mary and the women. It was so with the disciples the evening of the resurrection day. *"As my Father hath sent me, even so send I you"* (John 20:21). It was so with all to whom the charge was given, *"Go ye into all the world, and preach the gospel to every creature"* (Mark 16:15). Christ's resurrection is the beginning and the pledge of His victory over all the earth. That victory is to be carried out to its complete manifestation through His people. The faith and joy of the resurrection life are the inspiration and the power for the work of doing it. And so the call comes to all believers without exception: *"Therefore, my beloved brethren, be ye...always abounding in the work of the Lord."*

"In the work of the Lord." The connection tells us at once what that work is. It is nothing less than telling others of the risen Lord and proving to them what new life Christ has brought to us. As we indeed know and acknowledge Him as Lord over all we are, and live in the joy of His service, we will see that the work of the Lord is but one work—that of winning men to know Christ and to bow before Him. Amid all the forms of service, the one aim in the power of the life of the risen Lord is to make Him Lord of all.

This work of the Lord is no easy one. It cost Christ His life to conquer sin and Satan and gain the risen life. It will cost us our lives, too—the sacrifice of the life of nature. It needs the surrender of all on earth to live in the full power of resurrection newness of life. The power of sin and the world in those around us is strong. Satan does not easily give up his servants to our efforts. It needs a heart in close touch with the risen Lord, truly living the resurrection life, to be *"stedfast, unmoveable, always abounding in the work of the Lord."* But that is a life that can be lived because Jesus lives.

Paul added, *"Forasmuch as ye know that your labour is not in vain in the Lord."* I have spoken more than once of the mighty influence that the certainty of reward for work, in the shape of wages or riches, exerts on the millions of earth's workers. Christ's workers can, with assurance, believe that with such a Lord their reward is sure and great! The work is often difficult and slow, and apparently fruitless. We are apt to lose heart, because we are working in our strength and judging by our expectations. Listen to the message: *"Be ye...always abounding in the work of the Lord, forasmuch as ye know your labour is not in vain in the Lord."* *"Let not your hands be weak: for your work shall be rewarded"* (2 Chron. 15:7). *"Ye know that your labour is not in vain in the Lord."*

"In the Lord." This expression is a significant one. Study it in Romans 16, where it occurs ten times, where Paul used the expressions: *"Receive her in the Lord"* (v. 2); *"my helpers in Christ Jesus"* (v. 3); *"who also were in Christ before me"* (v. 7); *"beloved in the Lord"* (v. 8); *"approved in Christ"* (v. 10); *"who labour in the Lord"* (v. 12); and *"chosen in the Lord"* (v. 13). The entire life and fellowship and service of these saints had one mark—they were, their labors were, in the Lord. Here is the secret of effective service. *"Your labour is not in vain in the Lord."*

As a sense of His presence and the power of His life is maintained, and as all works are produced in Him, His strength works in our weakness. Our labor cannot be in vain in the Lord. Christ said, *"He that abideth in me, and I in him, the same bringeth forth much fruit"* (John 15:5). Do not let the children of this world, with their confidence that the masters whose work they are doing will certainly give them their due reward, put the children of light to shame. Let us rejoice and labor in the confident faith of the word: *"Therefore, beloved brethren, be ye...always abounding in the work of the Lord, forasmuch as ye know that your labour is not in vain in the Lord."*

Chapter 14

---◆---

Abounding Grace for Abounding Work

And God is able to make all grace abound toward you;
that ye, always having all sufficiency in all things,
may abound to every good work.
—2 Corinthians 9:8

*I*n the previous chapter we were motivated to abounding work—the spirit of triumphant joy that Christ's resurrection inspires as it covers the past and the future. This chapter assures us that we have the ability provided for this abounding work. *"God is able to make all grace abound,"* so that we may abound to all good works. Every thought of abounding grace is to be connected with the abounding in good works for which it is given. And every thought of abounding work is to be connected with the abounding grace that equips us for it.

Abounding grace has abounding work for its aim. It is often thought that grace and good works are in disagreement with each other. This is not so. What Scripture calls the works of the law are our own works, the works of righteousness that we have done. They are dead works—works by which we seek to merit or to be made fit for God's favor. These are the very opposite of grace. But they are also the very opposite of the good works that spring from grace, for which grace is given.

As incompatible as the works of the law are with the freedom of grace, the works of faith, good works, are essential and indispensable to the true Christian life. God makes grace abound, so that good works may abound. The measure of true grace is tested and proved by the measure of good works. God's grace abounds in us so that we may abound in good works. We need to have the truth deeply rooted in us. Remember, abounding grace has abounding work for its aim.

Abounding work needs abounding grace as its source and strength. Often, there is abounding work without abounding grace. Just as any man may be very diligent in an earthly pursuit, or a heathen in his religious service of an idol, so men may be very diligent in doing religious work in their own strength, with very little thought of the grace that alone can do true, spiritual, effective work. For all work that is to be really acceptable to God, and truly fruitful, not only for some visible result here on earth, but also for eternity, the grace of God is indispensable. Paul continually gave complete credit for his own work to the grace of God working in him. *"I laboured more abundantly than they all: yet not I, but the grace of God which was with me"* (1 Cor. 15:10). *"According to the gift of the grace of God given unto me by the effectual working of his power"* (Eph. 3:7). And he frequently called upon Christians to exercise their gifts *"according to the grace that is given to us"* (Rom. 12:6). *"But unto every one of us is given grace according to the measure of the gift of Christ"* (Eph. 4:7). It is only by the grace of God working in us that we can do what are truly good works. It is only as we seek and receive abounding grace that we can abound in every good work.

"God is able to make all grace abound toward you; that ye...may abound to every good work." Every Christian ought to praise God with great thanksgiving for the abounding grace that is thus provided for him. With great humiliation he ought

to confess that his experience of, and his surrender to, that abounding grace has been so defective. And with great confidence he ought to believe that a life abounding in good works is indeed possible because the abounding grace for it is so sure and so divinely sufficient. Then, with simple childlike dependence, he should wait upon God day by day to receive more grace that He gives to the humble (James 4:6).

Child of God, take time to study and truly understand God's purpose for you, that you may abound in every good work! He means it! He has provided for it! Make the measure of your consecration to Him nothing less than His purpose for you. And claim, then, nothing less than the abounding grace He is able to bestow. Make His omnipotence and His faithfulness your confidence. And always live in the practice of continual prayer and dependence upon His power working in you. This will make you abound in every good work. *"According to your faith be it unto you"* (Matt. 9:29).

Christian worker, learn here the secret of all failure and all success. Working in our own strength, with little prayer and waiting on God for His Spirit, is the cause of failure. The cultivation of the spirit of absolute weakness and unceasing dependence will open the heart for the workings of abounding grace. We will learn to credit all we do to God's grace. We will learn to measure all we have to do by God's grace. And our lives will increasingly be in the joy of God's making His grace abound in us, and our abounding in every good work.

- *"That ye...may abound to every good work."* Pray over this now until you feel that this is what God has prepared for you.
- If your ignorance and weakness appear to make it impossible, present yourself to God and say you are willing, if He will enable you to abound in good works, to be a branch that brings forth much fruit.
- Take into your heart, as a living seed, these precious truths: *"He staggered not at the promise of God through unbelief;*

but was strong in faith, giving glory to God; and being fully persuaded that, what he had promised, he was able also to perform" (Rom. 4:20–21), and, *"Faithful is he that calleth you, who also will do it"* (1 Thess. 5:24).

- Begin at once by doing lowly deeds of love. As a little child in kindergarten, learn by doing.

Chapter 15

---◆◆---

In the Work of Ministering

And he gave some, apostles; and some, prophets; and some,
evangelists; and some, pastors and teachers; for the perfecting
of the saints, for the work of the ministry, for the edifying of
the body of Christ.
—Ephesians 4:11–12

*C*hrist's objective, when He ascended to heaven and bestowed on His servants the various gifts that are mentioned, is threefold. The first aim of the gifts is *"for the perfecting of the saints."* Believers, as saints, are to be led on in the pursuit of holiness until they *"stand perfect and complete in all the will of God"* (Col. 4:12). It was for this that Epaphras labored in prayer. Paul wrote of this: *"Whom we preach,…teaching every man in all wisdom; that we may present every man perfect in Christ Jesus"* (Col. 1:28).

This perfecting of the saints is, however, only a means to a higher end: *"for the work of the ministry,"* to equip all the saints to take part in the service to which every believer is called. The same word is used in texts such as, *"which ministered unto him of their substance"* (Luke 8:3), and, *"ye have ministered to the saints, and do minister"* (Heb. 6:10). Two other examples of the

508

use of this word are found in 1 Corinthians 16:15 and 1 Peter 4:11.

And this, again, is also a means to a still higher end—*"for the edifying of the body of Christ."* As every member of our body takes its part in working for the health and growth and maintenance of the whole, so every member of the body of Christ is to consider it his first great duty to take part in all that can help to build up the body of Christ—whether by the helping and strengthening of those who are already members, or the ingathering of those who are to belong to it.

And the great work of the church is, through its pastors and teachers, to labor for the perfecting of the saints in holiness and love and fitness for service, so that each one may take his part in the work of ministering, so that the body of Christ may be built up and perfected.

Of the three great objectives with which Christ has given His church apostles and teachers, the work of ministering stands thus in the middle. On the one hand, it is preceded by that on which it absolutely depends—the perfecting of the saints. On the other hand, it is followed by that which it is meant to accomplish—the building up of the body of Christ. Every believer without exception, every member of Christ's body, is called to take part in the work of ministering. Every reader must try to realize the sacredness of his holy calling.

We must learn what the qualifications are for our work. *"The perfecting of the saints"* prepares them for *"the work of the ministry."* It is the lack of true sainthood, the lack of true holiness, that causes such scarce and weak service. As Christ's saints are taught and truly learn what conformity to Christ means, a life like His will become the one thing for which we live. His life was given up in self-sacrifice for the service and salvation of men. His humility and love, His separation from the world and devotion to the fallen, are seen to be the very essence and blessedness of the life He gives—the work of ministering, the ministry of love. Humility and love—these are the two great virtues of the saint; they are the two great powers for the work of ministering. Humility makes us willing to serve. Love makes us wise to know how to do it. Love is inventive. It seeks patiently and suffers long, until it finds a way to reach its purpose. Humility and love are equally turned away from self and its claims. Let us pray, let the church labor for *"the perfecting of the saints"* in humility and love, and the Holy Spirit will teach us how to minister.

We must look at what the great work is that the members of Christ have to do. It is to minister to each other. Place yourself at Christ's disposal for service to your fellow Christians. Count yourself their servant. Study their interests. Set yourself actively to promote the welfare of the Christians around you. Selfishness may cause us to hesitate. The feeling of weakness may discourage us, or laziness and comfort may raise difficulties for us. But ask your Lord to reveal to you His will, and give yourself up to it. All around you are Christians who are cold and worldly and wandering from their Lord. Begin to think what you can do for them. Accept as the will of the Head that you as a member should care for them. Pray for the Spirit of love. Begin somewhere—only begin, and do not continue hearing and thinking while you do nothing. Begin the work of ministering *"according to the measure of the gift of Christ"* (Eph. 4:7). He will give more grace.

We must believe in the power that works in us as sufficient for all we have to do. As I think of the thumb and finger holding the pen with which I write this, I ask, "How is it that during all these seventy years of my life they have always known just to do my will?" It was because the life of the head passed into and worked itself out in them. *"He that believeth on me,"* as his Head working in him, *"the works that I do shall he do also"* (John 14:12). Faith in Christ, whose strength is made perfect in our weakness, will give the power for all we are called to do.

Let us cry to God that all believers may wake up to the power of this great truth: every member of the body is to live completely for the building up of the body.

- To be a true worker, the first thing is close, humble fellowship with Christ the Head, to be guided and empowered by Him.
- The next is humble, loving fellowship with Christ's members serving one another in love.
- This prepares and equips us for service in the world.

Chapter 16

---◆---

According to the Working of Each Individual Part

[That we] *may grow up into him in all things, which is the*
head, even Christ: from whom the whole body fitly joined
together and compacted by that which every joint supplieth,
according to the effectual working in the measure of every part,
maketh increase of the body unto the edifying of itself in love.
—Ephesians 4:15–16

*P*aul was speaking here of the growth, the increase, the
building up of the body. This growth and increase has, as
we have seen, a double reference. It includes both the spiritual
uniting and strengthening of those who are already members
in order to secure the health of the whole body, as well as the
increase of the body by the addition of all who are as yet outside of it and are to be gathered into it. We spoke of the former
in the previous chapter—of the mutual interdependence of all
believers and the calling to care for each other's welfare. In this
chapter we look at the growth from the other side—the calling
of every member of Christ's body to labor for its increase by the
labor of love that seeks to bring in those who are not yet a part
of it. This increase of the body and building up of itself in love

512

can be only by the working in due measure of each individual part.

Think of the body of a child. How does it reach the stature of a full-grown man? In no other way but by the working in due measure of every part. As each member takes its part, by the work it does in seeking and taking and assimilating food, the increase is made by its building up itself. The work that assures the growth comes from within, not without. Similarly, in no other way can Christ's body attain the stature of the fullness of Christ. As it is unto Christ the Head that we grow up, and as from Christ the Head the body increases itself, so it is through the contribution of every joint according to the working in due measure of each individual part. Let us see what this implies.

The body of Christ is to consist of all who believe in Him throughout the world. There is no possible way in which these members of the body can be gathered in except by the body building itself up in love. Our Lord has made Himself, as Head, absolutely dependent on His members to do this work. What nature teaches us of our own bodies, Scripture teaches us of Christ's body. The head of a child may have thoughts and plans of growth, but they will all be vain unless the members all do their parts in securing that growth. Jesus Christ has committed to His church the growth and increase of His body. He asks and expects that as He the Head lives for the growth and welfare of the body, every member of His body, even the very weakest, must do the same, to build up the body in love. Every believer is to count it his one duty and blessedness to live and labor for the increase of the body, the ingathering of all who are to be its members.

What is needed to bring the church to accept this calling, and to train and help the members of the body to know and fulfill it? One thing. We must see that the new birth and faith and all insight into truth, with all resolve and surrender and effort to live according to it, is only a preparation for our true work. What is needed is that in every believer Jesus Christ be so formed, and so dwells in the heart, that His life in us will be the impulse and inspiration of our love toward the whole body and our life for it. It is because self occupies the heart that it is so easy and natural and pleasing to care for ourselves. When Jesus Christ lives in us, it will be as easy and natural and pleasing to live completely for the body of Christ. As readily and naturally as the thumb and fingers respond to the will and movement of the head will the members of Christ's body respond to the Head as the body grows up into Him, and from Him makes itself increase.

Let us sum this up. For the great work the Head is doing in gathering new members from throughout the world and building up His body, He is entirely dependent on the service of the existing members. Not only our Lord, but also a perishing world, is waiting and calling for the church to awake and give herself completely to this work—the perfecting of the number of Christ's members. Every believer, even the very weakest, must learn to know his calling—to live with this as the main purpose of his existence. This great truth will be revealed to us in power and obtain precedence as we give ourselves to the work of ministering according to the grace we already have. We may confidently wait for the full revelation of Christ in us—the power to do all that He asks of us.

Chapter 17

———————◆—◆———————

Women Adorned with Good Works

Women adorn themselves in modest apparel,
with shamefacedness and sobriety; not with broided hair, or
gold, or pearls, or costly array; but (which becometh women
professing godliness) with good works.
—1 Timothy 2:9–10

Let not a widow be taken into the number under
threescore years old, having been the wife of one man,
well reported of for good works...if she have diligently
followed every good work.
—1 Timothy 5:9–10

*I*n the three Pastoral Epistles written to two young pastors to instruct them in regard to their duties, "good works" are more frequently mentioned than in Paul's other epistles.[1] In writing to the churches, as in a chapter like Romans 12, Paul mentioned the individual good works by name. In writing to the pastors, he had to use this expression as a summary of their aim both

[1] In 1 Timothy six times: 2:10; 3:1; 5:10, 25; 6:18. In 2 Timothy twice: 2:21; 3:17. In Titus six times: 1:16; 2:7, 14; 3:1, 8, 14.

in their own lives and their teaching of others. A minister was to be prepared and completely equipped to accomplish every good work—an example of good works. They were to teach Christians—the women to adorn themselves with good works, to follow diligently every good work, and to be well reported of for good works. The men were to be rich in good works, to be zealous of good works, to be ready for every good work, and to learn to maintain good works. No portion of God's work emphasizes more definitely the absolute necessity of good works as an essential, vital element in the Christian life.

Our two texts speak of the good works of Christian women. In the first, they are taught that their adorning is to be not with fancy hair and gold or pearls or costly clothing but, as becomes women preferring godliness, with good works. We know what adornment is. A leafless tree in winter has life. When spring comes it puts on its beautiful garments and rejoices in the adornment of foliage and blossom. The adorning of Christian women is not to be in hair or pearls or clothing, but in good works.

Whether it is the good works that have reference to personal duty and conduct, those works of charity that aim at the pleasing and helping of our neighbors, or those that more definitely seek the salvation of souls—the adorning that pleases God, that gives true heavenly beauty, that will truly attract others to come and serve God, too, is what Christian women ought to seek. John saw the Holy City descend from heaven, *"prepared as a bride adorned for her husband"* (Rev. 21:2). *"The fine linen is the righteousness of saints"* (Rev. 19:8). If only every Christian woman might seek to adorn herself to please the Lord!

In the second passage, we read of widows who were placed upon an honor roll in the early church, and to whom a certain charge was given over the younger women. No one was to be enrolled who was not *"well reported of for good works."* Some of these are mentioned: if she had been known for the careful upbringing of her children, for her hospitality to strangers, for her washing the saints' feet, for her relieving the afflicted. And then there is added, *"If she have diligently followed every good work."* If her life had been devoted to good works in her home and out of it, in caring for her own children, for strangers, and for fellow believers, she might indeed be considered fit to be an example and guide to others. The standard was a high one. It shows us the place good works took in the early church. It shows how a woman's blessed ministry of love was counted on and encouraged. It shows how, in the development of the Christian life, nothing so fits for rule and influence as a life given to good works.

Good works are part and parcel of the Christian life, equally indispensable to the health and growth of the individual, and to the welfare and extension of the church. And yet, what multitudes of Christian women there are whose active share in the good work of blessing their fellow creatures is little more than playing at good works. They are waiting for the preaching of a full Gospel, which will encourage and help and compel them to give their lives to work for their Lord, so that they, too, may be well reported of as diligently following every good work.

The time and money, the thought and feeling given to jewels or costly clothing, will be exchanged for the true goal. Christianity will no longer be a selfish desire for personal safety, but the joy of being like Christ, the Helper and Savior of the needy. Work for Christ will take its true place as the highest form of existence, the true adornment of the Christian life. And as diligence in the pursuits of earth is honored as one of the true elements of character and worth, following good works diligently in Christ's service will be found to give access to the highest reward and the fullest joy of the Lord.

- We are beginning to awaken to the wonderful place women can take in church and school mission. This truth needs to be brought home to every one of the King's daughters, that the adorning in which they are to attract the world, to please their Lord, and enter His presence is only this: good works.

- Women, as *"the meekness and gentleness of Christ"* (2 Cor. 10:1), are to teach men the beauty and the power of the long-suffering, self-sacrificing ministry of love.
- The training for the service of love begins in the home. It is strengthened there; then it reaches out to the needy and finds its full scope in the world for which Christ died.

Chapter 18

Rich in Good Works

*Charge them that are rich in this world...that they do
good, that they be rich in good works, ready to distribute,
willing to communicate; laying up in store for themselves
a good foundation against the time to come,
that they may lay hold on eternal life.*
—1 Timothy 6:17–19

*I*f women are to regard good works as their adornment, men
are to count them as their riches. As good works satisfy a
woman's eye and taste for beauty, they meet a man's craving for
possession and power. In the present world, riches have a wonderful significance. They are often God's reward for diligence,
industry, and enterprise. They represent and embody the life-
power that has been spent in procuring them. As such, they
exercise power in the honor or service they secure from others.
Their danger consists in their being of this world, in their misdi-
recting the heart from the living God and heavenly treasures.
They may become a man's deadliest enemy. How difficult it is
for those who have riches to enter the kingdom of heaven! (See
Matthew 19:24.)

The Gospel never takes away anything from us without giving us something better in its place. It meets the desire for riches by the command to be rich in good works. The coin that is current in God's kingdom is good works. The reward in the world to come will be determined according to these. By abounding in good works, we lay up for ourselves treasures in heaven (Matt. 6:20). Even here on earth they constitute a treasure, in the testimony of a good conscience, in the consciousness of being well-pleasing to God (see 1 John 3), in the power of blessing others.

There is more. Wealth of gold is not only a symbol of the heavenly riches. It is actually, though so opposite in its nature, a means to it. As our text verse states:

Charge them that are rich...that they do good, that they be rich in good works, ready to distribute, willing to communicate; laying up in store for themselves a good foundation.

Make to yourselves friends of the mammon of unrighteousness; that, when ye fail, they may receive you into everlasting habitations. (Luke 16:9)

Like the widow's mite, the gifts of the rich, when given in the same spirit, may be an offering with which *"God is well pleased"* (Heb. 13:16).

The man who is rich in money may become rich in good works if he follows the instructions in Scripture. The money must not be given to be seen of men, but as unto the Lord. Nor must it be given as from an owner, but as from a steward who administers the Lord's money with prayer for His guidance. Nor must it be given with any confidence in its power or influence, but in deep dependence on Him who alone can make it a blessing. Nor must it be given as a substitute for the personal work and witness that each believer is to give. As all Christian work, so our monetary giving has its value alone from the spirit in which it is done, even the spirit of Christ Jesus.

What a field there is in the world for accumulating these riches, these heavenly treasures! In relieving the poor; in educating the neglected; in helping the lost; in taking the Gospel to Christians, and to heathens in darkness, what investment might be made if Christians sought to be rich in good works—rich toward God! We may well ask the question, "What can be done to awaken a desire for these true riches among believers?" Men have made a science of the wealth of nations and carefully studied all the laws by which its increase and universal distribution can be promoted. How can the order to be rich in good works convict hearts that its pursuit will be as much a pleasure and a passion as the desire for the riches of the present world?

All depends upon the nature, the spirit, of man. To the earthly nature, earthly riches have a natural affinity and irresistible attraction. To foster the desire for the acquisition of what constitutes wealth in the heavenly kingdom, we must appeal to the spiritual nature. That spiritual nature needs to be taught and educated and trained into all the business habits that go into making a man rich.

There must be the ambition to rise above the level of a bare existence, the deadly contentment with just being saved. There must be some insight into the beauty and worth of good works as the expression of the divine life—God's working in us and our working in Him—as the means of bringing glory to God, as the source of life and blessing to men, and as the laying up of a treasure in heaven for eternity. There must be a faith that these riches are actually within our reach because the grace and Spirit of God are working in us. And there must be an outlook of doing the work of God to those around us at every opportunity, in the footsteps of Him who said, *"It is more blessed to give than to receive"* (Acts 20:35).

Study and apply these principles. They will open the sure road to your becoming a rich person. One who wants to be rich often begins on a small scale, but never loses an opportunity. Begin at once with some work of love, and ask Christ, who

521

"became poor, that ye through his poverty might be rich" (2 Cor. 8:9), to help you.

- Why does the appeal for money for missions meet with such insufficient response? It is because of the low spiritual state of the church. Many Christians have no proper idea of their calling to live completely for God and His kingdom.
- How can the evil be remedied? Only when believers see and accept their divine calling to make God's kingdom their first care, and with humble confession of their sins yield themselves to God, will they truly seek the heavenly riches to be found in working for God.
- Never cease to plead and labor for a true spiritual awakening throughout the church.

Chapter 19

———————◆———————

Prepared unto Every Good Work

*If a man therefore purge himself from these, he shall be a
vessel unto honour, sanctified, and meet for the master's use,
and prepared unto every good work.*
—2 Timothy 2:21

*P*aul spoke of the foundation of God standing sure, of the
church as the great house built upon that foundation of vessels, not only of gold and silver, costly and lasting, but also of
wood and of earth, common and perishable (2 Tim. 2:19–20).
He distinguished between those who gave themselves to striving for words of praise and those who truly sought to depart
from all iniquity.

Paul gave us the four steps of the path in which a man can
become a vessel unto honor in the great household of God: (1)
the cleansing from sin; (2) being sanctified; (3) the suitability for
the Master to use as He will; and (4) the spirit of preparedness
for every good work. It is not enough that we desire or attempt
to do good works. As we need training and care to prepare us
for every work we are to do on earth, we need to be prepared
unto every good work that much more.

This is what constitutes the chief mark of vessels unto honor: *"If a man therefore purge himself from these."* A man must cleanse himself from that which characterizes the vessels of dishonor—the empty profession leading to ungodliness, against which Paul warned. We insist that every dish and cup we use be clean. In God's house the vessels must be clean that much more. And everyone who would be truly prepared unto every good work must first see that he cleanses himself from all that is sin. Christ Himself could not enter upon His saving work in heaven until He had accomplished the cleansing of our sins. How can we become partners in His work unless we first have the same cleansing? Before Isaiah could say, *"Here am I; send me"* (Isa. 6:8), the fire of heaven had touched his lips, and he heard the voice say, *"Thy sin [is] purged"* (v. 7). An intense desire to be cleansed from every sin lies at the root of fitness for true service.

"He shall be a vessel unto honour, sanctified." Cleansing is the negative side, the emptying out and removal of all that is impure. Sanctification is the positive side, the refilling and being possessed of the spirit of holiness, through whom the soul becomes God-possessed, and so partakes of His holiness. *"Let us cleanse ourselves from all filthiness of the flesh and spirit, perfecting holiness in the fear of God"* (2 Cor. 7:1). In the temple the vessels were to be not only clean, but also holy, devoted to God's service alone. He who truly desires to work for God must follow after holiness—*"To the end he may stablish your hearts unblameable in holiness before God"* (1 Thess. 3:13), a holy habit of mind and disposition, yielded up to God and marked by a sense of His presence, fit for God's work. The cleansing from sin secures the filling with the Spirit.

"Meet for the master's use." We are vessels for our Lord to use. In every work we do, it is to be Christ using us and working through us. The sense of being a servant—dependent on the Master's guidance, working under the Master's eye, instruments used by Him and His mighty power—lies at the root of effective service. It maintains that unbroken dependence, that

quiet faith, through which the Lord can do His work. It keeps up that blessed consciousness of the work being all His, which leads the worker to become humbler the more he is used. His one desire is to be *"meet for the master's use."*

"Prepared unto every good work." "Prepared." The word not only refers to equipment and fitness, but also to disposition, the cheerful readiness that keeps a person on the look out for every opportunity of doing his Master's work and makes him joyfully and earnestly desire to serve the Lord in every way he can. As he lives in touch with his Lord Jesus and holds himself as a cleansed and sanctified vessel, ready for Him to use, and he sees that he was redeemed for good works, they become the one thing for which he lives and proves his fellowship with his Lord. He is *"prepared unto every good work."*

- *"Meet for the master's use"*—that is the central thought. A personal relationship to Christ, an entire surrender to His disposal, a dependent waiting to be used by Him, a joyful confidence that He will use us—such is the secret of true work.
- Let the beginning of your work be a giving of yourself into the hands of the Master, as your living, loving Lord.

Chapter 20

— ◆ —

Furnished Completely unto Every Good Work

*Study to show thyself approved unto God,
a workman that needeth not to be ashamed,
rightly dividing the word of truth.*
—2 Timothy 2:15

*All scripture is given by inspiration of God, and is
profitable for doctrine, for reproof, for correction,
for instruction in righteousness: that the man of God may be
perfect, thoroughly furnished unto all good works.*
—2 Timothy 3:16–17

A workman who does not need to be ashamed is one who is not afraid to have his employer come and inspect his work. In hearty devotion to it, in thoroughness and skill, he presents himself approved to him who employs him. God's workers are to present themselves approved to Him to have their work worthy and well-pleasing unto Him. They are to be as workmen who do not need to be ashamed. A workman is one who knows his work, who gives himself completely to it, who is known as a working man, who takes delight in doing his work well. Thus, every Christian minister, every Christian worker, is to be a workman who concentrates on inviting and expecting the Master's approval.

"Rightly dividing the word of truth." The Word is a seed, a fire, a hammer, a sword, bread, and light. Workmen in any of these areas can be our example. In work for God, everything depends upon handling the Word correctly. Therefore, the one means of our being completely equipped for every good work is given in the Scripture that begins this paragraph—personal subjection to the Word and the experience of its power. God's workers must know that Scripture is inspired by God and has life-giving power in it. Inspiration is Spirit-breathed; as the life is in a seed, God's Holy Spirit is in the Word. The Spirit in the Word and the Spirit in our hearts is one. By the power of the Spirit within us, we take the Spirit-filled Word. Thus, we become spiritual. This Word is given for teaching—the revelation of the thoughts of God; for reproof—the discovery of our sins and mistakes; for correction—to remove what is defective and replace it by what is good; and for instruction—the communication of all the knowledge needed to walk before God righteously.

As one yields himself heartily to all this, and the true Spirit-filled Word gets mastery of his whole being, he becomes a man of God, furnished completely to every good work. He becomes a workman approved by God who does not need to be ashamed, rightly handling the Word of God. And so the man of God has the double mark—his own life is completely molded and his work is directed by applying the Word.

"That the man of God may be perfect, thoroughly furnished unto all good works." In the previous chapter we learned how the cleansing and sanctification of the personal life changes the worker into a vessel *"meet for the master's use, and prepared unto every good work"* (2 Tim. 2:21). Here we learn the same lesson: it is the man of God who allows God's Word to do its work of reprimanding and correcting and instructing. Every worker for God must aim to be equipped for every good work.

A worker, aware of how defective his preparation is, might ask how this furnishing for every good work is to be attained. The analogy of an earthly workman, not needing to be ashamed, suggests the answer. The earthly worker would tell us that he owes his success, first of all, to devotion to his work. He gave it his close attention. He left other things to concentrate his efforts on mastering one thing. He made it a life-study to do his work perfectly. Those who wish to do Christ's work as a second thing, not as the first, and who are not willing to sacrifice all for it, will never be fully equipped to every good work.

The second thing he will speak of will be patient training and exercise. Proficiency comes only through painstaking effort. You may feel as if you do not know how to work correctly. Have no fear. All learning begins with ignorance and mistakes. Be of good courage. He who has endowed human nature with the wonderful power that has filled the world with such skilled and cunning workmen will give His children the grace they need to be His fellow workers even more, will He not? Let the necessity that is laid upon you—the necessity that you should glorify God; that you should bless the world; that you should, through work, advance and perfect your life and blessedness—urge you to give immediate and continual diligence to be a workman equipped unto every good work.

It is only in doing that we learn to do correctly. Begin working under Christ's training. He will perfect His work in you and make you fit for your work for Him.

- The work God is doing, and seeking to have done in the world, is to win it back to Himself.
- Every believer is expected to take part in this work.
- God wants us to be skilled workmen who give our whole hearts to His work and delight in it.
- God does His work by working in us, inspiring and strengthening us to do His work.

- What God asks for is a heart and life devoted to Him in surrender and faith.
- God's work is all love; love is the power that works in us, inspiring our efforts and conquering its object.

Chapter 21

———◆◆———

Zealous of Good Works

*Who gave himself for us, that he might redeem us from
all iniquity, and purify unto himself a peculiar people,
zealous of good works.*
—Titus 2:14

*I*n these words we have two truths: what Christ has done to
make us His own and what He expects of us. In the first part
we have a rich and beautiful summary of Christ's work for us.
He gave Himself for us, He redeemed us from all iniquity, He
cleansed us for Himself, He took us for a people, for His own
possession. And all with the one objective that we should be a
people *"zealous of good works."* The doctrinal half of this wonderful passage has had much attention given to it. Let us devote
our attention to its practical part: we are to be a people *"zealous
of good works."* Christ expects us to be zealots for good works.

This cannot be said to be the feeling with which most Christians regard good works. What can be done to cultivate this disposition? One of the first things that awakens zeal in work is a
great and urgent sense of need. A great need awakens strong
desire, stirs the heart and the will, and rouses all the energies
of our being. It was this sense of need that roused many to be

zealous of the law. They hoped their works would save them. The Gospel has robbed this motive of its power. Has it entirely taken away the need for good works? No. Indeed, it has given that urgent need a higher place than before.

Christ needs our good works urgently. We are His servants, the members of His body, without whom He cannot possibly carry on His work on earth. The work is so great (with millions still unsaved) that not one worker can be spared. Thousands of Christians today feel that their own business is urgent and must be attended to; they have no conception of the urgency of Christ's work entrusted to them. The church must wake up to teach each believer his responsibility.

The world needs our good works as urgently as Christ needs them. Men, women, and children around you need to be saved. To see people swept past us in a river stirs us to try to save them. Christ has placed His children in a perishing world with the expectation that they will give themselves, hearts and souls, to carry on His work of love. Let us sound forth the blessed gospel message: He gave Himself for us so that He might redeem us for Himself, a people of His own, to serve Him and carry on His work—*"zealous of good works."*

A second great element of zeal in work is delight in it. An apprentice or a student mostly begins his work under a sense of duty. As he learns to understand and enjoy it, he does it with pleasure and becomes zealous in its performance. The church must train Christians to believe that when we give our hearts to the work of sharing in Christ's work of mercy and love, and seek the training that makes us in some degree skilled workmen, there is no greater joy. As physical and mental activity give pleasure and call for the devotion and zeal of thousands, the spiritual service of Christ can awaken our highest enthusiasm.

Then comes the highest motive, the personal one of attachment to Christ our Redeemer. *"For the love of Christ constraineth us"* (2 Cor. 5:14). Christ's love for us is the source and measure of our love for Him. Our love for Him becomes the power and the measure of our love for souls. This love, poured forth widely in our hearts by the Holy Spirit, becomes a zeal for Christ that shows itself as a zeal for good works. It becomes the link that unites the two parts of our text, the doctrinal and the practical, into one. Christ's love redeemed us, cleansed us, and made us a people of His own. When that love is believed in, known, and received into the heart, it makes the redeemed soul zealous in good works.

"Zealous of good works!" Let no believer look upon this grace as too high. It is divine, provided for and assured in the love of our Lord. Let us accept it as our calling. Let us be sure it is the very nature of the new life within us. Let us, in opposition to all that nature or feeling may say, in faith claim it as an integral part of our redemption. Christ Himself will make it true in us.

Chapter 22

———————◆———————

Ready to Every Good Work

Put them in mind...to be ready to every good work.
—Titus 3:1

" Put them in mind." The words suggest the need for believers to have the truths of their calling to good works set before them again and again. A healthy tree spontaneously bears its fruit. Even where the life of the believer is in perfect health, Scripture teaches us how its growth and fruitfulness can come only through teaching and the influence that exerts on mind and will and heart. For all who have charge of others, the need of divine wisdom and faithfulness is great in order to teach and train all Christians. Let us consider some of the chief points of such training.

Teach them clearly what good works are. Lay the foundation in the will of God, as revealed in the law, and show them how integrity and righteousness and obedience are the groundwork of Christian character. Teach them how, in all the duties and relationships of daily life, true religion is to be carried out. Lead them on to the virtues that Jesus especially came to exhibit and teach—humility, meekness, gentleness, and love. Explain to them the meaning of a life of love, self-sacrifice, and charity—entirely dedicated to thinking of and caring for others. Then carry them on to what is the highest, the true life of good works—the winning of men to know and love God.

Teach them what an essential part of the Christian life good works are. They are not, as many think, a secondary element in the salvation that God gives. They are not merely to be done in token of our gratitude, or as a proof of the sincerity of our faith, or as a preparation for heaven. They are all this, but they are a great deal more. They are the very purpose for which we have been redeemed. We have been created anew unto good works. They alone are the evidence that man has been restored to his original destiny of working with, through, and in God. God has no higher glory than His works, particularly His work of saving love. In becoming imitators of God and walking and working in love, even as Christ loved us and gave Himself for us (Gal. 2:20), we have the very image and likeness of God restored in us. The works of a man not only reveal his life, but also develop, exercise, strengthen, and perfect it. Good works are the very essence of the divine life in us.

Teach them, too, what a rich reward they bring. All labor has its market value. From the poor man who can scarcely earn a little money, to the man who has made his millions, the thought of the reward for labor has been one of the great incentives to undertake it. Christ appeals to this feeling when He says, *"Your reward shall be great"* (Luke 6:35). Let Christians understand that there is no service where the reward is so rich as that of God. Work is bracing; work is strength, and it cultivates the sense of mastery and conquest. Work awakens enthusiasm and brings out a man's noblest qualities. In a life of good works, the Christian becomes conscious of his divine ministry of dispensing the life and grace of God to others.

Good works bring us into closer union with God. There is no higher fellowship with God than fellowship in His saving work of love. Work brings us into sympathy with Him and His purposes. It fills us with His love. It secures His approval. And great is the reward, too, for those around us. When others are won to Christ, when the weary and the erring and the despondent are helped and made partakers of the grace and life in Christ Jesus for them, God's servants share in the very joy in which our blessed Lord found His reward.

And now the chief thing. Teach them to believe that it is possible for each of us to abound in good works. Nothing is so fatal to successful effort as discouragement or despondency. Nothing is more a frequent cause of neglect of good works than the fear that we do not have the power to perform them. Put them in mind of the power of the Holy Spirit dwelling in them. Show them that God's promise and provision of strength is always equal to what He demands. Show them that sufficient grace is always available for all the good works to which we are called. Strive to awaken in them a faith in *"the power that worketh in us"* (Eph. 3:20) and in the fullness of the life that can flow out as *"rivers of living water"* (John 7:38). Train them to begin their service of love at once. Lead them to see how it is all God working in them and to offer themselves as empty vessels to be filled with His love and grace. And teach them that as they are faithful in a little, even in the midst of mistakes and shortcomings, the acting out of the life will strengthen the life itself, and work for God will become in full truth a second nature.

God grant that the teachers of the church may be faithful to its commission in regard to all her members—*"Put them in mind...to be ready for every good work."* Not only teach them, but also train them. Show them the work there is to be done by them. See that they do it. Encourage and help them to do it hopefully. There is no part of the office of a pastor more important, more sacred, or fuller of richer blessing. Let the aim be nothing less than to lead every believer to live entirely devoted to the work of God in winning souls to Him. What a change it would make in the church and the world!

• Get a firm hold of the great basic principle: every believer, every member of Christ's body, has his place in the body solely for the welfare of the whole body.

- Pastors have been given for the perfecting of the saints with the work of ministering, of serving in love.
- In ministers and members of the churches, Christ will work mightily if they will wait upon Him.

Chapter 23

Careful to Maintain Good Works

I will that thou affirm constantly, that they which have
believed in God might be careful to maintain good works....
And let ours also learn to maintain good works for necessary
uses, that they be not unfruitful.
—Titus 3:8, 14

*I*n the first part of this passage, Paul charged Titus to state
confidently the truths of the blessed Gospel to the end, with
the express purpose that all who had believed should be careful, should make a study of it, to maintain good works. Faith
and good works were to be inseparable. The diligence of every
believer in good works was to be a main aim of a pastor's
work. Then Paul repeated the instruction, with the expression
"let them learn." As all work on earth has to be learned, so in
the good works of the Christian life there is an equal need of
thought and application and teachableness to learn how to do
them correctly and abundantly.

There may be more than one reader of this book who has
felt how little he has lived in accordance with all the teaching of
God's Word—prepared for, thoroughly equipped for, ready unto,
and zealous of good works. It appears so difficult to get rid of
old habits, to break through the conventions of society, and to

know how to begin and really enter into a life that can be full of good works to the glory of God. Let me try to give some suggestions that may be helpful. They may also aid those who have the training of Christian workers, in showing in what way the teaching and learning of good works may best succeed.

First, a learner must begin by beginning to work at once. There is no way of learning an art like swimming or music, a new language or a trade, but by practice. Let neither the fear that you cannot do it, nor the hope that something will happen that will make it easier for you, keep you back. Learn to do good works, the works of love, by beginning to do them. However insignificant they appear, do them. A kind word, a little help to someone in trouble, an act of loving attention to a stranger or a poor man, the sacrifice of a seat or a place to someone who longs for it—practice these things. All plants we cultivate are small at first. Cherish the consciousness that, for Jesus' sake, you are seeking to do what would please Him. It is only in doing that you can learn to do.

Second, the learner must give his heart to the work and must take interest and pleasure in it. Delight in work ensures success. Let the tens of thousands around you in the world who throw their whole souls into their daily businesses teach you how to serve your blessed Master. Think sometimes of the honor and privilege of doing good works, of serving others in love. It is God's own work, to love and save and bless men. He works it in you and through you. It makes you share the spirit and likeness of Christ. It strengthens your Christian character. Without actions, a man's intentions lower and condemn him instead of raising him. You really live only as much as you act. Think of the blessedness of doing good, of communicating life, of making others happy. Think of the exquisite joy of growing up into a life of charity and being a blessing to all you meet. Set your heart upon being a vessel fit for the Master's use, ready to do every good work.

Third, be of good courage, and fear not. The learner who says, "I cannot," will surely fail. There is a divine power working in you. Study and believe what God's Word says about it. Let the holy self-reliance of Paul, grounded in his reliance on Christ, be your example—*"I can do all things through Christ which strengtheneth me"* (Phil. 4:13). Study and take to heart the wonderful promises about the power of the Holy Spirit, the abundance of grace, and Christ's strength made perfect in weakness, and see how all this can be made true to you only in working. Cultivate the noble consciousness that as you have been created to good works by God, He Himself will equip you for them. Believe, then, that just as it is natural to any workman to delight and succeed in his profession, it can be natural to the new nature in you to abound in every good work. Having this confidence, you never need to faint.

Fourth, above all, cling to your Lord Jesus as your Teacher and Master. He said, *"Learn of me; for I am meek and lowly in heart: and ye shall find rest unto your souls"* (Matt. 11:29). Work as one who is a learner in His school, who is sure that none teaches like Him. Cling to Him, and let a sense of His presence and His power working in you make you meek and lowly, yet bold and strong. He who came to do the Father's work on earth and found it the path to the Father's glory will teach you what it is to work for God.

To sum up again, for the sake of any who want to learn how to work, or how to work better:

- Yield yourself to Christ. Lay yourself on the altar and say you wish to give yourself completely for God's work.
- Believe quietly that Christ accepts and takes charge of you for His work and will equip you for it.
- Pray much that God would open to you the great truth of His own working in you. Nothing else can give true strength.
- Seek to cultivate a spirit of humble, patient, trustful dependence upon God. Live in loving fellowship and obedience to Christ. You can count upon His strength being made perfect in your weakness.

Chapter 24

————————◆————————

As His Fellow Workers

For we are labourers together with God: ye are God's
husbandry, ye are God's building.
—1 Corinthians 3:9

We then, as workers together with him, beseech you also that
ye receive not the grace of God in vain.
—2 Corinthians 6:1

We have discussed Paul's teaching on good works. Let us
turn now to his personal experience and see if we can
learn some of the secrets of effective service from him.

In the text for this chapter, Paul spoke of the church as
God's building. As the Great Architect, God is building up the
church into a holy temple and dwelling for Himself. Of his own
work, Paul spoke as a master builder, to whom a part of the
great building had been given to his charge. He had laid a foundation in Corinth. To all who were working there he said, *"For*
we are labourers together with God....Let every man take heed
how he buildeth thereupon" (1 Cor. 3:9–10). These words are
applicable not only to Paul, but also to all God's servants who
take part in His work. And because every believer has been

called to give his life to God's service and to win others to His knowledge, every Christian needs to have the Word brought to him and taken home: we are God's fellow workers. How much it suggests in regard to our working for God!

As to the work we have to do, the eternal God is building for Himself a temple. Jesus Christ, God's Son, is the foundation. Believers are the living stones. The Holy Spirit is the mighty power of God through which believers are gathered out of the world, made fit for their places in the temple, and built up into it. As living stones, believers are at the same time the living workmen, whom God uses to carry out His work. They are equally God's workmanship and God's fellow workers. The work God is doing He does through them. The work they have to do is the very work God is doing. God's own work, in which He delights, on which His heart is set, is saving people and building them into His temple. This is the one work on which the heart of everyone who desires to be a fellow worker with God must be set. Only as we know how great this work of God is—giving life to dead souls, imparting His own life to them, and living in them—will we enter into the glory of our work. We will receive the very life of God and pass it on to others.

As to the strength for the work, Paul said of his work, as a mere master builder, that it was *"according to the grace of God which is given unto me"* (1 Cor. 3:10). For divine work, nothing but divine power suffices. The power by which God works must work in us. That power is His Holy Spirit. Study 1 Corinthians 2 and 2 Corinthians 3. You will see how absolute Paul's acknowledgment of his own powerlessness and his dependence on the teaching and power of the Holy Spirit was. The truth is that God's work can be done only by God's power in us. Our first need every day is to have the presence of God's Spirit renewed within us.

The power of the Holy Spirit is the power of love. God is love. All He works for the salvation of men is love. It is love alone that truly conquers and wins the heart. In all God's fellow workers, love is the power that reaches the hearts of men. Christ conquered and conquers still by the love of the cross. *"Let this mind be in you, which was also in Christ Jesus"* (Phil. 2:5)—the spirit of a love that sacrifices itself to the death, of a humble, patient, gentle love—and you will be made fit to be God's fellow worker.

As to the relationship we are to hold to God, let me say this. In executing the plans of a great building, the master builder has but one care: to carry out to the minutest detail the thoughts of the architect who designed it. He acts in constant consultation with him and is guided in everything by his will. His instructions to those under him all refer to one thing—the embodiment, in visible shape, of what the master mind has conceived. The great characteristics of fellow workers with God ought to be that of absolute surrender to His will, unceasing dependence on His teaching, and exact obedience to His wishes. God has revealed His plan in His Word. He has told us that His Spirit alone can enable us to enter into His plans and fully master His purpose with the way He desires to have it carried out.

We must have clear insight into the divine glory of God's work of saving souls. We must see the utter insufficiency of our natural powers to do the work. We must know that He has made provision to strengthen and guide us in performance. We will then come to a greater understanding that a childlike teachableness (a continual looking upward and waiting on God) is always to be the chief mark of one who is His fellow laborer.

Out of a sense of humility, helplessness, and nothingness, there will grow a holy confidence and courage. We will know that our weaknesses do not need to hinder us, that Christ's strength is made perfect in weakness, and that God Himself is working out His purpose through us. Of all the blessings of the Christian life, the most wonderful will be that we are allowed to be God's fellow workers!

- God's fellow worker! How easy to use the words, and even to understand some of the great truths they contain! How little we live in the power and the glory of what they actually involve!

- Fellow workers with God! Everything depends upon knowing, in His holiness and love, the God with whom we are associated as partners.

- He who has chosen us will equip us for His use, so that in and through us He might do His great work.

- Let our posture be adoring worship, deep dependence, great waiting, and full obedience.

Chapter 25

———————— ◆ ————————

According to the Working
of His Power

*Whom we preach, warning every man, and teaching every
man in all wisdom; that we may present every man
perfect in Christ Jesus: whereunto I also labour, striving
according to his working, which worketh in me mightily.*
—Colossians 1:28–29

*The mystery of Christ…whereof I was made a minister,
according to the gift of the grace of God given unto me
by the effectual working of his power.*
—Ephesians 3:4, 7

I n the words of Paul to the Philippians, which we have already
considered in chapter nine, he called upon them and encouraged them to work because it was God who worked in them.
This is one of the most momentous and comprehensive statements of the great truth that it is only by God's working in us
that we can do true work. In our Scripture texts for this chapter,
we have Paul's testimony about his own experience. His whole
ministry was to be according to the grace that was given to him

by the working of God's power. He said that his labor was a striving according to the power of Him who worked mightily within him.

We find here the same principle we found in our Lord—the Father doing the works in Him. Let every worker who reads this pause and say, "If the ever-blessed Son and Paul could do their work only according to the working of His power who worked mightily in them, how much more do I need this working of God in me!" This is one of the deepest spiritual truths of God's Word. Let us look to the Holy Spirit within us to give it such a hold of our inmost life that it may become the deepest inspiration of all our work. We can do true work only as we yield ourselves to God to work in us.

We know the ground on which this truth rests. *"There is none good but one, that is, God"* (Matt. 19:17). *"There is none holy as the* LORD*"* (1 Sam. 2:2). *"Power belongeth unto God"* (Ps. 62:11). All goodness and holiness and power are to be found only in God and where He gives them. Only He can give them to man, not as something He parts with, but by His own actual presence and dwelling and working. God can work in His people only as He is allowed to have complete possession of their hearts and lives. As the will and life and love are yielded up in dependence and faith, and we wait on God as Christ waited on Him, God can work in us.

This is true of all spiritual life, but especially of our work for God. The work of saving souls is God's own work. None but He can do it. The gift of His Son is the proof of how great and precious He considers the work, and how His heart is set upon it. His love never for one moment ceases working for the salvation of men. And when He calls His children to be partners in His work, He shares with them the joy and the glory of the work of saving and blessing men. He promises to work His work through them, inspiring and energizing them by His power working in them. To the individual who can say with Paul, "I also labour, striving according to his working, which worketh in me mightily," his whole relationship to God becomes the counterpart and the continuation of Christ's—a blessed, unceasing, momentary, and most absolute dependence on the Father for every word He spoke and every work He did.

Christ is our pattern. Christ's life is our law, and it works in us. Paul lived his life of dependence on God as Christ did. Why should any of us hesitate to believe that the grace given to Paul of laboring and striving *"according to the...working of his power"* will also be given to us? Let every worker learn to say, "As the power that worked in Christ worked in Paul, too, that power works no less in me." There is no possible way of doing God's work correctly except by God working it in us.

How I wish that I could take every worker who reads this by the hand, and say, "Come. Let us quiet our minds and hush every thought in God's presence, as I whisper in your ears the wonderful secret that God is working in you. All the work you have to do for Him, God will work in you." Take time and think it over. It is a deep spiritual truth that the mind cannot grasp nor the heart realize. Accept it as a divine truth from heaven. Believe that this word is a seed from which the very spiritual blessing of which it speaks can grow. And in the faith of the Holy Spirit's making it live within you, always consider: God works in me. All the work I have to work for Him, God will work in me.

The faith of this truth, and the desire to have it made true in you, will compel you to live very humbly and closely with God. You will see how work for God must be the most spiritual thing in a spiritual life. And you will again and again bow in holy stillness and acknowledge that God is working in you and will continue to work in you. Like Paul you can say, "I will work for Him according to the power that works in me mightily."

- The gift of the grace of God (Eph. 2:7, 3:7), the power that works in us (Eph. 3:20), the strengthening with might by the Spirit (v. 16)—these three expressions all contain the same thought of God's working all in us.

- The Holy Spirit is the power of God. Seek to be filled with the Spirit, to have your whole life led by Him, and you will become fit for God's working mightily in you.

- *"Ye shall receive power, after that the Holy Ghost is come upon you"* (Acts 1:8). Through the Spirit dwelling in us, God can work in us mightily.

- What holy fear, what humble watchfulness and dependence, what entire surrender and obedience becomes us if we believe in God's working in us!

Chapter 26

---◄◆►---

Laboring More Abundantly

By the grace of God I am what I am: and his grace
which was bestowed upon me was not in vain;
but I laboured more abundantly than they all: yet not I,
but the grace of God which was with me.
—1 Corinthians 15:10

And he said unto me, My grace is sufficient for thee:
for my strength is made perfect in weakness....For in
nothing am I behind the very chiefest apostles,
though I be nothing.
—2 Corinthians 12:9, 11

*I*n both these passages, Paul spoke of how he had abounded in the work of the Lord. *"In nothing am I behind the very chiefest apostles." "I laboured more abundantly than they all."* In both he told how entirely it was God who worked in him and not himself. In the first passage he said, *"Not I, but the grace of God which was with me."* Then, in the second, he showed how this grace is Christ's strength working in us. While we are nothing, we are told, *"He said unto me: My grace is sufficient for thee: for my strength is made perfect in weakness."* May God give us *"the spirit of wisdom and revelation"* (Eph. 1:17) and the enlightened eyes of the heart (see verse 18) to see this wonderful vision of a man who knew himself to be nothing. He was a man who gloried in his weakness so that the power of Christ would rest on him and work through him, and who labored more abundantly than all. What this teaches us as workers for God!

God's work can be done only in God's strength. It is only by God's power, that is, by God Himself working in us, that we can do effective work. Throughout this book, this truth has been frequently repeated. It is easy to accept. It is far from easy to see its full meaning—to give it the mastery over our whole beings, to live it out. This will need stillness of soul, meditation, strong faith, and fervent prayer. As it is God alone who can work in us, it is equally God alone who can reveal Himself as the God who works in us. Wait on Him, and the truth that ever appears to be beyond your reach will be opened up to you through the knowledge of who and what God is. When God reveals Himself as *"God which worketh all in all"* (1 Cor. 12:6), you will learn to believe and work according to the power of Him who works in you mightily (Col. 1:29).

God's strength can work only in weakness. It is only when we truly say, "Not I," that we can fully say, "but the grace of God...with me." The man who said, "In nothing am I behind the very chiefest of the apostles," first had to learn to say, "though I be nothing." He could say, *"I take pleasure in infirmities...for when I am weak, then am I strong"* (2 Cor. 12:10). This is the true relationship between the Creator and mankind, between the divine Father and His child, between God and His servant.

Dear Christian worker, learn the lesson of your own weakness as the indispensable condition of God's power working in you. Believe that to take time and to realize in God's presence your weakness and nothingness is the sure way to be clothed with God's strength. Accept every experience by which God teaches you your weakness as His grace preparing you to receive His strength. Take pleasure in weaknesses!

God's strength comes in our fellowship with Christ and His service. Paul said, *"Most gladly therefore will I rather glory in my infirmities, that the power of Christ may rest upon me"* (2 Cor. 12:9). *"I take pleasure in infirmities...for Christ's sake"* (v. 10). And he told how it was that, when he had besought the Lord that the messenger of Satan might depart from him, He answered, *"My grace is sufficient for thee."* *"Christ* [is] *the power of God, and the wisdom of God"* (1 Cor. 1:24). We do not receive the wisdom to know or the power to do God's will as something that we can possess and use at our discretion. It is in the personal attachment to Christ, in a life of continual communication with Him, that His power rests on us. It is in taking pleasure in weaknesses for Christ's sake that Christ's strength is known.

God's strength is given to faith, and the work that is done in faith. A living faith is needed to take pleasure in weakness, and in weakness to do our work, knowing that God is working in us. The highest exercise of a life of faith is to go on in the confidence of a hidden power working in us, without seeing or feeling anything. Faith alone can do God's work in saving souls. Faith alone can persevere in prayer and labor. Faith alone can continue to labor more abundantly despite unfavorable circumstances and appearances. Let us be *"strong in faith, giving glory to God"* (Rom. 4:20). God will show Himself strong toward him whose heart is perfect with Him (2 Chron. 16:9).

Be willing to yield yourself to the very utmost to God, so that His power may rest upon you and work in you. Let God work through you. Offer yourself to Him for His work as the one purpose of your life. Count upon His working in you to equip you for His service and to strengthen and bless you in it. Let the faith and love of your Lord Jesus, whose strength is going to be made perfect in your weakness, lead you to live even as He did, to do the Father's will and finish His work.

- Let every minister seek the full personal experience of Christ's strength made perfect in his weakness. This alone will enable him to teach believers the secret of their strength.

- Our Lord says, *"My grace," "My strength."* As we abide in Christ, and have Christ abiding in us in close personal fellowship and love, His grace and strength can work.
- Hearts completely given up to God, to His will and love, will know His power working in their weakness.

Chapter 27

---◆---

A Doer Who Works
Will Be Blessed in Doing

Be ye doers of the word, and not hearers only,
deceiving your own selves.
—James 1:22

Whoso looketh into the perfect law of liberty, and
continueth therein, he being not a forgetful hearer, but a doer of
the work, this man shall be blessed in his deed.
—James 1:25

God created us not to contemplate but to act. He created us in His own likeness, and in Him there is no thought without simultaneous action. True action is born of contemplation. True contemplation, as a means to an end, always causes action. There would never have been a separation between knowing and doing if sin had not entered the world. In nothing is the power of sin more clearly seen than this, that even in the believer there is such a gap between intellect and conduct. It is possible to delight in hearing, to be diligent in increasing our knowledge of God's Word, to admire and approve the truth,

552

even to be willing to do it, and yet to fail entirely in the actual performance. James warned us not to delude ourselves with being hearers and not doers. Thus, he pronounced the doer who works as blessed in his doing.

Blessed in doing. The words are a summary of the teaching of our Lord Jesus at the close of the Sermon on the Mount: *"Not every one that saith unto me, Lord, Lord, shall enter into the kingdom of heaven; but he that doeth the will of my Father"* (Matt. 7:21). *"Therefore whosoever heareth these sayings of mine, and doeth them, I will liken him unto a wise man"* (v. 24). To the woman who spoke of the blessedness of her who was his mother, He said, *"Yea rather, blessed are they that hear the word of God, and keep it"* (Luke 11:28). To the disciples on the night before His crucifixion He said, *"If ye know these things, happy are ye if ye do them"* (John 13:17). It is one of the greatest dangers in religion that we are content with reorganizing with pleasure and approval the meaning of a truth, yet do not immediately perform what it demands. It is only when conviction has been translated into conduct that we have proof that the truth is mastering us.

"A doer of the work, this man shall be blessed in his deed." The doer is blessed. The doing is the victory that overcomes every obstacle. It brings out and confirms the very image of God, the Great Worker. It removes every barrier to the enjoyment of all the blessing God has prepared. We are ever inclined to seek our blessedness in what God gives in privilege and enjoyment. Christ placed it in what we do because it is only in doing that we really prove and possess the life God has bestowed. When one said, *"Blessed is he that shall eat bread in the kingdom of God"* (Luke 14:15), our Lord answered with the parable of the supper (vv. 16–24). The doer is blessed. It is only in doing that the painter or musician, the man of science or business, the discoverer or the conqueror finds his blessedness. So, and much more, is it only in keeping the commandments and in doing the will of God that the believer enters fully into the truth and blessedness of fellowship with God and deliverance from sin. Doing

is the very essence of blessedness, the highest manifestation, and therefore, the fullest enjoyment of the life of God.

A doer of the work, this man shall be blessed in his deed. This was the blessedness of Abraham, of whom we read, *"Seest thou how faith wrought with his works, and by works was faith made perfect?"* (James 2:22). He had no works without faith. There was faith working with them and in them all. And he had no faith without works. Through them his faith was exercised, strengthened, and perfected. As his faith, so his blessedness was perfected in doing. It is in doing that the doer who works is blessed. The true insight into this will make us take every command, every truth, and every opportunity to abound in good works as an integral part of the blessedness of the salvation Christ has brought us. Joy and work, work and joy, will become synonymous. We will no longer be hearers but doers.

Let us put this truth into immediate practice. Let us live for others, to love and serve them. If you think you are not able to labor for souls, begin with the bodies. Only begin and go on, and abound. Believe that *"it is more blessed to give than to receive"* (Acts 20:35). Pray for and depend on the promised grace. Give yourself to a ministry of love. In the example of Christ and in the promise of God, you have the assurance. *"If ye know these things, happy are ye if ye do them"* (John 13:17). Blessed is the doer!

Chapter 28

The Work of Saving Souls

*Brethren, if any of you do err from the truth,
and one convert him; let him know, that he which
converteth the sinner from the error of his way shall save a
soul from death, and shall hide a multitude of sins.*
—James 5:19–20

We sometimes hesitate to speak of people being converted and saved by men. Scripture here twice uses the expression of one man converting another, and once of his saving him. Let us not hesitate to convert and save men, for it is God who works in us.

"Shall save a soul from death." Every workman studies the material in which he works—the carpenter the wood, the goldsmith the gold. Our *"deeds...are wrought in God"* (John 3:21). In our good works we deal with souls. Even when we can at first do no more than reach and help their bodies, our aim is the soul. For these Christ came to die. For these God has appointed us to watch and labor. Let us study the habits of these people. What care a hunter or a fisherman takes to know the habits of the spoil he seeks! Let us remember that we need divine wisdom, training, and skill to become

winners of souls. The only way to get that training and skill is to begin to work. Christ Himself will teach each one who waits on Him.

The church, along with its ministers, has a part to take in that training. The daily experience of ordinary life proves how often unexpected powers exist within a person. When a man becomes conscious and a master of the power that is in himself, he is a new creature. The power and enjoyment of life are doubled. Every believer has hidden within himself the power of saving souls. The kingdom of heaven is within us as a seed. Every one of the gifts and graces of the Spirit is also a hidden seed. The highest aim of the ministry is to awaken the consciousness of this hidden seed of power to save souls. A depressing sense of ignorance or powerlessness keeps many back. James wrote, *"Let him know, that he which converteth the sinner...shall save a soul from death."* Every believer needs to be taught to know and use the wondrous blessed power with which he has been endowed. When God said to Abraham, *"I will bless thee, and...all the nations of the earth* [will] *be blessed"* (Gen. 22:17–18), He called him to a faith not only in the blessing that would come to him from above, but also in the power of blessing that he would be in the world. It is a wonderful moment in the life of a child of God when he sees that the second blessing is as sure as the first.

"He shall save a soul." Our Lord bears the name of Jesus, Savior. He is the embodiment of God's saving love. Saving souls is His own great work. As our faith in Him grows to know and receive all there is in Him, as He lives in us and dwells in our hearts and dispositions, saving souls will become the great work to which our lives will be given. We will be the willing and intelligent instruments through whom He will do His mighty work.

"If any of you do err from the truth, and one convert him...he which converteth the sinner...shall save a soul." The words suggest personal work. We chiefly think of large gatherings to

whom the Gospel is preached. The thought here is of one who has erred and is sought after. We increasingly do our work through associations and organizations. *"If one converts him, he saves a soul."* It is the love and labor of some individual believer that has won the erring one back. It is this we need in the church of Christ—every believer who truly follows Jesus Christ looking out for those who are erring from the way, loving them, and laboring to help them back. Not one of us may say (as in Genesis 4:9), *"Am I my brother's keeper?"* We are in the world only and solely as the members of Christ's body, so that we may continue to carry out His saving work. As saving souls was and is His work, His joy, and His glory, let it be ours. Let each give himself personally to watch over individuals and seek to save them one by one.

"Know, that he which converteth the sinner...shall save a soul." "If ye know these things, happy are ye if ye do them" (John 13:17). Let us translate these Scripture truths into action. Let us give these thoughts shape and substance in daily life. Let us prove their power over us and our faith in them, by work. Is there a Christian around us wandering from the way, needing loving help and willing to receive it? Are there some whom we could take by the hand and encourage to begin again? If we are truly at the disposal of Jesus Christ, He will use us to show others the right way.

If we feel afraid, let us believe that the love of God dwells within us, not only calling but also enabling us to do the work. Let us yield ourselves to the Holy Spirit to fill our hearts with that love and to equip us for its service. Jesus, the Savior, lives to save. He dwells in us. He will do His saving work through us. *"Know, that he which converteth the sinner...shall save a soul from death, and shall hide a multitude of sins."*

- More love for souls, born out of fervent love for the Lord Jesus—this is our great need.
- Let us pray to love in the faith. As we exercise the little we have, more will be given.

- Lord, open our eyes to see You doing Your great work of saving souls and waiting to give Your love and strength into the heart of every willing one. Make each one of Your redeemed a soulwinner.

Chapter 29

———————— ◆ ————————

Praying and Working

If any man see his brother sin a sin which is not unto death,
he shall ask, and he shall give him life for them that sin not
unto death.
—1 John 5:16

And let us consider one another to provoke
unto love and to good works.
—Hebrews 10:24

These words in Hebrews express what lies at the very root of
a life of good works—the thoughtful, loving care we have
for each other, that not one may fall away. In Galatians 6:1 we
read, *"If a man be overtaken in a fault, ye which are spiritual,*
restore such an one in the spirit of meekness." Jude wrote of
Christians who were in danger of falling away: *"Others save*
with fear, pulling them out of the fire; hating even the garment
spotted by the flesh" (v. 23). As Christ's doing good to men's
bodies always aimed at winning their souls, all our ministry of
love must be subordinated to that which is God's great purpose
and longing—the salvation unto life eternal.

559

Praying and working must always go together in this labor of love. At times prayer may reach those whom words cannot reach. At times prayer may chiefly be needed for ourselves, to obtain the wisdom and courage for the words. As a rule, praying and working must be inseparable—the praying to obtain from God what we need for the soul, the working to bring to it what God has given us. The words of John here are most suggestive as to the power of prayer in our labor of love. We are led to think of prayer as a personal work with a very definite purpose and a certainty of answer.

Let prayer be a personal effort. *"If any man see his brother..., he shall ask."* We are so accustomed to act through societies and associations that we are in danger of losing sight of the duty resting upon each of us to watch over those around him. Let every member of our bodies be ready to serve any other member. Every believer is to care for the fellow believers who are within his reach, in his church, his house, or social circle. The sin of each is a loss and a hurt to the body of Christ. Let your eyes be open to the sins of your brethren around you. Do not speak evil or judge or helplessly complain, but love, help, care, and pray. Ask God to see your brother's sin in its sinfulness, its danger to himself, and its grief to Christ. However, God's compassion and deliverance are within reach. Shutting our eyes to the sin of our brethren around us is not true love. See it, take it to God, and make it part of your work for God to pray for your brother and seek new life for him.

Let prayer be definite. *"If any man see his brother sin..., he shall ask."* We need prayer from a person for a person. Scripture and God's Spirit teach us to pray for all society, for the church with which we are associated, for nations, and for special areas of work. This is necessary and blessed. But somehow more is needed in order to make those with whom we come into contact subjects of our intercession. The larger supplications must have their place, but it is difficult to know when our prayers are answered regarding them. But nothing will bring God so near, will test and strengthen our faith, and make us know that we are fellow workers with God, as when we receive an answer to our prayers for individuals. It will quicken in us the new and blessed consciousness that we indeed have power with God. Let every worker seek to exercise this grace of taking up and praying for individual souls.

Count upon an answer. *"He shall ask, and God will give him* [the one who prays] *life for them that sin."* The words follow on those in which John had spoken about the confidence we have of being heard, if we *"ask any thing according to his will"* (1 John 5:14). There is often complaint made of not knowing God's will. But here there is no difficulty. "[God] *will have all men to be saved"* (1 Tim. 2:4). If we rest our faith on this will of God, we will grow strong and grasp the promise: *"He shall ask, and* [God] *will give him life for them that sin."* The Holy Spirit will lead us, if we yield ourselves to be led by Him, to the souls God would have us take as our special care, and for which the grace of faith and persevering prayer will be given us. Let the wonderful promise—that God will give to him who asks life for them who sin—stir us and encourage us to our priestly ministry of personal and definite intercession as one of the most blessed among the good works in which we can serve God and man.

Praying and working are inseparable. Let all who work learn to pray well. Let all who pray learn to work well.

- Let us pray confidently, and if need be perseveringly, for an individual who needs a close walk with God, and for the faith that we can overcome with Him.
- In all our work for God, prayer must take a much larger place. If God is to work all, then our position is to be that of entire dependence, waiting for Him to work in us. If it takes time to persevere and to receive in ourselves what God gives us for others, there needs to be a work and a labor in prayer.

- Oh, that God would open our eyes to the glory of this work of saving souls, as the one thing God lives for, as the one thing He wants to work in us!
- Let us pray for the love and power of God to come on us for the blessed work of soulwinning.

Chapter 30

———————◆———————

"I Know Thy Works"

Unto the angel of the church of Ephesus...
in Thyatira...in Sardis...in Philadelphia...of the Laodiceans
write...I know thy works.
—Revelation 2:1, 18; 3:1, 7, 14–15

"*I know thy works.*" These are the words of Him who walks in the midst of the seven golden candlesticks, and whose eyes are like a flame of fire. As He looks upon the churches, the first thing He sees and judges is their works. The works are the revelation of the life and character. If we are willing to bring our works into His holy presence, His words can teach us what our work ought to be.

To Ephesus He said,

I know thy works, and thy labour, and thy patience, and how thou canst not bear them which are evil...and hast borne, and hast patience, and for my name's sake hast laboured, and hast not fainted. Nevertheless I have somewhat against thee, because thou hast left thy first love....Repent, and do the first works.   (Rev. 2:2–5)

There was much here to praise—toil, patience, and zeal that had never grown weary. But there was one thing lacking—the tenderness of the first love.

In His work for us, Christ gave us before and above everything His love, the personal, tender affection of His heart. In our work for Him, He asks us nothing less. There is a danger of work being carried on, and our even bearing much for Christ's sake, while the freshness of our love has passed away. Christ looks for the warm, loving heart and the personal affection that ever keeps Him the center of our love and joy. That is what Christ seeks. That is what gives power. Nothing can compensate for it. Christian workers, see that all your work is the work of love, of tender personal devotion to Christ Jesus.

To Thyatira He said,

I know thy works, and charity, and service, and faith, and thy patience, and thy works; and the last to be more than the first. Notwithstanding I have a few things against thee, because thou sufferest that woman Jezebel, which calleth herself a prophetess, to teach and to seduce my servants to commit fornication. (Rev. 2:19–20)

Here again the works are enumerated and praised. The last had even been more than the first. But then there is one failure—a false toleration of what led to impurity and idolatry. And then He adds His judgment, *"The churches shall know that I am he which searcheth the reins and hearts: and I will give unto every one of you according to your works"* (v. 23).

Along with many good works being done, there may be some one form of error or evil tolerated that endangers the whole church. In Ephesus there was zeal for orthodoxy, but a lack of love—here love and faith, but a lack of faithfulness against error. If good works are to please our Lord, if our whole lives are to be in harmony with Him, in entire separation from the world and its allurements, we must seek to be what He promised to make us, established in every good word and work. In His judgment, our work will decide our value.

To Sardis His message was this:

I know thy works, that thou hast a name...and art dead.
Be watchful, and strengthen the things which remain, that
are ready to die: for I have not found thy works perfect
before God. (Rev. 3:1–2)

There may be all the forms of godliness without the power and all the activities or religious organization without the life. There may be many works, and yet He may say, "I have found no work of yours fulfilled before My God, none that can stand the test and be really acceptable to God as a spiritual sacrifice." In Ephesus it was works lacking in love, in Thyatira works lacking in purity, in Sardis works lacking in life.

To Philadelphia He said,

I know thy works...for thou hast a little strength, and hast
kept my word, and hast not denied my name....Because
thou hast kept the word of my patience, I also will keep
thee. (vv. 8, 10)

On earth Jesus had said, *"He that hath my commandments, and keepeth them, he it is that loveth me"* (John 14:21). *"The Father himself loveth you, because ye have loved me"* (John 16:27). Philadelphia, the church for which there is no reproof, had this mark: its chief work, and the law of all its work, was that it kept Christ's Word, not in an orthodox creed only, but in practical obedience. Let nothing less be the mark and spirit of all our work—a keeping of the Word of Christ. Full, loving conformity to His will will be rewarded.

Christ said to Laodicea, *"I know thy works, that thou art neither cold nor hot....Thou sayest, I am rich, and increased with goods, and have need of nothing"* (Rev. 3:15, 17). There is not a church without its works, its religious activities, yet the two great marks of Laodicean religion, lukewarmness and self-complacence, may rob the church of its worth. There is not only the need for a fresh and fervent love, as Ephesus teaches us, but also the need for that poverty of spirit, that conscious weakness out of which the absolute dependence on Christ's strength for all our work will grow. It will no longer leave Christ standing at the door, but will enthrone Him in the heart.

"I know thy works." He who tested the works of the seven churches still lives and watches over us. He is ready in His love to discover what is lacking, to give timely warning and help, and to teach us the path in which our works can be fulfilled before God. Let us learn from Ephesus the lesson of fervent love for Christ, from Thyatira that of purity and separation from all evil, from Sardis that of the need of true life to give worth to work, from Philadelphia that of keeping His Word, and from Laodicea that of the poverty of spirit that possesses the kingdom of heaven and gives Christ the throne of all! Workers, let us live and work in Christ's presence! He will teach, correct, and help us, and one day give the full reward of all our works because they were His own works in us.

Chapter 31

———————◆———————

That God May Be Glorified

If any man speak, let him speak as the oracles of God;
if any man minister, let him do it as of the ability
which God giveth: that God in all things may be glorified
through Jesus Christ, to whom be praise and dominion
for ever and ever. Amen.
—1 Peter 4:11

Work is not done for its own sake. Its value consists in the objective it attains. The purpose of him who commands or performs the work gives it its real worth. And the clearer a man's insight into the purpose, the better equipped he will be to take charge of the higher parts of the work. In erecting a splendid building, the purpose of the day laborer may simply be as a hireling to earn his wages. The trained stonecutter has a higher objective—he thinks of the beauty and perfection of the work he does. The master mason has a wider range of thought. His aim is that all the masonry will be true and good. The contractor for the whole building has a higher aim—that the whole building will perfectly correspond to the plan he has to carry out. The architect has a still higher purpose—that the great principles of art and beauty might find their full expression in material shape.

With the owner we find the final end—the use to which the grand structure is to be put when he presents the building as a gift for the benefit of his townspeople. All who have worked honestly on the building have done so with some true purpose. The deeper the insight and the keener the interest in the ultimate design, the more important the share in the work, and the greater the joy in carrying it out.

Peter told us what our aim ought to be in all Christian service—*"that God in all things may be glorified through Jesus Christ."* In the work of God, a work not to be done for wages but for love, the humblest laborer is invited to share in God's plans, and to an insight into the great purpose that God is working out. That purpose is nothing less than this: that God may be glorified. This is the one purpose of God, the Great Worker in heaven, the Source and Master of all work, that the glory of His love and power and blessing may be shown. This is the one purpose of Christ, the Great Worker on earth in human nature, the Example and Leader of all our work. This is the great purpose of the Holy Spirit, the power that works in us, or, as Peter said here, *"the ability which God giveth."* As this becomes our deliberate, intelligent purpose, our work will rise to its true level and lift us into living fellowship with God.

"That God in all things may be glorified." What does this mean? The glory of God is this: that He alone is the Living One, who has life in Himself. Yet not for Himself alone, but because His life is love for men as much as for Himself. This is the glory of God, that He is the only and ever-flowing fountain of all life and goodness and happiness, and that His creatures can have all this only as He gives it and works it in them. His working all in all, this is His glory. And the only glory His creature, His child, can give Him is this: receiving all He is willing to give, yielding to Him to let Him work, and then acknowledging that He has done it. Thus God Himself shows forth His glory in us. In our willing surrender to Him and our joyful acknowledgment that He does all, we glorify Him. And so our lives and work are glorified, as they have one purpose with all God's own work: *"that God in all*

things may be glorified through Jesus Christ, to whom be praise and dominion for ever and ever."

See here the spirit that elevates and consecrates Christian service. According to Peter, *"If any man minister* [in ministering to fellow believers or the needy], *let him do it as of the ability which God giveth."* Let us cultivate a deep conviction that God's work, down to the details of daily life, can be done only in God's strength by *"the power that worketh in us"* (Eph. 3:20). Let us believe firmly and unceasingly that the Holy Spirit dwells in us as the power from on high for all work to be done for on high. Let us in our Christian work fear nothing so much as working in our own human will and strength, thus losing the one thing necessary in our work: God working in us. Let us rejoice in the weakness that renders us so absolutely dependent upon such a God and wait in prayer for His power to take full possession.

"Let him do it as of the ability which God giveth: that God in all things may be glorified through Jesus Christ." The more you depend on God alone for your strength, the more He will be glorified. The more you seek to make God's purpose your purpose, the more you will be led to give way to His working and His strength and love. I pray that every worker might see what a nobility it gives to work, what a new glory to life, what a new urgency and joy in laboring for souls, when the one purpose has mastered us—that in all things God may be glorified through Jesus Christ.

- The glory of God as Creator was seen in His making man in His own image. The glory of God as Redeemer is seen in the work He carries on for saving men and bringing them to Himself.
- This glory is the glory of His holy love, casting sin out of the heart and dwelling there.
- The only glory we can bring to God is to yield ourselves to His redeeming love to take possession of us, to fill us with love for others, and so through us to show forth His glory.

- Let this be the one purpose of our lives: to glorify God by living to work for Him, *"as of the ability which God giveth,"* and winning souls to know and live for His glory.
- Lord, teach us to serve in the ability that You give, so that in all things You may be glorified through Jesus Christ, *"to whom be praise and dominion for ever and ever. Amen."*

Book Six

———◆·◆———

Reaching Your World
for Christ

Contents

Chapter 1

The State of the Home Church

I have a deep burden on my heart for foreign missions, but I have an even deeper concern about the one thing on which missions most depends: the state of the home church. Of course, by *home church* I mean any church that supports missionaries in foreign fields.

I see vividly the worldwide need of the gospel message. Furthermore, openings exist for bringing the Gospel to every person throughout the world.

The piercing question is this: will the church be able to enter these open doors? The state of the home church is an all-important factor in the possible solution of the great challenges in missions. Indeed, I have recently seen new meaning in the words *the state of the home church.*

Everything in foreign missions depends on the home base. Everything depends on the ability and readiness of the church to respond to God's call. It is well worth our while to read what some concerned pastors and missionaries have said about the life of the church:

> As we contemplate the work to be done, we are conscious that the fundamental difficulty is not one of men or

573

money, but of spiritual power. The Christian experience of the church is not deep, intense, and living enough to meet the world's need. We need a more perfect manifestation by the church of the spirit of the Incarnation and of the cross. We need a new vitalizing of the whole church.

This renewal of the whole life of the church is indeed a great thing—an impossible thing, we are tempted to think. But does it seem so impossible when we get the conviction that God, being who He is, wills it? It does not seem so impossible when we saturate ourselves in the thought of the Gospels, with their repeated teaching, *"Ask, and ye shall receive"* (John 16:24).

It is also worth our while to read the statements of other church leaders on this subject. The following section contains a summary of the thoughts of key church leaders on the state of the church, written for our consideration.

Thoughts on Missions

The missionary problem of the church today is not primarily a financial problem. The problem is how to ensure a vitality equal to the expansion of the missionary program. The only hope of this is for Christians to obtain the more abundant life through Christ, which is given as we walk in the pathway of obedience to Him.

A crucial factor in the evangelization of the non-Christian world is the state of the church in countries that already have been evangelized. Until there is a more widespread consecration among the members of the home church, there can be no hope of expanding the missionary enterprise and making the knowledge of Jesus Christ readily accessible to every human being.

The most direct and effective way to promote the evangelization of the world is to influence Christian workers, and, indeed, the whole membership of the church, to yield themselves completely to the authority of Christ as

Lord. We must establish and preserve at all costs those spiritual habits that will surely give us spiritual power and Christlike witnessing.

Above all else, we need to have such a spiritual atmosphere throughout the church that the very character and spirit of Jesus Christ will live anew in the hearts of all His followers, and that, through them, His life may flow forth to the world lying in darkness.

We are driven back, at every turn, to the question of the spiritual condition of the home church. Does the church have sufficient vitality for the tremendous task to which it is called? We realize that the fundamental problems lie in these areas: the sincerity of the spiritual experience of the church, the quality of its obedience, and the intensity and daring of its faith.

There can be no forward movement in missions, no great offering of life, without a deepening of the spiritual life of church leaders and a real spiritual revival among church members. New methods can accomplish nothing unless they are begun, continued, and completed in prayer and permeated from first to last with the Holy Spirit. "Back to divine wisdom, back to the living power of Jesus Christ, back through prayer to the Source of all power"—this must be the motto of all missionary organizations, all church leaders, and, ultimately, all church members. This is necessary if the Great Commission of our Lord Jesus Christ is to be carried out.

Therefore, we recommend that every endeavor be made to spread the spirit and habit of prayer among all Christian workers, young and old. We are confident that when the entire church will devoutly pray for the coming of the kingdom, the triumph will already have been achieved.

We must make believers understand that it is only their halfhearted consecration and lack of faith that hinder the rapid advance of the work, only their own coldness that keeps back His redemption from a lost world. We must always bear in mind that He is eager and able to save the world, which has already been redeemed by Him. Alas, if only we, His professed followers on earth, were willing that He do so.

We frankly confess that it is futile to talk about making Christ known to the world unless there is a great increase of vitality in the members of the churches. It is the will of God that the most remote human soul would have the opportunity to know Jesus Christ as his personal Redeemer. Of this there can be no doubt. We are all aware that the opportunity and means are sufficient. The work halts only because the entire church is not yet in full submission to His will.

Other church leaders see and speak in similar words of the same great need. Cooperation, if it is to lead to unity, requires a spiritual revival, which must be in its very nature supernatural. The reinforcements that are needed are dependent on the spiritual state of the churches that are to supply them. The very religions that Christianity is to replace teach that its own life must first be lived on the supernatural plane, with the power of a living faith in a living God.

If our missionaries are to be fully and properly prepared to convince the world, they must go forth from a church in which the Spirit of Christ is evidently at work. They must go forth from a church in which the Gospel is continually and irrefutably proved to be, in very truth, *"the power of God unto salvation"* (Rom. 1:16).

Think on These Things

Let me beg every reader, whether minister or member, to look back over these thoughts on the condition of the church. Think about them until you come to realize the intense solemnity of what that condition implies, the place that God calls the church to take, and what is needed if God and the world are to find the church ready for the work that awaits it.

Before us lies a world dying in its need of the very message that the church of Christ alone can bring. The world in its need is accessible and open to this message as it never has been in ages past. The Lord Jesus Christ, having laid down His life to redeem this world, still waits for the message of His redeeming love to be brought to those for whom He died. But His church does not have the power or vitality or consecration that would make it possible for it to fulfill its blessed task.

A revival is greatly needed. Something must happen if the plea for prayer for that revival is to be carefully obeyed by God's people. Something must happen if prayer is to be truly effective. That something is this: the state of the church as it has been described must become an unbearable burden. We must learn to give ourselves no rest, and to give God no rest, until He makes His church a joy in the earth.

Chapter 2

The Present Crisis

A n article appeared in *The Missionary Record,* entitled, "The Present Crisis." The author of the article began by alluding to the serious decrease, in the last several years, in both the membership of the church and the number of young men offering themselves for the ministry. He said, in essence, "What sad proof this is of the lack of spiritual vitality in the church! What reason this gives for humiliation before God! What a call it is to the church to discover the cause of the evil and its remedy!"

In the course of his remarks, he expressed a thought of the deepest meaning in these words: "Membership in the church implies that the only true measure of our surrender to Christ and His service is the measure of Christ's surrender for our salvation." In other words, we should surrender ourselves to Christ and His service to the same extent that Christ surrendered Himself for our salvation.

The thought is one of unspeakable solemnity. Is it really true that the measure of Christ's devotion to God and to us in the sacrifice of the cross is to be the measure of our devotion to Him and the service of His kingdom? It must be true. Yet how few Christians take time to think this out. One almost feels that the minister who uses such an expression and has the vision of what it means could have no rest until he had lifted up his voice like a trumpet and called to the church, "Awake, you Christians, to your high calling—to have the same measure of devotion that Christ did in His surrender for you and your salvation."

Reflect on this thought until you realize something of its meaning; then let your heart respond and say, "Nothing less, by the grace of God, will be the measure of my surrender to the person and the service of this beloved Redeemer."

If a thought like this could take full possession of even a small number of Christians, what power there would be in their witness to others of what Christianity really means! What hope there would be of rousing the church to find out and to confess the reason that the membership of the church and the number of ministerial students are so sadly decreasing.

The article closes with an appeal to all ministers and church members to renew their efforts on behalf of true godliness, and to work diligently so that young people may be brought to the knowledge of Christ and to a complete surrender to His service. Have they not already been doing this? There is no reason to doubt it. But what is needed is the discovery that the low spiritual life that prevails throughout the church is the true cause of the alarming decrease in membership.

"The measure of the surrender of Christ for us and our salvation is the measure of our surrender to Him and to His service." If that is indeed to be regarded as the standard of church membership, how much more ought it to be the standard of the life and preaching of the minister! God has put an unspeakably solemn responsibility on the ministry. The whole tone of the church, the whole mind-set of the membership, depends on what rules the thoughts and heart and life of the minister. If the membership is to be lifted out of the worldly level, of which this decrease in the number of members is a sign, who is to do it if not the minister?

The God who has entrusted to ministers *the ministry of reconciliation* (2 Cor. 5:18) is the God who, by His Holy Spirit, worked in Christ the consecration that caused Him to give Himself as a living sacrifice. God will work a similar consecration in

His servants when they fall before Him, confessing their weaknesses and sins. Special prayer must be made for ministers, asking God to give them the vision of that great truth—that one standard of devotion to the salvation of men is required for both Christ and His ministers. If this vision comes to them, they, as the appointed leaders of the church, may be able to guide it in the way of repentance and restoration.

There is indeed a present crisis. In more than one church denomination, the same alarming disease has appeared. There is, indeed, a crisis throughout Christendom. Many leaders feel strongly that the church in its present state is utterly unfit and unprepared for the great work that God has put before it and expects it to undertake. Just read some of the thoughts of these men.

Professor Cairns recently asked, "Does the church have within itself at this moment the spiritual resources for so high and arduous a calling?" His profound conviction is that it does not. He said it is moving up to a situation that is too hard for it and for which it is not yet ready. And so, the matter of most urgent concern before the church, which dwarfs all others, is how it can obtain from the eternal God those spiritual reinforcements of His grace that will enable it able to meet the coming hour.

Dr. Denney said recently,

I speak only of the church to which I myself belong, but something similar, I believe, is true of almost every church in Christendom....The number of candidates for the ministry at the present time is less than it was a good many years ago. It is hardly a sufficient number to keep up the staff at home, to say nothing of supplying workers abroad. People are not coming forward as ministers, not coming forward as missionaries, because they are not coming forward into the membership of the Christian church at all. Something must happen to the church at home if it is going to even look at the work that has been put upon it [in foreign missions].

The solemn words of Dr. John Mott, a pioneer in the Young Men's Christian Association, are as follows: "I boldly say that the church has not yet seriously set itself to bring the living Christ to all living men!"

These statements are simply appalling. Imagine, the church of Christ not being able to hold its own—actually defeated and driven back by the enemy! Rich in the promise of the Father, it is, nevertheless, in spite of its perfection of organization, unable to gather in souls.

Do we not have good reason to say, as Joshua did when he fell on his face before the ark of the Lord, *"O Lord, what shall I say, when Israel turneth their backs before their enemies!"* (Josh. 7:8). The story of Joshua gives us the key to the question as to what is to be done to remove this terrible reproach on the church of Christ. God's answer was,

> *Israel hath sinned....Therefore the children of Israel could not stand before their enemies....Neither will I be with you any more, except ye destroy the accursed* [thing] *from among you. Up, sanctify the people, and say, Sanctify yourselves against tomorrow: for thus saith the* LORD *God of Israel,...O Israel: thou canst not stand before thine enemies, until ye take away the accursed thing from among you.* (vv. 11–13)

Something must happen to the home churches. What can it be but that God's people must fall on their faces before the Lord to confess their defeat with shame and humiliation? We must discover what it is that prevents God from giving that power and blessing with the Word that would give us the victory over the world. Individually and collectively, we must put away the accursed thing that makes it impossible for God to reveal His presence in power in the church as He longs to do.

"Up, sanctify the people, and say, Sanctify yourselves against tomorrow." Israel was reminded that God is the Holy One and that sin is the only thing that can rob us of His presence. Israel

was a holy people with whom holiness was the one secret of power and of blessing.

Joshua had used the same words when the children of Israel were about to cross the Jordan River: *"Sanctify yourselves"* (Josh. 3:5). At the Jordan River, God had shown His great power in bringing the Israelites through on dry ground. In this instance where Israel was defeated by its enemies, God would again reveal His divine power. This time it would be in teaching them to discover and to cast out the sin that had been the cause of defeat.

The same thing must happen to the church today if it is indeed to listen to the call for the army of God to move on to the great world conquest. The more we study these words from church leaders, the deeper will be our conviction that nothing less is needed than that we take our place with Joshua and the elders on our faces before God. There He will reveal the state of the church in such a way that will bring us to the end of all our hopes and plans.

There we will be brought, in utter weakness and in humble, persistent prayer, to urgently appeal to Him. We will entreat Him to give ministers and church members a revelation of sin on the one hand, but on the other, an understanding of the all-sufficiency of His grace to cleanse us and to make us holy. Such a revelation will induce us to give Christ His place as our Leader on the path of victory.

Nothing will teach a backsliding church that comes to repentance what the love of Christ is more than the exercise of His power in cleansing and delivering from sin. It is the experience of what He can do for us that will rouse in us true loyalty to follow Him as He leads us in the path of victory.

Chapter 3

---◆◆---

The Unsolved Problem

*T*he chief and most difficult problem of missionary work has not yet been solved. As I wrote in the last chapter, the most important problem of all is how the church is to be roused to a deeper and fuller life in Christ. Without this, there is no possibility of Christ being made known to all the world in this generation. Yet our church leaders have not shown us how to begin and what to do.

Dr. John Mott, in his book *The Decisive Hour of Christian Missions,* devotes the first three chapters to a survey of the mission field. He points out the hopeful signs, as well as the threatening dangers that urge immediate action. Chapter four of his book bears the title, "The First Great Requirement: An Adequate Plan." After pointing out the almost insurmountable difficulties that must be overcome before the thought and life of whole nations can be changed, he asks, "How is such a seemingly impossible task to be accomplished?" He answers that the first essential is for the church to have a plan to meet the situation—a plan adequate in scope, thoroughness, strategy, and methods. His chapter is devoted to pointing out the main features of such a course of action.

If the church's task in the mission field is so difficult that it cannot be undertaken without the development of an adequate plan, what are we to think of the far harder task to which the church at home is called? How are we to rouse Christians out of their apathy and train them to become devoted servants of Christ, full of enthusiasm for the King and His kingdom?

In a previous chapter, we saw how strongly, almost hopelessly, our leaders regard the present state of the church. They have stated the problem with terrible clearness, but they have left it unsolved. They have not given us any plan for bringing about a change, and as yet there is not much indication that the churches are preparing themselves for this work of supreme importance. Leading Christians to that deeper and more intense vitality, that more abundant life in Christ, without which the work cannot possibly be done, is a question of life or death.

It is with humble reluctance that I venture to make some suggestions as to what is needed if the churches are really to prepare themselves for the tasks ahead.

First of all, we will have to set clearly before ourselves and others the true calling of the church and of every believer. Christ expects everyone who knows His love to tell others about it. Christ requires everyone who is made a partaker of His redemption to yield himself, as the first purpose of his existence, to live for the coming of His kingdom. Christ asks and expects that, just as the loyal subjects of a king are ready in time of war to give their lives for the kingdom, so His redeemed ones, in the power of His Spirit and His love, will not live for themselves but entirely for Him who died and lives for them (2 Cor. 5:15).

As long as this calling is considered too difficult to fulfill and is not accepted as the very groundwork of the relationship between Christ and every member of His church, our attempt to lift the church into the abundant life will be in vain. Unless God's children can be brought to accept this standard, to consider it their highest happiness, and to believe in the power of Christ to work and maintain it in them, there will be little hope of their obtaining intense vitality, without which the church cannot fulfill its calling.

The second step is to discover the real cause of the evil, its terrible power over us, and our utter inability to overcome it. It will not be enough to confess that we have been unfaithful to Christ's charge, that it is our fault that people are perishing in darkness. We must go deeper than this. We must ask how it can be that, with our faith in Christ, there has been so little love for Him and the souls He has entrusted to us. How can it be that we could imagine that our activities were pleasing to God, while all the time we were grieving our Lord by neglecting His last and most cherished commands?

We will find that at the root of it all lies the selfishness that sought and looked to Christ for our own personal salvation; the worldliness that kept us from living in the power of His death and resurrection; and the self-satisfaction that rested content with a religion that operated, for the most part, in the power of human wisdom and had only the *"form of godliness"* (2 Tim. 3:5). We will have to be brought to the conviction that we need an entire revolution in our inner lives. The God on whom we counted to bring us out of Egypt, in conversion and pardon, must bring us, by a still more mighty experience of His grace, into that life of the new covenant in which God will dwell with us and walk with us.

Who is to take the initiative in all this? Should it be a missions conference, which, with regard to the foreign field, seeks to formulate and master all that is needed in connection with the spiritual work? Or can we count on each church to consider the question separately and to give time in its assembly or council or congress to deal with this subject as one of the most important that could be brought before it? Should each church lead the way in the deep humiliation and fervent supplication that are absolutely essential if the longed-for change is to come? Or should it be left to individuals to gather around themselves small groups to begin the work of confession and intercession for the power of the Holy Spirit, through whom alone the supernatural renewal can be accomplished?

Also, who are to be the agents who will carry out this work? We all naturally think of ministers as God's messengers, who have been given by Christ to perfect the saints for their work of the ministry in building up the body of Christ (Eph. 4:12). But ministers need prayer. Paul felt how absolutely dependent he was on the prayers of believers. Let us begin at once and implore God to raise up ministers who have the courage of their convictions, who will sound the call to a new repentance and a new consecration. May they, in bold faith, declare what Christ is going to do for the church if it will only yield to Him.

We will need to look to the ministers, but we will also need to encourage every Christian who is earnestly seeking to serve Christ to take part in the great crusade for winning soldiers for the Lord's army. Many are longing for someone to lead them into a life of liberty and devotion to Christ, which they have seen from far away but have never yet been able to attain. Let men and women take courage and speak out, telling those around them what happiness there is in a life spent for Christ and what unfailing strength can be found in Him.

Those who have already taken part in the great work of intercession for missions should begin to pray persistently for the renewal of the church around them. In this way, some hearts that have, so far, been content with the hope of heaven as the one aim of their Christian lives, will begin to wake up to the attraction of Christ's claim, as it is brought to them by living witnesses around them. And God will certainly hear our prayers and give His blessing.

God is able to awaken carnal Christians. Observe what happened in the book of Ezekiel:

> *Come from the four winds, O breath, and breathe upon these slain, that they may live. So I prophesied as he commanded me, and the breath came into them, and they lived, and stood up upon their feet, an exceeding great army.* (Ezek. 37:9–10)

In this undertaking, everything depends on the supernatural, on the all-sufficiency of God, on His infinite love and power. He yields Himself to be led by the prayers of His children to the place where His Spirit is to descend, and to the work that He is to do. Nothing less is needed than a new creation, a resurrection from the dead, which brings forth out of carnal, worldly Christians the new person in Christ Jesus, in which old things are passed away and all things are become new (2 Cor. 5:17). Nothing less than this is to be our aim and expectation. And the more absolutely we believe that God alone can, that God most surely will, revive the dead, the simpler and more unceasing will be our persistent prayer that God Himself will do for us what to human thought appears impossible.

One more word. Let us never forget that everything begins with and depends on the individual. Let no one who hears the call of God to this new consecration wait for the church to act or wait for his fellow believers to act. Let him offer himself with his whole being so that Christ may be magnified through him. Dear fellow Christian, begin at once, and give God no rest until Christ has the place in your heart that He claims. Let devoted loyalty to His kingdom be the fruit of intense attachment to His person. Let His love become a holy passion, and let Him find in you one upon whom He can count to seek, above everything and at any sacrifice, to make His name known to every individual.

Depend on it: God will use you to lift others around you into the fullness and the fruitfulness of the abundant life in Christ Jesus.

God grant that the unsolved problem may find its solution in the fervent prayer of His believing people!

Chapter 4

———◆———

Peace, When There Is No Peace

*D*uring the last ten years, there has continually come from one church or another the news of a decline in membership. This has become so widespread that reportedly today there is hardly a church in Christendom that is not suffering from the same problem. The disease is becoming chronic. I am surprised that no church has earnestly determined to examine the cause. I wonder why none of the church leaders has sounded the alarm and called on the whole church to cry to God for the discovery of the root of the evil and the secret of its removal. In the spirit of the deepest humility and love, I express the fear that the prophet's words are too applicable: *"They have healed also the hurt of the daughter of my people slightly, saying, Peace, peace; when there is no peace"* (Jer. 6:14).

Two years ago, the president of a well-known denomination made several comments about the state of the church. "To me it is questionable if any church is doing much more than marking time," he said. In other words, most churches are producing nothing, making no progress. "The atmosphere is impregnated with influences unfavorable to religious life," he added. But was that not much more the case in Corinth and Rome? Yet the power of the Holy Spirit brought the very atmosphere of heaven, the power of the resurrection life, into those churches. After mentioning many of the elements unfavorable to religious life, this Christian leader concluded: "Meanwhile, in my judgment, we have not yet touched bottom." Only when we have touched bottom can we go no lower.

In a recent article on this problem, the writer said, "The figures are unquestionably disappointing, though there is no reason for serious depression." Could it be that "serious depression" is just what God wants, and what is essential if we are to be fully convicted and see the evil as God sees it? The writer explained:

> There is an increase in the number of churches this year, and there is a marked increase in the number of Sunday school teachers. But the students are fewer by nearly seven thousand. Considering the greatly increased activity, the result falls far short of our hopes.

Does this not suggest the thought that building churches and increasing the number of Sunday school teachers is what man can do, while, in order to increase members and Sunday school students, we need a spiritual vitality in the ministers and teachers that none but the Holy Spirit can give?

Yet it is alarming that people in our churches are afraid of nothing as much as "serious depression." Men say that "in business or finance there are also times of depression, but they do not always last. A change comes, and business prospers again. We must keep up our courage and hope on."

However, are we not in danger of forgetting one thing? When the depression has to do with business and money, every man concerned is ready, with his whole heart, to do anything he can to bring about the change. But, tragically, this is just what is not the case in the church. How few there are who, with their whole hearts, yield themselves to the power of the spiritual life and do their utmost to win to Christ the souls that are drifting away from Him and His church.

The article mentions that only about one fifth of Sunday school students ultimately connect themselves with the church.

What a thought: millions of students are entrusted to the church for three or four years of their lives, and yet the church is powerless to influence them to become its members! If there is one problem that is worthy of the highest Christian statesmanship among our church leaders and needs the deepest waiting on God for the enlightenment and courage of His Holy Spirit, it is this unspeakably solemn one. How are these millions of young people, whom the church is now unable to influence, to be reached and won? The solution lies with God and with the believers who are willing to honestly face the situation. I am speaking of Christians who know what it is to have access to God and to receive from Him the teaching and power of the Spirit.

The chief suggestion that is given in the article in regard to the whole difficulty is contained in one word: *work.*

> There have been too many conferences and meetings to discuss work—it is better to do the work. The minister is to be pitied who does not know what he ought to do in his sphere of labor. He is most deeply to be pitied if he does not know the Source of true strength.

Yet this last part is just the crucial question. Judging by what is being written and spoken, it is the lack of much intense prayer and living faith that is the cause of all evil. God's promise is sure. But the lack of conversions, the decline in membership, the decrease in Sunday school students—all indicate that the power of God is little known. Nothing can be more dangerous than to tell people to work if their method of work is not what it should be.

If I meet a weary traveler who is on the wrong road and try to encourage him by telling him that he must go bravely forward, that he still will be able to go a long way before evening, I am deceiving him. I ought to tell him he is on the wrong road and show him where to find the right one.

The article says, "Considering the greatly increased activity in various organizations, the result falls far short of our hopes."

The activity may be two or three times as great, but if the worker has not learned to desire above all else the supernatural resources of God, which are given as the result of prayer for the power of the Spirit, all his work will be in vain.

No leader could do a greater kindness to the church than to help all its ministers gain a full understanding of the presence and power of the Spirit. When our ascended Lord spoke the words, *"Ye shall be witnesses unto me...unto the uttermost part of the earth"* (Acts 1:8), and, *"Tarry* [wait]...*until ye be endued with power from on high"* (Luke 24:49), He gave a law for all time to His servants in regard to the secret of work. Daily receiving the Spirit through fellowship with God is the only secret of successful work.

People sent letters in reply to the article, and more than one suggested that there are other causes than those that had been named! One mentioned the "lack of intimate Christian fellowship within the churches, which enables them to offer only a very small inducement to earnest souls." This writer noted that "this defect grows out of the lack of spiritual life, the prevalent neglect of Holy Scripture and exposition."

Another said that "in preaching, a personal appeal to the conscience and a direct effort for conversion are seldom witnessed. This is largely a result of the same cause [the lack of spiritual life]."

A third stated the following: "In many of our churches the great underlying doctrines and facts of the Gospel are scarcely ever referred to in preaching."

The question cannot be answered by simply saying that every minister knows what he ought to do. How many there are who have been doing what they could and yet have failed. Let us not think of it as demeaning the church when we invite our fellow believers to test their work according to the standards of the Word of God. When a doctor tells a man that his wife is suffering from a dangerous disease, he does not demean the man's wife; he is doing the greatest kindness as the first step toward healing.

Years ago, Charles Spurgeon spoke boldly about the decline. He was only warning against what has actually come to pass. There are thousands of hearts that feel deeply that the church of Christ is in dire straits. Let us beware of everything like healing *"the hurt...slightly,"* or saying, *"Peace, peace; when there is no peace"* (Jer. 6:14).

Let us rather listen to the word, *"Let mine eyes run down with tears...for the virgin daughter of my people is broken with...a very grievous blow"* (Jer. 14:17). In listening to that word from God, we will find healing.

Chapter 5

------- ▶◆◀ -------

Why Could We Not Cast It Out?

W hen we read the story of the demon-possessed child in Matthew 17:14–21, we see that the disciples felt ashamed that they were not able to cast out the evil spirit. Before, when Christ had sent them out to do the work, they had come back rejoicing that the evil spirits were subject to them. But here, in the presence of the Pharisees, they had been brought to confusion by their powerlessness. They felt it deeply, and they asked the Master to tell them what the cause of failure was. He answered with one word, *"unbelief"* (v. 20). They had not been living in communion with God and separation from the world; they had neglected prayer and fasting.

When the church begins to see that the shameful decline in membership is because of the loss of a power that it had in times past, when it confesses that it is beyond its reach to find the cause and the cure, then the church will learn to bow in penitent prayer for the Master to reveal to it the depth of the trouble and the only way out of it.

In this chapter I want to call three witnesses among the servants of Christ to show their thoughts on the state of affairs. Let the first be evangelist D. L. Moody. In an issue of the *Christian,* there appeared a letter from Mr. Moody to the *New York Independent* on the subject. He referred to a statement in a previous issue of that paper that "there are over three thousand churches [in certain denominations] in the United States that did not report a single member added by profession of faith during the year." Mr. Moody then asked,

> Can this be true? The thought has taken such hold of me that I cannot get it out of my mind. It is enough almost to send a shiver of horror through the soul of every true Christian. Are we all going to sit still and let this thing continue? Should we not lift up our voice like a trumpet about this matter? What must the Son of God think of such a result of our labor as this?

In answer to Mr. Moody, the *Independent* explained that some allowance must be made for the new churches founded within the year, for small churches without a pastor, and for others that failed to send any report. The editor expressed his disagreement with what Mr. Moody had said in his letter about modern biblical criticism and other causes of the evil. And then he proceeded to write:

> But, while all this is true, Mr. Moody does well to be astonished and pained at the thousands of churches that reported not a single member added by profession of faith last year. It is enough to send a shiver of pain through the soul of every true Christian.

Let us pause before we read on and ask, What should all this mean to the church?

Let Dr. Forsyth, an English Congregational theologian, be the second witness. In his book, *The Cruciality of the Cross,* he wrote:

> It is reported from most quarters in England that there is a serious decline in church membership. For this, several explanations are given. But it is well to face the situation, and to avoid excuses, and if we do, we may discover that the real cause is the decay, not in religious interests

or sympathies, but in personal religion of a positive and experienced kind, and often in the pulpit.

Religious sympathies or energies are not Christian faith. We have become familiar with the statement that there is as much good Christianity outside the churches as in. This is not quite false, but it is much more false than true. It would be true enough if Christianity meant decent living, nice ways, precious kindness, business honor, ardent philanthropy, and public righteousness. But all these fine and worthy things are quite compatible with the absence of personal communion with God, personal faith as Christ claims it, in the sense of a personal experience of God in Jesus Christ, personal repentance, and personal peace in Christ as our eternal life. Yet that is God's first charge to us, if Christianity is true. And it is this kind of Christianity that alone builds a church and its membership. Decay of membership in the church is due to a decay of membership in Christ.

Even among those who remain in active membership in our churches, the type of religion has changed, the sense of sin can hardly be appealed to by preachers now; and to preach grace is in many (even orthodox) quarters regarded as theological obsession and the wrong language for the hour, while justification by faith is practically obsolete.

The grace of God cannot return to our preaching, or to our faith, until we recover what is almost completely gone from our general, familiar, and current religion, the thing that liberalism has quite lost—I mean a due sense of the holiness of God. This holiness of God is the real foundation—it is certainly the ruling interest of the Christian religion.

Have our churches lost that zeal? Are we producing reform, social or theological, faster than we are producing faith? We are not seeking first the kingdom of God and His holiness, but only carrying on with very expensive and noisy machinery a "kingdom-of-God's industry." We are merely running the kingdom, and running it without the cross. We have the old trademark, but what does that matter in *"a dry and thirsty land, where no water is"* (Ps. 63:1) if the artesian well on our premises is growing dry?

Let us take to heart the lesson: it is the lack of positive personal religion, sometimes even in the pulpit, that explains the decline in membership.

Our third witness is the Reverend F. B. Meyer, who was an associate evangelist of D. L. Moody. In an address on Acts 19 and the anointing power of the Holy Spirit, he said,

> There are four different planes of power—the lowest is the physical, above that is the mental, above that is the moral, and above all is the spiritual. It is only when a man moves on the spiritual level that he has power with God and has power over unclean spirits.
>
> It is because too many ministers and too many Christian workers today are content to live upon the intellectual level, or upon the moral plane, that their work is powerless to touch the mighty stronghold of Satan.
>
> The first question, therefore, to put to every Christian worker is, On what level are you working; on what level are you living? For if you are speaking on anything less than the Spirit level, know that your life will be largely a failure.

He then told the story of the seven sons of Sceva. They had tried to cast out an evil spirit in the name of *"Jesus whom Paul preach*[ed]*"* (Acts 19:13). The evil spirit answered, *"Jesus I know, and Paul I know; but who are ye?"* (v. 15). And the man with the evil spirit leaped on them and mastered them so that they fled, naked and wounded.

F. B. Meyer then proceeded to say,

> We have been praying that God would send converts to the churches and stop this awful ebb. Still the people are leaving our churches, and the pews are empty. We have no additions, or few, to our churches; and, pray as

we may, we cannot avert it. Why? Why? Because the devil does not fear us. We have no power. The devil masters the church and masters the world, and here we are all powerless, and he says, *"Jesus I know, and Paul I know; but who are ye?"*

You remember the words of our Lord: *"How can one enter into a strong man's house...except he first bind the strong man?"* (Matt. 12:29). We cannot plunder the house, because we have not bound the strong man. We have not bound the strong man in our own houses. We do not know what it is to master the power of evil in our own hearts. How then can we rescue the men who are led captive at Satan's will? It seems to me we have got to get back to prayer. O God, forgive us for our prayerlessness! God knows what a prayerless people we are. I do not wonder at things being as they are.

Let us learn the lesson. The decline in membership is nothing more than what can be expected where the work is not done in the power of the Spirit and in prayer. The spirit of darkness that rules in the world, which, with its mighty attraction, draws men from Christ and His church, is too strong for us. Nothing and no one can give the victory except the Spirit of God working in us.

Should God's servants not be delighted to think that they have such a divine power working in them? Should they not yield with their whole hearts to its influence? Oh, let us turn to the Master to give us, in the very depths of our hearts, the answer to the question, "Why could we not cast this evil spirit out?" He will say to our hearts, "It is because of your unbelief. You did not believe in Me and in the power of My Spirit, and with prayer and fasting seek for it."

Chapter 6

—◆—

The Supernatural

S omeone once said, and I must agree, that "Christianity is nothing if it is not supernatural." It is only where that concept is fully realized and acted on that the true church can flourish. Let us try to understand what this statement teaches us in connection with our review of the state of the church.

It teaches us, first of all, that Christianity is a religion that came down from heaven and still has to be unceasingly received from there. It is ever dependent on the extent to which believers yield themselves to the immediate operation of the divine power.

Christianity points to God the Father and that unceasing action by which He works out everything according to the counsel of His will, even to its minutest detail. He is the God who *"worketh all in all"* (1 Cor. 12:6). It also points to Christ the Lord, to whom all power has been given, so that, just as He did His mighty works on earth, He may now live out and live over again in His people the life that He lived on earth. In the power of His resurrection, He will do even greater works than He did then (John 14:12). And Christianity points to the Holy Spirit, who proceeds unceasingly from the Father and the Son, who continuously works out in us God's plan according to the exceeding greatness of His power in us who believe (Eph. 1:19).

Just as Israel was brought out of Egypt by a mighty hand amid great and mighty wonders, so now the church is still upheld and guided by the omnipotent action of the triune God. This is not true just in regard to the great events of its history or the special interventions in its experience. It is likewise true in God's concern for every individual life, for all the work that is done from hour to hour by the feeblest of His servants.

Christianity is nothing if it is not, from beginning to end, through all and in all, the hidden, but direct and mighty, energy of the living God continuing and working out the great redemption that He accomplished in His Son. Beyond all that He has given in creation and providence is that special working of the power of the divine life in its infinite holiness, which continuously works in us that likeness to Him that is pleasing in His sight.

"Christianity is nothing if it is not supernatural." There is even more meaning in this statement. We also learn from it what man's disposition and attitude ought to be toward God his Redeemer—absolute and unceasing dependence. The more we exercise faith in the revelation of the supernatural, as we have it in God's Word, the more we will learn that the first of our virtues should be a deep fear of God, a holy reverence in the presence of His glory, and a consciousness of our impotence under the sinful, accursed state that characterizes everything in creation.

Humility and a sense of nothingness is the posture that suits us. Faith in what God can do, will do, is always doing, and is waiting to do still more abundantly, becomes the unceasing habit of the soul, as unbroken in its continuity as the breathing of our lungs. What at first appeared to be a difficulty becomes a deep joy as we spontaneously surrender our hearts to the mighty working of God and His life within us.

To some, the supernatural may appear unnatural. That is simply because they have never understood how the supernatural may become, in the true sense, most natural. When we allow God to take perfect possession, the movements of our spiritual lives can be as natural and joyous as our breathing.

However, for this we need the consciousness of how little our natural minds or hearts can take in this divine working. We need to learn that to know what the divine power can work in us is beyond the reach of human wisdom. The revelation of our redemption must be as supernatural as the redemption itself and its almighty action in our lives. From beginning to end, the work of grace is all, always, and in all things, the presence of God working and dwelling in us.

"Christianity is nothing if it is not supernatural." This statement teaches us still more. The more fully we yield ourselves to this statement, the more clearly we will discover that all the defects in our Christian life and in the church around us are due to this one thing: we have not taken our true place before this glorious God so that He can work out in us what He has promised.

In the church this question is always coming up: what can be the reason that Christianity has so little true power and so little fulfills all the wonderful promises that it makes? Read all the discussions that are going on; notice carefully all the plans and efforts that are suggested for enabling the church to exercise the power it ought to have and to enable it to influence men, either the masses of nominal Christians or the millions of unbelievers around the world. All these thoughts and plans center on what man's wisdom can devise and what his zeal and energy can accomplish. Everywhere, there is the thought that if believers will only keep up their courage and do their work faithfully, all must come out right.

How seldom do our ministers insist upon or stress the great truth that the Holy Spirit is our only power. An entire and absolute surrender to Him is our only hope. How seldom one hears from the church leaders, to whom the church looks for its guidance, the clear and unceasing summons: *"Brethren, pray"* (1 Thess. 5:25). We must pray more; we must *"pray without ceasing"* (1 Thess. 5:17). Prayer will bring blessing. The measure of prayer is the measure of power.

Every deeper insight into what Christianity is, into what our daily lives ought to be, into what the ministry is and needs, will lead us to one deep conviction: Christianity is nothing unless it is supernatural. Our Christian life and work will be a failure unless we live deeply rooted in the power of God's inspired Word, in the power of the Holy Spirit, and in the pressing prayer to which the promise of the Father will most surely be given.

All this brings us to our last lesson from this statement. There is no hope for the restoration of the church, no hope of its being lifted up into the abundant life that there is in Christ, no hope of its being equipped in holiness and strength for the work that is so urgently calling—that of making Christ known to every living individual—except in our return to God. Church of Christ, give God His place! And take your place of absolute dependence, of unbroken fellowship, of unceasing prayer, of living, confident faith, and see if He will not turn and bless us above all that we can ask or think.

Someone has said, "The one real lack today is a lack of spiritual life; the one great need, the realization of the constant presence and power of the Holy Spirit." As we have already learned, "Back to divine wisdom, back to the living power of Jesus Christ, back through prayer to the Source of all power" must be our motto.

The secret of all our strength for the work God has given us is absolute dependence on Him. God meant this to be an inconceivable privilege and honor. He intended for us to live in utter dependence on Him, just as His Son lived. Jesus, in fact, went to the grave to prove how surely God will work mightily for the one who gives himself up wholly to His will.

How strange that this concept of absolute dependence should cost us such trouble to understand and believe! Let the thought teach us our natural inability and incapacity for spiritual things, and bring us in a new surrender to accept the birthright that belongs to us as His children—the power of a divine life in Christ through the Spirit.

What we have seen of the state of the church, as revealed in its neglect and indifference to missions and its decline in membership, leads us to inquire as to the true cure of the evil condition. It is all comprised in one word—*supernatural*! Let us hold on to this thought as we continue exploring this topic.

We are naturally so inclined to listen to anything that calls us to take action, and so ready to undertake the fulfillment of divine commands in our own strength, that unless we are very careful, we may be deceived into putting our hope in what will turn out to be nothing but human devices.

Supernatural! Give the word its full force. Let us cultivate with our whole hearts a sense of God's power actively at work in us, an attitude of dependence and prayer and waiting on God, and a deep consciousness that God will work in us and in the church around us, above what we can ask or think. Then, the deeper we enter into the grievous need of the church and the world, the stronger will become our assurance that God is preparing us for deliverance.

However, remember the one condition—a habitual, unceasing, absolute dependence on Him. He must do all. He will do all for those who wait on Him.

Chapter 7

---◆---

Christ's Last Words

When our Lord ascended to heaven, He left behind three last statements. The very last was, *"Ye shall be witnesses unto me...unto the uttermost part of the earth"* (Acts 1:8). Then we read, *"When he had spoken these things,...he was taken up"* (v. 9). He left this world and His disciples with that one thought, *"the uttermost part of the earth."* A little while before this, He had said, *"Go ye into all the world, and preach the gospel to every creature"* (Mark 16:15). With that one thought in His heart, He sat down on the throne, longing for every child of man to learn to know Him and His love.

The second-to-last statement, which had just preceded the other, was, *"Ye shall receive power"* (Acts 1:8). As He sent them forth for the conquest of the world, He told them not to think of their own weakness or their own strength. They were to think of all the power in heaven and on earth that He was now to receive from the Father. This power, through the Holy Spirit, would work in them and give them the victory.

Then we have the first of the three last statements: *"Wait for the promise of the Father"* (v. 4). In Luke's account, Jesus is recorded as saying, *"Tarry [wait] ye in the city of Jerusalem, until ye be endued [clothed] with power from on high"* (Luke 24:49). The disciples so clearly understood those words, *"wait," "tarry...until,"* that they at once returned to the city. For ten days they continued with one accord in prayer and supplication, until, on the Day of Pentecost, they were indeed baptized with the heavenly fire and were all filled with the Holy Spirit and with power.

These three statements still express the relationship between Christ on the throne and His people. Just suppose for a moment that you were given the privilege of being caught up into paradise and of seeing and hearing what men may not know. You would, in the light and the power of that Spirit life, where words are eternally existing realities, be permitted to see the risen Lord on the throne, living with this one thought, *"the uttermost part of the earth,"* always in His heart, and always listening to the song of the redeemed from every people, nation, and language. How God waits and longs for the time when His love can reach every soul in the world! God loves the world; Christ gave His blood and His life for the world.

Moreover, you would know what a reality that second statement was, too, because you would see a Lamb standing *"as it had been slain, having...seven eyes, which are the seven Spirits of God sent forth into all the earth"* (Rev. 5:6). That holy symbol would show you how the Lamb on the throne lives to send forth God's Spirit wherever God's servants go, to enable them to make known His love and win souls for His kingdom.

You would also see the reality of the first of the three last statements, *"wait,"* which was interpreted by the disciples as a waiting that included much prayer and supplication. You would find there that the *"four and twenty elders fell down before the Lamb, having every one of them harps, and golden vials* [bowls] *full of odours* [incense], *which are the prayers of saints"* (v. 8).

The prayers of people here on earth have their place and their part before the throne of God. You would see the smoke of the incense in the golden censer with the prayers of the saints going up before God. And you would understand what it is so hard for us to realize: that the prayers on earth are indeed the condition for receiving power from heaven to extend the kingdom on earth.

And if, in the vision, as you saw that it was passing, you felt bold to ask the Blessed One, "Do you have a message to give me for Your people on earth?" you would not be surprised if His answer came, "Tell them in My name to remember My last three statements. I carry the ends of the earth, for which I gave My blood and My love, in My heart. Let them do so, too. I live on the throne to send forth the Spirit into all the earth. Let them believe My promise, yield wholly to My Spirit, and victory will certainly come. I am waiting to hear how much they are willing to have and to use; I am longing for more intercession and supplication, for more faith and prayer. Tell them to wait and tarry in prayer, and not to rest until they are clothed with power from on high. Oh, tell them the kingdom, and their Lord and King, wait for their prayers."

Will we not take these last words of Christ afresh into our hearts? Has not God brought them home to us lately with a new meaning? Has not the terrible indictment against the home church—its lack of fitness or willingness to undertake the glorious, Christlike task of bringing God's love to every individual—pierced some hearts at least? We have heard testimonies about the state of the church: its ignorance and its neglect and its rejection of the cross, its lack of the sense of holiness and crucifixion to the world, its neglect of the blessed truth of the Holy Spirit, its lack of loyalty to the Lord Jesus, its terrible feebleness in prayer. Have not these testimonies become to some of us a burden that we cannot bear?

Will we not turn away from all our devices and efforts, and listen, with new, wholehearted devotion, to the great charter the church has too long neglected, the last statements of the ascending Lord? To take the words that live in Christ's heart and let them live in ours will be the secret of wonderful happiness and irresistible power.

"The uttermost part of the earth." "All the world." "Every creature." Is it possible for the ordinary Christian in everyday life

to be so possessed by these words that, without effort or strain, they would be the spontaneous expression of his inmost life? Thank God, it is possible, where the love of God and Christ is poured out into the heart. Poor, simple men and women have proved it by the intense devotion with which they could sacrifice everything to make the love of Jesus known to others.

The love with which Christ loves us is a love that takes in the whole world. Of that love we cannot take just enough for ourselves and be indifferent to all the others who share in it. Such is the feeble, selfish, and unhappy life that so many Christians seek to live. In order to truly possess Christ and to fully enjoy Him, it is essential that we take in His love in all its fullness, that we yield ourselves to the service of that love, and that we find our happiness in making that love known to those who are still ignorant of it.

When the church is awakened and experiences in some measure the abundant life that there is in Christ Jesus, *"the uttermost part of the earth"* will become its motto. People will begin to understand that what fills and satisfies the heart of Christ in heaven is enough and more than enough to fill our hearts with the blessedness and beauty of likeness to Him. "Remember," He says, "My very last statement, as I ascended the throne: *'Ye shall be witnesses unto me...unto the uttermost part of the earth'* (Acts 1:8)."

You will recall that the second-to-last statement was: *"Ye shall receive power, after that the Holy Ghost is come upon you"* (v. 8). Yes, that is part of the last words of Christ: *"the Holy Ghost."* The Spirit of God was to be the divine empowerment that would carry them on irresistibly to universal conquest. He would sustain them through suffering and death, through long and patient labor, through many disappointments and trials. The victory was sure.

It has often been said that the Spirit flows from the cross. The Spirit is inseparably linked to the cross. In the fellowship of the cross, they could always count on the fellowship of the Spirit and His almighty power.

But, alas, how soon the church began to shrink from the cross and, without knowing it, began to lose that power of the Spirit, without which it is powerless to resist the power of the world. Oh, that God would raise up believers who could, as with a trumpet voice, sound out this last statement of Christ: *"Ye shall receive power, after that the Holy Ghost is come upon you."* Oh, that God would raise up believers who could lead the church in returning to the cross, with its crucifixion to the world, and in yielding itself to the glorious task of carrying the cross in triumph to the ends of the earth.

Let us implore our blessed Lord to write on our hearts this precious last phrase, too: *"the Holy Ghost."*

And then comes the first of the three last statements, *"Wait"* (Acts 1:4). The disciples spent their time of waiting in prayer and supplication. Church leaders have told us that to multiply the number of Christians who will individually and collectively wield this force of intercession is the supreme question of foreign missions. Every other consideration is secondary to that of wielding the forces of prayer.

Jesus Christ in heaven waits for our prayers. The world's conquest waits for our prayers. It has been said, "The essential task of evangelizing the world is the lifting up of the church into a fuller spiritual life." This lifting up of the church waits for our prayers. Let us, above everything, implore God for the spirit of prayer.

Does not the Holy Spirit of God take the central place in these last instructions of Christ? Without faith in the promise of the Spirit, the church will fail in its duty and lose the courage both to pray and to testify throughout all the earth. Should not everyone who desires to live for Christ and His kingdom entreat God to remove the terrible blindness that hinders believers from seeing that there is just one thing lacking in the church's work— the power of the Spirit—and just one thing required—that the church fall down in intense, fervent prayer to wait until it is clothed with power from on high?

Chapter 8

———————◆◆——————

Early Christianity

*I*n our last chapter we focused on the words of Christ, in which all God's power in heaven was promised to the church to enable it to fulfill the great task that Christ set before it. That power can be counted on in proportion to the measure of our faith and prayer. These questions naturally follow: How did the early church avail itself of that promise? Have we a right to expect its fulfillment in the same measure?

In his *Dawn on the Dark Continent,* Dr. Stewart compared the early church's missionary work with modern missionary work. He wrote,

> The religious life of the early Christians seems to have possessed some vitality or concentrated spiritual power that helped Christianity, possibly because they believed intensely what they knew. Whatever it was, those Christians were successful as unofficial missionaries....
>
> In the early church its force and expansive power depended at first, as it still depends, on its internal condition, that is, on its spiritual life. The church of our day needs to be reminded that spiritual enterprises require spiritual conditions of the very highest force. And when the latter are lacking, the success desired may also be lacking.

I make no apology for dedicating the rest of this chapter to quoting a report entitled "The Missionary Message." It shows the difference between the amazing vitality of the early church and the comparative powerlessness of the church of our day.

Regaining the Power of the Early Church

There could have been no Pentecost had it not been for the life, death, and resurrection of the Son of God. These provided a revelation of God. The cross revealed that He is absolute love and purity. The Resurrection revealed that He is absolute power. This revelation had to be given before the Spirit was given. Union with an impersonal absolute has in it no regenerative power; we need union with a personal God.

When that revelation had been made, and when it had been accepted by the common faith of the church, Pentecost became divinely inevitable. The barriers of human resistance were broken at last, and the encompassing, waiting, besieging sea of the Spirit rushed in. At last the living Father, through the Son, had found receptive vessels, and therefore the Spirit was given. From that point forward, believing men and women knew that no union with such a God could be too close and too steadfast. Their true lives were hidden with Christ in God, and all true progress in them was progress within the absolute revelation.

Is this too sweeping a statement as far as the Christian is concerned? Is it or is it not the view of the Christian revelation, that there is no limit to the efficacy of the Spirit of God in the life of man, except the measure of faith in those who receive it? Is it not true that all limitation and delay arise from the imperfect receptiveness of the Christian church?

What is implied in God's promise to give His Spirit to the Christian church? How far can we count on God to sustain and transform us? How near can we come to Him within the conditions of time? How far is it true that He is still literally creative in His world whenever and wherever He finds faith? Are there in Him unimagined resources of life simply awaiting the rise of faith, just as the riches of nature throughout the ages awaited the discovery and development of science?

When we endeavor to explain the difference between the amazing vitality of the early church and the comparative powerlessness of today's church, three possible explanations suggest themselves.

The first starts from existing facts and endeavors to explain the early records in the light of present attainment. This view says that the standard of judgment is the church as we know it, and that the actual life of the heroic age could not have differed in any real degree from the present church.

The second view is that these records of the first one hundred and fifty years of the church's life are true history. The contrast between the spiritual exaltation and achievement of that age and the comparative depression of our own lies in the fact that, for wise and good reasons, God has restricted the early gift of the Spirit and put us under a more rigid and limited dispensation.

The third view, like the second, holds to the truth of the records, but explains the difference between the early centuries and our own by saying that, while God remains unchanging in His grace, the church has failed to comply with the conditions of receiving it. Faith, according to this view, has gradually become depressed, and so the church has lost the expectancy that is the condition of all spiritual achievement.

Why have our prayers failed to overcome the remaining sin and tragedy in the Christian life? According to this third view, it is because the common faith and love of the church is far below the common faith and love of early days. The individual who lacks this faith and love cannot attain the ancient summit. The true remedy for such failure does not lie in abandoning the enterprises of faith as hopeless, while blaming the failure on God, but in flinging all our energies into the task of rousing the slumbering life of the church.

We must awaken it to a new community of faith and love, and press on from there to new personal attainment.

This view argues that the idea of God having restricted our spiritual resources has no foundation in revelation. Revealed truth declares that believers everywhere may count on the Spirit of God with the same assurance, as they rest on the unchanging providence of God. It also proves that, whether it is recognized or not, the whole missionary movement of the nineteenth century rested on a different foundation than ours. It began with William Carey's, "Expect great things from God; attempt great things for God." And its progress since then has been measured by the degree of expectancy, which again has depended on the depth and strength and grandeur of its idea of God.

Is the delay in the coming of the divine kingdom due to a lowering of the common faith of the church—a lapse of ages of time, a lapse as wide as the Christendom of the modern world? Are there unseen around us today all the illimitable forces of the divine Spirit that surrounded the first ages? Do they await only the rise of a generation stronger in faith and love than our own?

If so, then clearly the one true attitude for the church is to confess its historic sin and get ready for the most resolute and strenuous endeavor and prayer. Then the numbing mists of our common unbelief may be dispelled. Then the redeeming will of God in Christ may have free course in blessing the entire life of man.

If this third view is true, we have been attributing to the inscrutable will of God innumerable temporal and spiritual evils that are really the result of our fostering thoughts of God that are unworthy of His goodness, wisdom, and power. In this case, our whole perspective of God is being lowered and darkened by a false theory of His ways with people.

Are the same divine resources available today as in the early ages? The church is once more facing its duty to the whole world. It has been led by the providence and the Spirit of God into circumstances that are taxing its resources to the limit. Everywhere the question of our resources is coming to the forefront.

But there is surely common agreement that behind all these things there is an incomparably deeper need. Behind all questions of quantity lies the incomparably weighty question of quality. It is not simply the spiritual quality of our missionaries that is the crucial point; it is the spiritual quality of the church that is behind them. It is the spiritual character of the great masses of common Christians—their faith, their love, their hopes, their reception of the power of the Spirit.

A question arises and presses for an answer: at this moment, does the church possess the spiritual resources for reaching the world? Or, like Israel in the days of the prophets, is its existing spiritual attainment insufficient for the great world emergency that has broken upon it?

Valuable Lessons

How we need to learn these lessons from "The Missionary Message." With what force all the lessons that we need at this time are taught.

Seeking and finding the supernatural power of the Holy Spirit is the one condition of success in the work of Christ's kingdom. That power, as it manifested itself in the early church, is available for the church today.

All the feebleness from which the church is suffering, in its decline of membership and in its inability to fulfill its calling, can have no other cause but the lack of the presence and power of the Holy Spirit in its ministries.

How inconceivable that the church does not know and act upon the blessed truth that the Holy Spirit will work in it all that it needs of the divine strength for winning the world.

The plea for more prayer opens the certain path to the power of the Spirit in every work the church has to do.

Chapter 9

---◆---

Seven Times More Prayer

*R*ecently I took part in a World Missionary Conference. The reports that followed the conference greatly stress the supreme importance of prayer. I will begin this chapter with some excerpts from these reports:

> Prayer is the method that links the irresistible might of God to the missionary enterprise. That God has conditioned so largely the extension and the fruitfulness of His kingdom upon the faithfulness and loyalty of His children in prayer is, at the same time, one of the deepest mysteries and one of the most wonderful realities.

That paragraph is worth reading again. Here is another:

> How to multiply the number of Christians who, with clear and unshakable faith in the character and ability of God, will wield this force for the transformation of man—that is the supreme question of foreign missions. Every other consideration is secondary to that of wielding the forces of prayer. May the call go forth from this conference to the Christian churches throughout the world to give themselves as never before to intercession.

An entire chapter of one report is devoted to prayer, and especially the need of education in prayer. Here are a few paragraphs from that chapter:

> It is our conviction that none can pray his best, and few can pray with any fullness of effect, who has not received some careful training in the practice of prayer and has not acquired as well the grace of holy perseverance in it.
>
> We must emphasize the fact that encouraging and directing the prayer of Christian people is one of the highest forms of Christian service.
>
> We take for granted that those who love this work and carry it on their hearts will follow the Scripture's admonition to pray unceasingly for its triumph. To such, all times and seasons will witness an attitude of intercession that refuses to let God go until He crowns His workers with victory.
>
> Prayer is the putting forth of vital energy. It is the highest effort of which the human spirit is capable. Effectiveness and power in prayer cannot be obtained without patient continuance and much practice. The primary need is not the multiplication of prayer meetings, but that individual Christians should learn to pray.
>
> The secret and art of prayer can be learned only from the teaching of the Master Himself and by patient study of the best books on the subject.
>
> Sometimes it has seemed as if faith in the power of the Spirit and in His willingness to aid had been almost lost, and that we were now attempting to substitute human devices for spiritual power. All plans to deepen interest in missionary work must be devised and executed in devout prayer and solemn waiting upon the Lord.

These are indeed unspeakably solemn words. They lead us into the depth of the sanctuary. They open up to us the divine meaning and mystery of prayer as very few understand them. They call us to entreat God by His Holy Spirit to open our eyes so that we may know what prayer is in its spiritual reality.

Most Christians are content if they have some blessed experience of what prayer can do in bringing down blessings for their own needs, and maybe for the needs of others. Yet how seldom it is realized that prayer covers the whole divine mystery of man being in partnership with the triune God in working out the counsel of His will and grace.

All that God wants to do for the world, He does through people whom He has taken into His counsel. These people have yielded themselves fully to His will. His Spirit has taken possession of them so that they can pray with power in the name of Jesus. Such have the high honor that God will regulate the working of His Holy Spirit at their request. He will send His Spirit to go where and to do what they have asked.

This is indeed the mystery of prayer, that worms of the dust can become members of God's private council. The Holy One listens to such and becomes the Executor of their plans and wishes. Prayer brings forth the infinite and omnipotent resources of God, and God's saints have the honor of praying. No wonder the chapter from which I have been quoting concludes with these words:

> If the conference should lead some resolutely and irrevocably to enter into the school of prayer, the spiritual power of the church for the accomplishment of its great task would be immeasurably increased.

Now, how do all these excerpts relate to the subject of our book, the state of the church? First, they should deepen the painful conviction of how little the church knows how to pray and how unfit most of its members are to pray effectively.

We need time to get a full impression of what the Christian life means to most people, even those who are considered earnest. They have been taught to come to Christ for their salvation. They have found it, and they now seek to live in the world, looking to God for enough grace to enable them to live what they think are Christian lives.

They have no conception of the claim Christ has to an entire consecration of their whole being. They have no idea that it is definitely their great calling to live to make Christ King throughout the earth. The thought is entirely foreign to them that every day of their lives they are to pray, to labor in prayer, so that God's kingdom may come and so that God's Spirit may use them for His service.

When we compare this attitude with Scripture, the charge is brought home to us that the church is feeble and utterly unable to strive in prayer for the conversion of the world. I implore my readers to look back over all the excerpts in this chapter to see what ought to be, and what is not found to be, until the prayerlessness of the church becomes a burden too heavy to be borne.

After considering these things, the true Christian must surrender at once. He must wholly yield himself to become an intercessor.

When speaking of the work that needs to be done, Dr. Robson used this expression: "We will need three times more men, four times more money, seven times more prayer." That is, instead of twenty thousand men, we now need sixty thousand men; instead of ten million dollars, now forty million; instead of the amount of prayer being offered, now seven times more prayer.

If a congregation had at present three laborers in the field, it would not be impossible, if the right spirit prevailed, to increase that number to nine. If there were a Christian man who had given five percent of his income to foreign missions, it would surely not be too much, if a right sense of the claim of Christ came upon him, for him to give four times that amount— twenty percent. Would it then be thought impossible to believe that, when God's Spirit even now begins to work in the hearts of God's children, they will be drawn into seven times more prayer?

It is not only that we want the number of those who pray to be greatly increased, but even more we desire that those who already pray would accept the call for their part in the sevenfold. Quality is more important than quantity. Sevenfold is the sign of the quiet perseverance of Elijah that would not rest until the cloud had been seen. Sevenfold is the sign of the burning furnace seven times heated. Our hope lies in the new intensity of the prayer of those who already pray.

Christ *"offered up prayers and supplications with strong crying"* (Heb. 5:7), but He first offered Himself. Offer yourself to God, and a new power will come to offer up prayer without ceasing. Begin at once. Take each chapter of this book, and turn it into prayer. Take up the great subjects, and just speak your heart in communion with God. Again, go back to the quotations I have given. Make them food for prayer until your heart begins to understand what it means to give God no rest until He pours down His blessing.

There is an even more important message in these excerpts. They first refer to prayer for foreign missions. However, this book has to do with a subject on which missions is absolutely dependent—the spiritual life of the church. I included the excerpts to rouse the hearts of Christians to unceasingly pray for a revival. Without it, the church can never respond to the call of its Lord.

We may pray for the church at large, the church to which we belong, or the circle with which we are more closely linked. Regardless, let our prayer for missions lift up to God our first and primary desire—that His believing children who have known what prayer is may be stirred to a new intensity. That will lead them to ask that His feebler children may take courage and confidently expect Him to give them the Spirit of supplication, too.

Then will follow the prayer that His wandering children, who profess to trust in Christ but have never thought of what it is to live for His service, may, by the mighty movement of His grace, be brought to take their part in the great army of intercessors. In the ministry of intercession they will cry to Him day and night until He avenges them of their adversary (Luke 18:3).

Sevenfold more prayer. May God find His people ready for it.

Chapter 10

———————— ◆ ————————

A Holiness Revival

*H*ow is the church to be lifted to the level of abundant life in Christ? How can it gain the vitality that will prepare it for the work that God is putting before it? In answer to these questions, many will without hesitation say, "Nothing will help but a revival." Indeed, that alone is the something that must happen to the church.

As Mr. Oldham put it,

> If the World Missionary Conference had any meaning at all, it disclosed a situation so serious that nothing less than a tremendous spiritual revival can be adequate to meet it. It is a new and living understanding of God and of His purpose for the world that we seem most of all to need if there is to be an irresistible spiritual movement. Such a movement is the only thing adequate to the needs of the situation. Great tides of spiritual energy must be set in motion if the work is to be accomplished.

Yes, all perceptive believers will conclude that nothing less than a mighty revival is needed. Nothing less will rouse and prepare the church for the work to which God calls it. Yet there may be great differences in what is understood by "revival." Many will think of the power of God as it has been manifested in the work of evangelists like D. L. Moody and R. A. Torrey. They feel sure that what God has done in the past He can do again. They will perhaps hardly be able to understand me when I say that we need a different and a mightier revival than those were.

In those revivals, the chief purpose was the conversion of sinners and, in connection with that, the reviving of believers. But the revival that we need calls for a deeper and more entire upheaval of the church. The great defect of those revivals was that the converts were received into a church that was not living on a high level of consecration and holiness, and they quickly sank down to the average standard of ordinary religious life. Even the believers who had taken part in the work and had been stirred by it also gradually returned to their former life of clouded fellowship and lack of power to testify for Christ.

The revival we need is the revival of holiness. In this kind of revival, the consecration of one's whole being to the service of Christ for the rest of one's life is considered possible. For this we will need a new style of preaching, in which the promises of God to dwell in His people and to sanctify them for Himself will take a place that they do not now have.

Let me try to make this plain by an illustration from the history of Israel. When God redeemed His people from Egypt by the blood of the Passover and the deliverance at the Red Sea, this was only a beginning of what He intended to do. He had a higher purpose and a fuller blessing for them. He meant to dwell among them as the Holy One and to be their God. He meant to sanctify them as His people.

We find this twofold aim in the song of Moses: *"Thou in thy mercy hast led forth the people which thou hast redeemed"* (Exod. 15:13). That was the wonderful beginning. Then, *"Thou hast guided them in thy strength unto thy holy habitation"* (v. 13).

Just as God had said to Moses, *"I am the Lord, and I will bring you out from under the burdens of the Egyptians....And I will bring you in unto the land"* (Exod. 6:6, 8), the redemption from Egypt was only the foundation. The house to be built on it was the sanctuary, in which God dwelt in the midst of His people as the Holy One, to make them holy, too. Yet there were many Israelites who were brought out from bondage but were never brought into rest. They perished in the wilderness through unbelief.

When our Lord Jesus, in His farewell discourse, gave the promise of the Holy Spirit, He spoke of the new covenant blessing that would then be experienced: God dwelling in His people. *"If a man love me, he will keep my words: and my Father will love him* [and I will love him], *and we will...make our abode with him"* (John 14:23).

Paul wrote the words, *"That Christ may dwell in your hearts by faith...that ye might be filled with all the fulness of God"* (Eph. 3:17, 19). Dr. Maclaren has said that it seems as if the thought of Christ dwelling in our hearts has been lost in the church. In the Reformation, the great truth of justification—the bringing out from the bondage of Egypt—was restored to its place. But the other great truth of sanctification—the bringing into the land with its rest and victory—has never yet taken the place in the preaching and practice of the church that God's Word claims for it.

It is for this that we need a revival, that the Holy Spirit may so take possession of us that the Father and the Son can live in us, and that fellowship with them and devotion to their will and service will be our chief joy. This will indeed be a holiness revival.

A holiness revival! Has there ever been such a thing? There have been movements in the church that, though they have not been known by that name, have resulted in definite and intense consecration to God and His will. There have also been fuller manifestations of the Spirit that have left their marks in history. Many church leaders say that the Moravian ideal is what the church ought to aim at—every member ready for the work of the kingdom.

The Moravian community owed its birth to a true holiness revival. There were gathered together at Herrnhut, a small religious community, a number of refugees from Bohemia, along with a number of Christians of different sects, who hoped to find the Christian life as they sought for it. It was not long before disputes arose, and Herrnhut became a scene of contention and division.

Nikolaus von Zinzendorf felt this discord so deeply that he went down to live among them. In the power of God's Spirit, he succeeded not only in restoring order, but in binding them together in the power of devotion to Jesus and love for each other. More than once they had remarkable manifestations of the presence of the Spirit, and their whole lives became that of worship and praise. After they had been having nightly fellowship meetings for a couple of years, they were led to consecrate the whole community to the service of Christ's kingdom.

When John Wesley visited them, he wrote,

> God has given me at length the desire of my heart. I am with a church whose conversation is in heaven, in whom is the mind that was in Christ, and who so walk as He walked. Here I continually meet with what I sought for— living proofs of the power of faith, persons saved from inward as well as outward sin by the love of God shed abroad in their hearts. I was extremely comforted and strengthened by the conversation of this lovely people.

It was in a holiness revival that the Moravian missionary idea was born and realized.

A holiness revival! What was the great evangelical revival in England through George Whitefield and John Wesley but this? They had together at Oxford been members of "The Holy Club." With their whole hearts they had sought to live for God, to keep themselves separate from the world, and to devote their lives to the welfare of their fellowmen. They had not only sought deliverance from the guilt of sin, but also from its power. When their eyes were opened to see how faith can claim the whole Christ in all His fullness, they found the key to the preaching that was so mightily effective for the salvation of sinners.

What John Wesley did for the Methodists, General William Booth, as his disciple, did for the Salvation Army. Looking at the material with which he had to work, it is amazing how he inspired tens of thousands with a true devotion to Christ and to the lost. He accomplished this with his teaching of a clean heart and a full salvation.

If I remember correctly, one noted church historian has said that, along with Spurgeon, John Wesley and General Booth are among those whom God has most honored for winning many souls for Christ. Such a testimony has all the greater value because I know how far that particular scholar is from agreeing with the teaching of holiness as these men thought they had found it in God's Word. There may be great differences of doctrine, but no one can be blind to the seal God has set upon the intense desire to preach a full and entire consecration.

A revival of holiness is what we need. We need a preaching about Christ's claim on us that will lead us to live entirely for Him and His kingdom. We need an attachment of love to Him that will make His fellowship our highest joy. We need a faith in His ability to free us from sin's dominion that will enable us to obey His commandments in all things. We need a yielding to the Holy Spirit that will cause us to be led by Him in our entire daily walk. These will be some of the elements of a revival of true holiness. The church must learn to seek for this revival as for the *"pearl of great price"* (Matt. 13:46).

And how is it to be found? It will require much prayer. It will cost more than that. It will call for much sacrifice of self and of the world. It will require a surrender to Christ Jesus to follow Him as closely as God is able to work it in us. We must learn to look at a life like Christ's as the supreme goal of daily lives. We must have the very same mind that was in Christ.

May the prayer of the Scottish preacher Robert Murray McCheyne become ours: "Lord, make me as holy as a pardoned sinner can be." May it be offered by an increasing number of ministers and believers. Then the promise of the new covenant will become a matter of experience.

We need to hear preaching about God in His holiness, about Christ as our sanctification, and about the work of the Spirit as the Spirit of Holiness. When this preaching takes the place that it has in God's Word, God's people will have the power to do the work to which God has called them—making Christ known to every living individual. This promise will then be fulfilled: *"The heathen shall know that I am the* L*ORD*, *saith the Lord* G*OD*, *when I shall be sanctified in you before their eyes"* (Ezek. 36:23).

Chapter 11

———◆◆◆———

Christ's Claim on Us

*I*ndifference to missionary work prevails. The cause, many say, is that Christians are utterly unconscious of the claim Christ has on them. At conversion, their attention was directed to salvation from punishment, along with grace to help them to a better life. The thought that Christ had purchased them as a people of His own, *"zealous of good works"* (Titus 2:14), that through them He might from heaven continue and carry on the work He had begun on earth, never entered their minds. They knew that they ought to do good works as the proof of their love, but they never understood that these good works were service that Christ actually needed for the extension of His kingdom. They did not know that their whole lives, with all their abilities, were to be at His disposal for that purpose.

If there is to be a deep missionary revival, it will have to begin here: God's children who are striving to serve Him must get a new and far deeper insight into the blessedness of this claim of Christ. God wants them to be able to tell of it and to testify about the source of their motivation. They can pass on a power that will rouse Christians who have been living the self-ish life. Selfish Christians will be roused to a new thought that they never had before—the real blessedness of belonging to Christ. Only in this way will the world know that the love of God, in heavenly measure and power, dwells in Christians.

May God, by His Holy Spirit, open our eyes to see what this wonderful claim of Christ means.

What is the ground upon which it rests? That He is our God and Creator? This is only the beginning of it, and its power has been so obliterated by sin that something else was needed. And what a stupendous miracle was accomplished when the Son of God came to earth to unite Himself with us in all our sin and suffering. He not only suffered, but also endured the judgment of a Holy God, which we deserved.

Yes, so completely did He identify Himself with us that He stooped to bear our curse. He gave His life and His blood on our behalf. And He made us eternally one with Himself in His resurrection and ascension and in the glory into which He entered upon the throne of God. We are so completely one with Him that throughout the whole universe we will be known as His body, the inseparable companion and sharer of His place in the heart of the Father.

What is the ground on which Christ's claim rests? We need to think about Christ's sacrifice if this question is to be answered with a power that compels the heart. Is He not worthy of having your every thought and every ability yielded to Him—to be His completely and His alone?

That gives us the answer to the second question: what really is Christ's claim? It is nothing less than this: we should give ourselves for Him and to Him as completely as He gave Himself for us and to us. In chapter two, I used the expression—I cannot forget it, though I cannot grasp it—"The measure of the surrender of Christ for us and our salvation is the measure of our surrender to Him and to His service." This same idea was expressed by Dr. Denney in these words:

> We must seek to persuade men that a love like Christ's can only be answered by a love in kind, and that, for a Savior who came not only in water but in blood, there can be no adequate response that is bloodless. There must be a passion in the answer of our souls that reciprocates the passion of His love to us.

As we take in these words, we will begin to understand Christ's claim on us. He lived on earth, and now lives in heaven, in the fullness of a love for us that surpasses knowledge. In the same way, nothing can now satisfy His heart, or our own, but a love that on our part seeks to live every moment in His presence and for His pleasure.

Just as His love showed itself in a life of intense and unceasing action, so our love must be ready to wait on His will and to place our abilities at His disposal. We should be constantly on the lookout to see, not how much we can manage to keep for ourselves, but what else we can find to give Him who has given His all so unreservedly for us. There will then be no need for pleading for missionaries or for money. A group that loves Him will eagerly offer anything that the Master may desire.

Now comes the third question: how can we have the power to yield to Christ's claim and live in unbroken surrender to it? The thought comes readily to mind that it may be a very beautiful ideal, but how impossible it is to carry it out. Listen to Christ's answer: He Himself undertakes to settle all claims that He has upon us.

The love that gave itself on the cross, with the one thought of getting complete possession of us, is the love that in all its intensity and power watches over and works in us every hour of the day. When He gave Himself for us, He gave Himself to us. Surely a lost sheep can count on its strong shepherd to carry it back to its home. No less can each one of us count on the whole Christ, and count on Him constantly, to carry us. He is entirely ready to keep us from sin and to work out in us all the *"good pleasure of his will"* (Eph. 1:5).

Some ask the question, But why do we experience so little of His power? The answer is simple. We do not know it, we do not believe it, and we do not yield ourselves to it. The limited action of the Holy Spirit, hindered as He is by the spirit of the world, is the one cause of our failure. Christ calls for a passion of love toward Him that corresponds to His toward us. No power but His own love, dwelling in the heart and working there, can for a moment think of giving what He claims. He Himself, by His abiding presence, by His indwelling Spirit, by His unceasing working in us, must do all.

And this brings us to the fourth great question: how can a soul who longs to yield himself wholly to Christ's claim, make good his claim on Christ Himself to carry out all His work in us? The answer is simple and yet beyond the power of the human mind to fully grasp. Nothing less is needed than that the Spirit should glorify Christ in His claim on us and in our claim on Him. It is when we see how impossible it is for a person to really know and love Christ that we will come in our helplessness and cast ourselves at His feet. Then we will believe in the power of His Word to work in us a full faith in Him and all He has done and will do.

As we turn away from the world and from self and consent to be crucified with Him, we will find, in the fellowship of His death, the power through which He conquers sin. We will find, in the fellowship of His resurrection, the heavenly life through which He dwells in us, becomes one with us, and works out all His blessed purpose.

True love cannot rest until, by its divine power, it possesses the heart of the beloved one. God's love draws our love to itself and does not rest until our love has perfectly responded.

And now, this claim of Christ must be proclaimed in the church with a new power from on high. Who should proclaim it? It should be those who have yielded themselves wholly to it, who have given their lives here at home to let Christ work in them all that He wills. It should be those who are seeking with their whole hearts, even in the midst of conscious imperfection, to see Christ's claim fully acknowledged in the church.

When such believers begin to give themselves to prayer and supplication so that it might happen, hearts will begin to be touched. Christians, whether ministers or not, will begin to understand. They will see that for such an unspiritual, power-less church to be roused for the great work of making Christ's claim known to unbelievers around the world, nothing less is needed than the mighty power of the Spirit ruling in the hearts and lives of God's children. And every thought of the state of the home church and the crying need of the non-Christian world will be swallowed up in this one thought: Christ claims the world, and Christ expects everyone who has learned that claim to yield himself wholly to it and to live only to make it known.

Chapter 12

———————— ▶◆◀ ————————

The Promise of the Father

*T*he Holy Spirit is the promise of the Father. That promise includes everything we need. In order to truly know God, in order to experience and enjoy all that Christ is and has for us, in order to possess the true and full life that a child of God may expect even here on earth—everything depends on our being possessed and filled with the Holy Spirit of God.

We are absolutely dependent on the abundant measure of the Spirit that God is so willing to give and that He promises to give. Everything that reminds us of the fallen state of the church, of its unfaithfulness and lack of loyalty to Christ, of the terrible power that the world has over it, of its powerlessness to carry out its mission here on earth, is just another call: *"Turn you at my reproof: behold, I will pour out my spirit unto you"* (Prov. 1:23).

Ignorance prevails concerning Christ's cross and the holiness it offers. Christian ministers and workers are content to struggle on in their human efforts to save sinners. They do not give the Holy Spirit the first place that He must have. In view of all this, let us once again listen to the great promise that Christ gave His disciples when He was teaching them to pray. Let us see whether our hearts will not yield to this wonderful promise and turn to God for what He will so surely give.

Listen now to the promise of the Father: *"If ye then, being evil, know how to give good gifts unto your children: how much more shall your heavenly Father give the Holy Spirit to them that ask him?"* (Luke 11:13). In these words we find four deep and unfathomable mysteries. First, the mystery of the Holy Spirit whom God offers to give us. Second, the mystery of the Father's infinite willingness to give that gift. Third, the mystery of the Son of God, who came from heaven to bring the promise and to open the way for its fulfillment, and who now from heaven is the channel through whom the Father gives it. And fourth, the mystery of prayer, by which that great gift can be drawn down upon ourselves and others. If it were to please God to open our eyes fully to see the glory of these mysteries, we could not for a moment hesitate to give up everything to have the promise fulfilled in us.

The Holy Spirit

First is the inconceivable mystery of the gift of the Holy Spirit. Who is He? He is the Spirit of God. Just as a man has his life in the spirit that animates his body, the whole life and glory of Deity is contained in the Holy Spirit. The Spirit is the bond of union between the Father and the Son. He is the Spirit of the Father and of the Son, too. And this very same Spirit is to be the Spirit of our lives, dwelling in us as the hidden God, doing His work to reveal the Son and the Father within us. The Spirit of God dwells and works in us! The thought is so overwhelming that it compels us to worship and adore.

God has said that this blessed Spirit will be the life of our lives. He is given with the express purpose of working out in us all that God wants us to be and to do. He is given with the understanding that we never need to do in our own strength what God commands. The Spirit will work it in us. He comes as the whole God to take possession of the whole man. He will be responsible for the whole of our lives if we will yield ourselves to Him in faith. He will glorify Christ in us. As we look up to Christ, and through Him to the Father, the blessed Spirit will work in the depth of our hearts the likeness of God and His Christ.

The Father's Willingness

Now let us examine the second mystery, the mystery of the Father's inconceivable willingness to give this infinite gift. *"How much more shall your heavenly Father give the Holy Spirit to them that ask him?"* (Luke 11:13). Christ takes an illustration from the deepest experience of our daily lives. Have we not, as children, learned to know and trust and rejoice in the willingness of a father to give us the food we need? How natural, how easy, what joy it was, to live in that assurance of what a father would do!

Now, just think of what this phrase means: *"How much more shall your heavenly Father."* Think of His greatness. Think of His holiness. Think of His love and His tender compassion. Then say, "Do we not have good reason for the most unbounded confidence? The Father is just longing to fill us with His Holy Spirit." Oh, the mystery of this inconceivable longing of God to give us His Holy Spirit! Take time to take it in.

If He is so willing, why, then, do we so often pray and have to wait a long time for the answer? It is simply that *we* are not willing. We hinder Him. We do not yield our whole hearts and souls, our entire beings. We are not like a hungry child, for a hungry child will certainly be fed by his father. We are not ready to sacrifice everything and seek only what the Father longs to give.

Let us believe in the mystery of the Father's willingness to give the Spirit. It will draw us to come closer to God and, under the power of His love, to lay ourselves at His feet.

The Son of God

The third mystery is, Who is this who brings this wonderful message? No one less than the Son of God. As if to make unbelief impossible, God sent His only begotten Son as the Bearer of the good tidings. He came to prepare the way to deliver us from the power of sin. He came to yield His own body as a living sacrifice on the cross, so that He might then receive the Spirit from the Father to impart to us. Sin had so separated us and our whole being from God that it was only by death to the old nature, death to sin, that a new creation could be formed in which the Holy Spirit could dwell.

Here we have the reason why, in spite of the infinite willingness of God to give the Spirit, we find it so difficult to receive Him. Just as Christ could not receive the Spirit in His fullness of power to impart to us until He had died the death of the cross, it is only in the full fellowship of that death that we are made partakers of the fullness of the Spirit. It is when we are crucified with Him to the world, and when we live in Him as those who are dead to sin, that He can do His blessed work in us.

The Power of Prayer

The fourth mystery is the inconceivable power of my feeble prayer to draw down the Holy Spirit from heaven to work where and what I ask in the name of Jesus. Not only will the Father give me the Spirit, but He will send the Spirit at my request to other souls near me, and in distant lands. Yes, this is what prayer has done and is doing today. This is what it will far more abundantly do when God's children learn to believe the promise and take hold of His strength.

It is high time for the church to stop looking at prayer only in the light of our feebleness or our limited desires. We must begin to believe that God, in the mystery of prayer, has entrusted us with a force that can move the heavenly world and bring its power down to this earth. The prayers of 120 people at Pentecost brought down the power of the promised Spirit. When the church continues *"with one accord in prayer and supplication"* (Acts 1:14), the kingdom of heaven will again come down in power into the hearts and lives of people. This will be seen to an extent of which we have no conception at the present time.

The Proper Response

Oh, take time, children of God, and fall down in adoration in view of these four mysteries: the gift of the Holy Spirit, the infinite willingness of the Father to give Him, the blessed Son who is the channel, and the inconceivable power of the prayer of faith!

Let each of us ask and receive for himself. Yes, let us believe with our whole hearts that God gives, gives every day afresh, and gives in increasing power, His blessed Spirit to every child who asks in a right manner.

Let each of us believe in the power of prayer to bring the blessing to others. Let us cry to God continually that His children may learn to believe in His blessed promise and to live in the power of it.

As we think of what has been called "this Spiritless age," and the low state of spiritual life in the church, and the terrible need of the world, let us especially yield ourselves to the work of intercession. Let us allow the Holy Spirit to make us into believers who cry to God day and night until He pours out His blessed Spirit so that there is not enough room to receive Him. Let every prayer breathe the confident assurance, *"How much more shall your heavenly Father give the Holy Spirit to them that ask him?"* (Luke 11:13).

Seeking the Spirit

In *The Decisive Hour of Missions,* Dr. John Mott wrote,

The Reverend J. Goforth bears testimony that the results of the different evangelistic missions were in direct proportion to the extent the missionaries and Chinese Christians yielded themselves to God and sought the power of the Holy Spirit. He expresses the conviction that "if the church of Christ will humble itself under the hand of God, the Holy Spirit will confirm the preaching of the Word with unmistakable signs of His presence and power. I have the strongest of convictions that it would pay much, even manifold, for the church at home and abroad to cease for a season its busy round of activities and seek for the Holy Spirit's power as for hidden treasure. If we want to evangelize the world in our day, we must get back to the Pentecostal factor."

The church professes to believe that the Holy Spirit is the mighty power of God, that He will be given in answer to believing, persevering prayer, and that He will clothe His ministers with power from on high. Yet the church does not avail itself of this great promise and does not consider much prayer for the Holy Spirit as the first and all-important thing in the work of saving sinners. Is this not incomprehensible?

Our faith in the Holy Spirit is, to a great extent, simply intellectual. If it were not, we would count it our greatest privilege to ask and to receive the Holy Spirit in doing God's work. It would be impossible for us not to.

In order to do God's work, let us seek the power of the Holy Spirit.

Chapter 13

———————————◆•◆———————————

A Token of God's Displeasure

As we read in chapter two, the following words were spoken by Dr. Denney in reference to his own denomination. Unfortunately, these same words likewise apply to many other churches and many other denominations. I have expanded his comments in this chapter. Read his words carefully:

> I speak only of the denomination to which I myself belong, but something similar I believe is true of every church in Christendom. My denomination has 1700 congregations, and during the last five years the increase in its membership has been about 850 members. That is to say, every second congregation has added one member, and every other congregation has added none.

> The number of candidates for the ministry is much smaller at the present time than it was a good many years ago. It is hardly a sufficient number to keep up the staff at home, to say nothing of supplying workers abroad. People are not coming forward as ministers, nor are they coming forward as missionaries, because they are not coming forward into the membership of the Christian church at all. Something must happen to the church at home if it is going to even look at the work that has been put upon it [in foreign missions].

Just think of an insurance company, or any secular business, counting up the clients that it has gained through its agents during a year. What would it do if it received a report like the one the church has received? There would be an urgent order at once for a thorough investigation. Then there would be a review of all the methods and agents responsible for the decrease.

And what can be the reason in the church of Christ that this process of decrease has been allowed to go on? In his complete comments from which this excerpt was taken, Dr. Denney spoke of people who will not part with money or pleasure for the good of the church. Then he said, "I say the world is full of people like that, and what is worse, whoever is to blame for it, the church is full of them, too."

In every investigation in connection with a business undertaking, the aim is to lay the blame on the guilty one. Who is to blame here? The ministry as a whole? The individual ministers who are responsible for the decline? The congregations who, by their worldliness and lack of spiritual life, hinder the ministers? Or the governing bodies of the church because they have allowed things to come to such a crisis without sounding the alarm in the ears of the ministers and people?

We have asked questions that we do not know how to answer. Only God knows fully who is to blame. But God is willing to give us the courage and the honesty to find out and make confession, each on his own behalf, of what share we have had in this sad condition of the flock of Christ.

But apart from the question of blame, there is still the deeper question concerning the spiritual significance of the situation. What is the cause of the decline? Is it that the Gospel has not been faithfully preached? Is it, as some think, that higher criticism is beginning to do its work? Higher criticism is a method of biblical interpretation that has been used by some to critique the Scriptures from the standpoint of human reasoning, while at the same time discounting the Bible's inerrancy and inspiration. This method has been used for years, but in religious matters, it takes more than a generation for error to work out its evil consequences.

Is it, perhaps, that Christ is preached, that the doctrine is sound, but that the Gospel is preached with persuasive words of human wisdom and not in demonstration of the Spirit and power?

Or is it simply that worldliness and selfishness, along with the pleasure-seeking and money-loving spirit, have so poisoned the whole atmosphere that the Holy Spirit cannot reach through to win young hearts for Christ and His service? Can it be that churches have a reputation for being alive when they are truly dead (Rev. 3:1)? Is the whole church suffering from a low vitality that is not deep or intense or living enough to attract people to Christ and His service?

There is still another question that leads us deeper into the real condition of things: what does God think of it? When Joshua saw Israel defeated before its enemies, he felt at once that it was a sign that God had withdrawn His presence from His people. And God confirmed his thought: *"Israel hath sinned....Neither will I be with you any more, except ye destroy the accursed* [thing] *from among you"* (Josh. 7:11–12).

The decline in membership has this most solemn aspect—it is a token of God's displeasure. The promise by which the church alone can live, of the power of His Holy Spirit and His grace working with His servants, is not fulfilled. He has turned away His face in grief and great sorrow. That is the meaning of the dearth of conversions.

The church may rejoice in what it considers all the tokens of God's favor in the past. However, the lack of conversions and spiritual power is the sure sign that He has withdrawn the real proof of His presence—His saving power in the conversion of sinners. God, who answered Joshua when he fell on his face at the loss of God's presence, will come near to us as we wait for Him, and He will reveal the cause of our defeat.

And now, the last and the crucial question: what is to be done? The years have been allowed to pass by without any definite, full, and final dealing with the question. God waits to hear what we have to say and what we propose to do to put away the evil from us. This must happen before there can be any hope of our restoration to the position of a church in which He can dwell and work mightily for the honor of His name.

In the past, we had such high expectations of an increase in power for carrying on God's work. Yet now, God comes and reveals what little power we have, and how much we are lacking the one thing that Christ longs for and the angels rejoice in—the salvation of souls.

Let us turn to God, each one for himself. Let us ask Him to give us the spiritual insight into the true state of things that we need so much. When you pray, ask Him for the spirit of penitence that has been so lacking. Ask for the spirit of faith, a strong and living faith, that takes hold of Him and will not let Him go until He blesses us.

Allow me to end this chapter with the words of the Reverend C. Bardsley:

> How can we impress the mind of the church as a whole? The rank and file of the Christian church needs to grasp the truth that the evangelization of the world is the primary task, the central duty of the church. This will never happen, however, until a more definite lead in a more definite manner is given by the leadership of the church.
>
> How can they give that lead? First, they must be possessed of the truth themselves. They must be obviously full of this truth. They must be absolutely enthusiastic and deadly earnest themselves.
>
> Second, they must give opportunities to their people for intercession and praise for foreign missions. How much regular intercession and praise for foreign missions is there in the regular worship of our churches?
>
> Third, if evangelization is indeed the greatest task, it should dominate the gatherings of the church leaders

whenever they come together to consider the things of the kingdom of God. There are other matters of importance, but not as important. Let us put first things first when we are gathered together.

Chapter 14

---◆---

Contrition, Confession, Consecration

I have taken the title for this chapter from an article in a missionary magazine. The article gave an account of the powerful working of God's Spirit at a certain revival. In this revival, people who had been Christians for a long time were brought by the Holy Spirit into true brokenness of heart and penitence for sins in their Christian lives. When the contrition had fully mastered them, they confessed before both God and man what they had done. Faith that their confession was accepted gave them courage for a new consecration of mingled joy and trembling.

Does this story not teach us a lesson? Where God's children are brought face-to-face with a great evil that has been allowed in the church, His Holy Spirit will work the same deep contrition and penitent confession in answer to prayer. Without this confession, there can be no hope of restoration to full pardon or to true consecration.

The twofold charge against the church, that of neglecting its own members and neglecting the unbelievers entrusted to it, does indeed call for the deepest contrition. Somewhere along the way, there must have been a lack of watchfulness and prayer. There must have been a lack of spiritual life and power in the congregations concerned. There must have been, on the part of ministers—they will be the first to acknowledge it—a lack of the devotion and faith and prayer that would have faced the evil before it had attained such proportions.

The great thought that we must comprehend is the dishonor and the grief that we have caused God. He has been grieved by the neglect of the lost ones, by the reproach resting on the church of His beloved Son, and by the terrible thwarting of His strong desire to bless the world through the church.

Spiritual truth like this cannot be grasped by the natural mind. It is by God's Spirit alone that it can get full possession of our hearts. What is more, it takes time alone with God in order for Him to breathe and then to deepen the spirit of contrition. It takes turning away from the world and its numberless interests and waiting on God to bow and bend our hearts. Contrition must become such a reality that we feel something of the pain of a broken heart and offer this sacrifice to God as a felt, living reality. Where such contrition has been worked by the Spirit, He whose name is holy will come to dwell. He will dwell with him who has a contrite and humble heart.

Such contrition must first be found in secret, at least by some who mourn before God for their own state and the state of the church around them. However, then they will desire to help others. The church is a living body; each member cares for and suffers with the others. The contrite person will find like-minded believers to cultivate and strengthen this spirit of penitence and humility. By the grace of God, the gracious influence will spread. Ministers will begin to properly express God's claims and promises.

Let us ask God with our whole hearts to give the spirit of true, deep, abiding contrition to all who seek it. As we think of all the sins that are implied by this decrease of membership, we will feel the need of the conviction of the Holy Spirit to bring us into the right attitude before God. There are the sins of bloodguiltiness, of unfaithfulness in the discharge of our duty, of unbelief in not trusting God for His grace, of negligence in prayer and fellowship with God—all calling for deep humiliation.

After contrition comes confession. There is, I am sorry to say, a religion in which the confession of sin is too easy. People think that it is a matter of course that we sin, and they are sure that, if we only confess, God is ready to pardon.

This is not the confession God's Word speaks of. *"Whoso confesseth and forsaketh* [his sins] *shall have mercy"* (Prov. 28:13). That alone is the repentance that does not need to be repented of. As someone has said, "True repentance has restoring power; it never leaves you in the place in which you were."

Confession and forsaking sin make up true contrition, and this is why it is so hard for an honest person to confess his sin. He knows that God expects him to confess and forsake. But where contrition has been deep and true, the Christian will find that it is impossible for him to confess without forsaking.

Sin is very awful and God-dishonoring. It is not a simple or an easy thing to truly confess it. It means a transaction with God in which the sin is brought out, dealt with, and given up to God in the faith that He is righteous to forgive our sins and to cleanse us from all unrighteousness (1 John 1:9). Again, I say, nothing but the deep contrition that the Holy Spirit works can prepare us for true and full confession and forsaking.

Once this has been done in secret before God, then it is time to do it before man, too. However, the order may sometimes be reversed. In a group, under the moving of the Holy Spirit, the confession of one or more may help to rouse others to follow the example. But there is always a danger in this of superficiality. This is safe only if people are led from public confession to the inner chamber of their hearts, not to rest until they know that God has met them and accepted from them the sacrifice of a broken heart. Everything depends on knowing that there has been a definite transaction between God and the soul. This will give public confession its value and will help stir and strengthen others to follow in the same path.

Above all, full confession is what will give confidence for a full and entire consecration. A group of church leaders had this to say: "God is demanding of us all a new order of life, of a more arduous and self-sacrificing nature than the old." They added that we must "face the new task with a new consecration." Where the contrition and confession that I have spoken of have been full and true, a full and true consecration becomes possible, or rather, becomes a necessity to the penitent heart.

There are various ways of describing the terms of consecration. Keswick has one. Dr. Mott has another. Our godly fathers had their own. They had a deep reverence for God. They knew what it was to give themselves up to His will and to live lives of devoted service and holy fellowship with Him.

Thousands of Christians long to be helped to such a life, but they cannot understand how it can come about. May God raise up believers in the pulpit and in the pew who can testify to their fellow believers that Christ can keep strong the soul that trusts Him. He will not only keep him strong, but enable him to walk in His presence all the day!

The church needs to be lifted up out of its feebleness into the abundant life of Christ. But this can happen only if ministers and other believers take a new stand of separation from sin and the world, yielding themselves in a fuller surrender than ever before to follow Christ and live for Him alone. A revival among God's children cannot even be thought of unless the average standard of religion with which we have been content is replaced. This mediocrity must make way, through the power of faith and the Holy Spirit, for a much more tender walk with Christ and a much more complete yielding of our whole beings upon the altar of sacrifice.

Can it be that God is going to do this? Consider the shame and humiliation with which many ministers have looked at the result of their work. Consider the many church members who have confessed their share in the low vitality and feeble spirituality that had so much to do with it. Can it be that God will bring a wonderful blessing out of this? He is most willing to work contrition, accept confession, and strengthen for consecration.

And will He do it? That rests with us. The thought is unspeakably solemn, but the situation is just as solemn. He waits, He longs, He is working to draw His children to Himself. Oh, do not hesitate to bow before Him and listen to His voice: *"Not for your sakes do I this, saith the Lord God, be it known unto you: be ashamed and confounded for your own ways, O house of Israel"* (Ezek. 36:32).

Let us not wait for others to begin. If you have experienced any touch of God's Spirit as you have read and thought about the present crisis, if you have had any desire to pray that the mighty power of the Holy Spirit will breathe on the church, begin at once. Plead with God for His almighty grace, and do not rest until you know that, as a contrite penitent, your consecration has been accepted and sealed. Then go out as a living witness to help to bring Christ's call of repentance to the ears of His people. Lead all who will listen to the place of decision and full consecration.

Chapter 15

━━━━━━━━━ ►◆◄ ━━━━━━━━━

Repent!

The book of Revelation contains the letters to the seven churches of Asia Minor. In these letters we have a series of pictures of the conditions of several ministers and their people. They have been taken by Him whose eyes are like a flame of fire, searching out and showing forth the actual state of the church. Out of His mouth goes a sharp sword, for what He sees He speaks of in words of such divine power that they can touch the heart. After the many centuries that have passed, these words can still meet the needs of the churches of our day and work in us all that He teaches and commands.

The book of Revelation was written many years after Christ's ascension to heaven. Christ had finished His teaching on earth and had left the further instruction of His disciples to the apostles. Then, after keeping silence for more than half a century, Christ again desired to give some last words to the church on earth. What a solemn thought!

We have these words in the second and third chapters of Revelation. In them, Christ tells us what the smaller portion of the church is like. This part of the church pleases Him. Then He tells us what the majority is like. They are not what they should be. Christ gives the teaching for ministers to use to plead with the majority to return to Him as their Lord.

One of the central words in these letters is the word *repent.* There are only two letters, those to Smyrna and Philadelphia, in which the word *repent* does not appear. Of these two churches the Lord had only good to say. To Smyrna He said, "I know your tribulation and your poverty, but you are rich. Fear not!" (See Revelation 2:9–10.) To Philadelphia He said, *"Thou hast a little strength, and hast kept my word, and hast not denied my name....Because thou hast kept the word of my patience, I also will keep thee"* (Rev. 3:8, 10).

I praise God that there are churches on earth in which the majority satisfy the heart of the Son of God!

Then we have the letter to Thyatira, in which the word *repent* occurs, although not as an address to the minister of the church. There was much to be praised: *"I know thy works, and charity, and service, and faith, and thy patience, and thy works; and the last* [works] *to be more than the first"* (Rev. 2:19). But there was one evil: the woman Jezebel was allowed to spread her evil influence. God had given her time to repent, but she did not repent.

And then come four churches in which the word *repent* is used in the singular; in other words, it is addressed to the minister as well as the people. To Ephesus, after mentioning eight things in which they had proved their discipleship, He said, *"I have* [this] *against thee, because thou hast left thy first love"* (Rev. 2:4).

In all the highest relationships of life, love is everything. Between a mother and a child, a husband and a wife, a king and his people, love is the chief thing. And so it is between us and Christ. There may be diligence in His service, there may be zeal for the honor of His name, there may be patient endurance of suffering for Him, and yet Christ's heart can be satisfied with nothing less than the first love. This love is the compelling love that delights in His fellowship, yielding itself wholly to His personal influence and giving a living testimony about Him.

Amid all the activities of the church at Ephesus, true, tender love for Christ was lacking. It is about this that Christ said,

"Remember therefore from whence thou art fallen, and repent, and do the first works" (Rev. 2:5).

As we think of the failure of the church of our day in regard to making Christ known and its utter unfitness for taking up the work to which it is now being led, do we not here find the secret cause of it all, the lack of personal love for Christ? And does not the word of the Lord come to us, too: *"Repent...or else I will come unto thee quickly, and will remove thy candlestick out of his place, except thou repent"* (v. 5)?

To Pergamos He said, *"I have a few things against thee"* (v. 14). Their sin was that they tolerated false teachers. His word to them was *"repent"* (v. 16).

It is often said that higher criticism and its advanced teaching has much to do with the loss of power in our preaching and the lack of an earnest Christian life among believers. In chapter four of this book, I quoted a writer who said, "In many of our churches the great underlying doctrines and facts of the Gospel are scarcely ever referred to in preaching." He went on to say, "A personal appeal to the conscience and a direct effort for conversion are seldom witnessed."

I have heard more than one public testimony regarding the lack of the full and fearless preaching of Christ and His cross. Even those who are sound in doctrine themselves are still too silent in regard to exposing preaching that they know cannot satisfy the church's need or exercise divine power to salvation. Christ's command to repent is a call to us to evaluate whether our teaching is truly the proclamation of the message of God's inspired Word, or whether it seeks to please men by its excellency of speech and persuasive words of human wisdom.

To Sardis He said, *"I know thy works, that thou hast a name that thou livest, and art dead"* (Rev. 3:1). He then said, in essence, "I have found no works of yours completed before My God. Remember how you have received and repent."

Dr. Denney, in his address from which I have already quoted, spoke of many people who are *"lovers of pleasures more than lovers of God"* (2 Tim. 3:4). They refuse to give up anything for Christ's sake. I will repeat his words here: "I say the world is full of people like that, and what is worse, whoever is to blame for it, the church is full of them, too. As far as these people are concerned, the Christian religion is dead."

What an awful description—a church full of such people! And it was of this condition that Christ said, *"Thou hast a name that thou livest, and art dead"* (Rev. 3:1). It is to such a church today that Christ's first word is *"repent"* (v. 3).

To Laodicea He said,

> *I know thy works, that thou art neither cold nor hot.... Thou sayest, I am rich, and increased with goods, and have need of nothing; and knowest not that thou art wretched, and miserable, and poor, and blind, and naked.*
> (vv. 15, 17)

Do we not have here a true picture of a great many of our churches and our Christians—neither cold nor hot, but lukewarm, with *"a form of godliness, but denying the power thereof"* (2 Tim. 3:5), seeking and succeeding according to their own minds, uniting the friendship of God with the friendship of the world? As a result, the spirit of self-satisfaction and mutual self-congratulation is heard everywhere, with its deep undertone, "[We are] *rich, and increased with goods, and have need of nothing."* And Christ answers solemnly, "[Thou] *knowest not that thou art wretched."*

How does Christ deal with these lukewarm, self-satisfied Christians? He has, again, just that same solemn word for them, *"Repent"* (Rev. 3:19). Whatever the evil is, there is but one gate out of it—that hard, stern, but blessed word, *repent.*

Just think for a moment of the four churches that have been mentioned.

In Ephesus, the problem was a lack of love. Compelling love for Christ was no longer found.

In Pergamos, it was a lack of truth. They had forsaken the inspired Word. They tolerated the teaching of error.

In Sardis, the problem was a lack of life. They had a reputation that they were alive, but they were actually dead.

In Laodicea, it was a lack of fire. The baptism of the Spirit and of fire was no longer known.

Whatever the sin of a church may be, however closely the minister and people may be bound together in sin, Christ in heaven has one message, *"Repent."*

Think of what that means, coming from Him who gave His life to win our hearts for Himself. He is now seated on the throne in order to give repentance. He pleads with us by His cross and His blood. He seeks to touch the heart and break it with that love of His. With a voice of infinite holiness and tenderest compassion, He pleads with those whom His heart-searching words have warned and roused—just that one word, *repent.*

This is the word that He commissions the ministers of the churches to sound in the ears of His people, to bring near and to open up to them, to plead with them until they bow before it: *repent.*

He spoke the word, first of all, to the minister of the church himself. Whether he had been found lacking in love for Christ or in the truth of Christ or in the life of Christ or in the fire of Christ, He called him to repentantly come and receive His pardon and the new experience of His blessing and power. He then sent him forth to sound out with his whole heart the note of warning and of welcome: "Repent, O my people, repent."

We are accustomed to using the word *repent* in our missionary work or in ordinary evangelistic preaching. However, the ministers to whom Christ has committed the oversight of the churches—and the decline of membership proves what a lack of power there has been in their preaching and spiritual lives—are called to take up the word *repent* in its deeper meaning.

The church of Christ is on the decline. In the seven churches of Revelation, we have examples of the various

stages of spiritual decline in our churches today, and their impli-
cations. In the Ephesus stage, the defection begins with the
loss of the first love, even amid great zeal for the truth. In the
Pergamos stage, we discover a step lower: God's Holy Word is
no longer taken as the only standard of teaching. In the Sardis
stage, the evil becomes still more manifest: with a reputation for
being alive, the church is dead. In the Laodicea stage, it reaches
its full growth: people are so utterly unconscious of anything
wrong, so satisfied with themselves and with each other, so
blind to what Christ calls their wretchedness and nakedness,
that they proudly boast in their meetings and reports: *"Rich,
and increased with goods, and hav[ing] need of nothing"* (Rev.
3:17).

What a work it is for the ministers of the churches to take
that word *repent* from Christ's own lips while on their knees, to
bow to it with their whole hearts, and then in the power of His
Spirit to carry it throughout the church as the one great means
of revival and restoration!

Let no one think, "This message is too hard. Who can bear
it?" Listen to what Christ says of it: *"As many as I love, I rebuke
and chasten: be zealous therefore, and repent. Behold, I stand
at the door, and knock: if any man hear my voice, and open the
door, I will come in"* (vv. 19–20).

Do not be afraid, O minister of God, to sound the word
repent loudly and clearly. It is Christ's infinite love that speaks
the word, that will give the blessing with it, that will reveal Himself to His penitent people. Out of the fullness of a living faith in
the love of Christ, call believers to repent in the assurance of His
welcome and His blessing.

Christ closes each of these seven letters with these words:
*"He that hath an ear, let him hear what the Spirit saith unto
the churches"* (Rev. 2:7, 11, 17, 29; 3:6, 13, 22). Let the minister
of Christ take these words into the depth of his heart. Let him
pray and believe until he is sure the blessed Spirit is speaking
through him. Let him tell the church that the power of the Spirit
is working to reveal Christ and His love. And let him from this

point forward carry on Christ's work as never before. Let him be assured that, in answer to much prayer, the mighty power of the Spirit will secretly work and will restore God's children in the path of repentance to a new and more abundant life. Then, there will no longer be any reason to complain of the decline in membership or of a lack of loyalty to Christ and His service.

Chapter 16

———— ◆ ————

The Valley of Decision

*T*hese questions are often asked by believers: "What is it about certain Christian meetings that so influences people? What brings the power that is not felt in the ordinary services of the same speaker?" The answers are found in the fact that people are invited to come to the meetings with a definite need. Then they are helped toward a definite step for the fulfillment of that need.

Is this not the great secret of the success of our evangelists? They occupy people intensely and continually with the thought of their need of salvation and the possibility of their obtaining it at once. It is the same way in conferences on the spiritual life. People who feel burdened by the thought of their continual sinning and their powerlessness in seeking victory are invited to come and hear how deliverance can be obtained. The speaker's emphasis on making the right decision is the key. By this, he influences people to do and to be what they ought.

The same secret of success in preaching the Gospel can be found in other spheres. It is especially seen in the Students Christian Association. All who have heard Dr. John Mott or some other leader in the work know how the emphasis is placed on immediate decision. Years ago, Dr. Mott did a remarkable work among the students of Edinburgh. In his whole appeal to the will, the students were made to feel a contagious influence that gave them courage to hope for deliverance. His was not a teaching that people were to take home and think about. Some may have done so, but with most of them, help was found in Dr. Mott's confident emphasis on the real possibility of a present and immediate change.

This was the same emphasis that ran through all his work among Christian students. He pleaded for an irrevocable surrender to the vow of spending at least half an hour every morning with God. This caused many to give up habits of laziness and self-indulgence and, as a result, to consecrate the whole day to the service of God. It was on this account that he so often used the following words, both in speaking and writing:

> Next to the act of conversion, in which a man turns from sin to God, and after that, of the reception of the Holy Spirit as the power of a new life, I know of nothing that will aid a man so much in the Christian life as the undiscouragable resolution to spend at least half an hour in the morning alone with God.

The apparently simple act of the will in making the decision meant nothing less than a full surrender to live for God and His will.

It was that same call for decision that appealed so mightily and successfully for volunteers for the foreign mission field. This truth was underscored: Christ's command to preach the Gospel to every individual is a command to every disciple. The preacher preached this with all the urgency of a man who himself had yielded his whole being to Christ's service. Then an appeal was made to all who were truly willing to show their full allegiance to Christ. They were challenged to say whether there was any reason that they should not accept His call at once.

In *The Life of Douglas Thornton,* we read how he and a friend went out after a meeting into a field under the open heavens in perfect agony about this burden that was being laid on them. They did not rest until they had the courage to make a full surrender.

In the same book, we get a glimpse of the activities of Thornton and other totally committed men during a missionary conference in Liverpool. They threw themselves into the work of prayer and influencing others. Under the deep conviction that they had actually given themselves to Christ to receive in prayer His guidance and power, they proved what it meant to live wholly for the kingdom.

Dr. Mott has said that the book that has influenced him most in his life is John Foster's *Decision of Character.* The word *decision* is characteristic of his whole work and of that of his fellow workers in the great volunteer movement.

George Sherwood Eddy was a missionary and a delegate to the World Missionary Conference. He gave his testimony concerning the secret of his power:

> I remember fifteen years ago, before going to India, sitting down with my roommate, now in China, and saying to him, "What are we going to tell them out there on the field? What message have we got for people? Are we merely going to tell them about Christ? If so, it would be cheaper to send out Bibles and tracts. Can we tell them that we know Jesus Christ saves and satisfies, that He keeps us more than conquerors day by day?"
>
> I went on to say, "I am not satisfied. I do not feel that I have a message such as I need for people out there, or the experience, or the power. If we do not have these, do you not agree that the one great thing we need before we leave this country is to know Him?"
>
> From that day to the end of our student days, we rose every morning at five o'clock. From five to six we had an unhurried hour for the Word of God, and from six to seven an unhurried hour for prayer. These two hours each day changed our lives, and we were unspeakably blessed.

That valley of decision was to them truly the valley of blessing. And God has set His seal to it in the fruit of Mr. Eddy's work.

It is this note of decision that is too often lacking in our evangelical preaching. It is this note that will be greatly needed if slumbering or weak but well-meaning Christians are truly to be roused. People are content when they hear what they think is a profitable message. They carry away the impression that the message has made on them, and they hope that in some way or other an effect will be produced. And still they go on in that half-hearted religion, which they confess is wrong but which they cannot find the power to reject.

If God's Spirit begins to truly move in the church, the preaching will need an emphasis on decision that we have little known. The hearer must feel that he is called to face a crisis. He is to say whether or not he is really going to yield to Christ's claim and surrender his heart and life to His service. By the grace of God, the minister must seek to get hold of the hearer and not let him go until the decision is made.

Why have I written all this? I feel deeply that unless a call for believers to immediately repent is sounded throughout the church, unless they are reassured that they can be restored to a life of devotion to Christ, there is no prospect of a true response to Christ's claim.

The passages in chapter two about the powerlessness of the church and the disloyalty of Christians to their Savior ring in my ears. How I wish that every thoughtful, prayerful friend of missions could embrace these words and devote himself to comprehending their full meaning. Surely the questions would then come with tremendous urgency: "Can anything be done to bring Christians to a sense of their shame? Can they be brought to desire the restoration of that spirit of loyalty and devotion without which Christianity is just a form?"

Are we to look to the ministers to lead people to a conviction of what is wrong in their Christian lives, to a desire for what is better, to a faith in the possibility of an entire change in all who are willing to receive it? If so, we must have ministers in whom the Spirit of God works a faith in the power of Christ, a faith that will enable them to inspire their hearers with an entirely new hope.

And where are these ministers to be found? Surely there must be many whose hearts burn with the passion of Jesus Christ for mankind. But many are not conscious of the power God can exert through them. If they truly come to know the power of Jesus Christ to keep them loyal and true, they will have a message that will certainly reach some hearts.

Let loyalty to Christ—full, unflinching, wholehearted loyalty—become the keynote of their praying and their preaching. Let a few band themselves together to ask God for this one thing—full insight into the terrible condition of a church in which so few members are won to Christ by the preaching of the Word. Let them offer themselves to God for a new baptism of His Spirit and a new power to preach about the Day of the Lord and about His presence in the midst of His people.

Let them not rest until they begin to gather together, however few they may be, souls who are willing to be living witnesses that Jesus Christ does indeed save from the power of selfishness and the world. He does indeed enable ordinary men and women to live with His life so much in their hearts that the conquest of the world for Him is the greatest reality, the all-absorbing purpose, of their lives and their love.

Teachers of psychology and ethics tell us that the first step in breaking the power of an old habit or in cultivating an entirely new one is to take the initiative with full purpose of heart. Everything should be done, by pledge or public confession, to break away at once from the old and to commit oneself with no room for compromise. They say that the application of this principle will give, in many cases, the needed help to those who otherwise despair of deliverance.

This plan is just what is needed by the preacher who comes to call weak, sluggish Christians to a new life of loyalty and devotion. If believers can be brought to confess the error of their position, and their powerlessness to make it right, to believe that Christ by His Spirit can strengthen them to escape from the bondage in which they have been serving self and the world, they will find the courage to take the decisive step. Faith that Christ is able to keep them in a close relationship with Himself, which makes a life of consecration possible and most blessed, will enable them to step out in full surrender to His mighty power. The church will see what wonders God can do in those who wait on Him.

Let us simply have witnesses, in the pulpit or out of it, in whom the power of a living testimony sounds the notes of victory. Then we will find that God is faithful to give revival where otherwise all had been hopeless.

It is in the valley of decision that such preachers and such witnesses are found. It is in the valley of decision, that is, the valley of judgment, that a man feels utterly condemned and yet takes courage to believe in what Christ can make of him. There the church will find the secret of its lost power. It will find courage for a surrender to Christ and His service that seeks to know of no other standard than that of the love in which He gave Himself for us.

"Multitudes, multitudes in the valley of decision" (Joel 3:14). That will be the prayer of many. But please understand that we may not wait until multitudes are there. Let each one who hears the call of God go down, even if he is all alone, into the valley of decision, and yield himself as a willing sacrifice into His hands.

Chapter 17

---◆---

The Ministry

I feel that I have come to the most important and the most difficult chapter of this book. I cannot help thinking that a special appeal to ministers would rouse much thought and prayer. Under a deep sense of my insufficiency for the task of speaking to my fellow preachers, I will try to express the message that this book brings to the minister.

The first thought is the heavy responsibility that rests on the minister. We have been reading of the failure of the church and of the low state of spiritual life that is the cause of its failure. All this is, first of all, an appeal to the ministry. It comes with the question, Why is it that things are in such poor shape, and what is to be done to remedy the situation? Many church leaders lay the responsibility on the ministry. Take a look at the thoughts of some of them:

> As far as the interest of the church in missions is concerned, the minister holds the key to the situation.
>
> In the work of the ministers is found the secret of the real condition existing in the church.
>
> Invariably, a missionary pastor makes a missionary church.

There is no doubt that in order to rouse the church to a sense of its opportunity and privilege, the clergy must be reached and their enthusiastic cooperation secured.

On ministers, more than on all others, falls the duty of educating the church about its missionary calling and of supplying the people with the enthusiasm that will make the church equal in spiritual power to the present world situation.

Are we prepared to admit and accept this tremendous responsibility? Will we confess our share in the church's failure and yield ourselves, by the grace of God, at every sacrifice, to fulfill our task?

How is it possible that the majority of ministers have never realized what their duty is, or, when it was put before them, did not have the power and the courage to fulfill it? In answer to that question, we are reminded that the church as a whole must share the blame. It has never, through its theological colleges, trained its young students to fulfill this part of their high calling. Yes, it has tried to encourage ministers and members who are interested in missionary work to exercise all their influence. However, it has never clearly and strongly declared the truth that every minister and every member is to live and labor so that Christ may be made known to every living individual. These colleges have not trained ministers to carry out this task.

However, this explanation does not relieve us from the responsibility that God has put on us, and which He would have taught us, had we known what it is to live in continual prayer for His teaching. But this is another great defect of our theological training: how little we were taught that, in the true ministry, prayer is the first and most essential thing. It was not that our professors did not sometimes remind us of the need for prayer, but it was taken for granted that we knew how to pray and did pray.

Not long ago, I was told about two ministers who were talking on the subject, mourning that in their college training they had not been taught to acquire the secret of prayer. One said, "It is not that the subject was not mentioned, but it was not impressed upon us that prayer is the first secret of success in the ministry." The patterns of student life are naturally carried forward into the ministry, and we find it so hard to acquire the habit of truly effective prayer amid all the study and work that occupies our time.

Yet it is just in this matter of prayer that the responsibility lies on us so heavily. If we are to do our part, if we are to train our people to yield themselves to Christ's claim, we must, above all, learn to pray.

> How to multiply the number of Christians who with clear, unshakable faith in the character of God will wield this force of intercession—that is the supreme question of foreign missions. Every other consideration is secondary to that of wielding the forces of prayer.

> The primary need is not the multiplication of prayer meetings, but that individual Christians should learn to pray.... Every endeavor must be made to spread the spirit and habit of prayer among all Christian workers.

What a responsibility rests on the minister in the matter of his own intercession and in the training of God's people to take part in it!

I have spoken of the lack in our training, as theological students, of enthusiasm for missions and the power of intercession. I feel that I must mention something that goes still deeper. You have read more than once in this book that the lack of interest in missions and of devotion in prayer can be traced to the feeble vitality, to the low spiritual life, prevailing in the church. And it is just this that many ministers never learn at college: that the power to pray, and the power to teach others to pray, is entirely dependent on the depth of one's spiritual life.

Did our Lord Jesus not say, *"If ye abide in me, and my words abide in you, ye shall ask what ye will, and it shall be done unto you"* (John 15:7)? Many believers have resolved to pray more, but have failed, because they did not know this secret, that the average Christian life is not sufficient to provide power with God in prayer. It requires self-denial, a turning away from the world, and the sacrifice of what may appear legitimate to others. A heart that is given up to God and longs to be led by the Holy Spirit is needed if one is to claim all the wonderful promises in God's Word connected with prayer.

Listen once again to a passage from a church leader:

> The superhuman must be emphasized as never before since the days of the early church. Christians need a fuller, more constant, and more commanding realization of the personal presence of Christ.

That means there must be the experience of a closer daily fellowship with Him than is ordinarily thought possible. Read these two reminders:

> Conferences have been held where the work of world evangelization has received careful consideration, but there has been alarming neglect in facing the great central problem, namely, how to translate into actual experience these words of Christ: *"He that abideth in me, and I in him, the same bringeth forth much fruit: for without me ye can do nothing"* (v. 5).

> The missionary problem of the church today is not primarily a financial problem. The problem is how to ensure a vitality equal to the expansion of the missionary program. The only hope of this is for Christians to obtain the more abundant life through Christ.

Everything returns to this question: does the church have sufficient vitality for the tremendous task to which it is called? That sufficient vitality is what the ministers need first of all if they are to lead the church to it. On the ministers rests the responsibility of lifting the church up out of its feeble vitality into the abundant life that there is in Christ Jesus.

What a responsibility! *"Who is sufficient for these things?"* (2 Cor. 2:16). *"Our sufficiency is of God; who also hath made us able ministers...of the spirit"* (2 Cor. 3:5–6). God never lays responsibility on His servant without the assurance of sufficient grace for all that He expects him to be. Let this thought turn the sense of responsibility into prayer. And let all that we have learned about the absolute necessity and the limitless possibilities of prayer just lead us to cast ourselves upon God, in the confidence that He will equip us for the place that we are being called upon to take in the world conquest.

You remember the instance I gave in chapter sixteen, "The Valley of Decision," of the decision of two young students to give an hour each day to prayer. What do you think? Would it be too much for you to ask God for grace to spend half an hour, every day, in addition to your ordinary time, just to learn from Him the art of prayer and intercession? In that school you will get the necessary training for that power of prayer that will lead you into the abundant life of Christ as never before. Then you will be ready for the great work of lifting up the church into the same place of power and blessing.

With faith in God's promise, do not be afraid, but go down into the valley of decision. Let it be your firm resolve to spend that half hour with God in special prayer for your own need and the need of His church concerning the new consecration to the service of His kingdom. By the grace of God, the decision for that half hour may be a decision for a life of new devotion to God and His will.

The hesitation and self-reproach for unfaithfulness in the morning brings, unconsciously, a cloud all day. The decision to do God's will at any cost in the morning hour casts us upon Christ and makes the will strong for the whole day. And the decision for the day may give us courage for the next day and lead us on to a walk with God day by day.

What a responsibility rests on the ministers in this question of the feeble spiritual life of the church and in their commitment to pray to God to lift it out of its low state into the sunlight of His love.

Chapter 18

---◆◄---

A Plea for More Prayer

What a difference there is between the first mountain springs where a great river has its origin and the vast expanse of water where it reaches the sea and carries fleets of ships on its surface. Such, and even much greater, is the difference between prayer in the simplicity of its first beginnings and the incomprehensible mystery of what it becomes when it makes man a partner with God in the rule of the world. Instead of being the simple channel through which a child or a new convert obtains his request from God, it becomes the heavenly power that can channel all the riches of God and bring down the blessings of the Spirit on countless souls.

What a study prayer is! I do not know whether to thank God most for prayer in its blessed simplicity, in which it is the comfort of those who hardly ever go beyond their personal needs, or in its profound depths, in which it reveals to us how close and wonderful the union is between God and man.

I feel that I cannot end this book without once again attempting to point you to this latter aspect of it. I do so with fear and trembling. The thoughts are so wonderful and beyond our reach that I hardly venture to hope that I can make them plain. Yet, with God's help, I must make the attempt.

When God undertook the stupendous work of creating man after His own likeness, His great purpose was to have a being in whom He could perfectly reveal all the glory of His divine power. Man was to be here on earth what God is in heaven, the king and ruler. He was made in the image of God in this especially, that just as God is self-determined and is what He is by His own blessed will, so man also, as far as a creature dependent on God could do so, was to fashion his own character and being. Man was to prepare himself for the power of ruling others.

As we are told in Revelation 1:6, we have been made *"kings and priests unto God."* As priests, we turn our face godward to worship and receive His blessing. As kings, we turn manward to dispense that blessing in ruling and guiding others.

The great thought of God was to train man for the place that he is to have with Christ upon the throne. God's purpose was that man should rule in such a way that God would do nothing except through him, and that man should understand that he would do nothing except through God.

It is in this wonderful relationship that prayer has its mystery and its glory. God promises to give His Spirit and to exercise His power according to the will of man (when, of course, it is aligned with God's will). If man will avail himself of his high prerogative and fully yield himself to the Holy Spirit's teaching in regard to the will of God, God will make literally true what Christ promised: *"If ye abide in me, and my words abide in you, ye shall ask what ye will, and it shall be done unto you"* (John 15:7). The prayer of faith will remove mountains.

We are told that every aspect of nature seeks to clothe itself in a suitable body. The life in a tree creates for itself, in the fruit, the embodiment of its inmost nature. So it is with God, who is Spirit. The creation of man was not an afterthought, but part of His eternal purpose to reveal Himself completely throughout all creation.

The first step in that path was the creation of man out of the dust, in God's image and likeness. The next was the coming of the eternal Son to unite and forever identify Himself with human nature. Then followed Christ's resurrection from the dead and His ascension to heaven in His glorified humanity. And last of all came the outpouring of the Holy Spirit, by which the church became *"his body, the fulness of him that filleth all in all"* (Eph. 1:23). In that body Christ is to be revealed when He comes in glory, and in that body the Father will dwell in the Son. Throughout all eternity, man is to be the revelation of what God is, and through man Christ will rule the world.

It is in prayer that man takes his part even now in the rule of the world. As a preparation for his future glory, he, even now, in the holy priesthood of intercession, begins to understand what the inconceivable power of prayer can be. Prayer is the highest proof of the image of God in which we have been created. Prayer is the exercise of our kinglike privilege of ruling the world.

The point at which it becomes difficult for us to believe all this is when we are told that God is longing to pour out blessing but is prevented by His people. They are the hindrance. God allows His work to suffer loss, terrible loss, because He will not break the law He Himself made. He respects the liberty He Himself gave man. In infinite long-suffering, He bides His time until man becomes willing to pray and receive His blessing.

Let me repeat a thought from a previous chapter: We must make believers understand that it is only their halfhearted consecration and lack of faith that hinder the rapid advance of the work, only their own coldness that keeps back His redemption from a lost world. We must always bear in mind that He is eager and able to save the world, which has already been redeemed by Him. Alas, if only we, His professed followers on earth, were willing that He do so.

One would think that on hearing this people would say, "It is impossible. It cannot be true that millions are perishing because God's people are not praying." But it is true. However, it is a truth that the natural mind cannot grasp. It is only the Holy Spirit who can enlighten the heart to comprehend the spiritual reality of this wonderful partnership between God and His people in the salvation of the world.

One would ask, "How can the church be so foolish as to spend all its strength in doing a work that is comparatively a failure, that ends in a decline of membership, when it has the divine promise that in answer to prayer the power of the Holy Spirit can make the dry bones live?" There is no explanation but this: people hear the promise with the hearing of the ear, but the truth has no power over them. They simply do not yield themselves, in holy fellowship with God, to receive the Spirit and the Spirit-born conviction that prayer can bring down into their hearts the life that there is in Christ Jesus.

How often the complaint is heard that it is so hard to pray properly, to pray enough, to pray in power. The reason is simple: we think of prayer mainly as a means of getting blessing for ourselves. We think very little about yielding ourselves entirely to holy fellowship with God and to the self-denying sacrifice needed in bearing the needs of others.

We are hardly conscious of the fact that we are kings. No wonder we have so little confidence in our priestly access to God for the work of bringing down blessing on the world. A man's thoughts rule his actions; the ideas he fosters make his character. Oh, that God's children might take hold of the wonderful promise that whatsoever they ask in the name of Jesus, it will be done for them. (See John 14:13.) Oh, that they would learn to look upon themselves as God's chosen intercessors, the channels without whom His love cannot do its work. They may be sure that prayer will begin to have a new attraction and that fellowship with God will become their highest privilege.

I fear wearying my reader by the repetition of the chief thoughts of this book, yet these ideas are a plea for more prayer. Therefore, I will risk summing up once again what I think God wants us to consider:

The verdict of church leaders that the church is unwilling and unfit for doing the work God puts before it

The confession of the churches that they are powerless to keep hold of their members—the spirit of the world is too strong

The sad truth that both of these things are due to a lack of that spiritual life and power without which our work is in vain

The conviction that nothing but the power of God's Holy Spirit in our hearts and lives can cure the evil

The belief that God longs with all His heart to give His Spirit to the righteous person whose fervent prayer accomplishes much, so that He may lift His church to the life that it can have in Christ Jesus

As we study and pray over these thoughts, step by step, in God's presence, the mystery of prayer will open up to us. We will see that God has actually made us partners in the business, has made us kings and priests to dispense His blessings to a feeble church and a perishing world. We will hear a call to forsake that halfhearted, selfish, prayerless life in which we have lived, and to begin as intercessors to take our place before God. He assures us that He has put the renewal of the church into our hands, and that He will give to persevering, believing intercession the high honor of restoring His children to the life that He meant for them.

Let each of us take a prayer card and write on it the five points I have just mentioned. Let us think and pray over them until we realize that there is really something that needs to be prayed for. Let our hearts get so interested in the need that prayer becomes the spontaneous expression of our strong desire for God's blessing on His church.

Chapter 19

---◆---

Fear Not; Only Believe

Some people possess an easy optimism that they imagine to be faith in God. They think their easy optimism gives them the right and ability to claim every promise in God's Word. They do not understand how inseparably the words *repent* and *believe* are bound together. They have never learned that throughout Scripture a chief element in faith in God is a sense of powerlessness and utter helplessness.

I want to write here, as our book closes, about the place faith must have. We must give faith its place if we are to go forward with the certain hope that God's mighty power will be manifested in our own lives, in the church around us, and especially in our ministers. I am speaking of the power manifested as God works in us that deep, intense, living vitality that we are longing for.

In order to apply to ourselves Christ's words, *"Be not afraid, only believe"* (Mark 5:36), we must carefully note the attitude of the man to whom they were first given.

We find that Jairus was greatly troubled. His little daughter was at the point of death. He had fallen at Christ's feet and earnestly pleaded with Him to come and lay His hands on her. Jesus went with him. But all at once there was an interruption—a woman touched the hem of Christ's garment—and

Jairus feared that they may be too late. His worst fears were realized when messengers came to say, *"Thy daughter is dead: why troublest thou the Master any further?"* (Mark 5:35).

It was to this deeply distressed man, who had intensely implored Christ to come and was now brought to utter hopelessness by the news of his daughter's death, that He spoke the words, *"Be not afraid, only believe."* The soil had been broken up deeply. The heart was prepared to believe. Christ's precious word entered in and took possession.

Some of us are bearing the burden of a dead or a dying church. If we are going to take part in the work of rousing it and lifting it up into the abundant life that there is in Christ, we need nothing as much as a word like this. It will bring us the joyous assurance day by day that Christ is with us, that He will work through us, and that we can count on Him to give the blessing.

However, we must take the place that Jairus did, falling at His feet, greatly imploring Him to graciously and mightily intervene. Even when the news comes, "There is no hope; death reigns; all our efforts are in vain," we must still take courage and hold on to His Word. "Fear not; only believe" must be our motto. But it applies—I say it once again—only to the person who waits at Christ's feet in prayer and looks to Him alone. There we will learn that throughout all Scripture it is faith in the midst of seeming impossibility that waits and claims the fulfillment of the promise.

Think of Abraham, who *"was strong in faith, giving glory to God...being fully persuaded that, what he had promised, he was able also to perform"* (Rom. 4:20–21). As we persevere in prayer, take hold of definite promises, and earnestly appeal to Him to fulfill them, we will hold fast our confidence to the end through every obstacle.

We may find that as time goes on, as our insight into the deadly state of the church grows deeper, and as experience teaches us how very hard it is to rouse Christians to the full meaning of and to full surrender to the claims of Christ, our hearts will often grow faint and fail us for fear. Yet if we have made our covenant with Christ that we dare not go back, but are determined to hold on, we will find that just one word from our Lord, hidden in the heart and lived on day by day, will give strength in the time of greatest darkness.

Just think of the words of Christ in regard to what appears to man to be impossible. He had said of the young ruler, *"How hard is it for them that trust in riches to enter into the kingdom of God!"* (Mark 10:24). The disciples had asked, *"Who then can be saved?"* (v. 26). Christ's answer was, *"With men it is impossible,"* but He added, *"With God all things are possible"* (v. 27). And He said to the father of the demon-possessed child, *"All things are possible to him that believeth"* (Mark 9:23). These three sentences—*"With men it is impossible," "With God all things are possible,"* and, *"All things are possible to him that believeth"*—are a threefold cord that cannot be broken. (See Ecclesiastes 4:12.)

Impossible with Man

First, *"With men it is impossible."* It seems easy to say, and yet how difficult it is to realize it and act it out. What is it that hinders the church in this day from falling on its knees and pleading with God by His Holy Spirit to give revival? Nothing but this: people do not consider that the work that they must do is impossible for man. They consult, organize, and labor, oh, so diligently, and yet the members decline by the thousands. They cannot see that the work of winning people to become members of Christ and His church is a work that God alone can do through believers who have yielded themselves to the Holy Spirit. What a day it would be if the church were to fall down before God and bow in the dust with the cry: "O God, it is impossible with man."

Possible with God

We should then be prepared for the second lesson: *"But not with God: for with God all things are possible"* (Mark 10:27). At first sight this word also appears easy to accept. We are sure that there is nothing impossible with God. Yet when we ask whether God's servants really believe it, whether they wait on Him and expect His working with joyful confidence, we soon find out that they do not. How hard it is to get a deep impression of God's power and of His readiness to work out in us what He has called us to do. God is so little of a reality to us. How few take time with God so that the blessed sense of His holy presence can fill their hearts and strengthen them in their work.

Oh, all you who are beginning to take the state of the church to heart and to bear it as a burden before the Lord, do not be surprised if you have found it a hard thing. If you want to fully grasp the truth, *"With God all things are possible"* in regard to the purposes of your work and prayer, learn the lesson of bringing that blessed truth into contact with your daily work and prayer. Let its light shine into your heart, on your sphere of labor, on the church around you, and on the feeblest and most hopeless part of the church, until all your thoughts have this as their keynote: *"But not with God: for with God all things are possible"* (Mark 10:27). He is able to rouse the church out of its apathy and lift Christians into the abundant life.

He Who Believes

Now comes the third and most difficult lesson: *"All things are possible to him that believeth"* (Mark 9:23). It is something great to really believe that all things are possible with God, yet the soul may be troubled as to how and when that belief may come. This word of Christ throws the responsibility on us. It is to him who believes that God makes all things possible.

When Christ spoke that word to the father of the demon-possessed child, the man felt his responsibility so deeply, was so concerned that he might lack the necessary faith, that he cried out, *"Lord, I believe; help thou mine unbelief"* (v. 24). And Christ heard that prayer.

Our hearts may shrink back with the thought, "Is it going to depend on me whether this mighty God will do the impossible thing? I do not dare to bear the burden of this responsibility." But He is still waiting to strengthen our faith. Jesus Christ, the One who helped the father of the demon-possessed child, who said to Peter, *"I have prayed for thee, that thy faith fail not"* (Luke 22:32), who became man to bring us into fellowship with the omnipotent God, will give us the confidence to believe God. Jesus says, *"If ye abide in me, and my words abide in you, ye shall ask what ye will"* (John 15:7). Let us live in fellowship with the One who spoke these words. He will enable us to receive them until they become the joy and the strength of our hearts.

Able and Willing

If I have not given in this little book a deep impression of the church's great need of the Holy Spirit and His power, I have failed to fulfill my purpose. But I would fail even more if I were to part from you, my reader, without having helped you to this confident assurance: God is able and willing to work revival in answer to prayer and to fill the hearts of His children with a measure of the Holy Spirit that they have never known. As we look out upon a church that is feeble and faithless, let us listen to the voice of Jesus as He says, "Fear not; only believe."

What I have already said, I repeat here. The church around you may be in a dying state, with no possibility of being reached by human effort. I plead with you, look up to God. Wait before Him in prayer until stronger desire is stirred and faith rises to link itself to His omnipotence. Believe in the power of our Lord Jesus and in His tender relationship to you, as He watches over your faith. Believe in the power of the Holy Spirit, which is the promise of the Father and the birthright of the church. His power is surrounding you on every side and longing to get possession of you and those for whom you are praying. Let your review of the state of the church give you a knowledge of God and a trust in Him beyond what you have ever known or thought.

Chapter 20

———————◆———————

A Personal Word

We are about to part. Before we do so, I am most eager, if possible, to detain you and to ask you to come to a decision in regard to the great unsolved problem before the church.

This problem may be summarized in these words, which I quoted in chapter one: "The Christian experience of the church is not deep, intense, and living enough to meet the world's need." Also, in previous chapters of this book, I have given other quotations from various leaders, which emphasize the thought that the church lacks the vitality and devotion needed for the tremendous task to which it is called. The all-important question is this: how can the church be lifted up into a fuller spiritual life?

I boldly plead with you to ponder the question until you realize its tremendous solemnity and resolve that you will at least yield yourself as a living sacrifice for God to use for that great work. I ask every child of God to carefully consider the following thoughts.

Will you not take the time and thought and prayer to fully sense the terrible situation? Millions of people are still without the knowledge of Christ. The church has been created, set apart, and clothed with the Spirit for the one purpose of making Christ known to every human being without delay. But the great majority of Christians are utterly indifferent to this. A considerable number are apparently willing to help, but they are utterly unconscious of the urgency of the need or the solemn responsibility resting on them. Only a small number are seeking to yield themselves to fulfill their Lord's command at any cost.

God in heaven holds His omnipotence at the disposal of the faith and prayer of His people, but He is hindered by their unbelief. And Christ the Lord is grieved, oh, so grieved, because His love is so little known and honored by His people, and so little made known to those whom He longs to reach.

I ask you, will you not turn aside from the world and from people to take up this burden of the Lord? Will you wait on God to see if He will use you to help His church to some proper sense of shame and contrition for all this sinful neglect? I know no other way of restoration than for individual men and women to begin by pleading with God on behalf of the church, and by pleading with men on behalf of God. I plead with you, pointedly and personally, will you be one?

You may feel as if you do not have the enthusiasm or the faith for such an undertaking. You are not conscious that you have power with God as an intercessor. You fear that you may not be faithful in fulfilling your vow or in attaining that more abundant life to which you are asked to help lift the church.

I beg you, do not give way to such thoughts. Only one thing is needed: Are you willing to yield yourself up to God so that His Holy Spirit may get entire possession of you? This is surely what every Christian ought to seek. Review chapter twelve, "The Promise of the Father." Give time and heart to meditate on the wonderful mysteries: the Holy Spirit of God given to fill you with a divine life; the heavenly Father inconceivably willing to give the gift; the blessed Lord ready to teach you to pray and to lead you in the path that He took, through the death of the cross to the fullness of the Spirit; and your prayer, which can work the mighty wonder and bring the fullness of the Spirit.

Just follow the examples that Christ gives in Luke 11: a simple child trusting a father, a needy man persistently pleading with a friend. See if God will not pour out a blessing. Oh, remember that if you fail, you will be keeping open the path in which others fail, too. If you are strong and courageous, God will certainly use you to help others.

I know no other solution to the tremendous problem of lifting the church into a fuller spiritual life than this: Let each of us give himself for God to use. God is eager and able to do something for us that we have never yet known. Read Isaiah 6 until your awareness of your own powerlessness has been first deepened, then conquered, by the thought of the Holy God cleansing you with His fire. Oh, prepare yourself to say, "Here am I, here am I."

As we have already seen,

> There can be no forward movement in missions, no great offering of life, without a deepening of the spiritual life of the church leaders and a real spiritual revival among the church members....The one real lack today is a lack of spiritual life; the one great need, the realization of the constant presence and power of the Holy Spirit.

It is this we need to pray for—a revival of true spiritual life—not, in the first place, a revival among the unconverted. God has given that in past years, but it is as if the mission outreaches do not have the access or hold that they had formerly. It is as if God sees that the church is not living on the high spiritual level that equips it for bearing and rearing strong spiritual Christians. The converts come too much under the influence of a feeble spiritual life, and too many sink into worldliness and indifference.

We must plead with God for such a mighty renewal of the power of eternal life in His children's hearts that it will give them the intense devotion that marks a truly healthy soul. We need nothing less than the resurrection power of Jesus Christ.

I believe that there are three circles in every congregation: the large outer one of the scarcely saved; the small inner one of the truly devoted; and then the middle one of those who are always longing for a better life, and yet are so bound in their powerlessness that they know nothing of true victory. Let us think especially of these and plead for them that believers may be raised up, full of faith and the Holy Spirit, with the power to lead them to a clear vision of Christ. This will cause them to gladly and completely surrender to Him at once. And they will be assured of an all-sufficient strength for their lives in His service.

I plead with you to pray for missions, in all its different aspects, as never before. Yield yourself to the Holy Spirit for this work of intercession, and fervently ask God to bring the people in your congregation to such a life in Christ that it will make them a willing people in the day of His power. Set your heart on this. Give God no rest until His Spirit moves among His children in mighty power.

Cherish carefully the thought that you have yielded yourself to God to be set apart as an intercessor. He will work in you all the grace that is needed and give you the blessed assurance that you have power with Him. Live in the bold and holy confidence that God is ready to bless His church through you.

As this consciousness becomes stronger, you will be able to speak with others and testify, in the power of the Spirit, that God is really only waiting for prayer in order to give the blessing. Try to gather others who are of the same spirit for meetings and prayer. Help each other to realize that you are definitely and persistently expecting God to lift His church into the abundant life. Cry day and night for it.

Help all to feel that this should first of all be the object of definite, secret prayer. Secret prayer will be the proof that your life has now been given up to the Holy Spirit. Let united prayer then be a witness to God and your own heart that you are sure that secret prayer will be answered.

If you are a minister, try to find other ministers who will give themselves to this great work in the spirit of entire self-sacrifice, confident faith, and persistent prayer. Help each of them to come to the full sense of his calling and the confident assurance that God will hear. Remember these words: "If some are resolutely and irrevocably led into the school of prayer, the spiritual power of the church for the accomplishment of its great task will be immeasurably increased." Believe that when you take part in such a ministry of prayer, it will be to you the beginning of a new life of blessing and strength.

Let me appeal to all of my readers, men and women, children of God. As you lay aside this book, do not refuse the pleading with which it closes, but tell God whether you now present yourself as a holy sacrifice to be at His disposal for the work of His Spirit. Let each of you say, "Here am I," until your whole being bows before God in this living conviction: "God accepts me, God enables me, God will bless me. What He has never been able to do through me before, He can and will do now. I am His for the great work of helping to lift His church into the fuller life, which will overflow in blessing to a perishing world."

And let each one of us pray that every reader who has joined in the surrender may be blessed with a new discovery of what God will do through him.

Remember, everything depends in the first place on the individual yielding himself up.

Hints on Intercession

To be effective, intercession must be intelligent, definite, believing, and persevering. First of all, it must be intelligent. This means that we are not to be content with what others think or write. We must set ourselves with all our hearts to realize what it is that we are asking for. *"Thou shalt love the Lord thy God with all thy…mind, and with all thy strength"* (Mark 12:30). That applies to prayer, too. Let us apply it to the great unsolved problem that has been occupying us and now calls for our prayers: How can the church be lifted up out of its low spiritual state into the abundant life that there is in Christ Jesus?

If one is really to pray effectively, he must prove to God that he feels grieved at the low spiritual condition of the church, and that he has set his heart on the blessing of the abundant life in Christ.

Just think for a moment of the proofs we have had of that feeble life:

> We have the verdict that the church as a whole is indifferent to the call to do the work for which it was placed in the world; therefore, it is spiritually unfit for taking part in it.
>
> We have the confession of the churches of their decline in membership. It is a proof that they are unable to drive back the spirit of the world.
>
> Both of these symptoms indicate a lack of spiritual life and power.
>
> With this there is the absolute impossibility of doing anything to bring about a change.

Take time and think through these points. Pray to God to give you a vision of their terrible reality, the grief and dishonor they are to Him, the terrible loss of souls that they imply, and the part that you have in it all. Begin to admit what a great work it is that you are undertaking, to pray for that great revolution that is needed if a change is to come. Pray for your ministers, pray for your congregation, pray for the believers with whom you have fellowship in prayer, pray for the whole church, that God may show us all what the true state of the church really is.

Unless we are willing to take time, to turn aside from the world to give ourselves to the holy exercise of laboring and striving in prayer, we have no right to hope for deliverance. It is a hard work, a difficult work, a solemn work. But let us not try to serve God with that which costs us nothing. It cost Christ everything, His blood and His life, to conquer death and win for us a share in His abundant life. If God's intercessors are to have power to prevail, they must learn in deep humility and contrition to truly give their whole lives and strength to bear the burden of the state of their fellow Christians.

Now, let us look on the other side, the abundant life that is waiting for the church, and see what basis there is for faith and hope in prayer.

What is impossible with men is possible with God. God has given to His church the promise of the Holy Spirit, who has the divine power that will equip it for the work it has to do. The more we carefully study the state of the church—the worldly life of the majority of its members, the tremendous difficulty of rousing even a single congregation to a higher spiritual life, the lack of power in its ministers, even many who long for better times—the more deeply we will feel the hopelessness of having a true revival, one in which Christians will really yield themselves wholly to a new life in Christ Jesus. But let this impossibility be just what drives us into the arms of God and into a new faith in what He can do.

Think of how Christ has promised that the Father will give the gift of the Holy Spirit to those who request it. Think of that until your whole heart is filled with the assurance that God can, God will, God must (we say it reverently), give His Spirit where His believing people unite in wholehearted prayer and consecration.

With this, think of the very special power that has been given to prayer, and the boundless possibilities to which it gives us the key. Take time—if you want to exercise yourself in prayer and learn the art of intercession—to let all the promises of answers to prayer fill you with the confident assurance of what is going to come. This is one of the great privileges of prayer: it throws you upon God and opens your heart so that He may make His promises a personal gift to you.

Begin then, and take time. Just as you have examined the state of the church in its feebleness and sin, begin to study God's Word as if, for the first time, you were trying to find out what God has really promised to do for His church here on earth. Take Christ's teaching in the fourteenth through the sixteenth chapters of John, and believe that the power of the Holy Spirit is meant to make the following promise a reality: *"If a man love me...my Father will love him, and we will come unto him, and make our abode with him"* (John 14:23).

Take the experience of Paul, in all that Christ did for him, and regard that as a pattern of what God is willing to do now. Steadfastly ask God to definitely work in you, in those around you, and in His church in its low state, what He has promised. Do not rest until the vision of what God is willing to do fills your heart so that you can think of nothing else. You have given your whole life to be occupied with this as its chief aim; do not rest until your heart is fully possessed with it.

Then you will be prepared to take your place as an intercessor in power. Your prayers will become more intelligent, but also more fervent, more believing, and more persevering. You will begin to understand something of what prayer means in its fullness—a taking hold of God, a giving Him no rest, a going on to be persistent in prayer until faith receives the quiet assurance that God will give what is asked.

Pray, above all, for the gift of the Holy Spirit to have entire possession of both you and all God's children who are pleading for the new life. Pray fervently, determinedly, for the ministers who are willing to yield themselves to God's work. Pray for all ministers as the leaders of the flock of God. Give yourself as a whole sacrifice to God for the great work of seeking the revival of His church and, through it, the evangelization of the world.

God seeks intercessors. God has need of intercessors. God is concerned about the lack of intercessors. Do not rest until God sees that you are one.

About the Author

———◆◆———

*A*ndrew Murray (1828–1917) was an amazingly prolific Christian writer. He lived and ministered as both a pastor and author in the towns and villages of South Africa. Some of Murray's earliest works were written to provide nurture and guidance to Christians, whether young or old in the faith; they were actually an extension of his pastoral work. Once books such as *Abide in Christ, Like Christ,* and *With Christ in the School of Prayer* were written, Murray became widely known, and new books from his pen were awaited with great eagerness throughout the world.

He wrote to give daily practical help to many of the people in his congregation who lived out in the farming communities and could only come into town for church services on rare occasions. As he wrote these books of instruction, Murray adopted the practice of placing many of his more devotional books into thirty-one separate readings to correspond with the days of the month.

At the age of seventy-eight, Murray resigned from the pastorate and devoted most of his time to his manuscripts. He continued to write profusely, moving from one book to the next with an intensity of purpose and a zeal that few men of God have ever equaled. He often said of himself, rather humorously, that he was like a hen about to hatch an egg; he was restless and unhappy until he got the burden of the message off his mind.

About the Author

During these later years, after hearing of pocket-sized paperbacks, Andrew Murray immediately began to write books to be published in that fashion. He thought it was a splendid way to have the teachings of the Christian life at your fingertips, where they could be carried around and read at any time of the day.

One source has said of Andrew Murray that his prolific style possesses the strength and eloquence that are born of deep earnestness and a sense of the solemnity of the issues of the Christian life. Nearly every page reveals an intensity of purpose and appeal that stirs men to the depths of their souls. Murray moves the emotions, searches the conscience, and reveals the sins and shortcomings of many of us with a love and hope born out of an intimate knowledge of the mercy and faithfulness of God.

For Andrew Murray prayer was considered our personal home base from which we live our Christian lives and extend ourselves to others. During his later years, the vital necessity of unceasing prayer in the spiritual life came to the forefront of Andrew Murray's teachings. It was then that he revealed the secret treasures of his heart concerning a life of persistent and believing prayer.

Countless people the world over have hailed Andrew Murray as their spiritual father and given credit for much of their Christian growth to the influence of his priceless devotional books.

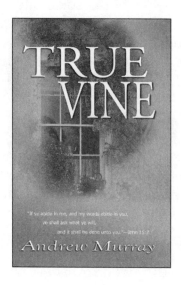

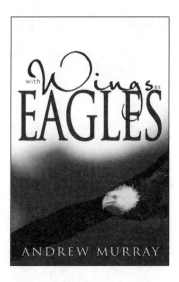

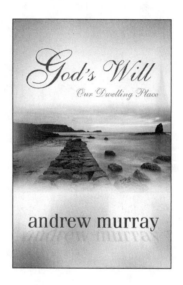

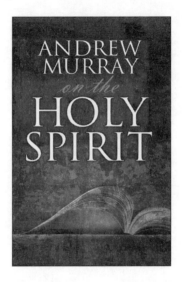